# THE SUBURBAN CHURCH

Architecture, Landscape, and American Culture Series

*Katherine Solomonson and Abigail A. Van Slyck, Series Editors*

*Medicine by Design: The Architect and the Modern Hospital, 1893–1943*
Annmarie Adams

*The Suburban Church: Modernism and Community in Postwar America*
Gretchen Buggeln

*Building Zion: The Material World of Mormon Settlement*
Thomas Carter

*Little White Houses: How the Postwar Home Constructed Race in America*
Dianne Harris

*Manhood Factories: YMCA Architecture and the Making of Modern Urban Culture*
Paula Lupkin

*Fallout Shelter: Designing for Civil Defense in the Cold War*
David Monteyne

*Designing the Creative Child: Playthings and Places in Midcentury America*
Amy F. Ogata

*Women and the Everyday City: Public Space in San Francisco, 1890–1915*
Jessica Ellen Sewell

*194x: Architecture, Planning, and Consumer Culture on the American Home Front*
Andrew M. Shanken

*A Manufactured Wilderness: Summer Camps and the Shaping of American Youth, 1890–1960*
Abigail A. Van Slyck

*The Architecture of Madness: Insane Asylums in the United States*
Carla Yanni

# THE SUBURBAN CHURCH

## *Modernism and Community in Postwar America*

GRETCHEN BUGGELN

Architecture, Landscape, and American Culture Series

MINNESOTA

UNIVERSITY OF MINNESOTA PRESS
MINNEAPOLIS • LONDON

Portions of chapter 2 were previously published in "The Shape of a New Era: Valparaiso's Chapel of the Resurrection in Historical Context," *The Cresset* (Lent 2010): 6–14. Portions of chapter 6 were previously published in "Form, Function, and Failure in Postwar Christian Education Buildings," in David Morgan, ed., *Religion and Material Culture: The Matter of Belief* (New York: Routledge, 2009), 193–213.



Published by the University of Minnesota Press
111 Third Avenue South, Suite 290
Minneapolis, MN 55401–2520
http://www.upress.umn.edu

Library of Congress Cataloging-in-Publication Data
Buggeln, Gretchen, author.
The suburban church : modernism and community in postwar America /
Gretchen Buggeln.
(Architecture, landscape and American culture series)
Includes bibliographical references and index.
ISBN 978-0-8166-9495-2 (hc) — ISBN 978-0-8166-9496-9 (pb)
1. Protestant church buildings—Middle West—History—20th century.
2. Architecture and society—Middle West—History—20th century.
3. Suburban churches—Middle West.
4. Midcentury modern (Architecture)—Middle West. I. Title.
NA5212.5.M63B84 2015
726.50977′09045—dc23 2015031931

Printed in the United States of America on acid-free paper



22 21 20 19 18 17 16 10 9 8 7 6 5 4 3 2 1

# CONTENTS

# ACKNOWLEDGMENTS

In 2005, during my first year teaching at Valparaiso University, I offered a seminar called the American Home. While searching for a case study for my students, I happened on the 1960 house designed for the university president by Chicago architect Charles E. Stade. My students and I discovered that Stade designed our 1959 chapel and several other buildings for a major campus expansion, yet, much to our surprise, next to nothing was known about him. In 2006, Valparaiso granted me a summer travel stipend to find out more. While visiting Stade parish churches in Midwestern suburbs, I encountered many people who had spent much time in his buildings but had never heard of him. I asked questions about the founding years of these congregations and had the opportunity to meet people who had served on postwar building committees. My curiosity grew, and what began as a simple task to find out more about one architect became a book-length project about the architecture and religious culture of the postwar suburbs—a story that was largely untold outside individual congregations and was rapidly being lost. I discovered two other significant Midwestern church architects, Edward Dart and Edward Sövik, and followed their postwar work, too, into suburbs from Minneapolis to Indianapolis.

A great number of people helped me on this journey of discovery, and it is a pleasure to thank them. Hands down, the richest and best part of my research was my acquaintance with two people who were instrumental in the architectural and religious life of this period: Edward A. Sövik and Martin E. Marty. Sövik, who died in 2014 at the age of ninety-two, was a brilliant architect who was generous with his ideas and insistent that in order for church architecture to serve God and human beings, designers and builders needed to understand the meaning of Christian worship and community. I am so grateful I had the chance to know Ed and learn from him about his early work and this exciting time for church architects. I was amazed by his knowledge, memory, and the scope of his contributions to church architecture. Much more remains to be written about the life and work of Edward Sövik.

Martin Marty has been an extraordinary help to me and this project. Although I move at a pace far, far slower than his own, his interest in the project was unflagging. I first approached him because in 1959 Stade had designed Marty's church in the new Chicago suburb of Elk Grove Village. I quickly recognized that Marty, as editor at *Christian Century* but more importantly as a parish pastor, understood the religious art and architecture of this period inside and out. He seemed to know every character I would mention, and he was constantly dashing to his shelves to pull out a relevant book or firing bibliographic references at me. Marty's assessment of this period in the life of the American denominations is critical but fair, and, as always, his acute perception is balanced by humor and love.

Early in the project, Jesse and Ramsey Stade Barlow shared important insights into Ramsey's father, Charles Stade, and generously handed me a box of his architecture books. I thank Della Olsen for inviting me to see Stade's house and providing original plans. People I interviewed extensively are acknowledged at the end of the book in my list of Sources for Research; I am grateful to all of them for their willingness to relive a time long past. Many others also played a role in this research. Although they are unnamed in this book, I hope they know how much I appreciate the time they gave to share memories or root around in drawers and long-forgotten boxes in search of old photographs or church bulletins. I met a number of extraordinary volunteer church archivists: Lyle Nelson, Marilyn Hermann, Joanna Seltz, Bette Hanna, Faith Albano, and Helen Danielson were especially helpful. Paula DeBois, at St. Augustine's Gary, has given an unfathomable amount of time to preserving Dart's building and the history of her congregation. Paula's important work offers proof that the stories of these postwar congregations continue to matter.

I had the pleasure of working in several professional archives, including those of the Presbyterian Historical Society, the American Institute of Architects (AIA), Luther Seminary, and the Art Institute of Chicago. Special thanks to archivists Nancy Hadley at the AIA and Kari Bostrom at Luther Seminary. Jane Nicoll created the Local History Collection and Archive for the Park Forest, Illinois, Public Library; cofounded the Park Forest Historical Society; and helped to create a Park Forest House Museum. She has worked tirelessly, in many capacities and for many years, toward the preservation of the history of that remarkable place. Anyone concerned with preserving the history of postwar suburban America is in her debt.

Professional colleagues have shown kind interest in my work and provided an example to follow. I am especially indebted to Catherine Osborne, Dale Dowling, Jeanne Halgren Kilde, Jay Price, Mark Torgerson, Peter Williams, and Victoria Young. Brian Wolfe offered his fieldwork on Stade and helped me with photography. Matthew Seymour shared his knowledge of Dart's life and work, and I look forward to seeing more from Matt on Dart. I was privileged to share portions of my work at the American Studies Colloquium at Princeton University and the Quadrant Program at the University of Minnesota. Many thanks to Bill Gleason at Princeton and Katherine Solomonson and Anne Carter at Minnesota.

My fabulous editor, Abigail Van Slyck, was invested in the success of this book from our first conversations about it several years ago. She gave her careful and intelligent attention to the manuscript several times, all the while juggling her responsibilities as college professor, administrator, and president of the Society of Architectural Historians. Her suggestions for improvement always made sense, and this is a much better book because of her. I am grateful as well to an anonymous reader who pushed this manuscript, and its author, in important directions. It is a privilege to be included in the Architecture, Landscape, and American Culture series of the University of Minnesota Press, and I thank the Press for the care it gives to complex architectural studies. I particularly acknowledge the expert assistance of Pieter Martin, Laura Westlund, Kristian Tvedten, and David Thorstad.

This research benefited from the generous financial support of several organizations. I am grateful for summer research grants from the Louisville Foundation and the National Endowment for the Humanities, and the book would still be in the research stage if not for an academic year faculty fellowship I later received from the National Endowment for the Humanities. Any views, findings, conclusions, or recommendations expressed in this book do not necessarily represent those of the National Endowment for the Humanities.

The community at Valparaiso University supported this project from Day One. I am thankful for two summer travel grants and a semester of research leave, as well as generous publication support. Even more important, I appreciate the community's steady interest in my research on church architecture. In 2009 I was awarded the Phyllis and Richard Duesenberg Chair in Christianity and the Arts. This chair has provided the resources required to complete my book and support my own and my students' ongoing education in Christian art and architecture. Phyllis and Dick have been extraordinarily generous to me and to Valparaiso University, and it has been a pleasure to know these two interesting, gracious, and supportive alumni.

Several Valparaiso colleagues deserve special mention. The late Gus Sponberg was a source of boundless encouragement and enthusiasm, and I miss our morning conversations in the coffee room about all things Midwestern. Richard Brauer has been a terrific resource because of his rich understanding of postwar liturgical art and our shared concern for the relationship between Christianity and the arts. My good friend and co-teacher Sara Danger has celebrated the joys of this project with me and cheered me on through the inevitable lows. Whether puzzling through the interpretation of words, images, children, or husbands, her friendship and insight have been invaluable these past ten years.

I am fortunate to have an appointment in Christ College, a small and collegial interdisciplinary honors college within Valparaiso University. For welcoming me to this unique scholarly community (and getting me through my first attempts at teaching Aristotle and Kant!), my thanks to former colleagues Marcia Bunge, Scott Huelin, Andrew Murphy, and Kevin Hoffman, and current colleagues Mark Schwehn and Bill Olmsted. Mel Piehl, my dean for nine years and a terrifically sharp historian of American religion, was especially supportive as an administrator and also offered his excellent editing skills at two important stages of the project. Friend and former colleague David Morgan inspired me by his scholarship at the intersection of art and religion and set an example of how to maintain a scholarly program at a small university. Colleagues Jennifer Prough, Samuel Graber, Edward Upton, Julien Smith, David Western, and Slavica Jakelic spur me on with their dedication to learning and teaching and their willingness to think broadly and imaginatively. Thanks also to Dean Peter Kanelos, Associate Dean Margaret Franson, former administrative assistants Vicki Brody and Kristin Nygaard, and current assistants Jo Ellen Zromkoski and Patrice Weil, all of whom furthered this work. Finally, I acknowledge my highly intelligent, humble, salt-of-the-earth Midwestern students who make teaching at Valparaiso such a pleasure, with particular thanks to three students who directly helped with this book: Mary Morales-Rivera, Jacob Just, and Gregory Maher.

Traveling scholars are always grateful for a good meal, a comfortable bed, or just encouragement on the road. For their kind hospitality and good cheer I thank my sister Kate Garred, my parents John and Carol Townsend, my mother-in-law Eleanor Buggeln, Anna Andrzejewski, Jan and Bill Breyer, Patricia Elliot, Suzanne and Doug Fagen-Smith, Mary Habeck, Laura and Mico Loretan, Martin and Harriet Marty, Sharon and Dave Oslin, Thom and Kristin Peters, Cheryl and the late Thorpe Running, Anne and the late Ed Sövik, and Kim and Steve Zimmerman.

My daughter Hannah and son John Henry now know a lot more about postwar church architecture than they ever wanted to. Among other church architecture detours, Hannah and our Scottish exchange student, Julia Melling, spent an uncommon spring break driving across the frozen north to Sioux Falls, South Dakota, wandering around obscure postwar churches and serving as conscripted research assistants. They said it was fun, but I'm sure they would have preferred a beach in Florida. John Henry patiently tolerated a distracted mom and many late dinners. He was a third grader when I started this research; now he occasionally lends his keen ear to help me craft a stubborn sentence. Finally, it simply would be impossible for me to write anything of this length without the love and support of my husband, John. He often had more faith in me and this project than I could muster on my own accord. Much of his suburban childhood was spent in a postwar modern church like those in this book, and he knows firsthand the value of such communities. This book (and, more significant, the completion of it) is for him.

INTRODUCTION

# New Times, New Architecture

## *Making a Place for Religion in Postwar Suburbia*

### A SUBURBAN SUNDAY MORNING, CHICAGO, 1957

The ranch house bustles with activity. Mom and Dad coax their three children into their Sunday best and lead them out the door and into the family station wagon. Driving down a major thoroughfare in their expanding suburb, they see several contemporary places of worship sitting comfortably among the newly built houses and schools, each making its presence known by a welcoming roadside sign and a distinguishing roofline or tower. As they pass the neighborhood elementary school, where their congregation held its first meetings and worship services, Mom and Dad remember both the excitement and the inconvenience of those early years.

Dad turns the wagon into a paved drive that leads to a large parking lot alongside their sprawling one-story church. Parents and children slide out of the car and walk to the sheltered entrance at the bend of the L-shaped building. In the narthex, friendly waves and hellos greet the family. Mom steers the children past the coatracks and glass-enclosed offices and down a long hallway with classrooms on either side. She drops her youngest daughter in a large, sunny room, and the little girl makes a beeline for a bright yellow chair at a low table. Under the watchful eye of her teacher, she busies herself with a craft project. Her older brothers scamper down the hall to their age-specific smaller classrooms where they say hello to their teachers and friends and prepare for the morning's lesson.

Children safely in their places, Mom walks back to the narthex, stopping in the Ladies' Restroom to check her hair in the anteroom's wide mirror. She smiles at another young mother from her Wednesday Ladies' Circle, and they share a quick conversation about an upcoming church bazaar that will raise money to support a missionary family in India. Following the sounds of the electronic organ, Mom moves toward the sanctuary, looking through the wide entrance until she spies the back of her husband's head. The sanctuary is full, even though the youngsters have lately been staying in the Sunday school wing for children's worship. While appreciative of the tradition of family worship, members of this busy congregation find it difficult to get everyone in the same place at the same time.[1] On Sunday mornings, multiple classes, worship services, rehearsals, and meetings use the building to full capacity. This congregation is just six years old and the building is still new, but it won't be long before the congregation will need to open the rear sanctuary overflow space on a regular basis.

Slipping into the polished wooden pew next to her husband, Mom relaxes into one of the few quiet daytime hours of her hectic week. Dad also enjoys the calm of the modern sanctuary, its high, peaked roof drawing his eyes forward and upward. With few decorations to distract his attention, his sight lands on the large, plain cross behind the altar, softly lit by indirect light from a hidden side window. He hears the choir shuffling into place in the rear balcony. Looking up at the laminated wood trusses, Dad remembers days of staining and painting as he joined others from the Men's Club to save the church money by completing much of the finish work. He wonders about the pesky leak coming into the flat-roofed office area. How can a new building already be causing trouble? As a member of the property committee, he is proud of the new church building and the amount of financial sacrifice it represents. He also knows firsthand how much work such a big building requires. At the dedication service one year ago, many details remained unfinished. There is still work to do.

The pastor, just a few years out of seminary, is as young and energetic as his congregation. He preaches on the call to faithfulness, reminding his listeners that the heart of the Christian is formed in the family as well as the church. In a culture that appears increasingly hostile to Christian moral principles, parents and church need to work together to raise this next generation. Communion follows the sermon, and the congregation files forward to receive the bread and wine at the altar rail. The words of the liturgy call up deep memories for some. Others, schooled in different denominations, are still getting used to an unfamiliar way of worshipping.

When the worship service ends, Mom and Dad make a special effort to seek out newcomers and help them feel welcome. One reason they chose this church over others was its friendliness, and they are determined to keep it up. Mom heads for the Sunday school wing to pick up the children. Dad joins the crowd of people moving out of the sanctuary, through the narthex, and into the open and spacious fellowship hall. Remembering the dark church basements of their childhoods, church members appreciate the daylight streaming in through the large windows. In the state-of-the-art kitchen, women of the congregation pour steaming coffee from large urns into china cups that they set on the pass-through to the fellowship hall. The dedication of the kitchen committee is revealed in the gleaming stainless-steel surfaces and top-quality appliances. All church members have benefited from this efficient work space, sharing church suppers around tables in the comfortable hall.

Looking around, Dad notices with satisfaction the many new faces, although he misses his friends who recently transferred to California and New York. Mom stops at a bulletin board to glance at the church calendar for the coming week. She'll be back again Wednesday for the meeting of her Ladies' Circle, and next Sunday it will be her turn to serve the coffee. Dad checks briefly with the congregation's scoutmaster. He and his eldest son will return to the fellowship hall Thursday evening when the boys and fathers will be working on earning their God and Country emblem. He looks forward to that time shared with his growing son. Mom and Dad gather their children and move to the narthex to retrieve their coats. The family makes its way to the parking lot as another stream of cars files in for the second service.

In postwar America, millions of suburbanites passed Sunday mornings in this kind of place, gathering together for worship and Sunday school.[2] During this heyday of the "seven-day-a-week" church, congregations filled their weekends and weekdays with Bible study groups, community meals, service projects, and recreational and social activities. For some parents, involvement consisted only of dropping off the children at Sunday school. For others, family life was so tightly bound to the church building and community that it felt like an extension of the home.

A 1957 church bulletin cover shows a well-dressed and well-behaved family walking to church in the suburbs (Figure I.1). This is certainly not a realistic picture of the Sunday experienced by the great majority of families, then or now. Without the accompanying text, it would be tempting to read this simply as a fantasy of postwar white culture and privilege, a "Happy Home" cliché. But alongside the photograph was an earnest plea emphasizing the need for the family to "lose itself in something greater than itself" so as not to become a "caricature of what great living ought to be." Suburban life without an ideal, without a commitment to "something greater," would be insular and even immoral, the writer argued. For many Americans, that "something" was to be found at church. Eyes forward, the family looked with anticipation to gathering at their house of worship.

Postwar church buildings—sanctuaries, social and education rooms, administrative offices, and recreational spaces—tell us about what mattered to these gathered communities. After World War II, as congregations recovered from the economic restrictions of wartime, flourished in a time of increased attendance and membership, and spread into the rapidly developing suburbs, they spent billions of dollars on architecture. They shaped their investment in bricks and mortar to match their contemporary spirit, often choosing modern architecture. Today, the many thousands of modern churches these congregations created are rendered almost invisible by their ubiquity. To present-day eyes, if they are noticed at all,

FIGURE I.1. Church bulletin cover for Sunday, August 25, 1957. From the Archives of Lutheran Church of the Good Shepherd, Moorhead, Minnesota.

they often appear as unremarkable, bland structures that lack the distinction of the colonial New England meetinghouse or the Gothic revival church. Yet their very ubiquity calls for attention. Why, in the decades after World War II, did the style and form of new American churches and synagogues take such an apparently radical turn?

In step with their changing ideas of worship and religious community, congregations sought revolutionary buildings—"Churches for Today" as they were called by a regular Sunday feature in the *Chicago Tribune*. By the 1950s, most congregations were building in one of two styles: what contemporaries referred to as "Colonial" (a traditional, American look with red brick, white pillars, and steeple) or "contemporary" (churches in new forms, of new materials, without extensive ornament) (Figures I.2–I.5). Both types were often called "modern" by ordinary churchgoers, reflecting the up-to-date features of the church complex and the overall facilities plan.[3] Many church leaders and architects were increasingly certain, however, that contemporary—and only contemporary—was the appropriate architecture for the postwar church.

For Americans and Europeans struggling to understand their dramatically different postwar world, the new religious architecture took on heightened importance. British architect Edward Mills captured the uncertainty of the times in the preface of his 1956 book *The Modern Church*. "The history of the last fifty years," he wrote, "indicates the chaos that results when the world turns its back on Christian ideals. Scientific discovery and development have out-paced spiritual growth, and man is no longer able to control his own inventions. Our civilization is indeed at a crossroads . . . the total destruction of the human race is within the realms of possibility."[4] This is heady stuff for the beginning of a book on church architecture! But Mills hastened to introduce the hope that Christianity brought—a message that could cause people to "live together as brothers." This precarious situation declared "the need for new methods of presenting [the Gospel] to the world," and contemporary architecture, he argued, needed to "play its part" in revitalizing the church. "If we do not build churches in keeping with the spirit of the age," Mills cautioned, "we shall be admitting that religion no longer possesses the same vitality as our secular buildings."[5] Reformers urged that new churches must offer a fresh solution to the needs of the day, a solution that should grow organically out of contemporary life and culture.

To a large degree, congregations answered the call. By 1963, organist Robert S. Baker could observe that in his travels across America, his "overwhelming impression" was of "stunning new sanctuaries in contemporary architectural style." Baker acknowledged that Americans were still building "more than our share of traditional New England churches, almost always in red brick with white trim and white pillars." He was surprised, nonetheless, at the range of congregations choosing contemporary architecture: even those with "a conservative theological emphasis,

FIGURE I.2. Charles Stade, Christ Evangelical and Reformed Church (Christ Church United Church of Christ), Des Plaines, Illinois, 1953, 1964. Photograph by Brian L. Wolf.

FIGURE I.3. Christ Evangelical and Reformed Church, Des Plaines, Illinois, sanctuary. Photograph by Brian L. Wolf.

FIGURE I.4. Charles Stade, Lutheran Church of the Holy Spirit, Elk Grove Village, Illinois, 1960, 1963. Photograph by the author.

FIGURE I.5. Lutheran Church of the Holy Spirit, Elk Grove Village, Illinois, sanctuary. Photograph by the author.

seem to have embraced the opportunity to build their new sanctuaries in an architectural vocabulary which speaks of our own time." He recognized that modern churches were relatively cheap to build, but he was not willing to claim that fact as the only reason for their acceptance. "Rather," he stated, "I congratulate the architectural profession on a major achievement in persuading the Christian church of today that it is not only meet and right but also its bounden duty to express the thrust of today's faith in sanctuaries which say to all that Christianity is not of a former time and no longer pertinent to our world but it is here now, alive, pulsating and very much concerned with today's world and its problems."[6]

Many contemporary observers of these buildings were not nearly as generous with their assessments. It is undeniable that the "modern" intentions of church architects and theologians often resulted in buildings that were and are disparaged as "modernistic"—second-rate, derivative designs shaped by the limited grasp ordinary architects had of the deceptively simple tenets of modernism, the whims of building committees, and bottom-line cheapness. Detractors referred to modern churches as "grocery store" or "gas station" churches, and decried their ugliness and vacuity. Even today, these buildings are apt to elicit a laugh, or at least a "What were they *thinking?*"

This book, using the architecture and experiences of approximately seventy-five Midwestern, suburban congregations, is an attempt to answer that question. What were church leaders, architects, and, perhaps most important, congregations, *thinking* when they designed, built, and used these churches? These buildings are a revealing repository of the history of American religion in the postwar years—its ecumenism, its optimism, and its liturgical and social innovation, as well as its fears about the increasing "irrelevance" of institutional religion at a time when cultural and social change and dramatic demographic shifts rapidly transformed society.

My focus is on modern church buildings and their congregations in the Midwest.[7] Because of the architectural importance of Chicago and Minneapolis, and the artistic leadership of Lutheran denominations (and Roman Catholics) heavily represented in Midwestern cities, the American conversation about new church design flourished there. The work of three architects—Edward Dupaquier Dart (1922–1975), Charles Edward Stade (1924–1993), and Edward Anders Sövik (1918–2014)—anchors the study. Dart, in Barrington, Illinois, and Stade, in Park Ridge, worked close to Chicago, and most of their church commissions were in the suburbs around this urban center and nearby Wisconsin, Indiana, and southern Michigan. Sövik's office was in Northfield, Minnesota, a short drive south of Minneapolis. His clients included suburban as well as urban and rural congregations, primarily in Minnesota, Wisconsin, the Dakotas, and Iowa.

These three men were at the top of their profession within the region, and all three achieved national acclaim for their religious architecture. Although their ecclesiastical designs are not well known today among architectural historians, the influence of their work was both broad and deep. Edward Sövik was the most theologically informed and articulate American church architect of his day. His impact on the conversations about Christianity and architecture in the postwar era, and his important church designs, make him a critical figure in this study. Edward Dart was a Chicago modernist whose commitment to excellent and innovative ecclesiastical design was noted by his architectural community and calls for recognition in the present. Charles Stade provides an example of the kind of prolific, regional church architect whose designs were especially in tune with the desires of postwar congregations, and his hundreds of high-quality buildings had a far-reaching impact.

One of the chief aims of this book is to recover the work of these important church architects and to place it in a larger architectural context. These three architects, and several hundred other leading designers like them, were primary shapers of the postwar religious landscape. In the Midwest where Sövik, Dart, and Stade lived and worked, contemporary church architecture became dominant in the late 1950s. By 1966, Sövik declared with pleasure, "It is a sort of comfort to architects in my part of the country that there is no longer any pressure from clergy or laymen which urges them to the gross dishonesty which is the imitation of historical styles."[8]

With its focus on the Midwest, this study contributes to a growing awareness of midcentury architectural regionalism. In 1955, architect Pietro Belluschi asked architects to attend to place and local tradition, pushing back against the unifying forces of modernism that he feared would wipe out regional distinctiveness.[9] Like Belluschi, midcentury architects could make a conscious decision to connect to the local tradition of building. But new architecture also unconsciously *shaped* regionalism. Because church building committees traveled locally to appraise new architecture, architects often replicated their own or their competitors' work at the request of these committees, in the process crafting a new local norm. Midcentury regionalism in church architecture was the outgrowth of architect and building committee design preferences, available materials such as regionally distinctive stone and brick, denominational concentrations, and even local weather patterns.

Just as a robust understanding of church architecture requires geographic context, it must be grounded in an understanding of theology and congregational life. Dart, Stade, and Sövik were Protestants, as were the great majority of their clients, and I focus on Protestant architecture and belief. Yet the denominational borders of architecture were so fluid, and the trends in contemporary religious architecture so sweeping, that Roman Catholics and Jews also shared in the conversation, and some Catholic churches and synagogues appear in this book.[10] The case study of Park Forest, Illinois, in chapter 7 places the architecture of the different faiths next to each other, and both similarities and differences are evident. Many of the same concerns shaped the architecture and suburban religious lives of all three groups. But the religious and cultural world described in these pages, centered on the work of these three architects, is primarily that of congregations with ties to mainline Protestant denominations.[11]

In addition to being Midwestern and Protestant, the historical subjects of this study are largely suburban. As geographer Justin Wilford has argued, thinking of religion as emplaced, as active within spatial constraints, is critical to understanding how it operates.[12] The 1950s, hopeful model of suburban community anticipated a sociospatial environment that would be open, modern, and coherent. This vision was instrumental in shaping the first postwar wave of suburban churches and determined much about the opportunities and limitations these congregations encountered.

I will define suburbs much the way a writer for *Fortune* described them in 1953—not as a particular demographic, but as a way of life. In answer to the question "What, where, and how big is Suburbia?" the writer replied: "Because it is a way of life and not a color on a map, it is very hard to define. It certainly cannot be bounded by arbitrary lines like city limits."[13] This writer included some sections of older cities that seemed very like the brand-new developments on the fringes.

The suburban "way of life" was centered on nuclear families in single-family homes that became receptacles for a vast array of new consumer goods and comforts. Some of these places were extensive housing initiatives by large-scale developers that turned Midwestern cornfields into new communities. Others were small-scale developments on the outskirts of cities or in smaller towns. As the Reverend Martin Marty, a keen observer of culture who began his professional career as a pastor in a new Chicago suburb, wrote in 1958, "The suburban complex is not a place but a state of mind that reaches everywhere from inner city to outer farm."[14] Marty felt that "suburbia" had increasingly broad economic and cultural significance, even to the lower middle class. What defined these neighborhoods were patterns of interaction, movement, and activity. A car was a necessity of life for suburban families, yet kids on foot or on bicycles could range freely across these landscapes, getting themselves safely to the adjacent schools, libraries, and recreation centers. Green spaces often surrounded both private and public buildings.

Suburban migration, a long-term trend, had been stalled by the Great Depression. After the war, movement to new suburbs exploded because of a mobile population, a growing middle class, the assistance of government mortgage programs, and a tremendous housing shortage in many cities. Literally millions of newly married couples were in temporary housing, often sharing space with relatives, and eager for a more permanent and comfortable residence. The boom was almost overwhelming in the Chicago area. In a May 1958 article titled "Bursting Point in Paradise: Chicago's 275 Suburbs Spilling over Their Limits as Populations Double, Triple, Quadruple," journalist Joan Beck listed communities that had almost quadrupled in population since 1950: Niles, Wheeling, Morton Grove. Others had more than tripled: Addison, Lincolnwood, and Hillside. And close behind in growth were Mount Prospect, Skokie, Park Forest, Westchester, Deerfield, Arlington Heights, Flossmoor, Hazelcrest, Highland, Mundelein, Northfield, Oak Lawn, and South Holland. Beck cited an estimate that by 1960 suburbs in Chicago's six-county metropolitan region would house 2.9 million people.[15] Congregations in many of these suburbs hired Dart or Stade to design a modern church for them.

Across America, such suburban growth was accompanied by the unprecedented proliferation of religious organizations. In 1958, the McGraw-Hill Corporation's Department of Economics produced a memo titled "The Boom in Church Building." With a light touch, the author declared, "And it came to pass in the 1950s that the prosperous times begat a growing number of churches, synagogues, temples, Sunday and parochial schools, hospitals and an expansive market for everything from acoustical materials to weatherproofing. Yes, as both clergy and businessmen would agree, verily it was a building boom. And it was good." A recent Gallup poll had indicated that 51 percent of Americans said they went to church the "previous week," and the lion's share of this growth was in the suburbs.[16] Growth began to surge in 1947, after a lull in church building during the Depression and

World War II. In 1947, $126 million was spent on churches; by 1953 this number had almost quadrupled, to just under half a billion dollars.[17] And the numbers kept leaping upward. As a prelude to a 1959 national meeting of architects and church builders in Los Angeles, Scott Ritenour, director of the National Council of Churches Church Building Department, stated that in 1958, $863 million had been spent on church buildings, and the U.S. Department of Commerce predicted that the number would reach $950 million in 1959.[18] Even without these figures, all one has to do is look around on a drive through the suburbs to see the legacy of this building frenzy.

In the new Twin Cities suburb of Roseville, for example, where developers quickly expanded onto farmland beginning in the late 1940s, "many thoughtful people realized that moral leadership must go along with industrial and business development if the fledgling city was to become the 'garden' its planners envisioned."[19] By 1973, Roseville Lutheran, St. Rose of Lima Catholic, Corpus Christi Catholic, North Heights Lutheran, Calvary Baptist, North Como Presbyterian, Resurrection Lutheran, Advent Lutheran, St. Christopher's Episcopal, Centennial Methodist, and St. Michael's Lutheran had all claimed a portion of the churchgoing residents of Roseville. This is a typical suburban, Midwestern assortment of Christian denominations: multiple congregations of Lutherans with at least one Roman Catholic parish and a fair representation of the other major American Protestant denominations and nondenominational community churches.

Although certainly not all suburbs were alike, the great majority of the thirty million people who lived in American suburbia by 1953 were homeowners pursuing a middle-class American dream. Recent work on American suburbs has aggressively countered the notion that life there was homogeneous.[20] But in the suburbs in this study, shaped by postwar consumerism and middle-class social concerns, residents led lives that, at least from the outside, looked quite similar. The lifestyle of the new suburbs was casual and contemporary, focused on the needs of "baby-boom" children. Many of the Midwestern churches being built during these years were in these new suburbs, as homes for congregations that were leaving the old downtowns or for newly formed congregations. As young suburbanites joined up, church membership grew rapidly; churches often claimed that their modestly planned sanctuaries were already bursting at the seams by the time of dedication.

From the very beginning, the expansion of suburban churches was eyed with concern by intellectuals and many church leaders. Marty and others watched the postwar revival of religion and worried that it was simply one of "faith in faith, a resurgence of an attitude directed toward no particular deity," the outgrowth of a culture that was focused on the pragmatic and technical, and not very thoughtful.[21] Marty cited the theologian Paul Tillich's warning that "if religion passes in America it will not be killed but will die of a surfeit of its own suburban excesses and successes."[22] Yet Marty, himself pastor of a new Lutheran congregation, the

Lutheran Church of the Holy Spirit in the Chicago suburb of Elk Grove Village, was also careful to point out that none of this suspicion justified abandoning the cause of the church in the suburbs (Figures I.4 and I.5). "The place where the American future is being shaped—whether or not we like the prospect—seems an excellent place for churches to be active."[23]

The legacy of the postwar suburban church has been powerful, yet its place in American religious life is not well understood.[24] In part this is because suburban life was so quickly disparaged by intellectuals as a vapid and self-serving existence. Books such as sociologist William Whyte's *The Organization Man* (1956), Sloan Wilson's popular 1955 novel *The Man in the Gray Flannel Suit*, and University of Chicago Professor Gibson Winter's *The Suburban Captivity of the Churches* (1961) set the tone. According to Winter, "suburban leadership is the antithesis of the prophetic note in the gospel."[25] Religious leaders urged American Christians to keep the tensions between faith and culture alive, not to take the easy road. It was difficult for them to see how Christianity could remain vital in comfortable suburbs, seemingly at a cloistered remove from the ugly problems of the day. From the outside, it was and continues to be easy to fit the churches into that picture of complacency. Even current revisionist histories, such as a study of Levittown, Pennsylvania, continue to invoke the idea of the "country club church."[26] This is far too one-dimensional an assessment of their nature and their complex role in suburban communities.[27]

Those who stepped over the church threshold were motivated by a variety of things: a sense of duty, personal desire for worship and spiritual growth, the hope of friendship, concern for the moral education of their children, a commitment to the flourishing of their communities, a search for an outlet for service, pride, even a patriotic civil religion, or just a desire to feel that they fit in. Some families and individuals had the opportunity to actively participate in shaping a new church, whether that was choosing an architect or choosing dishes for the new kitchen. Others walked into a building planned by others and learned something immediately about those people by what they saw and experienced in its spaces. A phrase commonly deployed in this era, the "seven-day-a-week" church, perfectly encapsulates the array of clubs and meetings available Sunday through Saturday in these suburban buildings. Equating busy-ness with emptiness, however, would be a mistake. As members of these congregations express over and over, they were young and ambitious, and their religious lives were rooted in meaningful activity. Spirituality was realized in practical work, much of which involved constructing, maintaining, and serving within their modern church buildings.

What made a church modern? "Modern" generally meant a rejection of deliberate copying from the buildings of a previous era, but it was more than an erasure of the past. Architects used industrial materials such as steel, concrete, large glass windows, and laminated wood beams, taking bold advantage of their physical attributes and celebrating their cheapness and efficiency without hiding the evidence behind paint or veneers. Edward Sövik's firm stressed the "use of familiar rather than exotic materials. Brick, clay tile, stone, solid wood and even unadorned concrete. Modern materials were used, but never imitatively."[28] Form was also a critical marker of modernism: clean and bold lines were better than fussy profiles that hankered after the past. Yet only a rare postwar architect—and an even rarer building committee—wanted to dispense with the Christian tradition in architecture. They often looked back over the sweep of Christian history to find meaningful links to the present and chose forms that might be appropriately worked in a modern idiom. These architects fit well with Sarah Goldhagen's idea of a "situated modernism," a modernism that rejected the authority of tradition but would "adopt *abstracted historical forms* if justified with modernist principles" and tended to prefer natural materials and textured surfaces.[29]

Although abstraction and simplification reigned, church designers recognized the ongoing importance of symbols, in both form and ornament. They insisted, however, that those symbols be fresh, meaningful, and spare, not what they saw as the excessive or irrelevant ornament of bygone times. In short, reformers envisioned the best new churches as buildings that were truly *of* their own times, *of* contemporary materials, *in* contemporary forms. In an age fraught with Cold War tensions and conspiracy theories, it should be no surprise that in religion, too, and in its architecture, Americans wanted clarity and openness.

This study draws out the dynamic between forward-looking church leaders, newly educated architects enthusiastic about the potential of modern design, and church building committees that tended to be cautious with their precious dollars. Many church architects, aware of the developments in Europe, felt that Americans were stuck in old patterns and were frustrated by the conservatism of building committees. Younger architects, in particular, suggested modernism to their clients. Sövik admitted that "in the beginning we sold it [modernism] on the basis of cost . . . people couldn't afford to build Gothic architecture; they might as well give up."[30] Soon, however, building committees chose contemporary architecture for its own reasons. Although a longing for beauty and awe never departed, the stronger impulse was for warm, comfortable spaces that engaged contemporary culture and integrated religious experience into the fabric of the modern world.

One can certainly find churches with Gothic and Colonial details from this period in the Midwest, but they tend to belong to older, wealthier congregations or denominations with strong bases in the Northeast and Southeast (Baptists and Presbyterians, for instance). Stade's Christ Evangelical and Reformed Church in Des Plaines (1964) is one example (Figures I.2 and I.3). Midwestern Lutherans, by contrast, were leaders in the modern church architecture movement, and a pan-Lutheran group founded the progressive and influential Lutheran Society for Worship, Music, and the Arts in Chicago in 1957. This progressivism came as something of a surprise to outsiders. The artist Albert Christ-Janer, writing in 1962, suggested that "one would expect this Church, so orthodox in theology and so conscious of its Old-World origins, to cling more tenaciously than any other to traditional forms in architecture. Instead, Lutheran congregations have led the way in the contemporary approach to religious design, often electrifying conservative communities with their modern churches." "In tradition bound America," he wrote, "the modernism of the Lutherans comes as something of a shock."[31]

The reasons for these denominational proclivities are not entirely clear. Even at the time, observers noted that, oddly enough, the more liturgical Protestant churches tended to be more adventurous in their architecture, and speculated that the anchor of liturgy freed them to experiment with design. The European connections of some denominations, such as the Lutherans and Roman Catholics, made them more aware of international architectural developments as well as the international crisis in Christianity and the powerful critique of business as usual in the churches. It is also evident that meaningful historical ties to a "Colonial" architectural tradition yoked some denominations and regions to historic forms. An abundance of Colonial churches were built in the postwar years, particularly in the Southeast, and there are compelling arguments that link a pro-American, conservative, Cold War mentality to this style of architecture, in churches as well as other private and public buildings.[32] A spirit of experiment and adventure, on the other hand, often marked the congregations that sought out a new horizon in religious architecture.

Congregations often made it plain that they did not want to build a shrine or a monument to themselves but a church that would be a servant in the community. In the dedication notes for Trinity Lutheran Church in Moorhead, Minnesota (1952), Sövik wrote, "The most important thing about a church is that it means something. It is a monumental building in the sense that it reaches our minds and spirits with ideas, and through it we speak to others and to ourselves."[33] Many building committees grasped this idea. They intended their buildings to fairly represent who they were and the message of the Gospel. Yet, in an era when architecture was in flux, money was scarce, and time was short, building committees, and architects too, had to make compromises.

Much has been written about the conformity of postwar suburban houses, and we might see these churches as just another way suburbanites desired to be like everyone else. But church buildings, and their congregations, simultaneously fit in and stood as a critique in their communities. They offered both comfort and challenge, "as a place pregnant with the possibility of another kind and level of human community . . . the church must celebrate its particular community in such a way as both to address but not to be swallowed up in general society; to address, not only with *grace* as that word is used in *Better Homes and Gardens*, but with the 'grace' as used in the New Testament."[34] Congregations intuitively sought this balance by asking their architects for something "attractive, not over pretentious," yet at the same time they wanted their church to "stand out" and have "character."[35]

As these often modest buildings indicate, these congregations had neither the resources nor the inclination to replicate the array of carefully orchestrated programming carried on by the large urban churches of earlier decades. Nor were these postwar churches a 1950s version of the later suburban megachurch. With their sympathetic architecture, they convey a connection to surrounding spaces and places, a belief in congregations integrated into their family-oriented communities. Congregations hoped their buildings would send a message about their faith, about piety and service. Understanding their church buildings as partners in evangelism, they believed they needed to be inviting yet vigorous, to look familiar yet still signify transformation.

A desire to make church architecture a "reflection" or "expression" of contemporary Christianity appears frequently in the writings of church leaders and church architects of the period. Modernism was a capable if somewhat unwieldy partner in this enterprise. Critics wanted the churches to go farther, to push modernism to its most challenging forms and thus disrupt comfortable ways of belief and practice. Suburbanites, not surprisingly, erred on the side of familiarity and comfort. This book tells the story of Midwestern architects and religious communities that sought to achieve a balance between comfort and challenge, and examines how modern church architecture took shape at the crossroads.

White, middle-class suburbia was fraught with prejudices, both sublimated and overt. Suburbanites often took comfortable privilege for granted and ignored the Americans who suffered as a result. Yet the 1950s suburban congregations that would put on a blackface minstrel show, by the 1960s were sending their teenagers on mission trips into the inner city and hosting summer schools for the children of migrant farmworkers.[36] Suburban churches were places of transformation as well as conformity. Critics of the postwar suburban church often seemed to pose a stark opposition—rare suburbanites were progressive, radical individualists, the rest were robotic conformists. Most human lives, however, fall somewhere in the middle of that spectrum. The architecture of the suburban church suggests where congregations placed themselves on that continuum.

This is not a comprehensive history, but a representative survey of architects, buildings, and congregations that played a role in shaping the religious culture of postwar suburban America. Church building projects were highly collaborative, and understanding why these buildings look the way they do requires knowing both the congregation and the larger body of work of the architect. The strength of my approach—centering the research on the work of three architects—is that it allows me to better understand the relationship between congregation and architect and to chart the work of the architects as they developed their personal styles and responded to challenges from their clients and their professional colleagues.

Like any approach, it also has limitations. In this case, by following these three architects, the study is less evenly representative of demographic features such as religious affiliation, class status, and race. It centers attention on congregations that would hire an architect rather than use a denominational architecture board or even stock plans. These congregations were typically mainstream, denominationally based, and solidly middle-class. This book is thus about a representative Midwestern collection of these congregations, primarily in the 1950s and early 1960s, as they worked with their architects to build religious lives in suburban America.

While researching this book I spent countless hours in suburban churches, wandering the halls with my camera, poring over dusty parish records often loosely filed in metal cabinets or placed in forgotten cardboard boxes and shoved into a dark closet. It was a joy and a privilege to meet those who remembered the active and hopeful congregational life of the 1950s and early 1960s. I am aware that because I primarily interviewed men and women still on the membership rolls, I have been talking to those who stayed active in parish life. That no doubt skews my results toward a more optimistic interpretation of the work these buildings and congregations did and continue to do. Nonetheless, my generous conversation partners were candid about both the successes and the failures of their architecture and the religious life it contained. Many times I have walked through a postwar suburban church in the company of those who remember the ground breaking, and I have been impressed by the mix of pride, gratitude, frustration, humor, and rich memory that the buildings recall. These conversations reveal the complex relationship between the spiritual and the material, the lofty and the practical, that is both a description of the way human beings experience architecture and a tension inherent in any group of religious beings living together. A delightful story about a full-blown historical pageant put on by a congregation segues easily into an account of God's blessings. A weakness or imperfection in architecture serves as a reminder of the limitations of human achievement. Classrooms evoke the memory of a wiggling crowd of little children and the way that faith moves through the generations—or does not.

In sum, these were functional, family-oriented buildings that provided stability when life seemed to be changing very fast. They represent an episode in the history of American Christianity, a period when the denominations expanded rapidly to meet the needs of an increasingly suburban population.[37] To outside observers (and some insiders as well) these buildings quickly came to represent a bourgeois suburban complacency, and by the mid-1960s the episode was passing. But these congregations and their church buildings were not simply about the status quo. Modern buildings required congregations to think anew about the structure and practice of their faith, and allowed them to plan for a dynamic future. The pattern of spaces, activities, and social interaction inside these buildings, all inflected to some degree with religious significance, formed a generation of Americans. Even today the sights, smells, and sounds of these churches recall a particular way of being religious in the postwar world.

This book begins with a broad view of the international conversation about modern religious architecture, showing why it was of such great interest and concern to both architects and many of their congregational clients. Midwestern congregations, through their architects and national and local denominational leadership, shared in a lively dialogue that linked the future of the church and its moral strength to architectural concerns, both programmatic and aesthetic. Advocates, in print and at national and local meetings for church builders, promoted modernism as a necessary means of revitalizing the church's message to the postwar world and carrying it into the future. Chapter 2 offers brief biographies of Sövik, Dart, and Stade, giving an account of their upbringing, their religious backgrounds, their formative experiences in World War II and at architecture school, and how those life experiences came together to shape their architecture.

The following three chapters take the reader into the church buildings, reconstructing the experience of the church-building and church-going suburbanite for whom these churches were an exciting departure from the past. Chapter 3 outlines the process of church building, a formative experience in the life of the postwar congregation. Drive and adaptability are evident in the generosity, hard work, and compromises common to the process. Fund-raising strategies, the design planning process, and a tendency to build in stages, or "units," illustrate the resourcefulness of these often young congregations. Chapter 4 is a close study of one ubiquitous and important postwar church type, the A-frame, which offers a window into how modern ideas and modern architecture were incorporated into the religious life of ordinary Americans. The A-frame church balanced old and new, allowing congregations to ease into modernism in a way that preserved a historical sense of church architecture. The form's efficient construction and relative cheapness also illustrate the practical considerations faced by postwar builders. Chapter 5 centers on the sanctuaries and the worship experience, which congregations understood as their central function. During the postwar years, an emphasis on the gathered congregation and the work of the people in liturgy led the denominations to reconsider the appropriate form of Christian worship space, and the axial plan increasingly gave way to a centralized one. Chapter 6 describes the important educational and fellowship spaces that also played a critical role in the religious lives of church members and neighbors who used those spaces for a variety of purposes. Social spaces reflected open and casual fellowship practices, while the Sunday school and education rooms reveal the influence of postwar thought regarding public-school education and a developing psychology of learning for all ages.

Drawing on the overview of postwar church building provided by the previous chapters, chapter 7 is a detailed case study of the religious life of one of the Midwest's most significant new suburbs, Park Forest, Illinois, the research lab for

William H. Whyte's important 1956 book *The Organization Man*. Here the architecture of Protestants is considered in neighborly dialogue with that of Jews and Catholics, in the full, suburban architectural context of houses, schools, and other public and commercial buildings. Park Forest's religious organizations balanced conformity, or "fitting in," with an expression of denominational or congregational uniqueness. Their architecture challenged, as well as complied with, architectural and social norms.

A historical account of these buildings and communities that stopped in the 1960s seemed to leave the story unfinished, for these suburban buildings still pose questions and present both problems and possibilities for congregations. The buildings live on. A final chapter thus tells the story of what has happened to some of them, and their congregations, in the ensuing decades. These churches continue to adapt to the ebb and flow of religious life in the suburbs. At the same time, they call up the memory of a few decades of extraordinary vitality, when religion, architectural modernism, and suburban growth coalesced to shape a remarkable episode in American religious life.

## A NOTE ON CHURCH NAMES AND DATES

Many of the buildings in this study have had multiple names. Sometimes this simply reflects inconsistency in spelling (St. Mark versus St Mark's, for example). At other times the names changed to reflect denominational activity. For instance, after the founding of the United Methodist denomination in 1968, a union of the Methodist Church (USA) and the Evangelical United Brethren Church, most Methodist churches added the word *United* to their names. For another example, in 1957, the Evangelical and Reformed (E&R) denomination merged with most of the Congregational Christian Churches into the United Church of Christ (UCC)—E&R churches became UCC. Finally, some church buildings have passed from congregation to congregation or even to secular purposes. Hope Lutheran in Park Forest became Celebration Ministries; Northlake Lutheran Church became Northlake City Centre. In the body of this book, I use the original names for these congregations and their buildings, as determined by period documents. In the appendices, I give the original name of the congregation as well as the name at the time of publication of this book (2015).

Dating these buildings requires some approximation. Rather than give the inclusive dates of a construction project, information not always clear from church records, I use the date of the first official use of the building, typically on or very close to its dedication date. Many of these buildings have date stones, which are useful, although frequently give a date one year or more prior to the actual completion of the building. Dedication dates better reflect the moment when architecture and congregation officially joined in service.

CHAPTER 1

# The Modern Church Movement

The postwar church building boom prompted much earnest conversation about what churches should look like and how they should function. Print resources multiplied, and building committees could often get their hands on the freshest advice for no more than the price of postage.[1] A wide range of books was readily available, from the most esoteric discussions of theology and liturgy, to straightforward and practical sources designed for building committees. Advice and opinion also proliferated via popular religious periodicals that were chock full of information about church architecture and the use and management of facilities.[2] Professional architecture journals frequently published articles about notable ecclesiastical buildings and trends in modern church design.[3] National ecumenical and denominational bodies provided consulting services for building committees and circulated photographs and printed materials filled with ideas about everything from acoustics to landscaping.[4] And, at national and international conferences, architects, church leaders, manufacturers, artists, and laypeople met in person to share information about building matters and discuss the relationship of architecture to mission. One architect claimed, "we are inundated with data, new and old ideas, constant reworking of similar themes and concepts."[5] Never before or since has so much concerted energy been directed toward American church design.

In 1959, Edward Frey, chairman of the Department of Architecture of the United Lutheran Church, told an assembly of architects and church leaders about two "exciting realities that have emerged" to shape the world of church design.[6] The first was a "really broad scale ecumenical enterprise" that drew the denominations together in common cause. Inspired by the 1948 inaugural meeting of the World Council of Churches in Geneva, in 1950 American Protestant leaders formed the National Council of Churches of Christ in the USA (NCC). The NCC, headquartered in New York City, became the central voice of the interdenominational

Protestant establishment in the postwar years.[7] Important differences in both belief and practice persisted among religious groups, but in the world of church building, ecumenism led to a widely shared conversation about architecture, a conversation in which Roman Catholics also played a major role. This Ecumenical Movement was closely tied to the Liturgical Movement (or, more broadly, "liturgical renewal"), which began among mid-nineteenth-century Catholics and by the mid-twentieth century had spread its concerns for renewed worship and congregational life to all the denominations. The Liturgical Movement emphasized that shared worship and shared work, grounded in biblical theology and history, were central and vital to Christian community.[8]

A second trend, according to Frey, was the emergence of a group of professionals devoting much of their time and resources to the problem of church building. Frey gave credit to church architects and liturgical designers, of course, but equally to those who wrote the books and magazine articles about all facets of the church building campaign, and those who advised congregations on building programs. National organizations helped coordinate and further these efforts. Among church architects, the most important were the Church Architecture Guild of America (founded in 1940; renamed the Guild for Religious Architecture in 1965), the Committee on Religious Architecture of the American Institute of Architects (organized in 1958), and the American Society for Church Architecture (organized in 1960).[9] Several divisions and committees of the NCC, particularly the Department of Church Building and Architecture and the Department of Worship and the Arts, provided leadership for the churches by offering information and advice and working closely with denominational architecture boards, church leaders, and architects. Not all the members of these organizations were immediately devoted to modern architecture, but convictions strongly trended in that direction. By 1960, it was hard to find a voice in any of these organizations that would advocate for anything but a contemporary approach to church architecture.

An educational film produced in 1958 by the American Institute of Architects and designed for church building committees illustrates the missionary zeal of these reformers.[10] The thirteen-minute production, titled *A Place to Worship*, commenced with images slowly fading in and out: "sky with floating clouds"; "Parthenon"; "classic Greeks at work." The narrator began: "Since the beginning of history man has devoted his best creative ability to building his place for worship. In each period of his history he has built his temple in the spirit of his time." As the film continued, images of Gothic and Renaissance churches were paired with medieval merrymakers and knights. Then the viewer was thrown into the modern world. City and highway noises accompanied a rapid-fire sequence of scenes of the city, the superhighway, and the suburb. "We live in a period of accelerated change, in the whirl of a technological revolution with all its untold human consequences," the narrator intoned. For "people who work in modern offices and factories, who live in modern communities, and drive to worship in streamlined cars, mere imitation of the architecture of past periods is out of place." Modern life, with its "new emphasis on the individual family, its material, emotional, and spiritual needs," required a religion "firmly anchored in the life of our day" and "best expressed by the architecture of our day." The film addressed the process of design and showed examples of modern churches and synagogues. The authors of the film, architects and churchmen, presented themselves as experts capable of guiding congregations embarking on building programs.

Pastors who contacted the national organizations to request educational materials sometimes doubted the ability of their congregations to welcome the message of modern church architecture. For instance, in 1958 the youthful Wilbur Canaday Jr., pastor of the Park Avenue Congregational Church in Arlington, Massachusetts, wrote that he had booked *A Place to Worship* and wanted the lowdown before showing it to his congregation. "I am wondering whether I should have previewed it first," he mused. "What I want to know is whether the examples shown in the picture are 'good' contemporary design, giving a fair picture of what we might expect if we went into contemporary. Of course in New England Congregationalism, it would have to be a 'conservative' contemporary, and I am also wondering whether the film would shock them out of their wits."[11] Building committees typically had no qualms about embracing the latest improvements in heating or insulation, or making the floor plan of the church building more convenient. It was much harder for them to let go of their ideas about what a church should *look* like, particularly their affinity for the sense of history and tradition conveyed in steeples, white pillars, or Gothic arches.

The experts did their best to convey their often novel opinions to the ordinary Americans who were seeking to make their faith visible in architecture. It is hard to calculate precisely the range of influence of these national bodies, although their publications are found in the files of many churches. Letters in organizational records document frequent requests for information, and much of the conversation made its way into broadly circulated publications such as *Your Church* or *Church Management*. One article by a Guild member published in the April 1962 issue of *Farm Journal Magazine* brought in "over 700 requests . . . for exhibits, slides, pamphlets, etc.—and these requests are coming from building committees."[12]

All three architects in this study were active participants in these conversations. Edward Sövik was able to use these organizations and their publications as a platform for his formidable thought. He served as president of the Guild for Religious Architecture and edited its newsletter, served on many national committees, and wrote a book and more than seventy articles.[13] Charles Stade's contributions were more practical and local. He contributed his enthusiasm for modern design, wrote a column, "From the Architect," in the national journal *Your Church*, and offered much helpful advice about the exchange between architect and building committee.

Edward Dart also attended national meetings of church architects and wrote occasionally for the popular press. His thoughtful church work shows that he was attentive to both architectural trends and new theological insights.

## MODERN CHURCHES IN AMERICA

Modernism in church architecture had its beginnings well before the postwar period. In America, historians of architecture might begin with Frank Lloyd Wright's Unity Temple in Oak Park, Illinois (1908), a Unitarian building that was innovative in its plan and use of steel-reinforced concrete. But the revolution in church architecture really began in Europe after the First World War, the result of sweeping reforms by church leaders and architects of many different places and Christian traditions. As one American lamented in 1953, Europeans had engaged in thirty years of "continual inquiring and sympathetic search for appropriate church architecture, a search that puts to shame the warmed-over gothic which we still accept so readily."[14] European architects began to lay the groundwork for a new church architecture in the 1920s, revolutionizing both design and structure. Auguste Perret's Catholic Church of Notre Dame in the Paris suburb of Le Raincy (1922–23) showed the potential of reinforced concrete—great volume with strength and lightness. A 1928 Lutheran church by German architect Otto Bartning achieved a similar effect of light and volume using structural steel. Another important early European example is Corpus Christi Catholic Church, Aachen, Germany, 1930, designed by the influential German architect and theorist Rudolf Schwarz (Figures 1.1 and 1.2). At Corpus Christi, a simple, stark white rectangular box with tower, plain, unornamented walls, and luminous interior, Schwarz demonstrated a new way of thinking about worship space, spatially and aesthetically. Strong, simple forms, dramatic lighting, and clarity of liturgical purpose marked Schwarz's pathbreaking building.[15]

A few early American experiments with modern church architecture drew notice and even acclaim, such as the Church of St. Clement (Episcopal) in Alexandria, Virginia (Joseph H. Saunders, 1948), a dark box lit by pinpoints of light, with the altar in the center. But tradition held sway. Americans who leaned toward modern churches faced articulate and persuasive opponents. In 1948, Elbert Conover, the middle-aged director of the Interdenominational Bureau of Architecture (founded in 1933), cautioned about "the encroachment of fads." Citing the church building's important evangelistic function, he insisted it must "be distinctively and easily recognizable as a place of divine worship"; it must "look like a church" and express "endurance, shelter and welcome" as well as "aspiration," to fulfill this function.[16] Among American Protestants, the final decisions about the design of church buildings typically rested on the shoulders of local, lay-led building committees, not architects or even denominational leaders, and these laypeople often came to the task with strong beliefs about what a church should look like.

FIGURE 1.1. Rudolf Schwarz, Sankt Fronleichnam (Corpus Christi), Aachen, Germany, 1930. Foto Marburg/Art Resource, New York.

Very few architects of this period rejected the notion that a church should "look like a church," but, together with their clients, they redefined what that meant. Conover believed his own times to be "the most difficult period in the history of church design" because of the tug-of-war between tradition and "something entirely new." His solution was to modify a historic style to give it contemporary meaning, and to fully modernize the church plan. Of the several hundred church plans reviewed by the Bureau in 1947–48, he noted, scarcely more than a dozen were of contemporary architectural style.

Ten years later, however, American churches were looking markedly different. Two iconic Midwestern churches from the late 1940s had a strong influence on

FIGURE 1.2. Sankt Fronleichnam (Corpus Christi), Aachen, Germany, sanctuary. Foto Marburg/Art Resource, New York.

shaping the new regional church design: Frank Lloyd Wright's First Unitarian Society Meeting House in Madison, Wisconsin (1951) (Figure 1.3), and Eliel Saarinen's Christ Lutheran Church, Minneapolis (1949) (Figures 1.4 and 1.5).[17] Wright's Madison meetinghouse had an especially far-reaching influence on the development of the Midwestern modern church because of its connections to the iconic Wright himself and the Prairie Style he popularized, but also because it was a striking form that combined warmth and human scale with drama. Many regional A-frames borrow ideas from this building, especially the sweeping prow on the north side of the building (see chapter 4). As a means of cutting costs, Wright used wood and stone as the primary construction materials, materials used by many suburban church designers.[18] The back of the worship room blended seamlessly into the social space of the parlor, and a similar spatial arrangement appealed to suburban congregations interested in both a less formal division of space and flexibility. Wright's building brought people together in comfort without sacrificing the dignity of the gathering, and its cozy, sheltering aspect appealed to a Midwestern audience. As one northern building committee noted, "One can worship in a tent, or in the great out-of-doors. But in a Minnesota winter, it's always good to have a place where people can gather in relative comfort, there to be strengthened in faith, to build up the body of Christ and to share the Good News.[19]

FIGURE 1.3. Frank Lloyd Wright, First Unitarian Society Meeting House, Madison, Wisconsin, 1946–52. Photograph by Adam Childers.

FIGURE 1.4. Eliel Saarinen, Christ Lutheran Church, Minneapolis, Minnesota, 1949. Photograph copyright Christ Church Lutheran, Minneapolis, Minnesota. 

FIGURE 1.5. Christ Lutheran Church, Minneapolis, Minnesota, sanctuary from choir loft during worship service, circa 1951. Photograph copyright Christ Church Lutheran, Minneapolis, Minnesota. 

Whereas the origins of Wright's meetinghouse were regional, the design of Christ Lutheran Church had strong ties to northern European church architecture. Eliel Saarinen, a Finnish immigrant and son of a Lutheran clergyman, designed Christ Lutheran at the request of its young pastor, William Buege. This established, middle-class congregation in a residential area south of the city center had been attempting to build a new church since before World War II, and the congregation anticipated something Gothic, like the new stone church built by Olivet Lutheran in Minneapolis at the same time (Hugo Haeuser, 1949). Pastor Buege, however, advocated for contemporary architecture, both because of his progressive outlook and his belief that only contemporary architecture would be affordable for his congregation. He traveled to the Cranbrook School in Detroit to pitch this modest parish project to Saarinen, challenging him to design a spiritually satisfying, inexpensive, modern church for a relatively small congregation. Critics still admire this intimate space, its unadorned simplicity, sensitive and dramatic indirect lighting, perfect acoustics (open brickwork on the north wall covers sound-abating material), soft colors, and warm, clean surfaces. Saarinen's earlier, larger Tabernacle

Church of Christ (now First Christian) in Columbus, Indiana (1942), is essentially the same form, as are Rudolf Schwarz's Corpus Christi and many other European churches of the 1950s. Christ Lutheran is one of the best of a common type of Midwestern postwar church: a long rectangular, high-ceilinged, processional nave with a slightly raised chancel at one end, a nearly flat roof, and a free-standing or attached tower near the entrance. Together, Wright's meetinghouse and Saarinen's churches brought ecclesiastical modernism to the Midwest in a manner that resonated with regional architects and congregations.

## ARCHITECTS AND DESIGNERS TAKE UP THE CAUSE

Architects who worked with building committees to design sacred spaces required special knowledge and skills. In the early decades of the century, denominational bodies had provided the primary oversight and guidance for church building efforts. In 1940, church architects formed their own mutually supportive, professional organization, the Church Architecture Guild. Members of associated professions were also valued Guild members, such as Henry Lee Willet of Willet Studios, a notable Philadelphia stained- glass workshop. The Guild's purpose was primarily educational, a goal reinforced by its close ties with the *Christian Herald,* an evangelical periodical that was eager at the time to publish articles and news relating to church building. Guild members were concerned about the lack of resources for architects and building committees, a condition they believed was in part to blame for the mediocrity of many American church buildings.

By 1959, the Guild had about 150 members, estimated to be designing about one-third of the new churches in America.[20] "Church work" was broadly conceived by Guild architects as not simply a matter of designing contemporary worship space, but creating spaces that met the many functions of the modern church. Guild members acknowledged that "the Church must play a bigger role in the life of the Community, with Spiritual refreshment and well as intellectual stimulants, cultural integrity and recreational opportunities. This creates the problem which we as Guild Architects are eager to solve."[21] Many viewed their line of work as one of service and sacrifice. They saw themselves as addressing critical social and spiritual needs through architectural design, including not just worship but educational, social, and administrative spaces.

Most of the Guild members were modernists. Philadelphia architect Harold Wagoner, Guild president from 1957 to 1958, was well known for his substantial and expensive church complexes in historic revival styles. Yet, even Wagoner was drawn to modern designs. Sövik recalled his good friend Wagoner telling him, "Ed, you are so fortunate you've never done a Georgian church," and Wagoner envied Sövik for his progressive clients.[22] In 1955, Frederick Webber, an older Lutheran pastor who had been a strong advocate for Gothic revival architecture and art, expressed his frustration that church architects were turning their backs on traditional church architecture. He complained about "this crack-pot Church Architecture Guild, or whatever they call it . . . They have annual conventions, exhibitions of photographs of Modern church buildings, and award prizes . . . usually they are careful to award the prize to some Smart Aleck type of extreme Modern."[23] The Guild in fact tended to represent a moderate vision of modernism, and later critics accused its members of not being modern *enough*.

When prominent architect and Guild member Walter Taylor was serving as director of the Department of Education and Research of the American Institute of Architects in Washington, D.C., he discovered a great need for a central clearinghouse of information among the different faiths. In response, he initiated a bibliographic project on religious architecture and in 1958 founded the Committee on Religious Architecture within the AIA, charged with pursuing specialized research for publication in the AIA's professional journal. A list of suggested members for this new AIA committee reflects both its ecumenical nature and its emphasis on critically acclaimed new architecture: in New England, Pietro Belluschi (MIT); for New York, Percival Goodman, a prolific architect of temples and synagogues; in the Midwest, Eero Saarinen (Eliel's son), Edward Sövik (one of the youngest architects represented), and Harold Spitznagel (a Sioux Falls, South Dakota architect with a strong national reputation). Other names on the list were Victor Lundy (Florida), Milton Ryan (Texas), James Hunter (Colorado), Paul Thiry (Washington), and Wayne Williams (California).[24] By the mid-1960s, acknowledging their shared concerns and the need for efficiency, the AIA made the Guild an affiliate member.[25] Guild members had been working with Catholic and Jewish as well as Protestant groups and aimed to increase their ecumenical base and bolster their reputation. At this time, the organization changed its name to the Guild for Religious Architecture and became deliberately interfaith in program and membership.

Edward Sövik became a director of the Guild in 1960, took over editorship of its newsletter in 1961, served as vice president in 1966, and assumed the presidency after the death of the incumbent later that year. Sövik aggressively moved the Guild toward greater professionalism and theological awareness, primarily through his voluminous writing and insistence on theological sophistication and architectural excellence. In 1961, at the National Conference on Church Architecture in Pittsburgh, Sövik delivered the address "New Visions for Church Builders" in which he powerfully articulated the mission of the church architect while he gently chastised the profession where it had failed to embrace modernism. He reminded his listeners, "We have insisted that *the great thing about Christianity is not that it is old but that it is alive*; that if the church is to speak to people in the twentieth century it should speak their language."[26] Practical needs were important, too, he acknowledged. Churches "ought to be comfortable, useful, efficient, durable, and very inexpensive while not appearing to be so."[27] These two points—that the church must be alive and it must be practical—had been commonly made throughout the 1950s, but Sövik blended them with a message full of strong theological content. He insisted, "The building is not simply a shelter which ministers to the body while the pastor ministers to the mind and Spirit. The building also ought to be a minister and to communicate the word . . . And if it doesn't function in this way, it isn't very functional."[28]

When Sövik first took over the Guild's newsletter, he used its pages to argue that liturgy and theology were both in flux, calling into question previous assumptions about what the church *is*, and the appropriate "atmosphere" or "psychology" of worship.[29] His questions were never just about architecture, but ultimately about the role of the church for individuals and society and the definition of true worship and piety. In his efforts to educate his peers, he also drew their attention to important organizations, notably the Roman Catholic Liturgical Arts Society (publisher of *Liturgical Arts*), the Lutheran Society for Worship, Music, and the Arts (and its journal *Response: In Worship-Music-The Arts*), as well as international publications, such as the German journal *Kunst und Kirche (Art and the Church)*. Sövik preached from the pages of the newsletter, reminding architects that they needed to be seekers of truth and to have their *own* vision and not rely on building committees to provide it. In 1965, he served as chair of the AIA's Committee on Architecture, and his leadership no doubt was an important force in drawing the AIA and the Guild closer together.[30]

Another national organization, the Chicago-based American Society for Church Architecture (ASCA), was an outgrowth of an annual Chicago trade conference of church building suppliers, which had begun in 1956 under the auspices of the Church Federation of Greater Chicago. It was broadly ecumenical from the beginning, and included Roman Catholics and Jews among its members. The ASCA held its own annual conference, as well as smaller regional meetings and workshops around the country, and published a journal (primarily of its conference lectures) from 1961 to 1976. Membership was a national and diverse mix of architects, theologians, pastors, and craftsmen, although the center of gravity of the organization remained in the Protestant Midwest. The ASCA's collaboration with the Guild and the NCC was frequent and friendly. Stade was heavily involved in the ASCA, and served as its president from 1964 to 1966. Dart and Sövik also participated in some of the ASCA's work, and Dart became a member in 1963.

When considering church architects as a professional body during this period, it is helpful to think in terms of generations. The three architects who anchor this study, and many of the church architects of their day, were of the World War II generation. Their architectural education took place in a postwar world where old designs and old ways of doing business were questioned as a matter of course. Modernism to them was a given, although in danger of becoming trite. They constantly pushed questions of honesty, authenticity, and quality. They had clear ideological reasons for designing as they did. And, like their often youthful suburban building committees, they were willing to take risks for what they believed was true and good. Observers note a shift in church architecture from the 1950s into the 1960s, and in part that is the result of this generational changing of the guard.

## CHURCH LEADERS AND THEOLOGIANS JOIN IN

Just as church architects joined together to sharpen their profession, the churches likewise desired to have a stronger and more coherent influence on architecture. Most denominations had some form of architecture committee that advised congregations, suggested architects to building committees, and sometimes provided plans. Their advice tended to be practical and their designs fairly conservative. What marked these denominational bodies after the war was their cooperation, resulting in an increasingly sophisticated theological, architectural, and social critique.

Two divisions of the NCC dealt specifically with church architecture. The first, the Bureau of Church Building and Architecture, was the descendant of the Interdenominational Bureau of Architecture and the branch most occupied with publishing brochures, coordinating the efforts of the denominations, and dispensing advice to architects and building committees.[31] The Bureau's close ties with the churches grounded it in the practical, with a tendency to recognize a variety of viable approaches to design and construction problems. Among its publications, an extensive series of twenty four-page leaflets titled *Briefs for Church Builders* began circulating in the late 1950s and early 1960s. Brief no. 1, dated 1956, was about as mundane as they came: "Church Parking." These booklets are full of practical wisdom about the everyday concerns of American churchgoers and their pastors, the sort of advice most eagerly sought by the churches. Because of its voluminous publications, the Bureau had a significant impact nationwide.

The other NCC wing that dealt directly with architecture was the Department of Worship and the Arts (DWA), housed in the Division of Christian Life and Work headed by Methodist theologian Marvin Halverson. The DWA's purpose was to make clear connections between art and theology for modern society because "the church should have a vanguard of men and women qualified to interpret the significance of contemporary art for the believer and able to make contact with the influential movements of our time in all of the arts."[32] DWA activities encompassed architecture, fine art, drama, literature, music, ways of worship, and later, the popular arts. The Department directed most of its efforts toward artists and clergy, and published important bibliographies of recent scholarly work on Christianity and the arts.

The DWA's Commission on Architecture, first meeting in 1954, was a fairly heady group whose focus was "professional and theoretical." Members were practicing architects, heads of schools of architecture, and prominent clergy.[33] The first committee included among its members the Reverend Darby Betts, president (Cathedral of St. John the Divine, and former rector of one of first modern churches,

St. Clement in Alexandria, Virginia, 1948), Edward Sövik, G. E. Kidder Smith (architect, photographer, New York Episcopalian), architects William Conklin, Frederick Dunn, Herbert Johe, Norman Nagle, John Oliver Nelson, and Harold Spitznagel, with Marvin Halverson integrally involved in the proceedings. Halverson was a learned theologian, a good conversationalist, and a close friend of New York intellectuals such as the theologian and philosopher Paul Tillich. He was a zealous and determined crusader who felt that the church had abdicated its role as a leader in the arts. Halverson wanted Christian art to carry a theological message that would challenge, rather than accommodate, culture.

Tension between the Bureau and the DWA Commission suggests the wide range of opinions and goals within the church architecture movement. The Bureau understood the everyday needs of congregations and was more sympathetic to their concerns. The Commission, while armed with tremendous intellectual firepower, was somewhat removed from the economic and social concerns of congregations. A tone of condescension toward ordinary Christians tends to creep into its records. One member acknowledged that building churches was "not a profitable business; too much underpaid psychiatry in it," and that "building committees are difficult but one can sometimes put a good building over on them."[34] Although the Commission hosted many interesting and lively conversations, few concrete suggestions emerged from these discussions. The Commission's discussions nonetheless remain a helpful indicator of national and international dialogue among intellectuals, and a measure of the aspirations of those with high theological and artistic standards for new church architecture.

One live topic of debate during these years was the place of symbol in architecture, either symbol of form (for instance, a church in the form of a fish) or decorative symbols (in stained glass, for example). The DWA, with its focus on artistic expression broadly defined, was particularly interested in the relationship of faith to symbol. Commission members noticed that some modernist church architects had become enamored with form, pursuing interesting, exotic, or symbolic geometries. For some, a cautionary tale was provided by Beth Shalom, Frank Lloyd Wright's new synagogue in Philadelphia, which Darby Betts called a kind of "program architecture" that was "uncomfortably reminiscent of those road side ice cream stands in the form of ice cream cones."[35] In April 1960, the Commission organized a dialogue centered on this question of symbolism, suggesting that the thoughtful use of culturally relevant symbols could be the antidote to nostalgic sentimentalism and a way of proclaiming the deeper meaning of modern forms.[36]

The two primary speakers at this New York event, with fiercely divergent points of view, were Julian Hartt, chairman of the Department of Religion at Yale University, representing theology, and Joseph Hudnut of MIT, the influential former head of the Harvard Graduate School of Design, representing architecture.[37] Dr. Hartt gave a long, erudite talk about the value of the symbolic in architecture. In response, Professor Hudnut declared that he disagreed with Hartt's argument for the need for overt symbols. Anything didactic, he argued, would sap the life out of the forms. Later that afternoon, Hudnut clarified his reservations. "I have a friend who built a church in the form of a triangle," he said, ". . . and he explained it to me as a symbol—he said it is a symbol of the Trinity. Now the fact that he had to explain that meant that symbol had no power. If you walk into a church and you don't realize the triangle is the Trinity and someone has to tell you—"Look—see—that is the Trinity"—the symbol is gone."[38] Rather than educating people to grasp opaque symbols, Hudnut argued, we should be teaching them about form and "the language of structure and space."

Despite hosting such animated conversations, the entire Department of Worship and the Arts, including the Commission on Architecture, struggled for visibility and influence and consistently lacked financial support. Around 1962, Halverson gave up, citing reasons that were "deeper and more complex" than a simple lack of funds. He attributed the DWA's miseries to "the profound estrangement of the Church from the arts and the culture as a whole."[39] Halverson's ambitions were grand: he wanted the church to have an influence over not just church architecture and liturgical arts, but the whole realm of human creativity. His aims were so sweeping, structural, and idealistic that perhaps failure was inevitable, especially given the depth of the chasm between these concerns and that of the typical American building committee, with its insistent needs and strained resources.

Clearly, the desire of building committees to answer to their own preferences was a burr under the saddle of tastemakers such as the DWA Commission members. The probable cause for these tensions was a difference in mood; most Americans did not share the intellectual angst of Halverson and his peers in New York. Founding documents of the DWA offer a glum assessment of contemporary society's "dehumanization," "impersonality," "loss of community," "alienation and anxiety," and the general "dissolution of older loyalties and ideals"—not exactly a close match for the optimism of a new suburban congregation.[40] A Congregational pastor from Omaha, for instance, wrote to the DWA in 1956 requesting advice about appropriate art to match his congregation's new contemporary education building. He was looking for a picture of Jesus and did not want to appear uncultured, but explicitly did not want the brooding Jesus by the French expressionist Georges Rouault, an artist often recommended to congregations by elites. Instead, he wrote, "I crave something fresh and expressive of searching, yet deeply peaceful."[41] Generally, architects and clergy were less dismissive of the instincts of ordinary Christians and eager to help them see the need for a new artistic vision.

In October 1961, at the same time the DWA was disbanding, Marvin Halverson, Alfred H. Barr (art critic and founder of the Museum of Modern Art), and Paul Tillich established a Foundation for the Arts, Religion, and Culture, an organization poised to take over the work of the DWA. Many of the members of this foundation had been active in the Department. By 1965, a new Center for Interfaith Research on Religious Architecture, another organization based in New York City, had also assumed some of the work of the Commission.

## A LIVELY PUBLIC CONVERSATION SPREADS THE WORD

In print and at local, national, and international meetings, Americans with a stake in the contemporary church speculated about its future and considered the role that architecture would and should play. They educated architects and building committees, critiqued recent church buildings, and built momentum. As a way of tracking this dialogue, we will join the conversation in three important places: the national conferences that brought congregations, architects, and church leaders together; architectural awards and exhibition programs that endorsed a selection of designs and practices; and international concerns and contacts that broadened the discussion.

The most important national conferences during the postwar period were those organized jointly by the Guild and the NCC's Department of Church Building and Architecture, beginning with the Cincinnati meeting in 1955, and called the National Conference on Church Architecture.[42] Sövik, reflecting on the value of these conferences after the Cleveland meeting of 1962, wrote to his peers: "The chance to see what others are doing, to listen to what a distinguished theologian and a distinguished architect are thinking, to talk at length with old and new friends—to be thoroughly submerged in ideas, opinions, reactions, controversy, hopes, possibilities, enthusiasms—these are great days."[43] Although attendance might be 1,500 people during these years, the audience was far greater because the best of the talks and notice of the awards were inevitably published in journals and magazines, such as *Your Church* or *Church Management,* and were collected in edited volumes. The Guild's *Newsletter* noted in preparation for the Detroit conference of 1958: "With the tremendous building and remodeling program now taking place in our country, the annual conference on church architecture is one of the most important gatherings of its type. Many of the churches which are planning to build or remodel will have their committees at the meeting to obtain information on plans, materials, and equipment."[44] In addition to architecture, conference organizers included representatives of related craft traditions and showcased their work. Exhibitions (primarily photographic) of both architecture and allied crafts were mounted and awards granted for both finished churches and projects under way (drawings and/or models). Moving the venue allowed regional participation and gave attendees the valuable opportunity to see and experience new church buildings in different parts of the country. Meeting sites included St. Louis (1957), Los Angeles (1959), Minneapolis (1960), Pittsburgh (1961), Cleveland (1962), Seattle (1963), Dallas (1964), Chicago (1965), San Francisco (1966), Miami (1967), and St. Louis again (1969). More than half were held in centrally located cities, and, after the 1953 meeting in Washington, D.C., none in the Northeast until a return to Washington in 1970.

Early conferences were heavily weighted toward the practical. For example, the 1959 conference in Los Angeles, the first West Coast meeting, included workshops titled "What Building Committees Ought to Do," "Selecting and Working with the Architect," and "How to Serve Recreation and Fellowship Needs." Attendees included "pastors, members of boards and building committees that are in the throes of deciding what kind of church they shall build."[45] The most highly attended sessions were those that went over the work of building committees, those that discussed changing worship practices, and those that addressed financial issues.

A closer look at the three-day conferences in Minneapolis (1960) and Chicago (1965) will illustrate how the conferences changed in content and tone during those years, from the peak of the church boom to the beginning of the decline. Participants increasingly forecast a difficult future as denominations struggled to adapt to a changing American culture. Both conferences had a regional focus and attendance was heavily local.

The Minneapolis meeting took place during three days in early May 1960. Besides the Guild and the Bureau, the conference was sponsored by local chapters of the AIA and local councils of churches. Minneapolis seemed a particularly apt location for such a conference, as many saw the region as "the cradle of modern church architecture."[46] And, after viewing the thirty-five churches on the conference tour, Guild members "all found it to be true." One church emphasized in the tour and discussion was First Christian (Roy Thorshov and Robert Cerny, 1954), very similar to Saarinen's Christ Lutheran.

The Minneapolis conference title, "The Modern Church: Its Message and Its Architectural Challenge," signaled the spirit of the meeting. Edward Frey gave a keynote address titled "Why What We Believe Should Determine What We Build" and set the tone for the panel discussions to follow. He reminded his audience that "it is necessary that our buildings fairly bristle with belief or the whole effort will fail to advance the Christian witness in our communities which are already overwhelmed with the smogs of secularism."[47] By the time of the Minneapolis meeting, church leaders were painfully aware of the many uninspired churches that had been built since World War II and believed that impatience and thoughtlessness were to blame. Frey stressed that the outward appearance of the building was not the first aspect to consider. "A faithful pastor . . . wrote to me some months ago" asking for "a picture or photograph of a fine contemporary church building, preferably in color, that he might hang up to stimulate the people's thinking about a new church building."[48] Frey's response was to encourage him to think not about appearance but about significance. "I see too much attractive design frankly contrived for sensual effect," he told the crowd in Minneapolis, "demanding attention by strong visual impact and delight, but unable to deliver any meaning beyond itself, once it has captured the eye."[49]

The Minneapolis conference was the largest to date and significant because of its aim to "relate the arts to church building for the first time at a major conference involving the public."[50] An emphasis on the vital need for beauty in churches was accompanied by exhibitions of architecture and craft, and architect Robert Durham of Seattle, the curator of the Guild's growing slide collection, showed his slides of outstanding recent European and American churches. Registration lists for the conference indicate that Stade, Dart, and Sövik were all in attendance, as were most other regional church architects of note. A postconference tour brought many attendees to Marcel Breuer's St. John's Abbey in Collegeville, currently under construction. St. John's, although not a design widely copied in parish churches, was an intriguing building, and furthermore the Abbey and St. John's College was a critical center in the Roman Catholic Liturgical Movement.[51]

At the awards luncheon, Guild president Walter Damon summed up the plight of the church architect in 1960, as he saw it. Working with "bewildered building committees," the architect must "understand how the church worships, must keep up with the latest standard for church schools and the program of the church; must know what sound materials to use, what new, better, and mass produced items can be used." He must also know "how to meet the needs of the church on its site, and how to combine all these into a House of God where its members can reach God in their worship, where its children learn about the triune God, and how to live as Jesus taught." Finally, all this must happen "in a place so sacred that unconsciously one bows his head, so inviting it says come unto me, so beautiful in a simple way, while at the same time majestic, that it tells the passer-by it is a Christian church, designed by man with the help of God, and for Him."[52] These are tremendously high expectations, and architects felt both excitement and the weight of responsibility.

By the 1965 Chicago conference, "Church Architecture: New Concepts in Education and Mission," seminars and lectures reflected a greater emphasis on wider social mission and the tone was more critical and pessimistic. Much conference programming concerned mission and its relationship to the built environment, spurred by concerns that youth were increasingly dissatisfied with the church. Paul Tillich, who claimed his earliest ambition was to be an architect, delivered the "prophetic" concluding address, "Honesty and Consecration in Religious Art and Architecture," in which he asked the audience provocative questions such as "Is it honest today to have churches at all? Do we need and do we still want places of consecration?"[53] He glorified the storefront and the house church, yet still confessed a belief that humans needed holy times and spaces to counterbalance the secular. The program included a variety of papers and panels on Christian education, the mission of the church in urban society, and the church's role in developing communities. Speakers included planners such as Stanley V. Hallett, head of the Church Planning Department of the Church Federation of Greater Chicago, who was instrumental in organizing the innovative religious life of the new city of Columbia, Maryland, around shared central facilities.

Church tours incorporated into the conference program included visits to three Stade churches: Bethany Theological Seminary in Oak Brook, Good Shepherd Methodist in Park Ridge, and St. John's Lutheran in Lincolnwood. Also on the tour was Dart's Lansing Presbyterian Church, which Sövik found set "a standard of imaginative space and careful detail in the humblest of sound materials."[54] Attendees visited some older Chicago-area buildings of significance, such as Frank Lloyd Wright's Unity Temple in Oak Park and Rockefeller Chapel at the University of Chicago. Mies's Chapel at the Illinois Institute of Technology was on tour, as was Minoru Yamasaki's North Shore Congregation Israel in Glencoe. Additional sites included education facilities and mission projects.

In Sövik's report to the Guild following the conference, he highlighted the Guild's name change (from the Church Architecture Guild to the Guild for Religious Architecture), emphasizing that it demonstrated "the interest in both an ecumenical and interfaith vision of service and understanding." He noted that the churches were increasingly focused on living in the "world" and "must turn away from the temptation to invest their energies in the building of institutions to the detriment of serving their communities." He appreciated Paul Tillich's talk and his serious question as to whether church buildings should even be built at all, particularly if they interfered with the ability of Christians to engage the secular world in all its complexity.[55]

One wonders whether the incorporation of speakers such as Tillich—of intellectual interest but not highly useful for most of the attendees—moved the conference in a direction that made it less helpful for church building committees. Henry Willet expressed concern that the national conference was becoming so cerebral and out of touch with "clients who still require places of worship and education facilities that fit *their* needs" that it no longer was serving the needs of ordinary architects and building committees. He urged the conference to continue to address "all the practical, realistic approaches to today's problems" and to restrain the "attempt of certain highly intelligent and able theorists to take over the conferences in order to promulgate their ideas to the exclusion of all else."[56] According to Willet, this turn had "led to discord, bickering and the driving away from the conferences those architects, clergy and clients who still feel they have the right to build the type of religious structure they believe their congregations need." Preachy rhetoric was not going to transform ordinary church building projects, he reasoned. Tensions such as these within and among organizations, often a clash between the practical and the theoretical, reveal the many and sometimes competing interests that all had a stake in the architecture of new churches.

One way the conferences continued to address building committees was by publicizing and promoting what the professionals deemed the best of the newest church architecture. The national organizations collected and circulated images of new churches worthy of notice and granted awards of merit to the best work.

Since the 1940s, a popular service of denominations as well as the Guild and the NCC committees had been the assemblage of traveling exhibitions of photographs of new churches. On the one hand, the practice of circulating images of "good" buildings, vetted by the profession, makes a great deal of sense. On the other hand, publicizing such images would have perpetuated the tendency of building committees to think in terms of design (not program, as many architects urged), and also might have discouraged originality. Nevertheless, it was a common practice, and even the Museum of Modern Art in New York had a hand in it, with its traveling exhibition of photographs of modern church architecture, showing twenty-four buildings from seven countries.

Although the records regarding the circulation of the images are sketchy, occasional documents reveal a busy travel schedule. For instance, in 1958–59, the Guild's traveling exhibition went to thirteen cities from Washington, D.C., to Madison, Wisconsin, spending anywhere from one day to two weeks at each site, where showings were often accompanied by lectures.[57] By 1965, the Guild collection primarily consisted of slides of contemporary church interiors and exteriors, their artistic details and even more serviceable areas such as meeting rooms and classrooms, but it also included interior and exterior views of traditional, Gothic, and colonial churches. The slides were grouped according to geographic region—"Midwestern" being one—and such classification may not only have reflected but perpetuated the growth of regional styles.[58] In 1962, the Guild was invited to send a special exhibition to the Coventry Cathedral Festival in England. It included twelve images from its recent traveling shows, including Stade's Valparaiso University chapel.[59]

Probably the most influential of these traveling shows was one organized by the NCC Commission on Architecture after its selection of eighteen "outstanding new churches" erected in America since 1930 was announced in April 1956 to much fanfare (Appendix A).[60] The list reflected the judgments of Walter Taylor and the other members of the Commission on Architecture of the DWA, who were asked to nominate up to twenty-five candidates. The winners were those buildings that received the most nominations. On the one hand, constructing such a list seems to be a somewhat arbitrary enterprise. But the list and its popularity show how much Americans wanted to know what to do about this new architecture, what they should consider "good" among the many modern churches, and the tastemakers were happy to oblige.

The judges emphasized not just the most striking and beautiful designs but the best use of materials to match limited budgets, and the fit between building and context.[61] Belluschi's Zion Lutheran, in Portland, Oregon, offered "a fine lesson in how beautifully and how very economically the new techniques and materials of our generation can be used to create a structure rich in all the warmth and vitality of the Christian tradition." Eero Saarinen's round chapel at the Massachusetts Institute of Technology was "particularly appropriate for a retreat in the midst of a scientific and tech community." Alden Dow's First Methodist in Midland, Michigan, was praised for how the extended glass areas related to the massive brick piers, "creating an interplay of light and shadow." Less expensive, innovative churches that made the list were the San Lorenzo Community Church in California (1941, 1953), created out of Bruce Goff's Quonset hut chapel moved from a nearby naval base and renovated, and Paul Schweikher's economical and efficient Methodist church in Plainfield, Iowa (1951) (Figures 1.6 and 1.7). The jury liked Schweikher's "flexible use of space" and the "simple and dignified" design. Of these eighteen buildings, all but one (St. Matthew's Episcopal, Pacific Palisades, burned in 1978) still stand.

Architectural awards programs such as the NCC's list offer insight into the direction of church design during these decades. Guild awards from the 1960 meeting in Minneapolis heavily favored the Midwest (eight of twelve awards). Awardees included Stade's Valparaiso University Chapel of the Resurrection (1959) and Dart's St. Augustine Episcopal in Gary, Indiana (1958), noted for its "fresh and creative" design.[62] The following year at the 1961 Pittsburgh conference, the jury gave most of the thirteen awards to West Coast architects, and the judges speculated that this was explained by "a lack of inhibitions on the part of western

FIGURE 1.6. Paul Schweikher, Methodist Church, Plainfield, Iowa, 1951. William C. Hedrich for Hedrich-Blessing, HB-15361-K, Chicago History Museum.

FIGURE 1.7. Methodist Church, Plainfield, Iowa, interior. William C. Hedrich for Hedrich-Blessing, HB-15361-F, Chicago History Museum.

architects and their "freedom from the slavery of tradition."[63] The 1965 winners awarded at the Chicago conference included Stade's Good Shepherd Methodist in Park Ridge and his chapel at Bethany Theological Seminary.

Many of the projects granted awards have enduring significance, but others languish in obscurity. All but forgotten, for instance, is Schweikher's Methodist Church in the rural community of Plainfield, Iowa, on the NCC list and called by Harold Hauf, the editor of *Architectural Record*, "the most significant" American church building of its day.[64] Even in this rural village of three hundred, the building committee was able to forge a remarkable connection with the national conversation about architecture. After a fire destroyed the congregation's former building in 1949, local farm supplier and building committee chairman James Roach and his wife Ruth sought the advice of editors of *Progressive Architecture* and *Architectural Forum*, the NCC's Bureau of Architecture (from which they requested forty-four publications), and the Museum of Modern Art in seeking an architect.[65] They communicated with both Eero Saarinen and Mies van der Rohe (who said he would do the project, but was delayed) before choosing Paul Schweikher. Mrs.

Roach continued to correspond with Peter Blake at the Museum of Modern Art while she worked on convincing the congregation that the modern church was not a passing "fad."[66] When the sixty-five-thousand-dollar church was featured in the Methodist magazine *Motive,* Elbert Conover, a reluctant convert to modernism in church design—after being asked "at least a hundred times" what he thought of the church—corresponded with architect and building committee and prepared a detailed analysis.[67] Plainfield's Methodist church is notable for its use of modern materials (exposed steel beams, concrete block, plywood, and copious clear glass) and its low profile. The congregation found it to be an inexpensive and extremely versatile building. A removable glass wall separating the worship from fellowship space allows the entire room to be used for either purpose. In the classroom area, large wooden panels swing down from a storage position parallel with the ceiling, dividing the space into individual rooms or opening up even more overflow space for the worship/social room.

At the dedication of the church, First Methodist's building committee celebrated its "modern, functional church that is a tribute to God and man . . . an example of living architecture, dedicating the best of today's materials to the worship of God."[68] The congregation was even able to speak in terms of Vitruvius's three principles of architecture: "utility, strength, and beauty." While it was certainly unusual to find such avid readers of *Architectural Record* in the Iowa countryside, this story illustrates the potential range of what might appear at first to be remote and elevated conversations. Clearly, this church was right in the middle of the most sophisticated architectural conversations of the day.

While church architects and theologians watched the inroads modernism was making across America, they continued to study the church architecture of postwar Europe through private travel, organized tours or international conferences, and reading on the topic in journals and books published at home or abroad. Seminarians in some traditions were introduced to ideas about the arts that were taking hold in Europe. Edward and Marie Schroeder, for example, lifelong enthusiasts of contemporary art, became interested in European art and architecture in part because while Ed was a student at Concordia Seminary in St. Louis he attended a serious noon "culture hour" led by professors on whatever topics struck their fancy. When their studies led to a year in Germany, the Schroeders spent their free moments traveling around, exploring and taking pictures of the new European churches.[69]

Northern European churches of the 1940s and 1950s were well known among American architects, especially the churches of such architects as Rudolf Schwarz, the Scot Basil Spence, and the Swiss designer Hermann Baur.[70] Perhaps more than any other European religious building of the 1950s, Le Corbusier's Chapel of Notre-Dame du Haut in Ronchamp, France (1954), drew international attention (Figure 1.8). Although universally admired as an architectural achievement,

FIGURE 1.8. Le Corbusier, Notre-Dame du Haut, Ronchamp Chapel, France, 1954. Ezra Stoller/Esto/Yossi Milo Gallery.

reactions to this now-iconic building were varied, revealing the diversity of concerns of the modern church movement. Set on a hill, this relatively small Catholic chapel with thick concrete walls is as much a piece of sculpture as a building. Marvin Halverson, upon visiting Ronchamp, had nothing but praise. "This pilgrimage chapel," he wrote, "moves in the direction of sculptural form, its massive fortress-like towers contrasting with the floating shape of the roof and flowing interior space. Both simple and complex, the building has been described also as "both strong and gentle at the same time, like the Gospel."[71] Halverson found this to be a universal expression of Christian truth, the work of a great artist. James Hudnut questioned the usefulness of such a singular space for meditation. He stated, "I found much sophistication, much to admire, but I could not accept the theory that some great ethical statement had been made."[72] For Hudnut, it was a beautiful curiosity. Sövik believed that Ronchamp, while a remarkable work of architecture, was impossible to draw on, being more of a virtuosic and idiosyncratic expression of one architect than a model for architecture of the Christian faith. "I am a great admirer of Corbusier's chapel at Ronchamp," Sövik wrote, "but I think that it suffers some from self-consciousness. It is too much Corbu's church, not enough the church of God's family."[73] Architects like Hudnut and Sövik were thinking of religious architecture not only as an expression of faith, but explicitly as a partner in the work of the church.

In May 1959, Halverson and Sövik were among the attendees at the first major international Conference on Architecture and the Church at the Ecumenical Institute of the World Council of Churches at Château de Bossey, near Geneva, Switzerland. Attendees visited churches in France and Switzerland, including Ronchamp, the Roman Catholic Church of the Sacred Heart in Audincourt (Maurice Novarina, 1952), several Basel churches, such as Thomas-Kirche (Benedikt Huber, Swiss Reformed, 1958) and churches by Hermann Baur and Fritz Metzger. In addition to visiting modern structures, attendees also looked for the historic roots of this architecture, viewing, for example, the eleventh-century abbey in Payerne, Switzerland.

The Château de Bossey meeting created a buzz among American church architects. Participation meant the opportunity to connect with the great church architects and architectural traditions of Europe. The American organizers were rather selective about the architects they wanted to represent the United States, and hoped to bring at least six. Halverson invited Walter Taylor, G. E. Kidder Smith, Eero Saarinen, and Pietro Belluschi, but none of them were available. Halverson was particularly keen on the young Ed Sövik. He wrote to a colleague in 1959 that he had talked with Sövik at his Northfield office, and found him "a most discerning person and altogether trustworthy."[74] In the end, architects representing the United States were Sövik, Robert Durham, Harold Spitznagel, and Kidder Smith.[75]

Conference participants crafted a "Statement on Architecture and the Church" containing thirteen guiding principles for church buildings (Appendix B).[76] Although not circulated as such, this document reads as a manifesto of the modern church architecture movement during the late 1950s. First were customary expressions of the need for an architecture that was accountable to modern times, used modern materials, incorporated modern ideas, and served community needs. Several of the points insisted on the autonomy of the architect: building committees should "leave the designer free to speak his mind and do his work." The document also stressed the responsibility of the architect to "understand his client's need in all its aspects." The most controversial of the statements regarding church architects was that they need not be Christians or even know anything about the problems of the church. What mattered was that they were "men of imagination, energy and artistic integrity" and that they "know the world as well as the Church." Sövik, who participated in the crafting of this statement, believed strongly in this point and continued to emphasize the primacy of talent and sensitivity over personal faith. (He remembers Lutheran pastor and liturgical consultant A. R. Kretzmann grumbling to him about this particular item in the statement, at which time Sövik did not let on who was behind it.)[77] The remainder of the points emphasized the importance of designing buildings that would "help the congregation to act corporately in the praise and service of God." Design should avoid distraction and be augmented by the best in modern furnishings and art. Overall, the document accentuated the connection between good architecture and a vital church: "if we provide buildings which meet the purposes of the Christian community in today's world, we may find that in tomorrow's world we will indeed be a truer Christian community." The Château de Bossey meeting was the first of several significant international conferences on the topic. Other major meetings were the International Congresses in Lucerne (1961), New York City and Montreal (1967), Osaka (1970), and Jerusalem (1973). Sövik thought international conferences were the most fruitful he attended, especially the 1959 meeting in Switzerland and the major New York meeting in 1967.[78]

Naturally, such exchanges resulted in constant comparisons between the new churches of North America and those elsewhere. European achievements in church architecture often served as a standard against which American churches seemed doomed to fail. In 1961, Stade expressed concern about the American infatuation with novelty and suggested, "Perhaps when we turn our searching attention to current European architecture, we will succeed!"[79] Speaking at the annual conference in Seattle in 1963, Martin Marty told his audience that he had found American church architecture lacking when compared to recent European churches: "Which architect among us is not uneasy in the presence of the post-war European churches, those startling statements in the midst of patently 'post-Christian' culture?" He argued that "Europe, against the background of a really and openly secular culture, is seeing the growth of religious architectural forms which communicate with audacity and simplicity to our day."[80]

Some American theologians and architects were embarrassed that their churches had gone soft while their European counterparts embraced struggle as the inevitable position of the churches vis-à-vis culture. But the patriot Henry Willet came to the American church's defense. At a Guild meeting in 1958, he spoke about his recent trip to Europe: "while Europe has done great work and we have always tended to set them on a higher pedestal because of their achievements, we in this country are doing things that may be surprising to ourselves."[81] Architect J. Eugene Wukasch registered a similar response to his 1961 tour of Europe: "I returned to America certainly refreshed and delighted by what I had seen, however, not convinced that the European church is doing better than we in this country." Wukasch's concerns centered on the function of the church building and the life of the congregation it supported and enhanced. "Is the large, well designed European church as effective as ours?" he asked. "Attendance records quoted seemed not to indicate so. While I am jealous . . . for the grand scale and ideal esthetics . . . I question if this same approach would serve as effectively in America."[82] Moreover, the European socioreligious dynamic was entirely different. European churches were often government-initiated and -supported, and church education programs were small and limited; thus, comparisons were flawed. Nonetheless, many Americans, particularly architects, were attracted to the boldness of European church design. Sövik and Stade both had extensive libraries of European books on church design and read through these volumes when seeking ideas for their own buildings. In this way, less well-known European parish churches likely had a more direct and consistent influence on American church architecture than the few European buildings, like Ronchamp, more widely publicized by the American popular press.

## THE MODERN CHURCH MOVEMENT FACES THE END OF THE BUILDING BOOM

Throughout the postwar years, optimism about the expansion of the churches and their architectural form generally prevailed, but critics expressed nagging doubts both from within and along the margins of the movement. By the 1960s, church designers more freely abandoned historical styles, and technological advances led to some truly remarkable forms. If the churches of the 1950s had been criticized for their lack of creativity and relevance to contemporary culture, now observers were staring at imagination run wild. At the national conference in Pittsburgh in 1961 Sövik remarked, "We used to have a great sense of accomplishment whenever we were able to persuade a congregation that they shouldn't harness themselves to a medieval or Georgian carriage . . . but now that the battle is pretty much won we realize that it wasn't a great victory after all." "To be 'modern' is not enough," he claimed. "A church building has to be quality architecture as well as twentieth century architecture."[83] Church designers increasingly looked for meaning in "light and shadow and depth and beauty."[84] "I think we are going back to the solid mass," said Harold Spitznagel.[85] Many of Dart, Sövik, and Stade's 1960s churches display heavier massing, more aggressive angularity, solidity, and inwardness.

Criticism of mediocre modern church buildings was often closely tied to criticism of religion in the suburbs and the associated resource drain from city churches. Already at the Los Angeles conference in 1959, Thomas K. Fitz Patrick argued that "too many times we have been frightened into the 'suburban solution' by ministers with an 'edifice' complex or by the foolish notion that the church must necessarily be as convenient as the country club."[86] He urged, "I am quite aware of the enormous difficulties one faces in maintaining a downtown church and all of the parallel problems. But the solution is not found in running away." A few years later at the Seattle conference, Reverend Marty spoke of "dormitory chapels" in the "pastures and plains of the suburbs" growing up in areas sapped of the kind of

Christian vitality that develops in the midst of struggle.[87] Sövik also, with his Lutheran stoicism, could come down hard on the comfortable suburban parish. Many new churches, he claimed at the Pittsburgh conference in 1961, "are as comfortable, as livable, as homelike, or perhaps as club like as they can afford to be . . . God has been made into a sweet old man . . . Isn't God God anymore? And have his people turned from being the church militant to become a bourgeois club?"[88] Between fears of the abandonment of the city, the supposedly mind-numbing effects of the suburbs, and concern over becoming too comfortable, there was ample incentive to criticize the suburban churches and their architecture.

Yet, while critics scolded the too-comfortable congregations, they also defended the human need for significant worship space. The future of religious art and architecture in an increasingly secular world was a matter of great concern, and moving aggressively toward social programs brought its own problems. Rabbi Julius Nodel fretted that religious organizations, as they drifted "increasingly into fields of politics, economics, sociology, housing and international relations, all dressed up in ecclesiastical vestments," were neglecting their essential spiritual function. "All the awe and beauty are going out of religion," he asserted, "supermarkets with crosses fail the churches' function of making man aware of essential and ageless values and life processes."[89] Architects and artists, not surprisingly, defended the important role of the church community as a creator of beauty and questioned the reality of the economic equation that suggested money not spent on buildings went to social programs. Although he did not advocate churches that suggested bourgeois comfort, Sövik noted that "there are too many people who are willing to make their church a token of poverty while they themselves live in three-car garage homes."[90] As Rabbi Nodel and Sövik expressed, balancing the use of resources between serving the congregation, serving the community, and honoring God was an aesthetic as well as a financial problem.

In the end, the slowdown in church building in the last half of the 1960s hardly sounded the death knell for church building, and modernism prevailed. In 1953 the irascible antimodernist Frederick Webber had predicted that, "while Modern is a craze just now, yet its very ugliness will prove its own destruction, for people will tire of it."[91] As the landscape of postwar America attests, people did *not* soon tire of modernism, although the goals of "truth" and "authenticity" proved as slippery as ever. Those who constantly evaluated the architecture of the new churches were correct to notice that good modern church architecture was rare, and difficult. Many postwar churches fell short of the mark. But it was not for lack of trying. Architects and building committees gave it their concentrated attention and earnest effort, and consistently sought to join architectural modernism to theological insight and social needs.

CHAPTER 2

# The "Form-Givers" of Suburban Religion

## *Three Midwestern Architects*

Thousands of churches, scattered throughout the American suburbs of the 1950s and 1960s, assert the vitality and reach of the postwar modern church movement. If you contact the congregation inhabiting one of these buildings, however, it is unlikely that you will find someone who knows the name of the architect. That name might be buried in boxes of uncataloged church records. Bulletins from church dedications often contain a statement of gratitude to the architect, and sometimes the architect had a page or paragraph to explain the modernism, symbolism, and significance of the building. This information might also appear, in preliminary form, in the fund-raising documents prepared by the congregation. Very rarely, one can catch a glimpse of the architect in a photograph of a ground breaking or dedication. Only scant documentary traces of the postwar church designers remain in situ. Yet thousands of suburban churches bear witness to their ceaseless activity.

What drew these architects to church design? Some were motivated by theological concerns, some fell into the business because of personal connections, others simply responded to the needs of the building market. High-profile national conversations promoted church design as a challenging field that required something special of architects. As one suburban Chicago church architect stated, there was only so much you could do with houses, but church architecture gave more room for "freedom of expression."[1] Church education wings, fellowship halls, and basement kitchens were no doubt not the most exciting aspects of these projects, but sanctuaries, especially, offered architects the chance to go beyond the ordinary, to think about *meaning* as well as function.

Architects were just one of many influences on postwar church design. Their production was determined by their education and experience and honed in their communities. Their imaginations were often constrained and occasionally stretched by their clients. But, as leaders of these projects, they, more than any other individuals, shaped the religious landscape of their time. Their theological and artistic commitments blended with the practical needs of congregations and resulted in a range of buildings from award-winning successes to forgettable experiments. Many architects developed a personal, recognizable style of church design, although these signatures evolved over time, in tandem with regional, national, and international design trends.

In order to understand the dynamics of postwar church design, and to grasp the relative influence of both personality and place, I follow the careers, buildings, and ideas of three Midwestern church architects: Edward Sövik, Edward Dart, and Charles Stade. These men together designed hundreds of modern churches, the majority for congregations in the greater Chicago region and the upper Midwest. Their personal beliefs varied, although all were members of Christian parishes. All three had top-rank professional training. Sövik and Stade were primarily church architects, but they designed other types of institutional buildings as well. Dart designed two dozen churches among his other works, which included numerous houses and several significant institutional and commercial structures. These three men are representative of the many church architects active in the two decades after World War II.

## EDWARD ANDERS SÖVIK: THEOLOGIAN OF SPACE

Edward Anders Sövik (1918–2014) was a theologian of space. His buildings, as well as his voluminous writings, reveal a man with very clear, normative ideas about the architecture of Christian worship and fellowship (see Appendix E for a list of Sovik's postwar churches). Intelligent, articulate, and persuasive, Sövik more than any other American Protestant architect shaped discussions about church architecture in the last half of the twentieth century. His influence extended into the world of Catholic architecture as well, particularly after Vatican II (1962–65). In fact, a recent backlash in Catholic circles against postwar, modernist churches points an accusing finger at those who listened too much to Sövik—proof of the power of his message and influence.[2]

Sövik was the son of Norwegian-American Lutheran missionaries to China, where he was raised and educated. In 1939 he graduated from St. Olaf College in Northfield, Minnesota, having studied art and English. He then studied painting during a year at the New York Art Students League. After college he enrolled for three semesters at Luther Theological Seminary in St. Paul, reading in theology and literature and contemplating a possible career in the China mission field.

After the attack on Pearl Harbor, Sövik enlisted in the U.S. Marine Corps. Following flight training in Pensacola, he was commissioned as a pilot in a nightfighter squadron in the Pacific, where he served his country with distinction and was awarded both a Purple Heart and a Distinguished Flying Cross.[3] In 1945

Sövik left active duty. A college mentor, the artist Arnold Flaten, had recognized the depth of Sövik's artistic talent and encouraged him to get his architecture degree, promising that together "we'll revolutionize church architecture for the Lutheran Church."[4] With this encouragement, Sövik visited various architecture schools and found that he did not like Harvard, suspected his technical skills were not good enough for the Massachusetts Institute of Technology, and was not drawn to any Midwestern schools such as the Illinois Institute of Technology or the University of Illinois. But the intelligence officer in his squadron had been "a Yale man and an architect" and Sövik felt comfortable at Yale.[5]

Sövik completed his architecture degree at Yale in 1949. Architecture schools were in flux in these years, experimenting with how to teach architecture and who should do the teaching.[6] Sövik was already focused on the goal of church design, although his formal classroom and studio education at Yale had little to do with religious structures. In fact, he related, it was difficult to find guidance for the design of churches. His last project in school was a college chapel design for St. Olaf. "I didn't get much help from anybody," he remembered. "Ed [Edward Durrell] Stone was my thesis critic . . . but he wasn't interested . . . I had encouragement from one of the other professors who was the head of the school at the time . . . a Lutheran and a thoughtful man but an engineer."[7] Sövik believed his Yale education was nonetheless invaluable both for technical training and for developing some sense of architectural tradition: "Yale still had some last gasps of traditional classical training. We had a class in architectural ornament . . . of course that didn't interest any students." Although "we didn't even read Vitruvius or Palladio . . . as soon as I got out of school I read it" with a "sense that I was in touch with history." Sövik believed that "as an architect . . . one ought to have the sense that he's part of a stream."[8] But he was clearly looking forward, too, particularly to the new churches of Europe. He struggled through Rudolf Schwarz's *Vom Bau der Kirche (The Church Incarnate)* in German and spent many hours in the Yale library.[9]

After graduating from Yale, Sövik moved back to Northfield, where he became busy with his young family and his architectural firm.[10] By 1953 he had entered a partnership with Sewell J. Mathre and Norman Madson (Sövik, Mathre, and Madson). Sövik quickly became known in the upper Midwest as a designer of modern churches.[11] He was universally respected among architects and theologians as an articulate spokesman and a strong and steady personality in a rapidly changing field. Although his reputation was national, he remained a regional architect—the great majority of his designs were for Lutheran churches in Minnesota, Wisconsin, and the Dakotas—and he worked best with congregations sympathetic to his theological vision. He was very persuasive and moved many congregations toward his ideas about theology and space. "The architect has to remember," he insisted, "that he is an architect and his committee [members] are *not* architects . . . he must be faithful to his duties."[12] Although he claimed he never wanted to be known as a "church architect"—just an "architect"—he nonetheless had a strong sense of his vocation within the church.

Sövik was a popular speaker at workshops and seminars, and his theological fluency made him an ideal architects' representative among pastors and church leaders. He often reviewed books for architectural publications, encouraging his colleagues to develop a broader awareness of international design.[13] Each time he visited New York he would stop by a favorite European bookstore to buy art and architecture books, many in German. In the 1950s and 1960s, "for a period of fifteen years," he remembered, "I read everything I could get my hands on."[14] These included books on church architecture—German, French, Italian, English—but also the makings of a substantial shelf on symbolism, such as Carl Jung's *Man and His Symbols* and Alan Watts's *Myth and Symbol in Christianity*. He also read intently the international literature on worship and liturgical studies, because "the issue of the Eucharist among Protestants and Catholics had a lot to do with the way you organize a church."[15] At one time Sövik was the American correspondent for the German periodical *Kunst und Kirche* (Art and the Church). Sövik's early life in China also shaped his perpetual interest in Asian design, and his library revealed an especially strong interest in Japanese art and architecture, an affinity shared by many architects of his day.

A snapshot of Sövik's firm in this era is provided by a letter sent to a potential client in 1962. "Our office has been largely, though not exclusively, concerned with church buildings," Sövik wrote. His staff of twenty registered and fourteen graduate architects (the firm had no engineering department) had worked on projects in "over a dozen states" and were currently designing a Norwegian church as well. "Our work doesn't fit into any of the various 'schools' of design now current," Sövik explained. "Nor have we found it possible to establish what one might call our own school . . . the possibilities are too various."[16] This statement is generally true of many of the church architects I encountered in this study. They were educated and open, looking broadly and internationally at contemporary trends in church design, and their work reveals a wide range of influences.

Sövik's buildings and his ideas about them evolved over the course of his long, productive career. Mark Torgerson, who wrote his dissertation on Sövik's work, offers a thorough account of Sövik's mature theology of architecture in his book *An Architecture of Immanence*. Torgerson focuses on key Sövik churches of the late 1960s and early 1970s as representative of Sövik's idea of the "nonchurch," a flexible space that enables a congregation to serve its community's multiple and changing worship, fellowship, and service needs.[17] Sövik's book *Architecture for Worship*, published in 1973, gave expression to ideas that had been percolating for more than a decade and is his best-known publication in the field of church architecture.[18] Churches such as St. Leo Catholic Church in Pipestone, Minnesota (Figure 2.1),

FIGURE 2.1. Edward Sövik, St. Leo Catholic Church, Pipestone, Minnesota, 1967–69. Les Turnau for Michael Myers Studio. Courtesy of SMSQ Architects.

or Westwood Lutheran in St. Louis Park (see Figures 5.6 and 5.7), both large, open, rectilinear, flexible spaces indicative of his work in the mid- to late 1960s, represent the beginnings of his "nonchurch" ideal.

Sövik's earlier churches illustrate a different way of thinking about church architecture. Notes from a 1954 meeting with church leaders reveal a young Sövik admitting he "didn't like the over-flexible design very well and thought people might rather spend more money and have a real place of worship."[19] Many of his early churches resemble Eliel Saarinen's designs, conveying both his appreciation for Saarinen's work and his knowledge of its roots in a popular type of northern European church. Sövik churches of this earlier period also reflect economy and innovation. One quirky church, a very early one in the small town of West Concord, Minnesota (Trinity Lutheran, 1952), is an inexpensive red brick with white trim split-level. Trinity Minnehaha Falls (1961), in a residential area in south Minneapolis, is an experimental, concrete form with nine peaked gables on each side filled with colored glass rectangles. Sövik called this use of folded plate concrete "sort of an architectural fashion" attractive simply because it was new technology, and he never used it again because "it just wasn't worth it."[20]

From the 1950s through the 1960s, Sövik's church buildings illustrate how he developed his theories of church architecture while simultaneously responding to the needs of his clients, changing architectural fashion, and what he perceived to be common but wrongheaded approaches to church architecture. Within the career of this influential architect, we see a mix of high-mindedness and practical necessity, enduring forms and occasional surprising experimentation. Sövik was a thoughtful, intelligent, and measured professional. A photograph of him as a young architect in 1956 amid the construction of First Baptist Church, Bloomington, Indiana, conveys his confidence and charisma (Figure 2.2).

FIGURE 2.2. Edward Sövik on visit to construction site of First Baptist Church, Bloomington, Indiana, 1956. Courtesy of First United Church, Bloomington, Indiana.

Sövik wrote extensively and lived a long and productive life, so we know much more about him than we do about most other church architects of the period. One of the clearest expressions of Sövik's mid-1960s thought about church architecture is a series of missives he wrote in 1964 to the congregation of the Northfield Methodist Church (Northfield, Minnesota) as they worked together to plan a new building. These twelve short essays, published in the congregation's newsletter, show Sövik as a clear and patient teacher who was confident in his ideas. Topics included "Why are church buildings so modern?," "The axial and central church," "Architecture as servant," and "Notes on the varieties of beauty."[21] In this last essay, Sövik wrote that beauty for the work of the church should be "of a direct and vigorous and unpretentious sort, like Jesus' words and actions."[22] Sövik stressed throughout his career, his own theological literacy notwithstanding, that to be good church architect required less in the way of theological knowledge and more in the way of an intuitive sense of good design, "direct and vigorous." All truly religious architecture, he believed, shared a concern for ethics and honesty. Furthermore, religious buildings, reflecting an ethic of love, "should be those which are kind, serviceable, unself-conscious, gracious, strong, and disciplined, for love has these qualities."[23] It required a sharp and flexible intellect to put architecture and Christian love together in so compelling a fashion.

Sövik wrote and spoke frequently about his hope for ecumenical understanding. He believed increasingly in the "possibility of all denominations worshipping together in the future," and avoided particular denominational architectural conventions as much as possible.[24] His architectural ecumenism was not an acceptance of many truths but an argument for a normative approach to Christian worship space. Two lectures delivered in 1966 at a Southern Baptist conference in Nashville, Tennessee, demonstrate his search for elemental Christian principles.[25] Sövik chose "kerygma," proclamation and witness, as the primary work of church architecture. Message and meaning, he insisted, could be controlled by the disciplined creativity of the architect and the humility and openness of the building committee. Two important truths were embedded in kerygmatic architecture: the unity of the body of Christ (denied, he asserted, by both the divided chancel and the auditorium plan) and respect for the incarnation, manifest in unabashed concern with "the finite, the ordinary, the secular, the everyday, the contemporary, the particular." Sövik's parish architecture reveals a skilled and thoughtful architect working with this ideal always in mind.

## EDWARD DUPAQUIER DART: ARTIST OF PURE FORM

Edward Dupaquier Dart (1922–1975) was a gifted and creative architect who in his short career designed several hundred buildings, among them many churches, twenty-five of which were built (see Appendix D for a list of Dart's churches). He was born and raised in New Orleans, steeped in a Southern sense of family and history. During the majority of his childhood, his family lived in a 1910 Colonial Revival five-bay, symmetrical white-clapboard house, decorated in impeccable, traditional taste by his mother. Dart claimed that growing up in New Orleans strongly influenced his architectural designs and sense of history.[26] His father and grandfather were lawyers, his mother a certified teacher and a devout Catholic. Dart was athletic, self-assured, and charismatic, somewhat less interested in school than in his exuberant social life. In 1936, his family sent him to boarding school at Woodberry Forest School in Virginia. After graduation, he enrolled at the University of Virginia.

War changed Dart's life, as it did for so many in his generation. In 1940, he joined the Naval ROTC program at the University of Virginia. In 1942, he enlisted. Having always loved airplanes, he chose aviation. In the navy he excelled as a student and pilot and found close friends. He became a marine and learned to fly dive-bombers, earned his wings in 1943, and joined the war in the Pacific soon after. Dart met Sövik out in the middle of the Pacific, both of them Marine Corps pilots; they became acquainted and later found themselves classmates at Yale.[27] The experience of battle, particularly the loss of several close friends, sobered Dart. After a brief leave in 1944 for more training, he returned to the Pacific in 1945. It was during this time, while waiting for assignment in San Diego, that Dart apparently began to draw and paint with deliberation, and wrote to Yale about admission to the architecture program.

In the fall of 1946, Dart moved to New Haven with his wife to begin architecture school. At Yale he was exposed to many of the great modernists of the era: Richard M. Bennett was chair of the architecture department at the time, and Pietro Belluschi, Marcel Breuer, Richard Neutra, Louis Kahn, Eero Saarinen, Harold Spitznagel, and Paul Schweikher were all in residence during his years in architecture school. He developed a friendship with Vincent Scully, who would become the preeminent American architectural historian of his generation.[28]

When Dart was a child in 1934, his father had taken him and his older brother Harry on a trek to Chicago to view the Century of Progress Exposition. This visit impressed Dart, and by the time he began his career in architecture, he had wholeheartedly embraced the modern spirit in architecture. His sister Susan, the author of his biography, explains the appeal of modernism in the postwar period: it was "fresh and new and clean; it was the essence of what we wanted after the turmoil of the war."[29] The first house Dart designed, a summer place for his parents in Thetford, Vermont, captured these characteristics—it was a cozy, modern house with big stone fireplace, wood plank walls, built-in bookcases, and large windows looking out onto the countryside.

Upon graduation from architecture school in 1949, Dart accepted an offer from the Schweikher and Elting firm in Roselle, Illinois. During the war he had spent some time at the naval base in Glenview, and his sister lived in the area. Dart's second Chicagoland residence was a small cottage in the northern Chicago suburb of Barrington, at the time still quite rural. He remained a resident of Barrington for the rest of his life.

Dart greatly admired the work of Paul Schweikher, but in 1950, after merely a year with this firm, he set out on his own and established an office at home. His early success as an architect was the result of his house designs. Edward Durell Stone, whom he met at Yale, asked him to design the "House of the Fifties" for *Good Housekeeping*. He subsequently designed another model house for readers of *Popular Mechanics*, as well as stock plans for the *New Homes Guide*. Many of Dart's houses won design awards and were featured in magazines and architectural journals. In 1951, for example, he won an award in a National Association of Home Builders competition for a tiny house with a central, open, 8 × 10-foot kitchen, made the focal point of the house after the "colonial idea."[30] This house had large windows to the rear but the front entry was through an enclosed, high-walled courtyard; sheltered garden entrances are likewise a feature of several of Dart's later churches. His choice of materials in his houses is also echoed in his religious architecture: flagstone floors, Crab Orchard stonework, brick and natural wood walls.

Dart's first church commission came in 1952 from his own parish, St. Michael's Episcopal Church in Barrington, a new congregation that was seeking to build its first church. Dart and others made several additions and modifications to the church over the years, increasing its complexity and decorative detail. The original building was a steel frame structure with a two hundred–seat sanctuary with a slate floor and clear glass windows, a small narthex, and a basement with hall, kitchen, and Sunday school rooms.[31] Stained-glass windows were installed in 1961, and a north wing and parish hall were added the following year. Dart's next church commission, St. Augustine's Episcopal Church in Gary, Indiana, won accolades from the architectural community.[32] A photo of the young Dart addressing the congregation at the fund-raiser "loyalty dinner" shows him standing beside a model of an earlier design for the church, a steel and stone rectangular building, similar to St. Michael's, that proved too costly for his client (Figure 2.3). His second design was a simple A-frame with graceful, inward-curving trusses, an elegant match for the new congregation's needs (see Figures 4.12–4.14).

Dart's reputation as a church architect grew.[33] From 1958 to 1960, he was working on six churches in Indiana and Illinois: St. Augustine's in Gary; Church of the Holy Family (Episcopal), Park Forest, Illinois (see chapter 7); Lutheran Church of the Atonement, Barrington, Illinois, a unique small church with a "hyperbolic paraboloid" saddle roof (Figure 2.4); St. Ambrose Episcopal Church, Chicago Heights, Illinois; Grace Lutheran, in Bensenville, Illinois; and St. Mark's Lutheran Church, Aurora, Illinois. These Dart churches are significantly different from one another and his interest in experimenting with geometric forms is apparent. Edward Sövik later remarked on this talent of Dart's: "I remember a project of Dart's when

FIGURE 2.3. Edward Dart at St. Augustine's Episcopal Church Loyalty Dinner, ca. 1956. From the Archives of St. Augustine's Episcopal Church, Gary, Indiana.

Louis Kahn was our design critic for a museum project. Ed's scheme was a three-pointed star on a pedestal, each wing a tetrahedron extending horizontally with a horizontal floor and sloping roof surface coming together at the center. A piece of pure formal geometry, structurally rational, handsome, spatially interesting and well-scaled."[34] Dart's papers at the Art Institute of Chicago show five other 1959–61 church projects (not built), all Episcopal. His early church work and personal ties to this denomination led to many of his church commissions.

By 1962, Dart's impatience with small house projects and administrative duties and his wish to design more substantial buildings motivated him to consolidate his practice with the notable firm of Loebl, Schlossman, and Bennett (Richard Bennett, chair of the architecture department when Dart was at Yale). Dart became the firm's principal architect in charge of design. Although his workload now included more high-profile, urban designs, he continued his work for congregations.

One of Dart's most celebrated ecclesiastical designs was St. Procopius Abbey in Lisle, Illinois, created for a Benedictine community in 1966–70 (Figure 2.5). This extensive complex on a hilly, eighty-acre site employs many of the same features he used in his later parish churches: long, unornamented expanses of brick or concrete wall, striking angles, indirect but strong, clear light sources, and a disciplined and restrained aesthetic. St. Procopius is a series of twelve interconnected buildings around a central, cloistered garden. He told the Benedictines, who wanted the building to fit unobtrusively into its suburban location, "I feel deeply that the simple and humble way Jesus lived has a lesson for me as an architect. He showed me

FIGURE 2.4. Edward Dart, Lutheran Church of the Atonement, Barrington, Illinois, 1959 (since demolished). Photograph by Matthew R. Seymour.

FIGURE 2.5. Edward Dart, St. Procopius Abbey, Lisle, Illinois, sanctuary, 1967. Photograph by the author.

beauty in the common and ordinary. That's why I'm drawn to materials such as brick, tile, wood, and textured concrete. They bear the imprint of man."[35] The abbey includes several small chapels and a seven-hundred-seat church with huge clerestory windows and a massive steel truss. The extreme simplicity of this primary worship space magnifies aspects of Dart's earlier ecclesiastical work, offering clarity and restraint fitting for a Benedictine abbey.

Dart had many substantial and successful projects during his last years, including the Pick-Staiger concert hall at Northwestern University. His last project, for which he has been best known, was Chicago's mixed-use Water Tower Place on Michigan Avenue. This project, begun in 1970, eventually ran to 3,100,000 square feet and $160 million. Dart wanted the challenge of such a significant project, but its complexity, the tensions of working with multiple clients, and extensive criticism beginning with the first drawings led to mounting stress. Dart died of an aneurism in 1975, before the building was completed.

At St. Procopius Abbey, Dart worked closely with Father Michael Komechak, and the two became friends. Father Komechak studied Dart's religious buildings extensively and unfortunately died in 2009, before he could write the book he had intended. At the time of Dart's death in 1975, Father Komechak wrote a eulogy published in *Inland Architect*. He recalled that Dart would say, "Buildings should have a feel and a smell to them." He "argued the need for an architecture of strength and earthy integrity" and he preferred what he called "dirty materials"—brick, tile, wood, and concrete—that could evoke the romantic and picturesque.[36] Sövik recalled, "Ed had an innate feeling for the relationship between structure and form." He was "intellectually sharp without affectation, sensitive but not artsy, gifted yet humble."[37]

Dart won more than thirty awards, eighteen of them from the American Institute of Architects. His churches range from the suburban buildings considered in this book to simple and elegant urban churches such as First St. Paul's Evangelical Lutheran, Chicago (1970), and the intimate Augustana Lutheran in Chicago's Hyde Park neighborhood (1968). Dart's buildings reflect his intuitive sense of sacred space, his respect for architectural tradition and materials, and the influence of his modernist teachers. Although known for his many houses and later large-scale-projects, Dart's 1975 obituary claimed that he was "best known for his churches, and at one time known as Chicago's leading church designer"[38]

### CHARLES EDWARD STADE: TASTEMAKER AND EDUCATOR TO SUBURBIA

Charles Edward Stade (1923–1993) was a prolific architect of parish churches.[39] For three decades he was devoted to the modern church movement, attended national church architecture conferences, and built nearly exclusively modern buildings.[40] His work is just now being rediscovered, accompanying the general upswing of interest in midcentury modernism.[41] Stade is an ideal example of the type of highly productive and influential church architect who had such a profound impact on American suburban church architecture in the postwar era.

The influences on Stade's development brought him naturally to a career in church architecture. After his confirmation in the Lutheran Church–Missouri Synod (LCMS) in his hometown of Des Plaines, Illinois, he attended the denomination's Concordia high school in Milwaukee for two years, where he pursued a rigorous theology and classics-based education before finishing his secondary education at Maine Township high school back home.[42] Charles's father and uncles worked in the construction business, and Stade's interest in buildings and design led him to an architecture degree from the University of Illinois in 1946. During World War II, he spent one year at the University of Wisconsin's U.S. Air Force meteorology program (ill health keep him from the war front). In 1948, he earned a graduate degree from the Princeton University School of Architecture and a certificate of design from the Beaux-Arts Institute of Design in New York. He won the Howard Crosby Butler Prize, named for a Princeton architectural historian (1872–1922) who wrote about religious architecture, and may have studied with Donald Drew Egbert, a Princeton art historian also having an interest in ecclesiastical buildings.[43] Longtime director of graduate studies at Princeton, Jean

Labatut, who was trained at L'École des Beaux-Arts in Paris and recognized for his expertise in urban planning and masterful teaching, was Stade's mentor, and Stade maintained a close relationship with Labatut throughout his life.

Following Princeton, Stade spent part of a year on a French Government Traveling Scholar grant, touring Europe to study buildings, particularly churches.[44] After Stade completed his studies and travels, he returned to Chicago and worked for a short term in the Chicago firms of Victor Charn and Holabird, Root, & Burgee. Soon he ventured out, establishing his own firm, Charles E. Stade and Associates, by 1951.[45] By 1952, he had settled in Park Ridge, where the firm remained until closing in 1981.[46] Stade's earliest partnership, with William Cooley, ended around 1955. Stade went on to have productive relationships with several other partners, including Maurice Dolan, Harry Anderson, and Leroy Bonesz.[47] Ill health (asthma) kept him working at home most winters, where he would meet with clients and associates in his study. Stade died in 1993 after suffering for many years from Alzheimer's disease.

Over the course of his career, Stade designed hundreds of churches (see Appendix C for a working list of Stade's designs).[48] His firm's church work is concentrated in the Chicago region, although he worked across the country and in Canada, primarily for LCMS expansion congregations in the 1950s and 1960s. He also designed several houses, some significant educational buildings and dormitories for college campuses, and, later in his career, retirement homes, municipal buildings, and park structures.[49] As his career progressed, Stade desired to move away from church work toward other sorts of institutional design, and he succeeded in some measure; his obituary in the *Chicago Sun-Times* described his firm as "focused on designing college and university facilities and nursing and retirement homes."[50] But that description ignores his copious early work, for the vast majority of his career output was small suburban churches.[51] A 1959 *Chicago Daily Tribune* article called him "one of the architects who has been in the forefront of modern churches."[52]

A 1958 record of building committee deliberations noted that Stade had "the largest church architectural office in Illinois" and the third largest in the United States, with "eight architects and a total of twenty people . . . doing work in fourteen states."[53] Another 1958 account recorded that "his office specializes in church work and to date they have done over 150 churches and allied buildings throughout the country and Canada."[54] Advertisements seeking designers for Stade's firm emphasized his ambition; one from 1963 requested "only persons of ability with intense interests in creative architectural design need apply."[55] Stade had a professional reputation for tough-minded excellence, and close friends and associates remember him as a very "bright and considerate" man.[56]

In the 1950s and 1960s, through his participation in national organizations, his travels, and his reading, Stade kept abreast of national and international developments in church architecture and brought this awareness to his parish designs. His library included books on English and German churches and European architecture in general; many of these books contain bookmarks or notes indicating ideas or images that attracted him.[57] Stade was a great admirer of the work of Frank Lloyd Wright. His daughter Ramsey tells a story of a chance meeting Stade had with Wright at the Guggenheim in New York City. Her father was deeply impressed, she relates, and never stopped talking about that moment.[58] In 1966, Stade wrote, "I suspect most architects inwardly desire some of Wright's genius and image," and it is evident in his work how much that applied to Stade himself.[59] In addition to Wright, he highly regarded the work of Michigan architect Alden Dow; every year he took his associates on a "pilgrimage" to Midland, Michigan, to see Dow's First Methodist Church (1952), a visit that "renewed enthusiasm and attention."[60] Aspects of Dow's church that would have appealed to Stade were Dow's choice of warm colors, natural materials such as cork flooring, and lush plantings. Along with Sövik, Stade was also attracted to the naturalism of Japanese architecture, in itself and as seen through the work of architects such as Wright and Dow.

These preferences can be seen in one of Stade's first buildings, a house he designed for himself in Park Ridge that is similar to Wright's small "Usonian" houses (Figure 2.6). The house demonstrates his careful attention to detail, as well as his insistence on quality materials and craftsmanship.[61] The red-brick structure is a one-story, two-bedroom, one-bath plan with a two-bay garage. Multiple floor-to-ceiling windows on the front of the house allow plentiful light into the study and the living room; these windows are separated by brick piers with integrated planters (a technique Stade often used in his churches). Along the front of the house, the wide eaves extend as pergola-type shades, allowing light to pass to the windows below, another technique visible in his early churches. Inside, there is the same attention to materials and detail, and efficient use of space, including many built-in cabinets and bookcases throughout the house. Like Sövik and Dart, Stade preferred unfinished surfaces—brick, wood, ceramic tile—to plaster and paint. The house was a shrine to Scandinavian modern design, down to the Dansk china and the surfeit of aqua (his favorite color, seen frequently in the geometric stained glass in his churches).[62] In his institutional architecture, Stade applied these same design elements: natural materials left exposed, attention to the effects of light and the integration of architecture and nature, and a sensible arrangement of spaces and built-in storage areas for comfort and convenience. Stade designed several other houses, as well as some parsonages, and he won a small-home design competition sponsored by the Chicago *Tribune* in 1946.[63]

Stade completed his first churches in 1952 and 1953. One of these was a Colonial addition to Christ Evangelical and Reformed Church in his hometown of Des Plaines. This, together with the 1964 sanctuary, is possibly the only complete Colonial church Stade ever designed (see Figures I.2 and I.3). Another building from these early years better indicates the nature of his future work. St. Paul Lutheran

FIGURE 2.6. Charles Stade, Stade House, Park Ridge, Illinois, 1951–52. Photograph by the author.

Church in Oak Lawn, Illinois, a small, $85,000 A-frame for an expansion congregation founded in 1950, dedicated in September 1954 (Figure 2.7).[64] St. Paul's low masonry walls, high-pitched roof over the sanctuary, flat-roofed education wing, and thirty-two-foot, integrated carillon tower are features on many of Stade's 1950s churches. In his architectural notes for the dedication bulletin, he argued for a religious architecture suited to the present day. He presented St. Paul as an "attempt to integrate contemporary materials and techniques into a true interpretation of today's design and construction potentials in religious architectural forms."[65]

One of Stade's most influential supporters was Reverend Oswald T. (O. T.) McRee, the executive director of Missions for the English District, LCMS, who was responsible for the construction and financing of new churches. The English District had a reputation as a place you could "let off steam," intentionally venturesome in matters of art and architecture and less rigid overall.[66] McRee was frustrated with the state of church building in the postwar years.[67] He discovered "Chuck" Stade's serious approach and teamed with Stade to design and build modern churches that incorporated contemporary liturgical art as well.[68]

The years between 1955 and 1963 were busy church building times for Stade's firm. A representative church from these years is Lutheran Church of the Resurrection (see Figures 2.8, 4.16–17), a suburban expansion parish in Yardley, Pennsylvania, an area Reverend McRee believed to have high growth potential. The LCMS

FIGURE 2.7. Cover of fund-raising brochure for St. Paul Lutheran Church, Oak Lawn, Illinois, 1953. Courtesy of St. Paul Lutheran Church, Oak Lawn, Illinois.

chose Reverend Robert Stade, Charles's brother, to form the new congregation. Stade first designed a parsonage for this suburban site, completed in 1954. Ground breaking for the church took place in December 1955, and the congregation dedicated its new building the following May.[69] A fuller description of Stade's A-frames is given in chapter 4.

Rare correspondence from the Yardley building project documents the kinds of details Stade negotiated with his brother, Reverend McRee, and the building committee. For instance, the architect advocated a curved sidewalk leading to the church, "much better than the straight line approach" and consistent with a naturalistic aesthetic.[70] There was apparently some discussion about the materials used in the chancel, and when flagstone was chosen, Stade was pleased. "I'm real glad Ted [O. T. McRee] went along with the stone," he wrote to his brother. "It should really be a honey of a chancel!"[71] The chancel contrasted the orange-red brick with a dark stone panel behind the altar and the built-in stone and wood altar, lectern, and pulpit (see Figure 2.8). In these letters one senses Stade's youthful enthusiasm and gets a picture of the family working together. Stade wrote to his brother,

FIGURE 2.8. Charles Stade, Lutheran Church of the Resurrection, Yardley, Pennsylvania, 1956, sanctuary. Cortland V. D. Hubbard for Hedrich-Blessing, HB-19791-B, Chicago History Museum.

"As for the drapes, Mom came to the office last week with a very fine color and fabric selection. She told me that she was going to send this on to you for your approval . . . I'm real anxious to actually see your church."[72]

In addition to his many parish projects, in the late 1950s and early 1960s Stade worked extensively for Valparaiso University in Indiana, designing administration buildings, a library, dormitories, and a president's house. His most notable structure on campus is the Chapel of the Resurrection (1959) (Figure 2.9).[73] The Valparaiso chapel was the most significant commission of Stade's career, and according to his daughter he felt it was his greatest work.[74] Conversations with the university began in the fall of 1955, when Stade was just thirty-two, and he and his associates worked on the initial plans for nearly a year.[75] This project benefited from occasional input from Jean Labatut (1899–1986), Stade's mentor at Princeton.[76] A university chapel was a different sort of commission for Stade, one of remarkable size and importance. Stade and the Reverend A. R. Kretzmann, pastor of St. Luke's Lutheran on Belmont in Chicago and a liturgical consultant, traveled around looking at examples of new chapel architecture in Germany, England, and the United States.[77] Although campus architecture until this point tended to be Georgian (Colonial) or collegiate Gothic, times were changing. Adventurous work, while not without critics, earned a great deal of praise, and several new university chapels won national attention. In Chicago, Mies van der Rohe's Robert F. Carr Memorial Chapel at the Illinois Institute of Technology (1952) was a rectilinear, steel frame with a precast concrete roof on brick walls. Other notable modern chapels of the period were Eero Saarinen's round Kresge Chapel at the Massachusetts Institute of Technology (1955) and his A-frame Kramer Chapel at Concordia Seminary, Fort Wayne, Indiana (1954–58; see chapter 4).

A European building often mentioned in connection with the Valparaiso Chapel is Basil Spence's Coventry Cathedral in England, built next to the ruins of the medieval parish church of St. Michael that had been bombed by the Germans in 1940. A preconstruction drawing from 1952 shows the striking comparison, particularly the monumental size of the buildings, the zigzag nave wall, and the relationship between the Valparaiso Chapel's star-shaped chancel and the star-shaped "Chapel of Unity" at Coventry (smaller as actually built) (Figure 2.10). Although this cathedral was not completed until 1962, Spence won the design competition in 1951, and his designs circulated widely.[78] Stade almost certainly saw Spence's early drawings, although the parallels between the two buildings are far from exact. Stade used local materials, such as an elongated, orange-colored brick and limestone, and the nave windows are L-shaped in cross section, a Wright characteristic. The Valparaiso Chapel displays both the regional and international influences that shaped Stade's work.

Stade's Valparaiso commissions energized his creativity. His A-frame churches had been popular with congregations, but it bothered him that he was doing so

FIGURE 2.9. Charles Stade, Chapel of the Resurrection, Valparaiso University, 1959. Courtesy of the Valparaiso University Archives.

many.[79] He and many of his peers were eager to experiment further with form. By the mid- to late 1960s, churches generally had heavier massing, more aggressively asymmetrical geometry, and less ornamental detail. Stade's designs during these years responded to the changing tides of fashion, but also reflect his increased maturity as an architect and the greater means of some clients. By the later 1960s, Stade was designing more campus and other institutional buildings but continued to design churches and chapels. The striking chapel at Associated Mennonite Biblical Seminary in Elkhart, Indiana, is representative of his later institutional work (Figure 2.11).

Stade acquired national status as a church architect and his designs won multiple awards from the AIA and the Guild.[80] He was vocal in the church architecture movement, often serving as an associate editor for *Your Church* magazine and as a public speaker (Figure 2.12). Although all of Stade's work demonstrates his commitment to modernism, his knowledge of the history of ecclesiastical architecture meant that he consciously took what he considered to be the best of the tradition

FIGURE 2.10. Basil Spence, drawing for proposed Coventry Cathedral, 1952. Copyright RCAHMS (Sir Basil Spence Archive). Licensor www.rcahms.gov.uk.

FIGURE 2.11. Charles Stade, Chapel of the Sermon on the Mount, Associated Mennonite Biblical Seminary, Elkhart, Indiana, 1965. Photograph by the author.

into the future. He believed an architect could learn from the past without copying or simply modifying it. In 1960, reflecting on the importance of a historical consciousness for architects, he wrote:

> Before a man becomes an architect he has studied and travelled and poured over the lore of past building. Before he is capable of setting his own ideas on paper, he is informed as to what others before him have thought and worked. Memories of his own childhood will in part predetermine his approach; he may want to capture some of the colored-glass splendor that once made its way across his Sunday blue-serge . . . he may want to purge his past of dim and shadowed memories of gloom. He may have caught in a corner of his mind's eye a structural solution, a beam or a cornice or a window recalled from his trip to Europe or his view of a slide lecture at an architect's convention. All this goes into making up his approach to designing . . . Studied repudiation is arrogant if not anarchic; it seems to deny the notion of the communion of the saints and substitutes an errant form of individualism for the community of creators.[81]

Stade's eyes were always open for attractive features of both historical and contemporary church architecture, and he had the ability to blend these influences seamlessly. His expansion for a Gothic Presbyterian church in La Grange, Illinois, demonstrates his sensitivity to architectural precedent together with his talent for incorporating the advantages of modernism into a historic church (Figure 2.13). When lengthening the long, narrow nave, Stade added bright, enclosed exterior arcades down the length of each side, lit though expanses of windows in his signature rectilinear pattern of aqua and tan glass.

As his career progressed, Stade expressed frustration with the moniker "church architect" and with small projects and the whims of church building committees. His friend Martin Marty, for whom he designed the parish church in Elk Grove Village, remembers him as a complex man who knew his limitations and "feared he was grinding things out."[82] The care with which Stade applied himself to knowing and appreciating the work of other architects was an inspiration, but also might have limited his confidence and originality. Marty believed that Stade "knew he didn't measure up to the giants of the age." But Stade was especially successful at moving building committees to a place that was better than where they started, educating them about architecture and design while accommodating their needs and budgets, and delivering high-quality, well-designed, satisfying, and enduring buildings. Marty praised the worshipful quality of Stade's sanctuaries, which are "instinctively ready for liturgy."[83]

In 1966 Stade addressed the American Society of Church Architecture as its outgoing president. Following a sweeping account of church architecture, he argued that currently, in the mid-1960s, the church faced turmoil within and challenge

# An Architect's Notes

By Charles Edward Stade, M.F.A.

Associate Editor, *Your Church*

FIGURE 2.12. Charles Stade as an associate editor for *Your Church* (July–August 1965): 8.

from without. "Churches have never been so busy or confused," he said, urging the church to express its theology in its art, encouraging artists, architects, and ministers to "join together in creating forms that will best present the meaning of their beliefs."[84] This sentiment, that church architecture was a shared enterprise grounded in belief and beauty, was at the core of Stade's architectural practice. He valued integrity in himself and in his relationships with his clients. He mused, "If I were asked to select one quality that an architect must surely possess, I would choose sincerity . . . the opportunity to create a church building, a symbol of living, doing, growing faith, is a wonderful thing! It must be approached with humility, concern, and a willingness to bend all one's energies and talents towards finding the significant form for that particular church."[85] Now, as Stade's reputation rises again, his buildings, from ordinary A-frame churches to college chapels and dormitories, testify to a well-trained and fastidious architect whose work was rooted in his time and place.

Sövik, Dart, and Stade all consistently incorporated the central tenets of architectural modernism into their church designs. Highly educated in their profession, committed to the church, and alert to the direction modernist principles were leading American and European church architects, they sought to create inspiring places for worship and congregational life in the Midwestern suburbs. But these

FIGURE 2.13. Charles Stade, expansion to First Presbyterian Church, La Grange, Illinois, 1962. Photograph by the author.

important architects never worked alone. Church building projects are complex processes of collaboration and compromise between architects and the building committees that hire them. Among the other talents these three architects possessed, they were able, patiently and persuasively, to convince their client congregations of the timeliness, relevance, and necessity of their modernist ideas, leading congregations to become enthusiastic partners in the modern church movement.

CHAPTER 3

# From Dream to Dedication

## *The Shared Work of Church Building*

William Clark, in his popular 1957 volume *Building the New Church*, warned that "one should never approach a church building project with the idea that it is going to be a simple process. Quite the contrary is the truth."[1] Planning and building a modern church required patience, hard work, and optimism. Pastors, many of them fresh out of seminary and bound up with brand-new congregations, became deeply involved in projects of a nature and financial magnitude beyond their experience. Suburbanites faced an endless string of new expenses and were strapped for cash. Overextended denominations were often not much help. Church members with no specific knowledge of architecture often served on postwar church building committees. Yet, despite the enormity of the task and the lack of experience of the participants, church records reveal little hesitation. The postwar suburban generation found significance in *doing* things—organizing, building, and serving. These buildings meant something especially important to those who gave their time and energy to planning, offered their resources to pay for them, and contributed their labor to the construction process. As James Hudnut-Beumler suggests, time, effort, and resources put to a building project could be an offering to God.[2]

Church records and published advice repeatedly cite several primary motivations behind the building boom. "The most frequent of these," wrote John Scotford in 1955, "is the cry, 'Where shall we put the children?'"[3] Another motive, closely related to suburbanization, was the rise of the automobile. The implications of automobile traffic were significant. The difficulties and dangers faced by pedestrians, the parking crisis around older centrally located churches, the dissolution of former parish and community boundaries with the increasing mobility of Americans, and the consequent increased competition among congregations for membership all pushed congregations toward large suburban lots where there was space to grow and park. Children and automobiles were two tangible forces prompting the church building boom. But practical material and social factors alone do not explain the energy behind these projects. While suburban churches contained many spaces for recreation and social interaction, they remained churches first, and the spiritual motivation behind a building project is evident in congregational minutes, fund-raising materials, and memories.

In the 1950s, few doubted the need to form new congregations and build suburban churches. Many postwar Christians saw a secular world chipping away at their beliefs and moral standards, and believed they needed to work hard to sustain religious life in their communities and encourage Christian faith in their children. Church buildings were not a mere expression of the status quo but a bulwark against decline.

New or relocated congregations very deliberately went about organizing and canvassing their mission fields. Many churches have early documents that record the growth of suburbs and project their futures. In Moorhead, Minnesota, for example, the churches and the city documented the membership of all Moorhead churches and offered population statistics as well as information about banks, auto registrations, utilities, industry, the value of recent construction, and even the number and location of grocery stores, all useful information for the planting of churches.[4] Moorhead's Lutheran Church of the Good Shepherd was typical in asking its congregation to keep its feet on the ground while dreaming big. In a letter from the earliest days of its gathering, church leaders called members to "meet with us for a general discussion on what type of church building we might plan. To begin with, we are erecting only what we absolutely need. But we must do some long-range planning . . . It is important for us to crystallize our thinking on future plans even though we are not formally organized."[5] Although just beginning, Good Shepherd's small congregation had no doubt that its efforts would succeed. There was an enormous amount of guesswork to this planning. Would a residential community grow, and with it the need for churches? Where was the best place to buy property? How large might a new congregation of fifty to one hundred people become in five years? Ten years? Congregations tended to be ambitious, buying as much land as they could find and afford, and stretching their budgets to get the most building for their dollars.

A lot of legwork undergirded the growth of congregations. On the developing south side of Fargo, North Dakota, Carol and Dean Ferguson, members of Olivet Lutheran, recall that "as a street filled in, we'd go and make the evangelistic call."[6] In Lansing, Illinois, Coloradan James Peterson, a student from McCormick Theological Seminary in Chicago, rang 2,400 doorbells in the summer of 1954 to survey the community's religious needs.[7] And, in Elk Grove Village, a brand-new suburb northwest of Chicago (incorporated in 1956 by Centex Developers of Texas), Martin Marty marched up one side of each street and down the other, ringing the doorbells of everyone who moved in, eventually visiting 1,800 homes.[8] The English

District of the LCMS had charged him with the task of gathering a church in the developing area northwest of Chicago. Longtime Church of the Holy Spirit member Gerry Russell remembered his twenty-eight-year-old pastor "barreling down the road in his little Corvair," full of energy and enthusiasm.[9] Marty and Father Ward Morrison, the priest sent to Elk Grove Village by the Roman Catholic Diocese, became good friends and shared the work of welcoming new residents.

In St. Louis Park, the largest suburb west of Minneapolis, Westwood Lutheran grew in a decade from a small mission church to, by 1954, a congregation of two thousand members, including one thousand Sunday school–age children, thanks largely to this kind of grassroots organizing.[10] Westwood's energetic thirty-one-year old pastor, Norman Nielsen, was an organizational genius with a congregation willing to do the work.[11] Some of Westwood's members served on St. Louis Park's "Welcome Wagon—a non-denominational greeter group of 75 families who introduce themselves to every new family which moves to the Park." Furthermore, everyone who came to the door of the church received a letter from the pastor and a personal visit. The parish worker would ask them, "Do you belong to a church? Would you *like* to belong to a church? Our church?" If the answer was yes, the newcomer was quickly connected to Westwood. If the answer was no, the parish worker would give them a list of all the St. Louis Park churches. In 1953 alone, Westwood made four thousand such house calls. "This is sound public relations," explained Reverend Nielsen. "We are interested in having people come to our church, but primarily bent upon having them go to church, whether it be Westwood or some other of their own church."[12] Westwood members could expect a yearly visit by a parish worker toting a "talent sheet" on which parishioners would note their skills and interests, to be matched with church needs. Nielsen called this "tried and true principles of organization, old fashioned neighborliness and elbow grease—plus plenty of Christian faith and effort." In 1954, 80 percent of the members were active in the church's work in some capacity.

The work of building was a central occupation of many postwar congregations, work that could extend for quite a number of years. One common characteristic of the postwar church building project was the tendency to design and build in stages, as resources allowed, buildings playing catch-up to material needs. Congregations thus often approached an initial building project as a "first unit" in a larger scheme.[13] It was up to the congregation to decide which aspect of the church complex to build first. Some new congregations began with education wings and held worship in a temporary smaller chapel or assembly room.[14] Westwood Lutheran's first buildings, for example, were devoted to education and recreation; the sanctuary came later. This was a useful strategy if the congregation's primary concern was accommodating a Sunday school. At the same time, there were strong arguments for beginning with a sanctuary. Worship was the heart of congregational life, communicated most clearly the nature of the organization—and, as many noted, was also the setting in which people were likely to be most generous with their financial contributions.

## THE WORK OF SERVICE: SUBURBAN BUILDING COMMITTEES

Postwar churches took shape according to the wishes of the church building committee, the client. The constitution of these committees varied from place to place. Pastors might sit on the committee but were not typically in charge. Nonetheless, they were often key collaborators in the process, particularly in matters of theology and practice. It frequently fell to them to guide the church toward an understanding of its total program, the functional needs that would direct design decisions.[15]

A small congregation might have ten members on the committee; larger churches could have dozens of members assigned to specific building-related tasks. Committee members tended to be professionals with some knowledge of business and finance, although it is not uncommon to find representatives of the building trades, educators, or even artists on these committees. Experts advised that building committees should represent the varied interests, ages, and professions in the congregation in order to best communicate the needs of all and to gather broad expertise. One of the hallmarks of the newer suburban congregation committees was the surprising youth of their members, no doubt one reason so many congregations freely chose contemporary architecture.

Although building committees were comprised largely of men, women were not always relegated to the kitchen or furnishings committees. Gender balance on building committees varied. The character of individual congregations and the personalities of their leaders (and to some extent the practices of a denomination) determined committee structure. Most widespread, however, was the assumption that because women played essential roles in congregational life (largely hospitality and education), their input was necessary at the planning stage. The ten-member building committee of First Presbyterian Church in La Grange, Illinois, included three women: Gladys Dutton representing the women's association, Betty Morse for Christian Education, and Betty Ackerman because, as she said, "I was complaining about the kitchen and they said, 'Why don't you get on the committee?'"[16] Ackerman attended every meeting, and remembered that it was a productive working group.

Once the building committee formed, tasks and meetings multiplied. Committee members researched the congregation's needs, investigated recently built churches, and learned to manage a building project. After developing a list of potential architects, the committee arranged for brief, preliminary interviews (often frustratingly brief, according to the architects) in which candidates had an hour or two to pitch their experience and expertise. Because of church networks and regional denominational structures, it was common for architects to gain commissions from clients within their own denominations. The great majority of Sövik's and Stade's clients were Lutheran. Many of Dart's commissions were from Episcopal congregations. At St. Augustine of Canterbury Episcopal Church in Benton Harbor, Michigan, the Building Planning Committee interviewed five architects before selecting "Mr. Edward D. Dart an Episcopalian from Chicago."[17] It made sense for building committees to hire an architect who knew their religious tradition from the inside. Sövik remembered "in those busy post WWII days . . . there was a substantial tie between the ability to design a good church and the religious affiliation of the architect . . . Catholics tended to hire Catholic architects, Lutherans Lutheran architects, and Reformed church people, Presbyterians or Methodists. Synagogues were almost always designed by Jews."[18]

As in most stages of the design and building process, price was an important factor and very much on the mind of the building committee. Fees recommended by the AIA were standard (6 percent minimum), but many architects won commissions by underbidding their competitors (not the architects in this study, however), and some architects charged more. Stade encouraged committees to be wary of church architects who promised unusually low fees, offered free sketches, and labeled themselves adherents of a specific "style." A good architect, he insisted, looked at the program, budget, site, and denomination before offering any design ideas.[19]

In 1965, after years of experience working with churches, Stade provided his "Recipe for a Good Building Committee." "Take approximately ten dedicated laymen," he wrote.

> Set forth the following needed incentives:
> 1. A wish to see, really 'see,' the disparate forms of beauty and ugliness.
> 2. A willingness to do discriminating reading on the subject of church architecture to be well and wisely informed.
> 3. A readiness to cover many miles and to study many structures.
> 4. A deep desire to understand their faith and the concepts engendered by that faith.
>
> Combine all these with an able and informed architect and the results will be a building of beauty and distinction speaking coherently in the language of today.[20]

Stade wanted an educated committee, one that would be open to the advice of artists, architects, and experts. He reiterated the words of many church leaders who were certain that no great church building would ever be built by a committee that did not thoroughly know itself, its faith, and its needs.

Most building committees fell short of this ideal. They were often unprepared, hurried and harried, and apt to make bad decisions that privileged money, square footage, and low maintenance over theologically based program concerns. Even so, Stade recalled one committee that had read "Tillich, Hammond, Frey, Sittler, Marty, and White" (all important, rigorous intellectuals writing about the problem of church architecture) and had traveled hundreds of miles to meet with architects and view their work.[21] It seems clear, however, that expediency and economy were the driving forces behind many church construction projects. To be fair, the committee itself often had a tough job communicating plans to the congregation. Committee and congregation did not always see eye to eye, with the congregation tending to be more conservative.

One role of the committee was to ease the adjustment to the modernist aesthetic. Building committee members deliberated with the architect about architectural style and expense, and in the process learned a rationale for modernism in religious architecture. The committee then had the task of convincing reluctant, or at least skeptical, congregational members. A sensitive and successful committee, such as that of St. Luke's Methodist in Indianapolis, understood that "there were people who had a hard time getting their heads around something that looked strange on paper" and worked carefully to educate the congregation as well as themselves.[22] But many church records, especially in the immediate postwar years, reveal tension surrounding design choice, occasionally leading to a loss of members. Modernism was a departure from the familiar, and dissent regarding aesthetic choice was a common part of the building process. The "church must look like a church" argument was heartfelt among many people in the pews, and there the rhetoric of the modern church movement had to do its work. Modernizing the social spaces, offices, and Sunday school facilities, however, was enthusiastically welcomed without controversy.

Church building consultants, affiliated with denominations or operating as solo practitioners, could help the committee and the congregation find their way through the building process—ascertaining the advisability of the project, determining location, and teaching the congregation how to raise funds, work with the architect, and navigate construction. William Clark emphasized the work of the public-relations committee, a central group of individuals responsible for communications between architect and congregation as well as the local media. Positive publicity alerted the wider community to the character and aims of the congregation. It could potentially deliver "glorious benefits for the church—more building funds, more new members, a powerful rise in morale for the older members."[23] Numerous positive news clippings in church records prove the success of this strategy. The local press used church building projects to display the general moral and material progress of their communities. Ground breaking for Olivet Lutheran in Fargo was attended by three local TV stations, and radio and newspaper reported the event in detail. The congregation responded, "We are most grateful for the news media coverage and for the keen interest shown by the general public."[24] Even the first phase of a building project could take years to complete, and it was the task of building committees and consultants to keep up interest and forward momentum in order to see the project through to completion.

## THE WORK OF FUND-RAISING, FROM BAKE SALES TO BANK LOANS

The cost of these new churches ranged from less than $25,000 to over $1 million. Even a smaller $100,000 church in 1955 would be equivalent to close to $900,000 in 2014 dollars, no small accomplishment for a congregation of young members just getting started financially.[25] The denominations, invested in expansion, could be important financial partners that offered construction grants or loans and provided consulting services, but church records also reveal irritation at the lack of help the denomination was able to offer. Sometimes other congregations in the denomination went out of their way to give a new congregation a leg up financially, as when a Lutheran congregation in Dodge City, Iowa, mortgaged its own building to help the Our Savior congregation get started in Austin, Minnesota.[26] A forward-thinking congregation would establish a building fund long before it was needed, but this was difficult, if not impossible, for new congregations. Most congregations needed to raise enough money to secure and minimize the required bank loan and mortgage payments. Even the least expensive buildings usually required significant fund-raising and unleashed often extraordinarily effective grassroots campaigns.

Consultants emphasized selling a vision rather than a specific plan. John Scotford counseled congregations that, "Instead of saying 'This is what we will build; let's go get the money,' there will be less complaint from the cautious if the sales talk is 'Here is what we want; now we must find out how much we can raise toward it.' Few can object to a campaign on this basis. It really puts the proposition up to the people."[27] During this period, the rise of professional fund-raising gave congregations another consulting option. With or without the assistance of a professional fund-raiser, however, the campaign was the work of the people. Through publicity, group meetings, and face-to-face canvassing, committee members spread a vision for the congregation's future. Buildings were typically funded by a mix of sources: the building fund, cash raised prior to construction, denominational support (depending on the denomination), cash raised during construction, and loans.

Effective communication within the congregation was fundamental. Building committees often prepared attractive illustrated booklets that stated the needs of the congregation and its vision for the future. These are telling historical documents that often communicate a strong sense of urgency. In 1953, St. Paul Lutheran, in Oak Lawn, Illinois, a brand-new congregation, printed a brochure with a sketch of the proposed new church, crisp and contemporary, on the cover (see Figure 2.7). Drawings such as these provided the motivation for congregations to give generously to a building project. This image anticipates a St. Paul church that would settle comfortably into a landscaped suburban setting, isolated from other buildings. Except for the aspirational chancel end, with its tower rising through the text above it, the church appears low and solid, with a direct and inviting path to its front door. Inside the brochure was a history of the congregation, the project description (highlighting the two large Sunday school halls, the assembly hall, and the modern kitchen), the financial status, and opportunities for memorial gifts. This one hundred thousand–dollar building project, already under way, represented "the united efforts of our people, working shoulder to shoulder, hand in hand, heart to heart, in an inspiring demonstration of Christian love." The pastor noted: we "aim to serve the community by proclaiming the message of the Gospel which alone gives true solution to the pressing problems of life and the courage to face the mysteries of death." An urgent message of service to the broader community was a critical component of these fund-raising campaigns.

Successful fund-raising forged a connection between generosity and faith. Our Saviour Lutheran in Lansing, Illinois, asked its members to "Stand Up and Be Counted: Help Finish the Job," and quoted 2 Corinthians 9:11: "Your very giving proves the reality of your faith." This brochure, circulated in advance of the canvass, attempted to allay concerns and fears. It anticipated questions and provided answers. For instance, for those who wondered why the congregation was moving out of town, the church replied, "To provide parking facilities and expansion of our church and Sunday School." To those concerned about the amount of debt, the brochure explained, "We have made a careful study . . . and we feel certain we are within the limits of our capacity to repay." One church member even penned a campaign poem:

So when God looks down upon this earth
Welcome the privilege of giving aid in building his church
"Stand up and be Counted" and let your heart throb
Then sign the pledge for the canvasser// "Help Finish the Job"[28]

The photographs in these brochures were effectively motivating, especially the images of masses of children crammed into small spaces. Other images showed metal folding chairs in the aisle of temporary worship spaces, adult study groups awkwardly placed in offices or even kitchens, and crowded parking lots. The focus was most often on the physical and spiritual needs of children, suggesting the importance of the building campaign for their future. On the cover of its fund-raising brochure, St. Luke's Methodist, Indianapolis, had a single sentimental image of a pensive young girl with her hands folded (Figure 3.1).

The "All-Member Canvass" and the "Loyalty Dinner" were elements of many church building campaigns. In the canvass, individual members received information and pledge cards and then a member of the fund-raising team paid a house call. Suburbanites were financially stretched, and there was certainly some squirming during these intentionally "low-pressure" visits. Furthermore, pledging to a major building project was risky if you knew your company might transfer you to a new community soon. In Park Forest, the United Protestant Churches printed

FIGURE 3.1. Fund-raising brochure for St. Luke's Methodist Church, Indianapolis, Indiana, 1964. Courtesy of St. Luke's United Methodist Church, Indianapolis.

a comprehensive booklet that anticipated this problem. Question: "Will we be expected to contribute to a church building fund even if we are temporary residents?" Answer: "Remember that you and your children have been blessed by churches in other communities which were built by others. You may go to another city where others have already built the church for your use."[29] Arguments such as these made church building and growth a shared national concern.

First Baptist, Bloomington, Indiana, executed its substantial building project with an unusually high degree of congregational involvement. As an older congregation, First Baptist had some resources at its disposal yet still needed to raise $175,000. Pastor W. Douglas Rae inspired a building committee of eighty-three members and fifty-one canvass workers to successfully pursue an exceptionally democratic program. The program brochure told the congregation: "we face a decisive hour in the progress of our church. Ours is a dynamic church, but the lack of space and modern facilities limits the spiritual growth of our children and the membership growth of our Sunday school."[30] The need was "especially acute among our children when we consider the necessity of developing young minds in the atmosphere of Christian community."[31] For further incentive, the church's weekly building program printed this notice: "overheard . . . last Sunday two visitors standing in the lobby and waiting for a folding chair seat in the aisle, one said to the other 'this is the last time we come to this crowded place!'"[32] These arguments—a sense of arrival at a critical crossroads and an appeal to Christian responsibility—are typical of postwar building campaigns.

Fund-raising was directed to every member, even the children. At First Baptist's Loyalty Dinner at Indiana University's Alumni Hall, November 9, 1954, a full program included an invocation, a presentation about the congregation's history, singing "Faith of Our Fathers," and detailed instructions on the building plan, how to pledge, and the mechanics of the canvass. The canvass workers carried out an "organized, intensive face-to face-solicitation in the homes" of not just members but Sunday school parents and others who were affiliated with the congregation. They asked for "nothing complicated or high pressure," just "a generous and sacrificial portion of weekly income."[33] In general, churches considered weekly pledges better than cash gifts, because a weekly amount was easier to promise up front, and the frequent reminder of the obligation to the building project kept members engaged in the work. Church members often recall their struggle to keep up with pledges that represented considerable sacrifice.

Although many congregations faced heavy debt that was difficult to shed, debt was not always such a bad thing for a congregation. For a church on the move, debt could be exciting, at least initially, because it meant something was happening. Jacquelyn Protsman believed the men in her Lansing, Illinois, church thought "a good church should be in debt . . . if everything is all paid off there's something wrong."[34] Debt also raised the opportunity for creative action. At First Baptist, the building project newsletter noted, "one woman is making and selling salad dressings. Another is going to wash and set her own hair for the duration. One is taking up babysitting."[35] Even the youth got involved: "Bobbie Cook, son of Mr. and Mrs. Robert Cook, has given up 'comics' for the duration."[36] While struggling to pay mortgages and make ends meet, church members gave generously. Small sums could add up, but more important, they signified personal investment in the church building project, and thus in the congregation's future.

## THE COLLABORATIVE WORK OF SUBURBAN CHURCH DESIGN

Design and financial considerations went hand in hand, and there were always compromises. Many decisions had long-term implications—placement of choir, orientation of the sanctuary, and the choice of artwork would all become part of the congregation's common practice and identity. From the congregation's perspective, given the common scarcity of funds, it was of the utmost importance to get building value, and more often than not that meant the most space for the least cost. Although the architects in this study insisted on quality materials, choosing cheaper materials was an effective way to cut costs and one reason many church buildings from this time have not fared so well. Stade always strove to convince his clients that a high-quality building cost less in the long run, and that has proved wise advice. Sövik decried such falsities as "plastic philodendrons," "chairs that look like leather but are really imitations," and other "little deceits and dissimulations" intolerable in church buildings.[37] Yet such shortcuts often allowed congregations to balance tight budgets.

According to architects, the usual building committee had practical concerns about style, cost, and fees, but not necessarily the searching questions about theology and meaning the most thoughtful designers hoped for. Architects such as Sövik, Dart, and Stade were successful in part because they encouraged congregations to ponder those questions. As important as the meetings between architect and building committee were, there is very little documentation of their content in the written record. The memories of participants, however, suggest that design was frequently a two-way street, with architects often presenting several ideas before finding one that was both appealing and affordable to a client. Betty Ackerman, for instance, of First Presbyterian, La Grange, recalled many meetings with Stade or his representative at which there was a lot of "give-and-take," and this seems typical.[38] Both parties started with the same idea—that the church should be "contemporary" to fit the needs of the modern world—and together they had to discover what that meant in terms of both program and architecture.

Sövik, Dart, and Stade insisted on keeping church design from becoming its own cloistered enterprise, and sought to integrate their work into the wider architectural conversations of their day. But they did not believe that creating churches was a routine, secular matter, and this is evident in the way they worked with congregations. Stade tried to hire architects of different faiths to diversify the theological understanding of his firm, and regularly attended services of the congregations for which he was designing buildings.[39] He claimed that he was essentially a servant of the congregation's needs. "I don't take into account my private beliefs, preference for worship or taste in architectural styles," he claimed. "It's not my church I'm designing—it's the congregation's."[40] Nonetheless, Stade had strong ideas about what constituted the best contemporary church architecture, and, while accommodating, he nudged his clients toward more sophisticated theological and architectural understanding.

Sövik's partnership with First Baptist, Bloomington, illustrates what an architect could accomplish with a capable and patient client. The unusually complete church building records document eight full years of planning and a high level of attention to detail. This was the first of Bloomington's established churches to go out to areas of new development and build a modern church. The fact that the democratic process at First Baptist was so unusually thorough—all major building decisions went before the whole congregation for a vote—was remarked on in the press. Sövik himself doubted the efficiency of the process: "the architects were at first dubious about the possibilities of allowing an entire congregation to make so many decisions"; he felt a small committee would be better. Each working committee actively solicited input from all constituents, from the scouts to the choirs, and the entire project worked surprisingly well.[41] Running such a committee and project could easily become a full-time job. The committee noted in July that "our chairman has been devoting the major part of his waking hours to this building project and has had to relegate his automobile business and professional duties to his spare time."[42] A suggestion box revealed the personal concerns and desires of members of the congregation: air conditioning, several small kitchenettes, multiple broom closets, a drinking faucet in the choir room, a sheltered entrance without steps, playground, "two well drained dressing rooms" next to the immersion baptistery, and bench cushions.[43] From the congregation's point of view, as these suggestions indicated, it was important to avoid the practical problems of the past, such as inadequate storage space, physical discomfort in the warm season, too many steps, inflexible spaces, or the inability to make a cup of coffee when and where it was needed. It is perhaps not surprising that issues like the choice of pew cushions and architectural style often became flash points, because they directly connected with the physical and aesthetic comfort level of each parishioner.

Reverend Rae and the building committee looked extensively for a church architect and contacted Sövik in 1954.[44] Before Sövik even entered the picture, however, the committee had collected suggestions and produced a lengthy thirty-two-page document detailing the church's building needs. One of the hopes of the congregation was that the building would be "so simple and meaningful and honest, that no one will be made afraid by lavish appointments or pretension in any form."[45] A not insignificant motivation for the restrained modern church was to "strike a contrast with St. Charles Church," the Gothic, Catholic church next door, in keeping with the Baptist "nonauthoritarian" tradition and "the spirit of [the] congregation."[46]

The most important congregational discussions about architectural design and its relationship to mission typically took place in the planning stages of a building project. Building committee representatives would educate themselves by visiting other newly built churches. Members of Zion Lutheran in Galesville, Wisconsin, for instance, visited new churches in Minneapolis and St. Paul before deciding on "the more contemporary style of architecture." Then, "after much discussion and more church visits," they chose Sövik as architect.[47] This would have been no later than the spring of 1950, when Sövik was still little known. The congregation began with the education wing, completed in 1952. A new pastor arrived in 1953 with "some reservations about the type of architecture to be used" for the new sanctuary, so the building committee again visited churches in the Twin Cities. In November 1954, at a full congregational meeting, the members voted once again to hire Sövik to design a contemporary building. At each of these stages, the congregation was called upon to think carefully about what its statement in architecture would communicate, and what modern architecture could offer.

Congregational notes about Zion's 1954 meeting, the largest meeting in the church's history, are instructive. "Architect E. A. Sövik of Northfield, Minnesota, first presented a church of modern design with a flat roof, which he had presented about a month previously. He then introduced a second plan with modification, a plan with pitched roof."[48] Clearly, there was some discussion about the choice of style, for "it was pointed out that the contemporary design was the church of the future because young architectural students are taught contemporary design only and are no longer trained in classical styling. A wealth of new materials and construction techniques are available today." Many in the congregation remained opposed, but in the final vote more than 80 percent favored contemporary design.

The illuminating building committee records of one of Stade's clients, St. Peter Lutheran in Arlington Heights, Illinois, record a similar process. In the fall of 1957, members of the congregation proposed that their old building had run out its usefulness and it was time to build anew. After getting an appraisal for their current property, they started scouting for a new site in the growing suburban areas of Arlington Heights. A planning committee met in December and sent one subcommittee to study new schools (an attached day school was anticipated) and another to study churches.[49] Without yet deciding to relocate, the congregation went ahead and purchased a fifteen-acre tract of land in an area of new development. In May 1958, the building committee began interviewing six architects, including Stade. Stade's presentation on June 19 stressed the nature of his firm (eight architects, twenty employees), the extent of his church work (150 buildings in fourteen states), and his tendency to build "mostly contemporary type of churches, expressing the religion and the feelings of the people through materials used for the building." Stade informed the committee that he worked, as did most church architects, first by making preliminary drawings and crafting a master plan for approval, then creating working drawings, and finally supervising the construction. His fee would be the standard, AIA-approved 6 percent.[50]

In early August, the committee asked Stade to begin preliminary drawings. In November, he led a discussion in which he showed slides "of various church buildings and discussed architecture, facilities, and approximate costs of these churches." In early December, Stade presented three study plans for consideration; a week later he came back with two more. At that point, the committee was able to agree on a cruciform, rather than a rectangular, plan. Carl Klehm, chair of the building committee, recalled meeting with the architects frequently as they hammered out the design: "They worked with ovals, squares, rectangles, triangles, and finally came up with a cross-shaped building" that seats 750, "yet has no worshipper more than fifty feet from the chancel."[51] Early in the process, Stade asked the committee to think about acoustics, sight lines, heating and cooling, lighting, beauty, and to understand all the liturgical uses of the space. Most of the discussion apparently focused on the sanctuary design, although the project would also include the standard support facilities, a new school, and a gym. All this time Stade was also providing ideas for remodeling the old church and school, in the event that the church decided not to move.

Finally, on December 28 the committee voted to relocate to the larger plot, "being convinced that relocating on our new site would mean a greater and steady growth for the congregation than we could attain by remaining in our present site; and realizing our Lord was giving us an opportunity to write another glorious and blessed chapter in the history of St. Peter Lutheran Church for the Kingdom Sake."[52] At this time, St. Peter finally officially resolved, in a congregational meeting, to hire Stade. This was a substantial commission for him, perhaps one reason he worked so diligently for the congregation even before he signed the primary contract. By March the proposed budget was more than $850,000 (almost $7 million in 2014 dollars). The records note an extended discussion on details such as the heating system (electric was cheaper to install but more expensive to run), the choice of interior and exterior stone, the "cathedral glass" for the anticipated Good Shepherd window behind the altar, the need for a women's committee to plan the kitchen, and the possibility of creating space for a future pipe organ. The congregation broke ground for the new church in June 1959 and it was dedicated in May 1961 (Figures 3.2 and 3.3).

For Roman Catholic parishes, building projects were typically in the hands of the clergy, although the laity participated in the process. The collaboration between

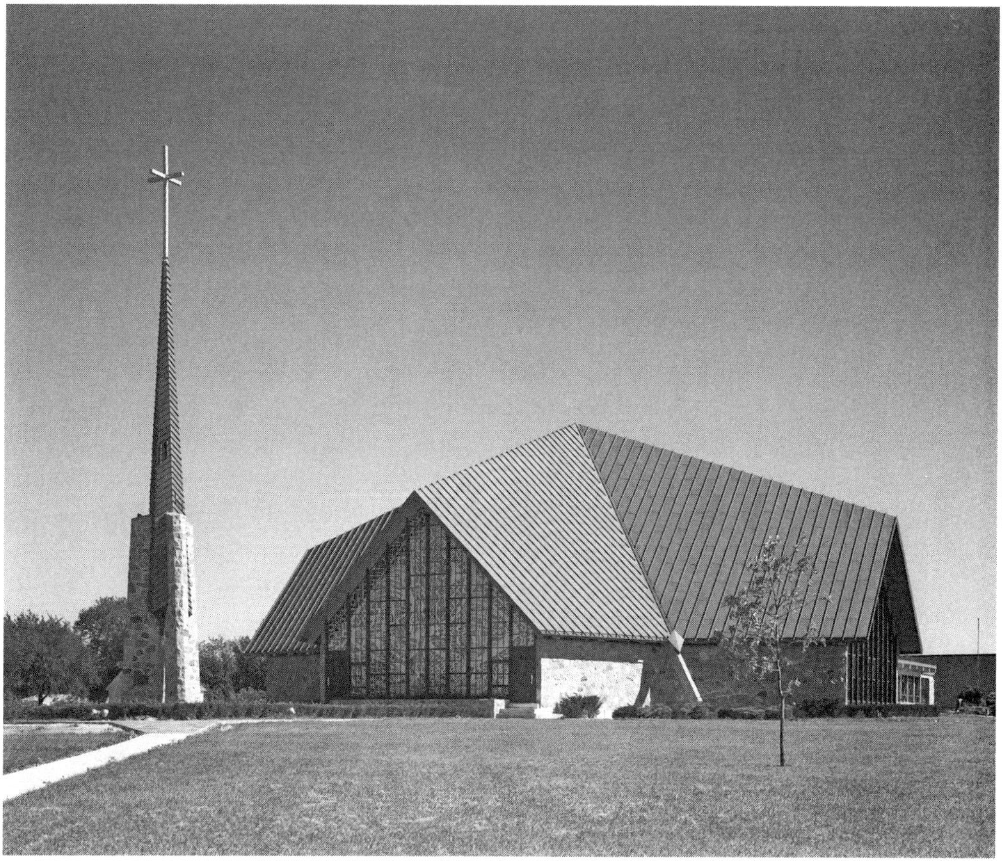

FIGURE 3.2. Charles Stade, St. Peter Lutheran Church, Arlington Heights, Illinois, 1960. Hubert Henry for Hedrich-Blessing, HB-25219-H, Chicago History Museum.

Sövik and St. Leo Church in Pipestone, Minnesota (1967–69), illustrates this exciting time in the life of the Catholic church (see Figures 2.1 and 5.27).[53] Father Bernel Deslauriers, pastor of St. Leo since 1948, and a new young assistant, Father Brian Willette, a recent graduate of St. John's University in Collegeville, Minnesota (a center for modernism and liturgical renewal), led the building project. St. Leo's old building, a small Gothic church, was falling apart. Deslauriers had already engaged an architect for the new building, but Willette pressed him to tour recent churches in the area and rethink his choice. Willette then asked Father Aelred Tegels (editor of *Worship*, the influential Catholic liturgical journal) and designer Frank Kacmarcik, both of St. John's, to send a list of architects they admired.[54] After a survey of these recommendations, Deslauriers and Willette chose Sövik. Together, these men spent about a year talking about architecture, liturgy, and belief. "It was like a proseminar," Willette remembers, "very, very exciting." The design became "more forthright, simple, and straightforward over time," and the group

FIGURE 3.3. Charles Stade, chancel at St. Peter Lutheran, Arlington Heights, Illinois, during the dedication ("ready for liturgy"), 1961. Courtesy of St. Peter Lutheran Church, Arlington Heights, Illinois.

was drawn to what seemed "authentic" and "earthy." Willette remembers standing together out on the prairie, looking at the "wide-open spaces" and trying to imagine architecture designed to protect and facilitate, one that would grow out of the earth—what they jokingly called "cow pasture architecture."[55] Sövik called the sanctuary "incarnational," explaining that "that is why it is made of earthy and familiar materials, and why its concrete framing appears as forthrightly as it might in a factory building, and why there is no self-conscious attempt to make a building which is 'out of this world.'"[56] In language that suggests why Sövik was such a persuasive advocate of modern church architecture, he stated:

> "St. Leo's church was not intended to be strange or majestic or impressive. Its materials are generally familiar and ordinary. But it was intended to be beautiful: its proportions, the relationships of materials and colors, the special sequences, and the other aspects of the design were intended to be so combined that people would have a

> sense of that indefinable thing called beauty, and that wonder would recall to them the great mystery of our lives under God."[57]

It is no wonder Sövik was so effective with congregations from many denominations, able to transcend theological and liturgical differences.

St. Leo's parish was involved in this "visioning" process. After the old building's demolition, services took place in the open space of the school gym, where the congregation had the opportunity to experiment with different seating configurations. Sövik, Kacmarcik, and Tegels all led educational sessions and workshops. Although the local bishop at the time was quite conservative, Pipestone was a long way from his seat, and some clever politicking enabled the St. Leo team to evade his potential objections to the modern design of the new church.[58]

## ALL HANDS ON DECK: CONSTRUCTION AND COMMUNITY LABOR

After many weeks of working together with the architect on the design and budget for a church, the building committee sent the plans out to contractors for bids. Ideally, when the bids were opened costs would be within 10 percent of the architect's estimate.[59] If the costs were too high, the congregation had to scale back the plans and/or put construction on hold while it raised more funds. Delays posed a challenge for mission, and they were also risky because both labor and material costs regularly rose during this time. At First Baptist, Bloomington, the large committee assembled in the old church carefully pored over five bids ranging from $306,000 to $450,000 well into the night, finally choosing the lowest bidder, Gwaltney Brothers of Indianapolis (Figure 3.4). Before signing the contract, First Baptist brought down the cost by deleting a fellowship hall, replacing the thermopane glass, terrazzo, and asphalt tile with something less costly, choosing cheaper toilet partitions, and agreeing to do the interior painting themselves.[60]

Many of the stories congregations tell about their postwar building projects focus on moments when members rolled up their sleeves and contributed their labor to the cause. First Baptist, Bloomington, requested that people with technical expertise on materials and specifications or educational facilities speak up and volunteer.[61] Photographs of the building process reveal that this was a family affair, beginning when each child was asked to bring a shovel to the ground breaking, a common practice for these congregational milestone events (Figure 3.5). "One of the most inspiring features of the entire program," noted the congregation, "has been that some two hundred people [out of 296 families] have given actual work, participating in the laying of several thousand feet of tile, and carrying the burden of the paint work" (Figure 3.6).[62] In retrospect, "this contribution of skills and semi-skilled work brought a new sense of Christian community which was of far greater value than the actual money saved by the free labor."[63] Fifty years later, Bob Stout pointed proudly to a wooden screen hiding the coat racks that he and two

FIGURE 3.4. The building committee of First Baptist, Bloomington, Indiana, opening bids with Edward Sövik seated in background at right, 1956. Courtesy of First United Church, Bloomington, Indiana.

other members built according to Pastor Rae's design.[64] It was exciting to watch a church building in progress. At Olivet, Fargo, "Side-walk superintendents [were] already in evidence at the site of the construction."[65] Dean Ferguson recalled, "we were proud . . . we'd watch it every day."[66] Parishioners remembered that when the laminated trusses were delivered for St. Augustine's, Gary, Indiana, the entire neighborhood seemed to turn out to watch the trucks unload and the workmen raise the beams.[67]

During construction, the presence of the architect or his representative was often a point of contention for building committees who wanted the architect on the job as much as possible. Such supervision varied, often for financial reasons. Before signing a contract with St. Augustine of Canterbury in Benton Harbor, Michigan, Dart calculated that he simply could not afford the amount of supervision requested. He wrote to the vicar asking that payment for site visits come in the form of a per diem, because traveling the 150 miles to Benton Harbor would be time-consuming and expensive. He hoped for a competent contractor who would permit him to keep these visits to a minimum.[68] Changes during the course of construction are common on most building projects, but churches, with their multiplicity of concerns and interests, are especially susceptible. Because so many

FIGURE 3.5. Ground-breaking ceremony for First Baptist, Bloomington, Indiana, 1956. Courtesy of First United Church, Bloomington, Indiana.

postwar materials and methods of construction were relatively new or even experimental (such as the materials and methods used for the A-frames discussed in the next chapter), unanticipated construction problems could plague congregations. New technologies were exciting, but they also required careful supervision. One way or another, through the inevitable bumps in the road, congregations made their way to joyful dedication ceremonies, at which they packed into their new sanctuaries and pledged the use of the building for the service of God.

## CRAFTING CURB APPEAL

Congregations paid a great deal of attention to the siting, external symbolism, and curb appeal of their new churches. Well versed in the mechanisms of postwar consumerism, advocates spoke frankly about the importance of the building as an advertisement in a world in which potential consumers had many options for how to spend their time and money. They realized they were up against some stiff competition. For one thing, "the suburban church is probably not very imposing or

FIGURE 3.6. The congregation of First Baptist, Bloomington, Indiana, works together to finish the sanctuary, 1957. Courtesy of First United Church, Bloomington, Indiana.

attractive as a building, has financial problems, and usually cannot compete with the downtown church as far as music, staff, and programs are concerned." Furthermore, there was the problem of competing activities: "For many suburbanites, it is more fun, and fashionable, to get in the family car on Sunday mornings and head for the hills or the beach; or just pass away the time working on the car or in the yard."[69] Choosing the site was a significant first step in not just taking care of the flock, but in evangelizing the neighbors. "The site will greatly determine the effectiveness of the only confrontation the Church will have with some of the passers-by," noted O. T. McRee, so "in the selection of the site consideration will be given to the nature and habits of the community."[70] Grounds as well as building were important, because they could send a message of open friendliness, making it clear that the church was not designed for "a private group in seclusion" but open to the community.[71] Most congregations did not think of themselves, or their buildings, in isolation. As St. Paul Lutheran in Oak Lawn, Illinois, announced, "we have planned a church which will be in harmony with the natural beauty and the contemporary homes and schools of our community."[72]

Architects preferred to be included in the site selection process, but often congregations purchased land before engaging a designer, largely because waiting to buy land limited choice significantly. In some communities land was already scarce. Hillside Methodist, for instance, considered itself very fortunate to have secured one of the last remaining sizable plots in Evanston, Illinois.[73] Because Americans were feeling less bound to the denominations of their childhood, church planners warned congregations that they could no longer expect indiscriminate loyalty. Proximity to new homes was a fortunate advantage. Some communities had local councils of churches that helped regulate the formation and placement of new Protestant congregations. Rather than clustering churches all together in a new suburb, planners argued that it was best to space them more evenly throughout the community, both for reasons of traffic control and to encourage people to attend churches close to their homes.

Location was also determined by zoning regulations (regarding site development and parking requirements) and the wishes of neighbors who had concerns about traffic and noise. Automobiles often determined the location of the building on its site. Congregations were of two minds about where to place the parking. Parking out front could be unsightly, yet a full parking lot also invited newcomers. On the large suburban sites in this study, a side parking area was a common solution, sometimes with a drive and loading/unloading area near the street side entrance (although anecdotal evidence suggests the drop-off was rarely used on Sundays) and additional parking to the rear. Churches found that members rarely used main entrances facing outward in favor of the rear entrance closer to parking. As much as possible, a yard-like setting was created, an environment much more akin to that of new houses and schools than shopping centers, demonstrating that congregations conceptualized these buildings as domestic rather than commercial.

The subsequent history of these postwar congregations proves the value of a good location near new housing with a visually appealing and car-friendly orientation, as a dedication Sunday photograph of St. Peter Lutheran, Arlington Heights, illustrates (Figure 3.7). In Fargo, Carol Ferguson of Olivet Lutheran remembers, "after we moved in the congregation grew so fast, just 'cause of the location, I think."[74] Numerous articles and conference talks centered on landscaping, but in reality it was lower on the list of priorities, a task often performed by the members of a congregation after the church was occupied. One of the reasons for the initial low priority given to landscaping might have been the belief that the church would expand further onto the property in the near future. As the suburbs flourished, trimmed shrubbery (in part to shield neighbors from headlights) grew to frame the new churches. Expanses of lawns and flower beds contributed to an inviting scene.

## WHERE THE DREAM BEGAN: THE "FIRST UNIT" OF THE SUBURBAN CHURCH

First-unit buildings, often the core of a new church project, could be perplexing problems for architects. The congregations' budgets were tiny, their needs and

FIGURE 3.7. The congregation of St. Peter Lutheran, Arlington Heights, Illinois, at dedication, 1961. Note the proximity of new houses and the parking lot full of automobiles. Courtesy of St. Peter Lutheran Church, Arlington Heights, Illinois

expectations enormous. As time has shown, many "temporary" first-unit buildings were called upon to serve into the indefinite future. Certain options, such as the use of folding chairs rather than pews, were suitable in the short term, but an architect who cared deeply about good design could hardly be satisfied with the requirements of these projects. Sövik said that he gave up designing first-unit buildings as soon as he realized that they were by definition flawed and that the architect was rarely called back to complete the next unit. Building committees were "so urgent about saving every nickel," he said, and wanted to strip the first-unit project to a minimum so they could "get to the next unit."[75]

Charles Stade's first-unit buildings were typically small A-frames with a reduced office/education wing. Edward Dart's first units were varied and interesting. In fact, he became something of an expert on the problem. In the winter 1963 edition of *Your Church*, a popular magazine for pastors and church leaders, Dart published an article titled "The Nature of the First Unit."[76] "Picture a building," he wrote, "that is schoolhouse, social hall, restaurant, meeting area, and, at some times, theater and, at all times, a church. The first unit of a master church building plan must include all of this with a building budget between $30–70,000." This demanded creativity and practicality from the architect, all without losing "an unmistakable churchlike quality." "It must," Dart insisted, "reflect the feeling and spirit of a church and not, as frequently happens, appear to be a replica of the local Legion hall." The best first-unit buildings, then, would be worshipful and coherent yet flexible and adaptable. Dart argued that the architect should consider the future use of the first-unit building.

In practice, this was not Dart's particular strength. He had a flair for designing intimate worship spaces with unique character, and because of this they were at once successful buildings yet sometimes impossible to integrate easily into a later, expanded structure. His saddle-roofed Lutheran church in Barrington is one example (see Figure 2.4). A form such as this could not be easily blended into a new sanctuary or adapted to use as a fellowship hall, although it could exist as a secondary chapel. It is hard to know, however, how much design authority to attribute to architects in many of these cases. Building committees at this first stage were desperate for space, and with their minimal resources often eliminated more expensive design choices.

The first-unit challenge is illustrated by Dart's St. Augustine of Canterbury Episcopal in Benton Harbor, Michigan (1962). Dart designed this church for a mission congregation with a very limited budget. This space was intended as a short-term solution for a congregation expecting eventually to add a classroom extension and a larger sanctuary. The congregation requested that their first-unit building, about 4,300 square feet total, include a worship space that could seat 175, a vestibule (narthex) that might be used as overflow space, bathrooms, coat rooms, utility rooms, administration areas, a kitchenette, and four classrooms that could each be partitioned into two spaces or opened into fellowship space.[77] And, "the spirit of the Sanctuary building shall reflect in every way the total and unmistakable feeling of a church." All for a budget of $65,000.[78]

St. Augustine's formed in 1960 when St. Stephen's Episcopal Mission in Benton Harbor (an integrated congregation) combined with members of all-white St. Paul's parish in nearby St. Joseph, Michigan, who were living east of the St. Joseph River. With a spirit of openness and adventure, the congregation approached the design process. Vicar Bruce Wheeler drove down to Gary to view Dart's 1959 church of the same name. He was impressed by "the simplicity of the structure, and asked the committee to seriously consider Mr. Dart."[79] Dart was by then an acclaimed architect, and the building committee knew the proposed project was small, but Dart accepted the commission.[80] The committee wanted something that "stood out" and had character, but at the same time was "attractive, not over pretentious." St. Augustine's is rectangular in plan, a sanctuary and narthex over a raised basement

FIGURE 3.8. Edward Dart, St. Augustine of Canterbury Episcopal Church, Benton Harbor, Michigan, 1962. Photograph by the author.

(Figures 3.8–3.9).[81] The upward sweep of the roof is arresting (originally topped by a large, simple cross). Dart managed to meet the needs of St. Augustine's congregation in this interesting building with a unique sanctuary and profile, but the building definitely has not lent itself easily to expansion.

Another very small Dart first unit, All Saints Lutheran in Orland Park, Illinois, has worked well as the core of an expanding suburban church. All Saints organized in 1961 and soon after purchased an eight-acre tract next to a new high school. The denomination instructed the small congregation to spend no more than fifty-eight thousand dollars on its building. Dart designed a two-hundred-seat sanctuary with an economical extension containing a few offices, a multipurpose room, and necessary service areas. The simple sanctuary has a distinctive roof that appears like a tightly stretched three-planed tent over low vertical walls. The congregation intended this to be just the first phase of "a complete complex of church buildings, including facilities for an extensive young people's program."[82] A new sanctuary, sympathetic to Dart's original, was finally built in 1986, and the first sanctuary turned into a fellowship hall. Dart's first unit was a mere three thousand square feet, cheaply made of inexpensive materials. Even today the church feels residential, with an inviting, human-scale entry and unpretentious, low-scaled rooms.

FIGURE 3.9. St. Augustine of Canterbury, Benton Harbor, Michigan, sanctuary. Courtesy of St. Augustine of Canterbury Episcopal Church, Benton Harbor, Michigan.

## THE WORK CONTINUED: BUILDING A SECOND CHURCH

When anticipated church growth did ensue, architects faced the corresponding problem of adding on to a first-unit building that no longer served the needs of the congregation. In the mid-1960s, Dart designed the second church of a Methodist congregation in the rapidly growing northern suburbs of Indianapolis. This venturesome congregation split off from a downtown church, Central Methodist, in 1952, and hired the well-known Philadelphia architect Harold Wagoner to design a first-unit building. Wagoner produced a modified Colonial Revival complex: red brick, white pillars, central steeple (1955–56). There was never a formal worship space in this structure; the congregation held services in the "Fellowship Hall," a large, open area filled with metal folding chairs, the intention being that, as soon as possible, the church would build a "true sanctuary." The congregation already had a reputation for progressive thinking, and under the leadership of a graphic designer, the building committee managed to convince the congregation to go in an entirely different direction. Committee members visited churches throughout Indiana and the region in 1964, and they told potential architects, "we want a *significant* church."[83]

Given the bland conservatism of the earlier structure, it is remarkable that the congregation turned to Dart and fully embraced a robust modern design for its next building, especially because Indianapolis was "not known for adventure in architecture."[84] It is possible that the congregation contacted Wagoner again at this time, but attention soon turned to Dart, most likely recommended by Ray Thompson, a young architect on the building committee. Pastor Richard Hamilton recalls that Dart was different from the other architects considered. For one thing, he began with conversation rather than pictures, asking questions such as "Let's suppose the Wagoner building were not here and you started fresh. What would you want?" The congregation responded, "a sanctuary that would be a true sanctuary."[85] Dart's vision for the church included a thorough overhaul of the old structure, encased completely in the new. The historic Georgian disappeared in favor of something altogether different for Indianapolis. Some of Dart's ideas were intended to save the congregation money—for instance, using a central corridor between the old and new buildings, rather than an open courtyard (thus using all enclosed space). He also removed the steeple (sold to the Church of God of Prophecy) and designed an open tower suitable for a carillon.

When estimates came in for Dart's initial design, the cost was beyond the means of the congregation, so cuts were made. Rather than reduce the size of the badly needed sanctuary, the committee decided to postpone some of the construction, including a chapel, some classrooms, and a library/parlor. Dart's church, "one of the most striking in the Indianapolis area," according to the *Indianapolis Star*, had a restrained, geometric, and unrevealing exterior, a low entrance passageway, and a simple and serene sanctuary (Figures 3.10 and 3.11).[86] The interior space, with its powerful beauty, was more readily accepted than the unusual exterior, which is still referred to in Indianapolis as the "Lego church."

As the experience of these three architects and their clients indicates, there were many compromises in the design and building process. In order to grasp the significance of these projects for the postwar congregation, understanding the process of building is as important as evaluating the outcome. Building projects taught and rewarded generosity, resourcefulness, and adaptability to new ways of seeing and doing. Both old and new congregations used building projects not simply to create usable space but to energize their people and programs, to literally shape future generations of religious life in America.

The architect bore the burden of leading the conversation toward successful design choices. It was in these building committee meetings that many ordinary suburban Americans learned the vocabulary and rationale for the modern architecture that increasingly surrounded them. In 1963, the acclaimed architect Pietro Belluschi, who had worked with numerous church building committees, told a group of architects and laymen in Seattle, "the architect must find within himself

FIGURE 3.10. Edward Dart, St. Luke's United Methodist Church, Indianapolis, Indiana, 1967. Courtesy of St. Luke's United Methodist Church, Indianapolis, Indiana.

the eloquence to explain and to convince, and such a task does not always come easy to a creative temperament which fears compromise and is impatient with the limitations of lay committees and with the general difficulty of defining Art."[87] Stade, Dart, and Sövik were fortunate that many of their church clients were open to learning about the new architecture and willing to take a few risks. When seeking to understand these buildings today, it is important to recognize the limitations of building committees, the many steps of the planning process, and the potential stages of the building never realized. Naturally, while aiming for an uncertain future, congregations and architects sometimes missed the mark.

The *process* of building was absolutely formative in the life of these congregations. As sociologist Robert Wuthnow has noted, by doing things locally—building, naming, transforming—people build a "sense of spatial attachment" to community.[88] These building projects marked a hopeful time of life for the generation who built them, and they provided a means for members of the congregation to establish durable bonds with the church and each other. Helen Danielson, of Good Shepherd, Moorhead, remembers the building phase as especially thrilling. "It was always kind of exciting," she says, "and everyone seemed to be working together and we wondered if we'd have the same camaraderie when the building was all done."[89] Similarly, in Park Forest, Illinois, a member of First Church of Christ, Scientist recalled the efforts of the congregation to sustain the early years of the

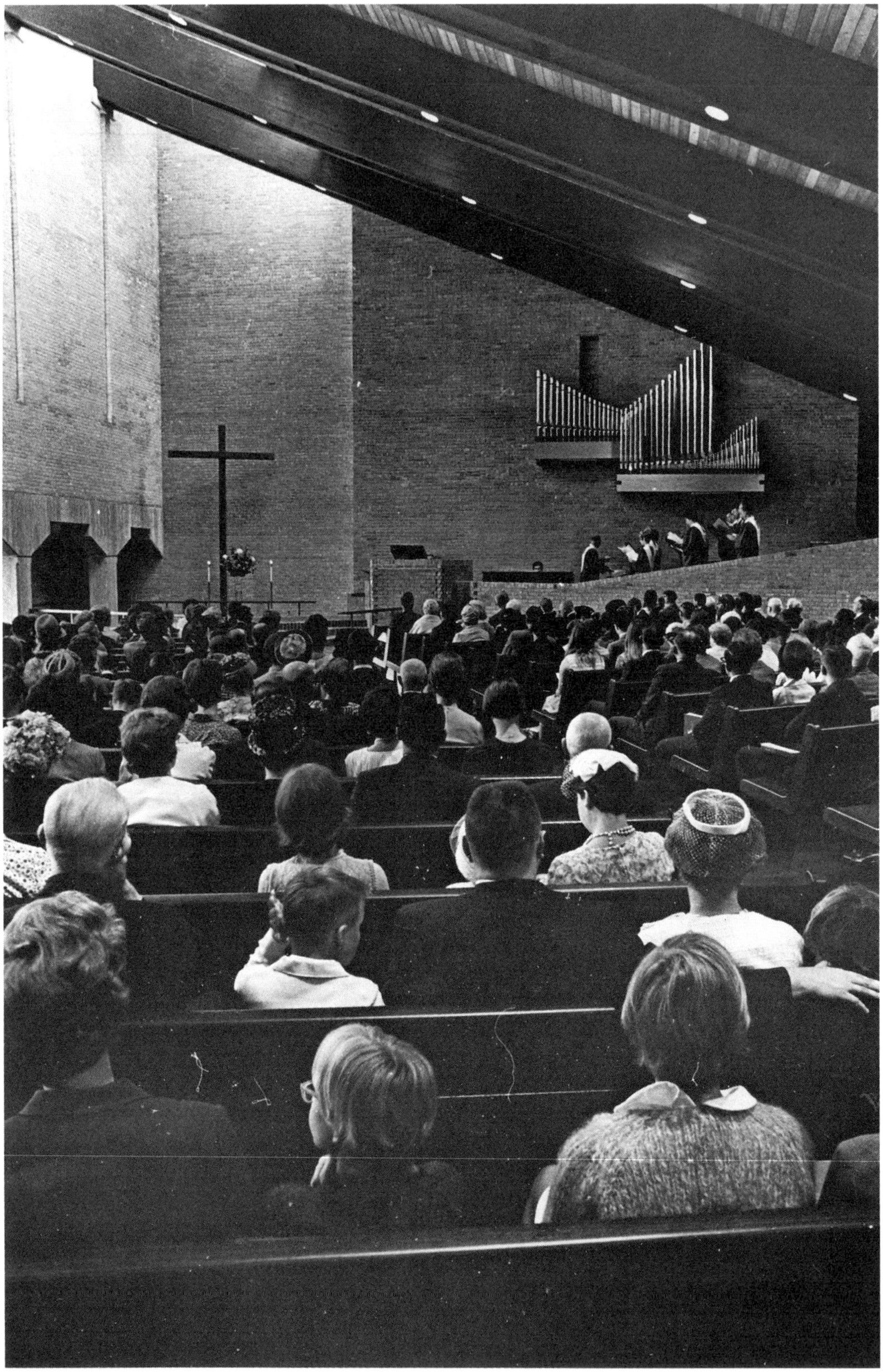

FIGURE 3.11. St. Luke's United Methodist Church, Indianapolis, Indiana, sanctuary interior at dedication, 1967. Courtesy of St. Luke's United Methodist Church, Indianapolis, Indiana.

Sunday school: "We all worked hard, no one was battle-weary, and never since have I had a church experience where members showed so much dedication."[90] The memory of a community energetically focused on the task of building and growing is typical among those who experienced this period in the life of the suburban church.

Evidence just as clearly reveals that building a church was no easy endeavor. Many of the strategies for completion of a building project—a first-unit beginning, aggressive fund-raising, and widely distributed labor—required generosity and sacrifice. This set a pattern for the involvement of this generation in the life of the suburban church. When the last swath of paint had dried, when the pews were set in place and the kitchen appliances installed, the work of the church in the community could begin in earnest. The many decisions made in the design and building process had lasting ramifications for religious programming, social activities, and even the character of each congregation.

CHAPTER 4

# The A-Frame Church

## *Symbol of an Era*

As the previous chapters have shown, the modernist movement in American church architecture had to negotiate a complex and often competing set of factors to gain momentum: the centuries-long weight of tradition in religious building, the aesthetic and theological concerns of diverse church leaders and thinkers, the keen imagination and professional ideals of church architects, and the pragmatic but often unfocused pressures of lay congregational building committees. On top of all this, the severe financial limitations on most suburban churches meant that, with rare exceptions, cost and efficiency were vital considerations.

In the Midwestern suburbs, one particular design offered a solution that seemed to balance all these competing interests: the "A-frame" church. Within a few years of its introduction, the A-frame became one of the most common postwar church types. For both aesthetic and practical reasons, Midwestern suburban congregations frequently chose this versatile form. The popularity of the A-frame extended well beyond this region—countless A-frame churches also were built from California to Florida, and from Canada to South Africa. A-frames tended to show up anywhere new congregations needed quickly built, inexpensive houses of worship. The form soon spread across most Christian denominations, and there is even the occasional A-frame synagogue.[1]

The extraordinary popularity of the A-frame, however, was short-lived. At first deemed an attractive design solution that combined aesthetic appeal, religious symbolism, and cost efficiency, the A-frame's very popularity and ubiquity began to be liabilities. By the mid-1960s, although A-frames continued to be built, the form was distinctly out of favor among architects and church leaders. In 1966, New York architect Edward Larabee Barnes told his audience at the San Francisco meeting of the National Conference on Religious Architecture that the A-frame was partly to blame for the blasé suburban church, one of the chief culprits in "vacuous banal sprawl."[2] Barnes berated "the little architect who simply builds an

A-frame roof (because it points up) and puts a glaring A-shaped window back of the altar (because stained glass is religious) and tells himself at the same time that his building is modern (because it has an A-frame), this little architect is fooling himself and the building committee."[3]

The rise and fall of the A-frame is an object lesson in both the shifting tides of the postwar church architecture movement and the increasing disillusionment with the architecture of suburbia. It is an ideal vehicle for assessing the practical concerns, theological imperatives, and symbolic needs of the postwar American congregation. The initial, successful match between the A-frame church and the aspirations of congregations indicates its special correspondence with the new postwar religious culture. The A-frame balanced the tensions suburbanites navigated—religious, economic, and cultural. It met the "looks like a church" criterion while signaling a contemporary spirit. Yet, in just over a decade, the A-frame church became the whipping boy of an architectural establishment that harbored a profound sense that modernism, particularly in church architecture, had fallen short of its potential to be fresh and new. This chapter locates the A-frame's origins, describes its variations, and seeks to explain its tremendous popularity and eventual decline.

The classic A-frame consists, technically, of a rigid, triangular frame in which the steeply pitched roof extends to the ground and doubles as side walls. "A-frame," as the term was broadly and colloquially applied to churches by postwar Americans, however, went well beyond this narrow definition; it generally meant a building whose dominant shape was a triangle, having a steeply pitched roof that often rested on low side walls. The gable end of these buildings almost always fronted the street, a dominant facade that became a familiar sight along the main thoroughfares of suburban neighborhoods. Inside, two ranks of pews separated by a central aisle typically faced a clearly demarcated, slightly raised chancel. Examples in this chapter will range from buildings of the classic triangle to those with substantial vertical walls under the eaves, but all have a geometry defined by a visually dominant, steeply pitched roof and low walls. This is a rather expansive definition, but one that fits the way ordinary people understood the A-frame form in the postwar years.

American A-frame churches range from extremely simple, prefabricated structures to relatively expensive, architect-designed examples. They came in a variety of materials and sizes. Integral towers or steeples (often prefabricated) sometimes appeared on these buildings, although an independent vertical element, such as a bell tower, was also common. Whether cheap or expensive, architects most often lifted the steeply pitched roof over low side walls and set in a ribbon of windows, mitigating two frequent complaints about A-frames: their interior darkness and lack of usable space where the walls meet the floor.

Prefabricated A-frames were an economical choice for congregations with small budgets and a salable product for manufacturers looking for a design easy to manufacture, ship, and erect on site. Unified Church Structures Company of Mt. Clemens, Michigan, for instance, sold a type of "A-frame" with a lower-pitched roof.[4] Their kits used plywood, laminated timbers, and treated cedar or brick veneer exteriors. Le-wood prefabs by the Lehigh Cement Company provided another option—precast, pre-stressed concrete slab churches.[5] The mission chapels division of Creative Buildings, Inc., advertised a 150-seat, twenty-thousand-dollar A-frame that could be erected in just four days.[6] These were not buildings intended to last for the ages, but they provided cheap and quick "churchly" homes for small congregations.

Substantial, architect-designed A-frames appealed to suburban congregations with more money and greater expectations. These custom A-frames could be framed in wood or steel, but a better solution, laminated wood trusses, or "glulams," became widely available (Figure 4.1). At the turn of the twentieth century, the antecedents of the glulam industry began in Europe; by the 1930s, American manufacturers were turning out the product.[7] Wartime innovation developed waterproof adhesives that enabled even the exterior use of these timbers. One glulam manufacturer, Unit Structures, Inc., claimed that its trusses were "strong as steel

FIGURE 4.1. Construction photograph of Immanuel Lutheran Church, Des Plaines, Illinois, ca. 1956, showing erection of laminated trusses. Courtesy of Immanuel Lutheran Church, Des Plaines, Illinois.

and even more fire-resistant, these time-tried and time-proved arches have been used from coast to coast in churches of every denomination" and for "every style of church building."[8]

The artist and critic Albert Christ-Janer, writing in 1962, explained that "Although still not equal in plasticity to reinforced concrete, nor in strength to steel, wood is now capable of a far greater range of performance than ever in its past. One result is the development of an entirely new kind of wooden frame, based on the arch rather than the ancient post-and-lintel system."[9] Laminated trusses brought the overall cost of construction down considerably by eliminating complicated joinery; the joints, or bends in the frame, were molded right into the truss. The truss bore the weight of the roof down to the ground, eliminating the need for load-bearing side walls. Laminated trusses were not inexpensive, but they minimized the cost of labor and other materials.

In the records for Stade's Lutheran Church of the Resurrection in Yardley, Pennsylvania, is a sixteen-page brochure from Timber Structures, Inc., for the year 1955, which displays the wide variety of trusses available. The brochure shows several church interiors employing "cathedral arches," or "adaptations of the Tudor, Gothic, or Parabolic types with or without special decorative build-up." The roof slope of the standard Timber Structures glulam went up to forty-five degrees. Custom trusses were also available. Glulam manufacturers also sold tongue-and-groove solid wood sheathing, typically three and one half inches thick, for use as roof decking. This interlocking decking, partner to the glulam arches, resulted in an appealing wood ceiling and obviated the need for any other ceiling treatment. The beauty of the laminated wood trusses and the uninterrupted interior height they allowed appealed to both architects and building committees. The A-frame offers one especially notable instance of how the ease and economy, as well as the aesthetic appeal, of new building technology influenced postwar church builders.

Imagine the building committee of an older congregation long in need of a new worship space still clinging to prewar plans for a stone or brick church with Gothic details but discovering that such a building was no longer remotely within budget. Or, think of a start-up suburban congregation, strapped for funds but determined to build something substantial and meaningful. The architects working with such congregations had to find their way through unrealistic expectations and conflicting aims. As Stade argued, these congregations simply could not afford the size and style of the building they had imagined. He suggested drawing an equilateral triangle and designating the three angles as "cost, quantity, and quality." The architect would point out that the building committee could have "two of the three, but never *all three*." In other words, with their typically limited building budgets, congregations could have a very fine, small church or more space in a less expensive building. But the A-frame, Stade noted, was a bargain all around: "the so-called A-frame church with low masonry walls and high roof (laminated trusses and wood decking) will be less costly than churches of high masonry walls and low-pitched roofs."[10] For a building committee that wanted its "money's worth," Stade promoted the A-frame as a prudent choice.

Pasadena architect Culver Heaton's Christ the King Lutheran Church in Reseda, California (1954), offers an early example of the economic virtues of the A-frame for a new congregation. The congregation wanted "a building that tells a message, built on a budget."[11] Pastor David Seward was convinced that "there must be a way for a mission church to avoid confusion with a gymnasium . . . or a cracker box!" and to "inspire reverence" in passersby. Seward's congregation had the very small budget of twenty-five thousand dollars but a firm commitment to building a respectable church. Heaton designed a simple and flexible A-frame using a modular system of beams with a small flat-roofed administration wing. The sanctuary, with its natural redwood walls, seated 150 in a space "so simple that it could be built at an absolute minimum of cost and yet create a worshipful atmosphere thus eliminating the need for expensive theological ornamentation." The story of Christ the King, its congregation's desire for both low cost and "worshipful atmosphere," illustrates both the aesthetic appeal and the practical utility of the A-frame church.

## MORE THAN A CLICHÉ: THE DIVERSE ORIGINS AND COMPLEX DEVELOPMENT OF THE A-FRAME CHURCH

The postwar A-frame church emerged out of a matrix of national and international historical and vernacular influences, economic necessity, and contemporary design. Although its origins are diverse, in the American context a few iconic buildings by prominent architects are often cited as the "prototype": Frank Lloyd Wright's First Unitarian Society Meeting House in Madison, Wisconsin (1949–51), and especially Eero Saarinen's Kramer Chapel for Concordia Seminary in Fort Wayne, Indiana (1953–58). The influence of Wright's meetinghouse on the Midwestern buildings in this study is certain (see Figure 1.3). Regional architects, Stade in particular, admired the prow-shaped chancel roof and adapted it frequently. Architect Henry Kamphoefner argued admiringly that in Wright's design, "the whole auditorium becomes the spire, for the roof and walls slope up to a point, so that the entire mass ascends. This daring concept puts the steeple under the roof, and gives the whole structure a symbolic upward reaching."[12] The drama of the sweeping roof, Wright's celebrity, and the meetinghouse's earthy, Midwestern associations, its rough stone emerging out of a hillside, combined to ensure a positive reception. Although not technically an A-frame structure (and it might seem unfair to Wright's genius to call it that), in the popular mind this was an important example of this type of building.

Eero Saarinen's Kramer Chapel is the dramatic focal point of a seminary campus made up of small-scale academic and residential buildings with broad gables and lower-pitched rooflines, a plan Saarinen modeled on a vernacular northern

European village (Figure 4.2). In this design, Saarinen strove "to capture simultaneously the tranquility of the Lutheran Church and its stern morality, the exhilarating thrill of belief and the demanding devotion of conviction" under the "the same kind of white winter sky you see in northern Europe."[13] With its contrasting roofline and an austere interior reminiscent of his father's Christ Lutheran in Minneapolis, Saarinen's chapel significantly enhances the campus.

A recent Saarinen retrospective argues that this "A-frame church was subsequently copied by architects all around the world."[14] Some Saarinen scholars today consider Concordia one of the architect's "less successful" projects and argue that, beyond this campus, once the A-frame lost its original vernacular reference, it became even less compelling and more derivative.[15] These claims simultaneously attribute too much influence to the chapel and downplay the strength of the original idea. At the time of construction, both the architectural and the religious establishments lauded the design. If Kramer Chapel appears "less successful" today, that may have more to do with subsequent derision of the common A-frame rather than Kramer's inherent weakness.[16]

FIGURE 4.2. Eero Saarinen, Kramer Chapel, Concordia Seminary, Fort Wayne, Indiana, 1958. Copyright Concordia Theological Seminary. Photograph by Alexandre Georges. Courtesy of Concordia Theological Seminary.

It is not clear how early Saarinen began thinking of a church along these lines. Visions of A-frames might have been bouncing around in his head long before the 1950s; Jennifer Komar Olivarez claims that "Eero was thinking of the A-frame solution for a church long before the Concordia commission," based on an intriguing sketch she found in an undated letter from Saarinen to Florence Knoll, a letter she believes dates from the 1930s.[17] Yet there were a number of other A-frame churches in the United States by the time Kramer Chapel was finished, and both European and American examples had appeared in the architectural press. Regardless of the originality of Saarinen's idea, it is clear that Kramer was not *the* prototype, although it was a particularly important and influential example.

These signature buildings certainly impressed many architects and even inspired copies, but the A-frame's genesis is much more organic and complex. On the one hand, what could be more common and historically proven than a small, processional, rectangular church with a peaked roof? One might understand the A-frame as just the latest incarnation of the basic form of the gable-fronted, spired churches popular among virtually all American denominations by the early nineteenth century. Yet there are more specific historical and cultural connections. In his personal library, Charles Stade had a copy of an English volume, *Fifty Modern Churches*, published by the Incorporated Church Building Society of London. Several small mission churches (for new congregations) in the final pages of this work bear a strong connection to the smaller postwar American A-frames.[18] These were temporary, functional buildings in which practicality trumped other considerations. Several had a chancel at one end and a stage/classroom at the other, with a curtain or moving wall that could isolate the chancel from sanctuary-turned-social hall.[19] An early American A-frame, Harris Armstrong's award-winning limestone and redwood church for the Lutheran Church of the Atonement in Florissant, Missouri (1952), had just such a curtain hanging from the ceiling in its three hundred–seat, closet-lined sanctuary, allowing the congregation "to close off the chancel when the nave is used for meetings"(Figures 4.3–4.4).[20] The small kitchen was in a passage along one side of the sanctuary, facilitating that space's use as a social hall. A cluster of offices separated the sanctuary from the classroom wing addition. Initially, the sanctuary itself was also used for educational purposes.

The A-frame's connection to English ecclesiastical architecture, however, is more than a functional link between the needs of the English mission church and the new church on the American suburban frontier. There is a strong formal connection between postwar A-frames and a common prewar American type of English Gothic masonry structure with a pitched roof and simple rectangular chancel, an aesthetic and historical connection that added some gravitas to the new suburban church. This earlier church type prepared the way for the acceptance of the modern A-frame. Grace Lutheran Church in Western Springs, Illinois, by the Chicago architect Herbert A. Brand is a hybrid form that illustrates the often

FIGURE 4.3. Harris Armstrong, Lutheran Church of the Atonement, Florissant, Missouri, 1952. Harris Armstrong Collection, University Archives, Department of Special Collections, Washington University Libraries.

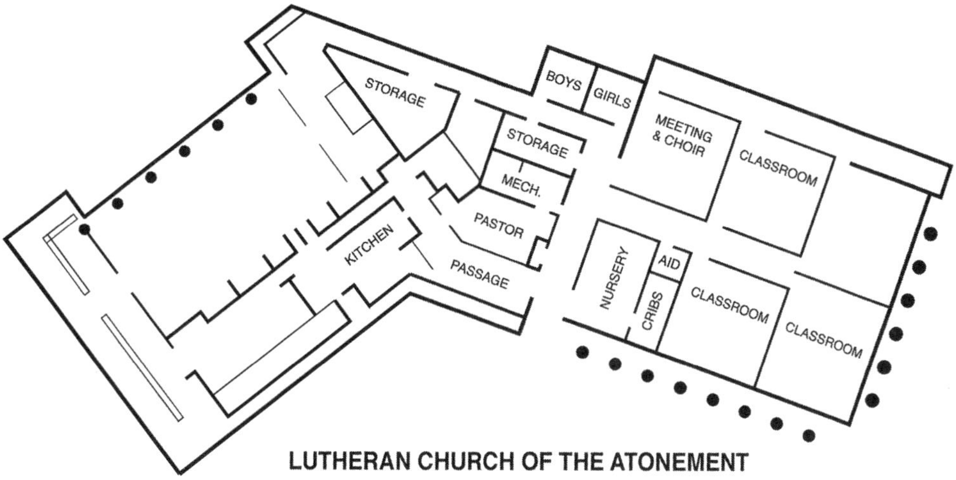


FIGURE 4.4. Lutheran Church of the Atonement, Florissant, Missouri, plan. *Your Church* (January–March 1956): 11. Redrawn by Jacob M. Just.

incremental evolution from Gothic to contemporary (Figure 4.5). The designer of this 1952 church consciously moved in the direction of the modern. He expressed his understanding of modern building: "We have followed the precepts of 'contemporary architecture,' i.e. form follows function, the materials used are apparent in the structural functions and the design is built around the uses to be made of the structure and the climatic conditions." Thus, an honest use of materials and attention to place and function registered that something was changing. The architect "omitted all useless ornament and all 'Gothic' features. No arches are needed, so the triangle, the symbol of the Trinity, is used throughout . . . Clean and simple lines . . . attract attention to this small church of different and contemporary design."[21] The church's exterior appearance, the "cardinal velour dossal" (ornamental chancel cloth), and "richly colored stained glass" window had more to say to the past than to the future. Yet, by "studiously" avoiding the Gothic, architect and congregation made an intentional decision to be "traditional, yet contemporary," language often used to describe early A-frame churches.

Four A-frame churches made the list of notable buildings compiled by the National Council of Churches of Christ in 1956 (Appendix A), and together they demonstrate the potential of the form in various permutations. Wright's meetinghouse was the first. The second, St. George's Episcopal Church (1954) in Durham, New Hampshire, shows the balance of past and present indicated in Brand's Grace Lutheran. For the Durham congregation, architect John A. Carter had proposed "a gothic church in the modern style." He used concrete block construction, covered

FIGURE 4.5. Herbert Brand, Grace Lutheran Church, Western Springs, Illinois, 1952. Photograph by the author.

by stone, and three-inch plank roof on laminated arches to create "the classic Episcopal nave and a greater sense of height" in a space "both grand and intimate."[22] The expression "modern gothic" shows up time and again in postwar descriptions of A-frames, particularly among the liturgical churches, an appropriate encapsulation of the blend of old and new these buildings embody.

A third A-frame on the NCC list, St. Stephen's Episcopal Church (Brooks and Coddington, 1953), shows the ability of the A-frame, despite its dominant roof and low walls, to convey openness to nature (Figure 4.6). On the campus of Ohio State University in Columbus, this church, with its broad expanses of plate glass along one side and at the rear of the sanctuary, was, according to the rector, intended to "express the vitality and strength of today's Christian church" while still preserving the past. The rector noted the congregation's courage in choosing a radical design that sent an "open message of warmth and welcome."[23] The natural wood (although the frame is steel), large windows, and intermediate planters dissolve the barrier between inside and outside.

The fourth and final A-frame on the NCC list, A. Quincy Jones's St. Matthew's Episcopal Church in Pacific Palisades, California (1953, destroyed by fire in 1978), had a squashed, sheltering, airy form. In the West, a more rugged setting and a relaxed attitude shaped a distinctively low and rustic variety of A-frame. A church

Side windows of *Thermopane* overlook a landscaped terrace which separates the church from the Parish House. Clear glass was used in preference to stained or colored glass. Earth pockets for planting occupy the space between plane of wall and the diagonally set windows.

This is St. Stephen's Episcopal Church, selected by the National Council of Churches' Commission on Architecture as one of the 18 outstanding new buildings constructed in the last 25 years. Like thousands of others, we visited the church to admire it, and to ask questions of those who had a part in creating it.

**Q.** Why and how did the church come into being?

**A. Dr. Thorp**—We needed to provide a better service to our community and especially to provide a new type of religious experience for the students and faculty of a growing university.

**Q.** What were the main considerations in planning this church?

University Center is split level. Lounge, study and library occupy upper level. A recreation room is below. Behind is a two-story Sunday school with kitchen and multi-purpose room on the first floor. Glass doors open out onto the terrace. Church offices and corridor connect Sunday school and church at rear of terrace.

LOF GLASS

FIGURE 4.6. Brooks and Coddington, St. Stephen's Episcopal Church, Columbus, Ohio, 1953. Sanctuary interior shown in Libby-Owens-Ford advertisement, n.d. Author's collection.

bulletin found in the records of Dart's Presbyterian church in La Porte, Indiana, shows a similar church amid new suburban construction in the mountain West, Gateway Presbyterian Church in Colorado Springs (Rico and Fairbanks, 1960) (Figure 4.7). Americans popularly identified the less traditional, contemporary A-frame with the Western states.[24] For instance, an Indianapolis newspaper called the local Park Heights Church of God's inexpensive A-frame (1957), "a contemporary structure of California design."[25]

While the A-frame was growing in popularity in America, 1950s Europeans tended to prefer other church types. English architect Edward Mills's 1956 book *The Modern Church* illustrated the contemporary European preference for the tall, rectangular nave with the low-pitched roof, the type favored by Sövik. But Mills did include several notable European A-frames that indicated the form's vernacular roots. Architect Maurice Novarina's Notre Dame de Toute Grâce du Plateau d'Assy, a Roman Catholic chapel in the French Alps (1937–38), is a heavy stone structure with a low-pitched, low-eaved A-frame in the manner of the local Savoie chalets. Another A-frame Mills esteemed, St. Anselm's Anglican Church in Vancouver, British Columbia (Semmons and Simpson, ca. 1954), employed local stone and stick timber in a simple design in which "the full power of the triangle form is exposed to the congregation inside, with no side walls to screen the base of the roof beams that spring from the earth to the infinite."[26] Commentators were adept at dignifying this simple form with such effusive language.

The vernacular resonances of the A-frame contributed to its appeal in the American context. Like the Savoie chalets that inspired Notre Dame de Toute Grâce, American contemporaries cited vernacular sources for A-frame churches. Warren Weber's precocious Cedar Hills Congregational Church in Portland, Oregon (1951–52) was a simple A-frame chapel that was a riff on the "thatch hut."[27] Paul Beidler's design for a timber and concrete block memorial A-frame chapel in Pennsylvania derived from "the early stone barns of Pennsylvania, an indigenous expression of American art."[28]

The A-frame's vernacular European and American roots were the subject of a 1954 *Architectural Forum* article titled "The Tent Form—A Village Gothic for Today." An image of a thirteenth-century church in Kaarina, Finland, accompanied the claim that "predecessors of the modern 'tent' form are the old village churches of northern Europe, with steep wooden roofs that shed the heavy snows."[29] "More and more rural and suburban congregations are turning to single, high-gabled roofs for their new churches," the author noted. In practical terms, the "bold simplicity of the form fits well with modern concepts of worship; its economy appeals to the many church groups with limited budgets." But the "deep traditions" that shored up its appeal were significant. "It is the old north country church, boiled down to a new structural clarity appropriate to the times, yet retaining the best of old essentials: the warm, neighborly personality, the humble aspiration and some

FIGURE 4.7. "Churches for New Times," showing Gateway Presbyterian Church, Colorado Springs, Colorado. Bulletin cover from 1961. Courtesy of Presbyterian Church of La Porte, Indiana.

of the medieval magic." The warmth, humility, and tradition inherent in the design appealed to the postwar building committee.

Another vernacular source was in the present, not the past—the fashionable A-frame home or vacation cabin. This popular building type included architect-designed houses as well as commercial buildings, but found its most common expression in a widely reproduced, inexpensive dwelling. As Chad Randl has demonstrated, by the later 1950s and into the 1970s, the inexpensive A-frame vacation cabin was a popular, middle-class, do-it-yourself entry into the rapidly expanding second-home market. By the 1960s, consumers could buy an A-frame kit house from one of several companies for less than a thousand dollars.[30] The A-frame connoted relaxed informality, and its snow-shedding roof made it an especially practical choice for a mountain retreat. With the rise of the A-frame cabin, a less formal and more rustic type of A-frame church grew in popularity, particularly in the West.

In addition to blending with tradition, nature, and the vernacular, the form could be an agile vehicle for modernism. With the rising popularity of folded concrete and formal experimentation, playful treatment of the A-frame increased. Some of the most striking modern churches of the postwar years, like the A-frames, had a simple, processional sanctuary with a dominant roof. Pietro Belluschi's Trinity Lutheran Church in Walnut Creek, California (1956), was one such modern suburban church roundly praised by the architectural community (Figure 4.8).[31] The pastor of this suburban congregation, Alwin L. Rubin, had served for a decade at Zion Lutheran in Portland, Oregon, where he worked with Belluschi on one of the architect's earlier modern churches (1948–50). Pastor Rubin came to Walnut Creek blazing with enthusiasm for modern church design, and his young congregation hired Belluschi to build this fieldstone and redwood structure, a truncated A-frame.

Belluschi and his partner on the project, Walter Netsch, took advantage of the truss structure to set the stone-clad concrete side walls inside the roof plane; at the top of the wall, a horizontal obscure wire glass panel connects to the glulams, allowing a soft natural light to reflect up off the wall.[32] Other light comes from the end wall sidelights surrounding the large redwood reredos—now stained glass, but originally a translucent light gray. This intriguing building not only brought "something new to church architecture in the Bay Area" but stood as "proof of the large savings inherent in brilliant structural solutions."[33]

With this wide range of expression and varied influences, it is no wonder Americans found multiple significant resonances in the A-frame. As noted, they bore a relationship to low, medieval parish churches that connected them to historical church architecture. Second, they were informal, natural, and human-scaled, like a chapel in the woods. Third, because of their simple, straightforward geometry, their ability to be pared down to an essence, and the correspondence

FIGURE 4.8. Pietro Belluschi and Walter Netsch, Trinity Lutheran Church, Walnut Creek, California, 1956, sanctuary. Photograph by the author.

between their form and function, they fit the modernist bill. Finally, contemporaries found the form itself appropriately symbolic—as praying hands, as a triangle representing the Trinity, as the tent for God's people on the move, an inverted ark, or even a cave for quiet renewal. Reverend A. R. Kretzmann wrote, "There is talk of 'A' frames—that's good! From the Words of Christ there comes the assurance that he is Alpha and Omega, the Beginning and the Ending—so the form becomes a symbol." Kretzmann and others noted that the church is "God's people in the wilderness of the world, pitching their tents along the road to the Promised land," and so, again, "the form becomes a symbol."[34] Grace United Presbyterian in Park Forest seized many of these metaphors to define its 1959 A-frame church: "It is like a ship—like an ark. It is a haven . . . reminiscent of the tents of Jewish nomads, open at both ends."[35] Some architects dismissed such overt architectural symbolism as cheap and trite, but Kretzmann disagreed. "We do well," he argued, "as we sit and talk with one another about building, to insist that what it says by its form is important."[36] The building and dedication records of many congregations demonstrate agreement with Kretzmann's enthusiasm for the A-frame as symbol.

A church building with metaphoric resonance was of great benefit to congregations wanting to send a clear message via their architecture. Church building experts addressed the need for visibility, asking, "How can the external form of a church 'speak' effectively to the multitude of those who have little understanding of religion?"[37] Besides the obvious presence of a cross or a steeple, a "strong upthrust into the sky" could be provided by the form of the building itself. Furthermore, the sense of history, nature, and ease of A-frame buildings made them a place of visual and cultural respite on an ever-changing and demanding postwar landscape. Minoru Yamasaki's First Methodist in Warren, Michigan (1957), is a small A-frame with an asphalt shingle roof brought down to meet glass walls about five feet above the floor, creating the sense of a suspended tent. Between the sanctuary's solid side walls and a surrounding landscape wall, a protected garden offered a sense of security. This church displayed "delight and serenity," "brightness," "clarity," and "calmness."[38] Yamasaki stated, "I feel that it is very necessary in this chaotic society that buildings should be serene. So often buildings which are restless and chaotic, as our society is, tend to transmute this quality into our life, but really this is one part of our environment that should be secure and stable and should give us a kind of attachment to the life we live on earth."[39] The A-frame church offered the security and stability desired by postwar congregations.

A-frame churches are identified by the triangular elevation and rectangular plan of their sanctuaries. The rest of the church plant was also standardized, most frequently consisting of low, one-story wing(s) that contained classrooms, offices, and social spaces. These wings were easily added or enlarged, appealing to congregations that required staged building. Such wings also contributed, however, to the nondescript character of many of the churches, aspects of the building virtually indistinguishable from elementary school wings or even a small-scale commercial strip. But the entire building, including the wings, could also be elegant and distinctive, as many of the following examples will show.

## SÖVIK'S EUROPEAN-INSPIRED A-FRAMES

Ed Sövik designed few A-frames, although his first church to be built was an A-frame chapel for Riverside Bible Camp near Story City, Iowa (1950). The camp community had enthusiasm but not much money, so construction was cheap and labor was provided by the client. Sövik chose wood frame and concrete block construction on a concrete slab and purchased stock four-pane barn windows (Figure 4.9). With its steeply sloped roof and metal cross on top (now missing) it looked the part of a rural chapel for a camp village. Another early Sövik A-frame was the small church with basement he designed for the Moravian Church in Northfield, Minnesota (ca. 1951–52), a tiny congregation of "basically three extended families." "What they wanted," Sövik recalled, "was something cheap" and he admitted, "I really didn't know a lot about church building."[40] When asked why he chose the A-frame, he replied that it was "such a simple thing, so cheap" and referenced Saarinen's Kramer Chapel (not yet built in 1950), a remark that suggests that because the origins of the A-frame were obscure to architects, they might have

FIGURE 4.9. Edward Sövik, Riverside Bible Chapel, Story City, Iowa, 1950. Photograph by the author.

tended to focus on memorable examples. Exterior features like the porch entrance and cupola give the Moravian church the feel of a rural chapel, but inside it is a bare-bones A-frame.

Also in the early 1950s, Sövik designed a small A-frame for a church in rural Chatfield, Minnesota (1953; just about half of the original A-frame sanctuary remains as a remodeled narthex area).[41] This church had long, tapering brackets under the low eaves and was clad in vertical boards with a dark stain. A more substantial Sövik A-frame, First Lutheran, Onalaska, Wisconsin (1954), has similar tapering brackets, an exterior clad with both stone and stucco, two small gables, and a delicate spire (Figure 4.10). These churches are clearly reminiscent of "the old village churches of northern Europe" invoked in the *Architectural Forum* article of 1954. Sövik had left the A-frame behind by the late 1950s, so his Calvary Lutheran Church in Park Rapids, Minnesota (1959), is a surprising exception (Figure 4.11).[42] A close design parallel is found in a 1954 German Catholic church by Marcel Felton, St. Engelbert Catholic in Westphalia, most tellingly similar in the elongated diamond shape of the wood casing around the steel trusses in the sanctuary interior (a motif seen on the chancel end of Calvary's exterior).[43] The Calvary church records indicate a lengthy process of design and compromise. The architect first presented the building committee with a rectangular building with a high ceiling,

FIGURE 4.10. Edward Sövik, First Lutheran Church, Onalaska, Wisconsin, 1954. Photograph by the author.

like Eliel Saarinen's Christ Church Lutheran. A plan for a cruciform building followed. Budget concerns likely caused the congregation to scale back original plans, ultimately choosing an A-frame.

It is interesting to note that the discourse of the gathered church (see chapter 5) was claimed by the architect and assumedly grasped by the Calvary congregation, despite the axial plan and more traditional layout of the sanctuary. The interior had a central altar raised three steps above the nave floor, surrounded by an altar rail and centered on a simple cross hanging on the chancel wall. The character of the interior is simple and humble, and indeed the modest chancel area is very close to the first row of pews. In a newspaper account of the new church, the architectural firm declared that the sanctuary took a form that united nave and chancel and brought the altar close to the people, "a family gathered about the table of the Lord." Furthermore, the "use of brick inside and out, and the generous use of glass remind the worshipper that his worship is a part of his life in the world, not an occasion for isolation and detachment."[44]

Although these examples show that Sövik would design an A-frame, and his congregations occasionally asked for them, his A-frame clients tended to be small congregations with tight budgets. On the whole, the 1950s axial churches he designed were more likely to be similar to Saarinen's Christ Lutheran Church in

FIGURE 4.11. Sövik and Mathre, Calvary Lutheran Church, Park Rapids, Minnesota, 1959. Photograph by the author.

Minneapolis, a regional (and regional Lutheran) preference. Numerous Minnesota A-frames exist, however, including an intriguing Catholic example worth noting, St. Francis Cabrini in Minneapolis (1947, Long & Thorshov, with Robert Cerny). In this early, laminated truss structure, the wing of the church was designed as the rectory, an exceptionally domestic version of the A-frame church type.

### DART'S PLAYFUL EXPERIMENTATIONS

When working with the congregation at St. Michael's Episcopal in Barrington, Illinois, Dart's first commission, he initially offered them sketches of three potential churches for their consideration. One was the modern, rectangular church the congregation selected. The second was a Georgian colonial, a type of church Dart never built for a congregation. The third was an A-frame with transept, spire at the crossing, built into a hillside.[45] These sketches demonstrate that Dart had the A-frame in his repertoire from the beginning, one typical choice among several for the postwar congregation. Dart's Church of the Holy Family (Episcopal) in Park Forest, Illinois, is a type of A-frame (see chapter 7), more like Stade's work than any of his other churches, although still distinctively Dart's design.

Dart's St. Augustine's Episcopal in Gary, Indiana (1959), is the most well known of his A-frame churches, a dramatic little church with a sweeping upturn to its

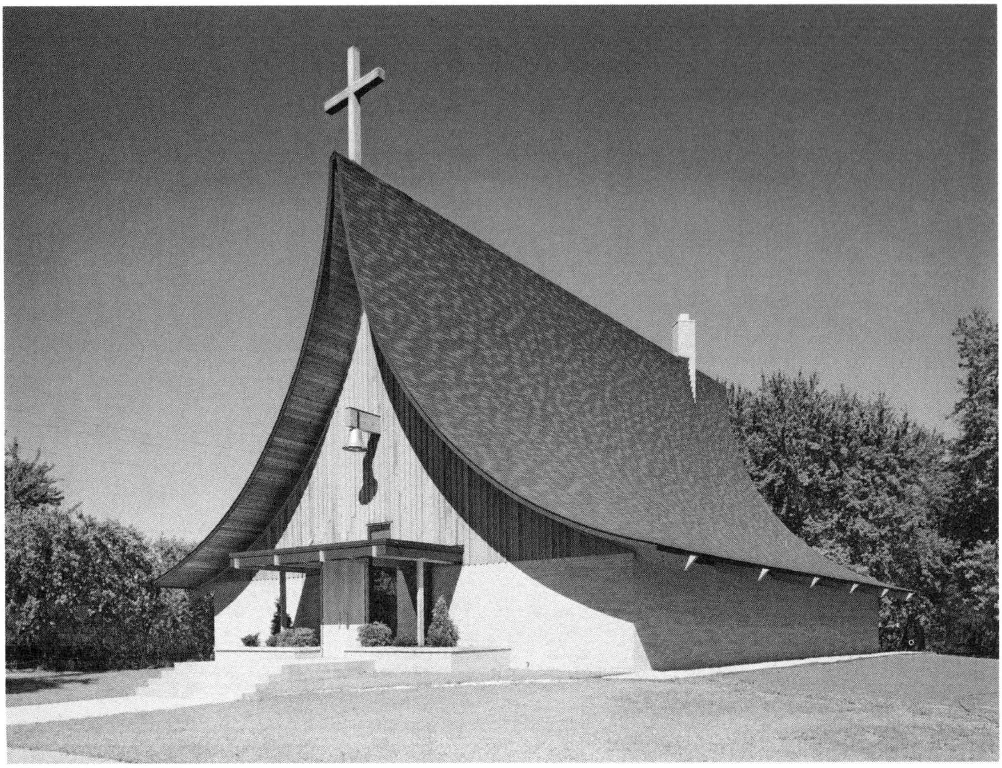

FIGURE 4.12. Edward Dart, St. Augustine's Episcopal Church, Gary, Indiana, 1959. Hubert Henry for Hedrich-Blessing, HB-22641-A, Chicago History Museum.

roofline and ample use of natural redwood surrounded by a solid, low stone wall, with a narrow band of windows under the eaves (Figures 4.12–4.14). The church as built is rectangular in plan with a full, open basement housing meeting space, kitchen, and restrooms. The first floor, besides the sanctuary with its small, glass-enclosed vestibule/narthex and rough wood rear organ gallery, has only an office, sacristy, and robing room behind the chancel. A very different Dart example, the Lutheran Church of the Atonement in Barrington, Illinois (1959), was a modified A-frame with an unusual hyperbolic paraboloid roof that bent down in the middle, giving it a whimsical flair (see Figure 2.4). Grace Lutheran in Bensenville, Illinois (1961), is the simplest of Dart's axial churches, yet even there his signature is plain. With its deep, bracketed eaves, open trusses, and narrow windows, this inexpensive building evokes the Gothic.

## A MOST POPULAR CHOICE: STADE'S DISTINGUISHED A-FRAME FOR THE AMERICAN SUBURB

Charles Stade's architectural legacy will be in large part defined by the suburban A-frame. Because he designed so many, over about fifteen years, these commissions

FIGURE 4.13. St. Augustine's Episcopal Church, Gary, Indiana, sanctuary. Hubert Henry for Hedrich-Blessing, HB-22641-H, Chicago History Museum.

allow us to see both the way Stade's interpretation of the form developed and the influence of location and congregational preference. In 1955, the Reverend Oswald T. McRee, executive secretary of missions for the English District of the Lutheran Church–Missouri Synod, wrote:

> Almost all of our churches are designed by Charles Stade . . . They are all of the same type of construction consisting of no basement (except for an occasional heating room). The floor is poured reinforced concrete as are the footings. The walls are of solid masonry. The roof consists of heavy roof timbers with laminated trusses or beams. Over the nave section we usually have a high pitched roof over 2" roof planking. Over the educational and office areas we have a flat roof.[46]

This, in a nutshell, is Stade's standard, suburban A-frame church. Although he adapted the form to site and congregation (often including a basement or lower story), his A-frames have a stylistic clarity and consistency, a technical excellence,

**ST. AUGUSTINE'S EPISCOPAL CHURCH** | Gary, Indiana

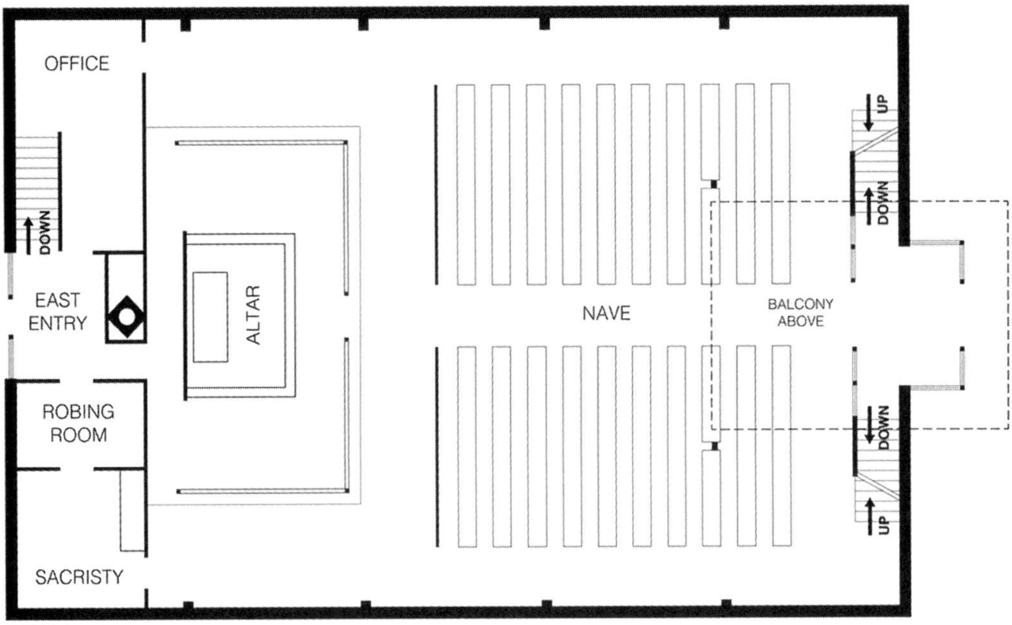


FIGURE 4.14. St. Augustine's Episcopal Church, Gary, Indiana, plan. *Your Church* (November–December 1960): 21. Redrawn by Jacob M. Just.

and often a quality of finish that distinguishes them. Stade and his associates probably designed well over one hundred A-frames. His daughter Ramsey noted that "it was a popular and current style . . . and Mr. Emrich (Stade's later partner) could finish them quickly."[47]

Two suburban Chicago examples of Stade's earliest A-frame churches, both begun in 1952 and dedicated in 1954, are St. Andrews Lutheran, Park Ridge (Figure 4.15), and St. Paul Lutheran, Oak Lawn (see Figure 2.7). Both display an asymmetrical chancel end, with the roof slope extending to the ground on one side only, where it also intersects a flat-roofed extension containing ancillary spaces. St. Paul was a new suburban parish. The building's distinguishing feature was a thirty-foot tower incorporated into the chancel's gable end. (The original church is now buried within a much expanded sanctuary.) St. Andrews was the new building of an established congregation, replacing its 1912 frame building on a central site in Park Ridge. The most unusual aspect of St. Andrews is the redwood-framed, rectangular side windows that extend from the ground to gables a significant height above the eaves.

In the mid-1950s, Stade began work on two very similar A-frame churches for congregations where he had family connections, Lutheran Church of the Resurrection (1956), a new congregation his brother pastored in Yardley, Pennsylvania, and

Immanuel Lutheran (1957), his family's parish in Des Plaines, Illinois. Resurrection epitomizes Stade's economical suburban A-frames (Figures 2.8, 4.16–17). With a total budget of around one hundred thousand dollars, this mission church made the most of an efficient, one-story plan with two main wings joined by a central narthex.[48] To the right of the narthex were the office and a hall leading to the restrooms, pastor's study, and kitchen. Straight ahead, one entered the meeting room/social hall/education/sanctuary overflow space. To the left, a side entrance leads to the rear of the nave. The original stairs to the choir/organ loft were in a small, enclosed space outside the nave. Stade's architectural notes indicate that, in a spirit of honesty, "all of the interior walls are brick, all ceilings exposed, laminated trusses, purlins and beams stained only to preserve their natural beauty."[49]

The Des Plaines congregation wanted to replace its 1876 brick Gothic church, intending "that the new church be of contemporary style."[50] Here Stade elaborated his already customary A-frame for a congregation with more money but less land. This was not a small project; the completed church cost more than three hundred thousand dollars, in part because of amenities and top-quality materials (Figures 4.18 and 4.19). This plan is also roughly L-shaped, but with a full basement under both wings, containing a fellowship hall/Sunday school area, kitchen, and nursery. The sanctuary was larger than the one in Yardley, seating five hundred, and the trusses angle down before reaching the side walls, allowing for aisles between truss

FIGURE 4.15. Charles Stade, St. Andrews Lutheran Church, Park Ridge, Illinois, 1954. Photograph by the author.

FIGURE 4.16. Charles Stade, Lutheran Church of the Resurrection, Yardley, Pennsylvania, 1956. Cortland V. D. Hubbard for Hedrich-Blessing, HB-19791-D, Chicago History Museum.

and wall. Stade was moving toward a preference for a freestanding tower, budget permitting, and designed a forty-foot Lannon stone tower topped by a thirteen-foot cross. A sculptural steel grill with Christian symbols is attached to the stone. At the chancel ends of both buildings the eave deepens toward the ridge and the windows are banded with louvers at regular intervals, evoking Wright's Madison meetinghouse. The nave side windows at Immanuel are L-shaped in cross section, as they are at the Valparaiso University Chapel, their rectangular panes randomly filled with colored glass. This is likely the first building in which Stade used the zigzag wall as a means of preventing direct light from distracting the forward-facing parishioners.

Inside, the Resurrection and Immanuel sanctuaries are alike in concept but have a differing degree of finish. At Resurrection, the chancel is paved in flagstone, while at Immanuel Stade used Italian travertine marble. In both, a reredos effect is provided by the recessed stone panel illuminated by side windows and electric lights. Stade designed simple and "honest" chancel furnishings, characterized by heavy brick or limestone bases firmly rooted in place. At Resurrection, even the

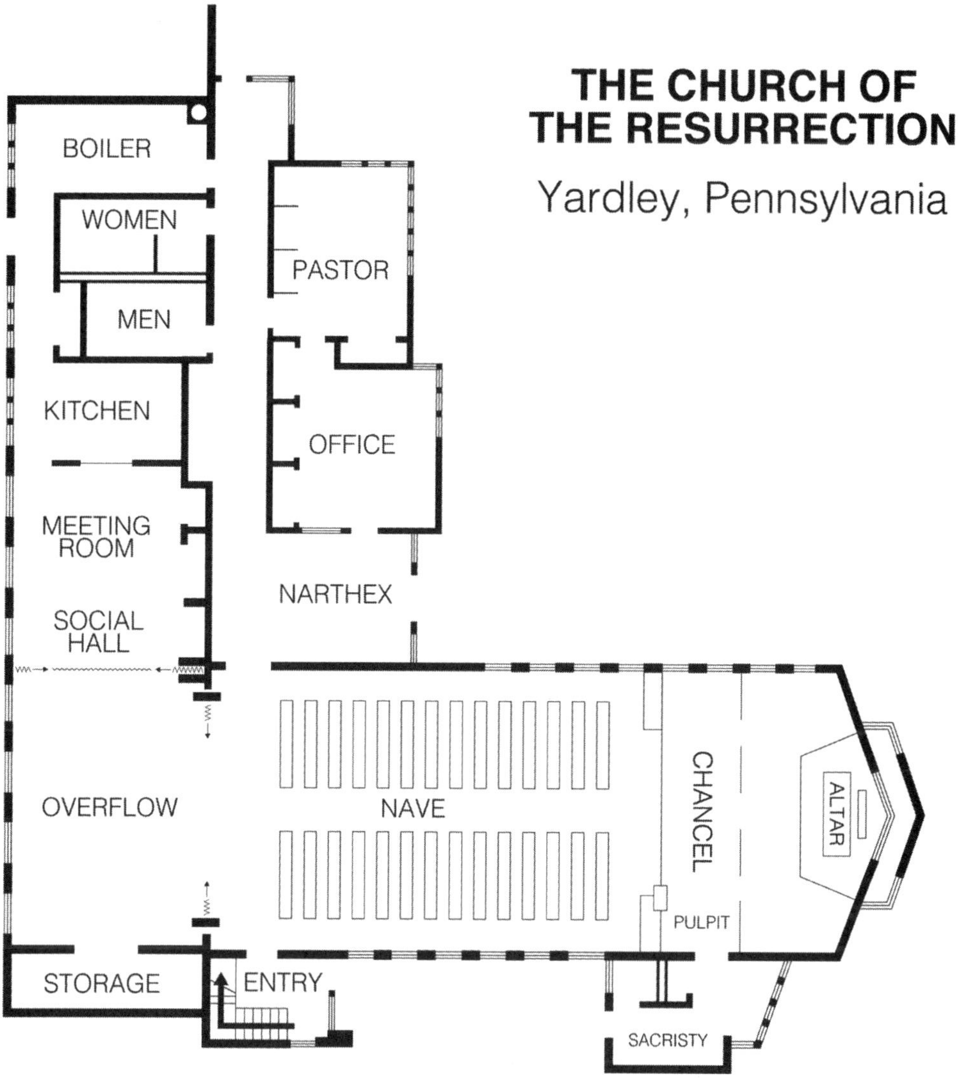


FIGURE 4.17. Lutheran Church of the Resurrection, Yardley, Pennsylvania, plan. *Your Church* (October–December 1959): 23. Redrawn by Jacob M. Just.

altar itself and the massive altar rail have a brick base. At Immanuel, the furnishings incorporate more metalwork and use higher-quality polished stone. Stade was familiar with the building resources in Chicago. In Pennsylvania, he scouted local brickyards, trying "to find a local stone that would look well on the chancel wall and a brick to work with the stone."[51]

While the Yardley church brought Stade's A-frame to the more traditional eastern United States, another Stade church, Lutheran Church of the Ascension, in northeast Atlanta, introduced the contemporary A-frame to a rather conservative

FIGURE 4.18. Charles Stade, Immanuel Lutheran Church, Des Plaines, Illinois, 1957. Hubert Henry for Hedrich-Blessing, HB-20907-A, Chicago History Museum.

FIGURE 4.19. Immanuel Lutheran Church, Des Plaines, Illinois, chancel. Photograph by Ken Kehe, *Des Plaines Suburban Times.* Courtesy of Immanuel Lutheran Church, Des Plaines, Illinois.

region of the South. On an eight-acre plot donated by the developer of a middle-class subdivision, the congregation dedicated its new church in June 1958 (Figure 4.20).[52] Ascension sits on a wooded hillside and, like Stade's similar Lutheran Church of the Good Shepherd in Palos Park, Illinois (1956, extensively remodeled), appears to be a one-story church but has a full lower story open to the side and rear.[53] The simple sanctuary, seating about 150, is marked by a north-facing, thirty-foot, clear glass chancel wall with scattered, random- pattern colored accents in a rectangular grid, a Stade trademark. The open basement social hall was divided by curtains into classroom spaces. *Your Church* magazine designated Ascension as "one of the earliest examples of contemporary church architecture in Atlanta—an area where Georgian, or Colonial, 'style' predominates."[54] Although the A-frame was quite common elsewhere by the late 1950s, "it was viewed with some reservations and some expressed misgivings, not only by members of the community, but also by some staunch parishioners." But soon the congregation grew to appreciate the church, and it drew a constant stream of visitors, including curious building committees and architects from elsewhere.

Another church Stade designed during these same years is Zion Lutheran in Kalamazoo, Michigan (1956) (Figure 4.21), one of his most dramatically sited and

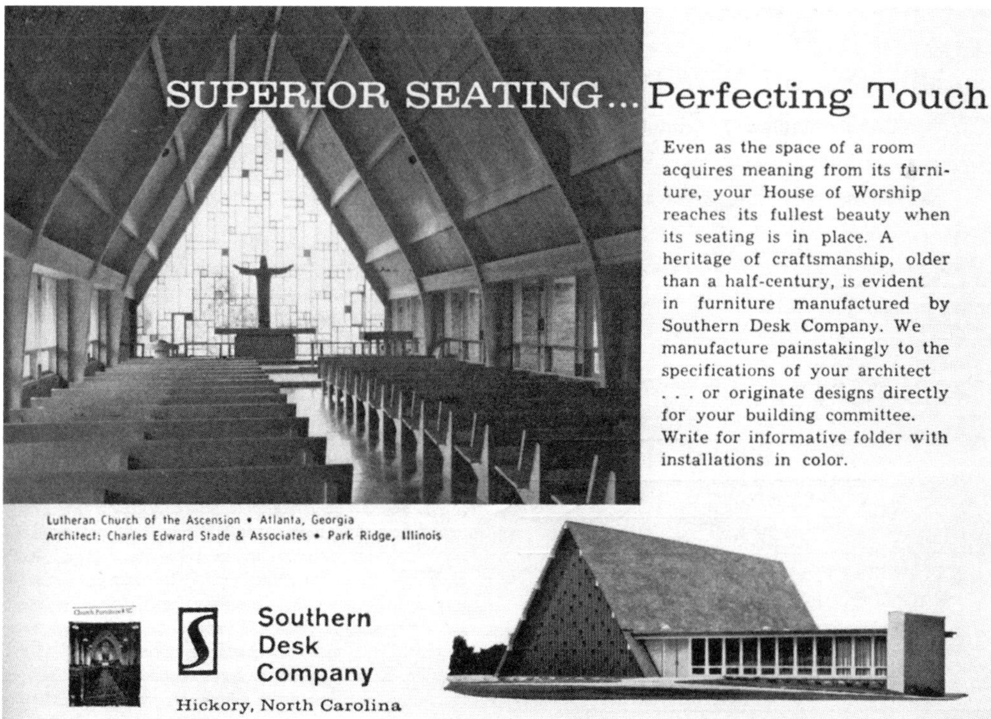


FIGURE 4.20. Charles Stade, Lutheran Church of the Ascension, Atlanta, Georgia, 1958. Advertisement in *Your Church* (January–March 1961): 22.

FIGURE 4.21. Charles Stade, Zion Evangelical Lutheran Church, Kalamazoo, Michigan, 1956, sanctuary. Photograph by the author.

configured A-frames. Here he placed three large gabled dormer windows on each side of the nave and filled the openings with clear glass in an angular muntin pattern; natural light fills the sanctuary. Members of the Zion congregation believe these windows were in part a response to the beautiful wooded hilltop site and reflect Stade's interest in "allowing the beauty of the trees and skies to come in to us as we worshipped."[55] In other cases, such as Stade's 1959 Pilgrim Lutheran in Hamilton County (Indianapolis), Indiana (1989), dormers were a later addition by a congregation desiring to bring more light into the sanctuary.[56]

Several Stade A-frames from the early 1960s show the range of expression he developed, often relaxing the traditional rigidity of the form by altering the roofline. Stade designed at least one parabolic church, for a Methodist congregation in suburban Chicago (Figure 4.22). In Tucson, Arizona, he worked with the local architectural firm of Jobusch and Friedman to create Fountain of Life Lutheran Church, dedicated in 1961 (Figure 4.23). This A-frame, with its lower sloping roof, looked much more like Gateway Presbyterian Church (Figure 4.7) than earlier Stade A-frames. The copper altar and open-backed pews with no ends contributed to the more casual atmosphere. Behind the altar, a large open window framed a view of the mountains. Stade designed a spare version of this flattened A-frame for the Villa Park Christian Church (Disciples of Christ) in 1960 (Figures 4.24

FIGURE 4.22. Charles Stade, Northbrook Methodist Church, Northbrook, Illinois, 1960. Photograph by the author.

FIGURE 4.23. Charles Stade, Fountain of Life Lutheran Church, Tucson, Arizona, 1961. Postcard in author's collection.

FIGURE 4.24. Charles Stade, Villa Park Christian Church, Villa Park, Illinois, 1959–60. Photograph by the author.

and 4.25). In the Chicago suburbs, this church seems especially open; one can see straight through the clear glass from chancel to narthex end. Because of the denomination, this church also included a large, concrete baptismal pool, visible just under the clear chancel window behind the altar.[57] Stade's St. Paul's Lutheran Church in Glen Burnie, Maryland (1963), shows both the western influence, with a somewhat lower pitch to the roof, and the heavier massing of 1960s churches (Figure 4.26). These later Stade churches illustrate the drift from the "Modern Gothic" to a more confidently contemporary A-frame.

As a rule, the churches Stade designed for Methodists or Presbyterians tend to be visually simpler than his Lutheran churches, although budget sometimes allowed these buildings to in fact display expensive materials and details, and it does not seem that denominational considerations had much effect on the design, with the exception of the choice of chancel fittings. Winnetka Presbyterian Church of Winnetka, Illinois (1961), is an excellent example of a larger Stade A-frame with top-quality finishes, its stone exterior adding elegance and weightiness (Figure 4.27). The original structure, with sanctuary (seating five hundred with overflow space), fellowship and education areas, and offices, cost nearly four hundred thousand dollars. Several later additions created a sprawling church plant, but even the original building, erected when the then-small congregation had significant financial limitations, shows material aspiration, with its walnut and oak furnishings, polished slate floors, and garden courtyard. Although this was a new congregation,

FIGURE 4.25. Villa Park Christian Church, Villa Park, Illinois, sanctuary. Baptismal pool is in front of clear-glass chancel window; choir seats are to right. Aqua, rust, gold, and gray-colored glass fills the sanctuary side windows. Photograph by the author.

FIGURE 4.26. Charles Stade, St. Paul's Lutheran Church, Glen Burnie, Maryland, 1963. Reprinted with permission of The Baltimore Sun Media Group. 

FIGURE 4.27. Charles Stade, Winnetka Presbyterian Church, Winnetka, Illinois, 1961. Photograph by the author.

not all the members were adventurous with their design choices. Church records indicate a "passionate split of opinion as to whether the design of the new building should be contemporary or traditional."[58] In the end, the congregation decided to build a contemporary church for both practical and theological reasons: "It cost 30 percent less, and was far cheaper to heat and maintain." Furthermore, the congregation noted that its Presbyterianism was correspondingly "sound and essentially simple."[59] This church was "simple" relative to the Gothic church the congregation might have built but was a rather expensive and elegant version of Stade's A-frame.

Stade's work demonstrates the wide popularity of the A-frame in the Chicago suburbs, and his examples stand next to those of many other architects. His former partner William Cooley, for instance, with whom he worked in the early 1950s, favored the A-frame in its many permutations. Cooley's churches can be gimmicky, but there are fine examples among many denominations, proving the A-frame's regional appeal. In Park Forest, Cooley designed Grace United Protestant and First Baptist (see chapter 7) as A-frames. It is striking how easily these churches—those by Stade, Cooley, and their peers—fit into the postwar suburban Chicago landscape, one reason they are often overlooked today. The muted colors of the minimally adorned, stone or brick chancel wall often match the materials of surrounding homes, and, although the peak of the sanctuary roof can achieve significant height, the solidity of the downward-sloping roof visually anchors the A-frame to its site at ground level. On new suburban lots, Chicago-area A-frames typically sit at the back of an expanse of green lawn that fronts the street, mimicking the front yard of many a postwar suburban house.

Although it is easy to dismiss the A-frame as unimaginative, as did critics in the 1960s, examples by these three architects show both considerable variety in cost and finish, as well as the ability of the form to bend according to the design preferences of an individual architect. Stade's many A-frames are graceful, solid, and functional, with his signature showing in the character of the chancel and its fittings, his use of stained glass, and a standard arrangement of nonworship space under a flat or nearly flat roof. Sövik generally stayed away from the A-frame as he developed his theology of architecture, although several of his earliest religious buildings demonstrate how an architect could play with the form while engaging its roots in regional European building traditions. Dart's occasional A-frame experiments tend to invoke historical precedent in creative ways. Perhaps most significantly for the architect–client relationship, the ongoing production of A-frames by all three architects demonstrates the powerful influence of suburban congregations' conservative desires and limited means on realized church designs.

## AN INTERNATIONAL PHENOMENON: THE RANGE OF THE A-FRAME

For reasons both practical and cultural, A-frames were a common choice in the Midwest and West and in other geographic regions marked by rapid development and a fresh aesthetic, such as Florida, Canada, South Africa, and Australia—places in the English-speaking world with similar development patterns. Although some A-frames were quite large, most were small in scale and informal. And while there are many urban examples, often squeezed onto small lots, they were especially popular in suburban or rural areas. Examples of the A-frame are everywhere, sometimes appearing in unlikely places, such as Stade's Lutheran Church of the Ascension in Atlanta, where they helped usher in modern church architecture to a more conservative region. Harold Spitznagel's widely published First Congregational Church in rural Spencer, Iowa (1954), or his First Presbyterian Church in his hometown of Sioux Falls, South Dakota (1957), for example, do not draw attention today but won architectural awards at the time they were built. Kahaluu Methodist Church on the Hawaiian island of Oahu (Wimberly and Cook), a $12,500 rural chapel, exemplifies the A-frame form's far-flung popularity and adaptability.[60] The building, of concrete block, heavy timbers, and dimension lumber, seated just seventy-five people. Given the Hawaiian climate, this church needed no side walls; sliding screen doors led to gardens enclosed behind a garden wall. Victor Lundy's Lutheran Church of St. Paul (1959) in Sarasota, Florida, also has sliding glass side panels that open to porches under the wide sweep of the reverse-curve arches, "an appropriate solution in a mild climate."[61] A basic typology for the A-frame to an extent follows regional lines: more open, flatter forms in the Southwest, an emphasis on timber details in the Northwest, "Colonial" brick A-frames with white trim in the Southeast (a common form that was both Colonial and contemporary), heavier structures mixing light-colored stone and brick in the Midwest, experimental modernism in the Northeast.

Besides region, another important element of the matrix, of course, is the critical variable of architect: Charles Stade's A-frames, no matter where they are or how regionally or denominationally inflected, still look like Stade's work, especially in their details. Because of the range of the Lutheran Church–Missouri Synod's English District, Stade's A-frames can be found north of the border as well, where they cross regional and denominational influences. Stade's churches in Canada, although they still look unmistakably like Stade churches, had to accommodate not just local taste and practice but Canadian building codes. For the Evangelical Lutheran Church of St. Matthew, for instance, in Scarborough, Ontario, Toronto architect Michael Bach adapted Stade's drawings according to local norms.[62]

The popularity of the postwar A-frame abroad sprang from needs similar to those of the American suburban church. South Africa offers a non-American case study that shows the versatile A-frame church in another postwar setting. South African religious bodies in this period, like their American counterparts, encouraged the establishment of small congregations in areas of new development, and this led to their version of a church building boom. The South African churches asked the same questions Americans were pondering: What does it mean to be contemporary? How can we meet the theological and social needs of our day? Many of the new South African churches were roughly A-frame in form, and here also the fit was based in both modern needs and historical memory. In South Africa, the form evoked "the eighteenth-century Cape with its whitewashed walls, steeply pitched thatch roof and florid gables."[63] Because of the smaller size (five to six hundred worshippers) and limited budgets of these new congregations, A-frames were a sensible choice. South African architect P. Roelf Botha, writing for the international community, noted the symbolism of the inclined roof and triangular form evoking the Trinity. He also praised the advantages of glulams and steel reinforced concrete as cost-saving and efficiency measures. An example is the Reformed Church in Alberton, by Verhoef, Smit, and Viljoen, illustrated on the cover of *Your Church* magazine in 1961 (Figure 4.28). In South Africa, as in the American Midwest, architects typically designed flat-roofed wings and added freestanding towers. A-frame churches in New Zealand and Australia followed a similar pattern of church expansion.

## FAMILIARITY BREEDS DISCONTENT: THE DECLINE OF THE POSTWAR A-FRAME'S APPEAL

The most famous of all postwar A-frames is the Air Force Academy Cadet Chapel, in Colorado Springs, Colorado, completed in 1963 (Figure 4.29). The controversy surrounding its design illustrates the form's strengths and weaknesses and its

FIGURE 4.28. *Your Church* cover (October–December 1961) showing Reformed Church in Alberton, South Africa, by Verhoef, Smit, and Viljoen.

FIGURE 4.29. Walter Netsch, United States Air Force Academy Chapel, Colorado Springs, Colorado, 1963. Courtesy of National Archives at Denver.

weakening hold on the imagination of church leaders and, by extension, congregations. On a campus starkly rectilinear and modern, architect Walter Netsch of Skimore, Owens, and Merrill proposed a striking chapel, a tubular steel frame made up of equally sized tetrahedrons rising to seventeen sharp spires. When Congress received the preliminary drawings in 1955, conservatives railed at the design, finding it weirdly modern, and they deployed the same suspicion they directed at most liberal-leaning projects of the day. Architectural critics, on the other hand, by this time frustrated by the conservatism of American church design, scoffed at its traditionalism. Joseph Hudnut of the Harvard School of Architecture, for instance, conceded that by building the chapel entirely out of aluminum, Netsch expressed modernity. But this notion of modernity was a superficial one, an "exploitation of a new technique," and Hudnut ultimately dismissed the design as "Gothic Revival in sheet metal."[64] What had been the strength of the A-frame—its blend of past and present—now seemed a liability to architects. Neither fish nor fowl, the Air Force Academy Chapel drew wildly divergent reactions. Critics from the church world, such as editor William Clark, questioned the design from a theological and liturgical point of view. Clark found it to be a building in which content was "squashed by form," meaning that by serving a romantic ideal, "dominating its environment in a manner similar to the cathedrals in villages in Europe," the designers neglected to think about how the building would actually work as a worship space.[65]

The disillusionment with the A-frame that showed during the Air Force chapel discussions had become widespread by 1960. In fact, progress in church design was often defined as movement away from this overused form. As architects experimented further, form itself, rather than materials or degree of ornament, marked the true modernist spirit. And that meant leaving behind the traditional sanctuary shape, finally blowing apart the constraints of the past. Stade, master of the A-frame, was bothered that he was doing so many of them. Congregations continued to ask for them because they gave a sense of soaring heavenward, but to a skilled designer they quickly became structurally boring.[66] When the Church Architecture Guild awarded Harold Spitznagel's A-frame First Presbyterian, Sioux Falls, South Dakota, notice at its 1960 Minneapolis conference, the building was already damned, as it were, with faint praise. "This is a teepee church," the jurors wrote, "and it seems to me to be the best of all of them. I think we are not going to do any more teepee churches in my office."[67] The writer was probably Sövik, who was chair of the awards committee. Even an award could not entirely reclaim a building dismissed as a "teepee church."

Although the basic A-frame form has never entirely fallen out of favor, by the early 1960s enthusiasm was waning. By the mid-1960s most mainstream American denominations came to the conclusion that a long rectangular sanctuary with altar at one end was no longer workable if the members of the congregation were to truly participate in worship. Both the exterior design of the building and the ritual it fostered inside lagged behind the newest thought in worship and architecture.

A-frame churches proved to be an easy target for criticism as they appeared to "multiply like a virus" across the continent. The form seemed too common, too facile, a hasty solution to a more profound spiritual problem. Others noted the growing gap between European modernism and the 1950s American church. A Catholic stirred by mid-1960s changes in liturgy noted, "Those who have seen the significant new churches of Europe of the past thirty years and the more recent American churches will understand the scope of the change in the interior and exterior visual image over the so-called traditional peak-roofed church of the more recent past."[68] European churches seemed to reflect more clearly the changes in the church and to speak more directly to the world. The A-frame church type was simply too inflexible, no longer "modern" at all to the eye that sought innovation and saw cliché in any recognizable form. The peaked roof church represented a late vestige of traditionalism in religious architecture.

In part, this critique reflected the cultural divide between European-leaning intellectuals and ordinary Americans who wanted practical and familiar "modern" solutions to design problems. But in the midst of the earnest soul-searching among church leaders in the 1960s, no alternative solutions were offered. Critics tended to cast their dissatisfaction, their yearning for something else, in emotional and vague terms. Edward Larabee Barnes, for example, waxed poetic: "I see buildings where space and light are everything, where one senses the very cubic volume as if *it* were real and tangible. I see quiet, all white interiors with dim back light and high sky windows. I see simple prime forms—the triangle, the cube, the pyramid and sphere—and I see continuous unbroken surfaces all in one material rather than a riot of textures and colors."[69] This kind of opaque language did not easily translate into a building program.

The popularity of the A-frame in the 1950s in fact speaks to a common dissatisfaction with modernism's severity and coldness. A 1952 *Architectural Forum* article had lauded a new A-frame, the Oneonta Congregational Church in South Pasadena, California (March, Smith, and Powell). The writer demonstrated how the church's seven glulams gave "a stately rhythm to the nave" and rendered it "warmer than many an antiseptic example of modern design. In spite of its halfway position between past and present, it is successful." This building has an informal, domestic character. On four suburban acres, it "fits its environment, becomes a neighborly rather than an awe-inspiring building."[70] Oneonta Congregational and others like it achieved what Robert Woods Kennedy called the "New Empiricism," an "effort to humanize the esthetic expression of functionalism," a type of modernism that, while lacking "extreme clarity," was a regional expression by lesser-known architects that conveyed "warmth, humanity, flexibility."[71] The A-frame church spread over the American landscape as the advance guard of modernism, cautiously and incrementally purifying the church's relationship with its past.

In the 1950s, the A-frame was evocative rather than trite. It succeeded because of its familiar associations, both vernacular and historical, its symbolic resonances, its "friendliness," and its economic efficiency. It became a tried-and-true model lesser architects might follow successfully, unlike the more adventurous postwar church types that were growing increasingly experimental and even bizarre in shape. The form became "boring" or "unimaginative" only after its popularity peaked and the meaning of the A-frame shifted to the pedestrian. Yet the A-frame never disappeared from the architecture scene, and it still appeals to designers and congregations. Japanese architect Shigeru Ban's "cardboard cathedral," erected to serve, temporarily, the religious community in Christchurch, New Zealand, which lost its cathedral in a devastating 2011 earthquake, is nothing but a very large, evocative, and serviceable A-frame church.

Never as pervasively "vacuous" as its critics decried, the style left many simple and functional church structures across the Midwestern landscape, along with a few outstanding examples with more appeal and endurance. However it is judged, the A-frame is inextricably linked with the immediate post–World War II American suburb, and conveys the character and values of that episode in the history of American religion.

CHAPTER 5

# The Suburban Sanctuary

## *A Home for the Worshipping Community*

The heart of the modern suburban church was worship. Worship space, called the sanctuary or simply "the church," was the primary distinguishing feature of the church building.[1] As the example of the A-frame demonstrates, churches were identified and classified by the shape and character of their sanctuaries, the most symbolic and distinctive aspect of the church complex. Together, architect and building committee aimed for dignified, beautiful, and functional worship spaces that suited the ritual of coming before God for prayer, preaching, the Eucharist (or communion), and singing. Here also they strove to address the spirit of the age, striking a tone that asked the congregation to look with fresh eyes at age-old practices. Church leaders emphasized that the sanctuary should instruct people as to why they were there, and more fundamentally, show them *who* they were.

Worship spaces had to work well physically in order to support the particular ritual of the denomination and congregational practice. Working well was a matter of having the right floor plan and liturgical fittings, successful acoustics, proper lighting and color, fitting accommodation for musical instruments and singers, and plentiful seats for the congregation arranged in a convenient and meaningful fashion. What makes a Christian sanctuary work well, however, is not a set of static features but a successful response to both historical and contemporary theological imperatives. In the postwar period, experts encouraged congregations to think in new ways about how the body of Christ should assemble and act in worship.

Working well was not simply a matter of putting the pews, altar, and pulpit in their proper place. Church leaders and their congregations also desired that their sanctuaries feel appropriate for the task of divine worship. This more ambiguous "feeling" of the sanctuary included what was harder to articulate than a floor plan: the proper ambiance for worship, a sense of temporal community under the canopy of the supernatural. Contemporary experts such as the theologian Paul Tillich spoke of this mysterious spiritual quality as the "numinous." Ordinary postwar Protestants might not have used or understood this term, yet they, too, as John Scotford noted, were on a "quest for the experience of the presence of God."[2] One of the tasks of the modernist architect was to make that presence manifest in meaningful ways. Even the most venturesome congregations generally wanted a mix of past and present in a place that had a stillness and serenity different from the workaday spaces of their world.

Postwar worshippers would have been familiar with two common prewar church types: the informal, auditorium church and the more formal, neomedieval sanctuary. In the 1960s, historian James White identified these traditions as "revivalism" and "romanticism," and noted that they represented broad cultural movements that affected all the denominations, leading to a loss of distinctive denominational expressions in architecture by the early twentieth century.[3] The auditorium church, well documented by Jeanne Halgren Kilde, was a nineteenth-century development that adapted lessons from the theater in fashioning informal worship spaces with broad, high stages and rows of seats fanning outward and upward from the pulpit, the institutionalization of the revivalist manner of worship. Today's megachurches descend from this type of church plan. The "romantic" sanctuary, on the other hand, supported more formal worship in an axially oriented space.[4] This kind of sanctuary, preferred by the majority of Protestant congregations by the 1920s, provided a long rectangular seating room (nave) with a central aisle facing a clearly demarcated, elevated chancel area containing a central altar, pulpit, often a font and separate lectern, and sometimes choir seating at the rear or sides.[5] Both types of prewar churches, auditorium and axial, had generally been rendered with historical references, formal and decorative details such as Gothic pointed windows, heavy Roman arches, or classical columns. Both separated the congregation from the performance of the service led by pastor and choir on a stage or in the raised chancel. These two types comprised the prewar legacy of Protestant worship space and the frame of reference for the postwar building committee.

Planning a new sanctuary differed significantly from any other phase of the building program, and a sizable portion of postwar church-building advice centered on this task. Arguments about the proper shape and character of the sanctuary were in large part theological. Church leaders considered the nature of the relationship between God and the worshipping community, the relationships among worshippers themselves, and the role of the church in the world, and they asked architects to translate those ideas into material form. New arrangements for seating were not simply for convenience, but were designed to prompt a reorientation of worship. Contemporary art was not about looking fashionable, but about communicating an important message in an idiom that resonated with postwar audiences in a way that would challenge them and deepen their Christian convictions.

The leaders of the modern church movement expected each aspect of the visual and material culture of worship to send a timely and relevant theological message.

Many of the concerns embodied in church design remained the same throughout the postwar period, chief among them this "quest for the experience of the presence of God." In one of the NCC's *Briefs for Church Builders,* Reverend Scott T. Ritenour, director of the department of Church Building and Architecture, took up the subject "Creating the Atmosphere of Worship." The most important characteristic, he claimed, was a sincere "reverence" that corresponded with "the degree of respect and adoration tendered to God by his people."[6] Throughout the 1950s and well into the 1960s, a considerable degree of formality persisted in much sanctuary design, particularly in the retention of an axial plan. This was generally not unprincipled conservatism on the part of building committees and congregations, but a belief that more formal spaces would preserve the "atmosphere of worship" and sense of God's presence. Members of all the major denominations preferred worship spaces that were distinctly different and special. When the congregation of St. Luke's Methodist, Indianapolis, for instance, told its new architect Edward Dart that they wanted "a sanctuary that would be a true sanctuary" they meant that they wanted something out of the ordinary, a space with the "atmosphere of worship."[7] This sanctuary would not have to copy the worship spaces of the past—in fact, they preferred that it would not—and St. Luke's did look remarkably modern to its community. But they wanted a modernism that retained formality and dignity.

Among architects and theologians in the postwar period, the form, arrangement, and even ornamentation of the sanctuary was never a settled question but a topic of constant inquiry and debate. The general trend was to think of the congregation as a family gathered to share the work of worship. Encouraged by church leaders and architects who continued the work of liturgical revival, congregations increasingly saw themselves as a unified body, not a collection of isolated and passive listeners to scripture, sermons, and music. To many church leaders and architects, forward-facing worshippers sitting in rows of pews, peering down a long nave toward pastor and choir, seemed less and less likely to achieve community goals or to square with new theological emphases. By 1959, Sövik unambiguously stated, "the central scheme is preferable to the axial scheme."[8] The tendency, as Sövik declared, was away from an axial plan toward a more centralized arrangement that supported the worship of the gathered community.[9] For most denominations, this meant that the congregation increasingly assembled around the altar, the central focus of the worship space.

As we shall see, however, the shift toward centralized plans happened gradually and unevenly. Axial-plan churches remained popular throughout the 1960s, and experimental sanctuary shapes could mask a rather traditional interior arrangement and practice. As Albert Christ-Janer and Mary Mix Foley noted in 1962, regarding the examples in their book *Modern Church Architecture*, "Many of the designs shown in this book, even those exhibiting the most daring and advanced structural systems, commonly enclose a standard, rectangular plan."[10] Even in these rectangular-plan churches, however, more subtle changes in the demarcation of the chancel area, a more unified ceiling treatment, or an angled seating plan could significantly diminish the sense of separation between chancel and nave.

Along with increasing spatial experimentation, throughout the postwar years the material character of the sanctuary moved deliberately toward more simple and humble furnishings and decor. On the one hand, this was the natural result of the adoption of a stripped-down, modernist aesthetic. But there was a theological reason for simplicity as well. A church building with "a glamor focusing attention upon itself" did not serve the work of the church.[11] Rather than imposing Houses of God, churches should witness to their living, working purpose as "shelter for a Christian family."[12] Designers allowed the natural colors and properties of materials (including contemporary building materials such as metal frame windows or laminated wood) to show. Neomedieval ornament, a common feature on the "romantic" prewar churches, largely disappeared. Olive green or gold textiles and aqua-colored glass spoke to a contemporary color palate that did not favor dark purples or reds. For many people, even buildings that today might appear superficially modern—for instance, Herbert Brand's "modern" neo-Gothic A-frame church in Western Springs, Illinois (see Figure 4.5)—appeared markedly contemporary.

Critics complained that congregations adopted only surface modernization of the sanctuary without truly embracing a design that would change the nature of worship. But even the experts disagreed as to the most suitable form of worship space. Minutes of the first meeting of the NCC's Commission on Architecture, May 27, 1954, record a spirited discussion about sanctuary design.[13] Marvin Halverson critiqued the "inappropriate use of the divided chancel" by Protestant congregations who didn't understand their own democratic traditions. Sövik agreed that architecture and arrangement of worship space should reflect doctrine, as well as "those aspects of modern Christianity not reflected in dogma" yet evident in "the spirit of the faith today"—which enlarged the possibilities considerably. Architect Richard Neutra, although not in attendance at the meeting, argued in a letter he sent to Halverson that "'forward-facing toward the holy' is properly part of all religious ritual; that direction is an organic need, a dictate of nature." Here and elsewhere commission members considered Christian precedent, most particularly the example of the early church. Walter Taylor "mentioned interest in the Early Christian pattern of worship where the faithful gather around the communion table," and Reverend Darby Betts concurred, stating that worship "should be a family gathering, not a performance." Reverend Betts liked the idea of people moving toward the altar from all sides, a pattern of movement that would make them aware of each other and their combined role in the liturgical expression of their faith. The multiplicity of opinions presented by these experts suggests how difficult it was to come up with any definitive solution. It is also evident in this and similar sources that the divided chancel plan (with chancel and nave clearly demarcated, often with a significant rise to the chancel) and an axial plan were not necessarily considered the same thing. Axial-plan churches, such as Rudolf Schwarz's rectangular sanctuary at Aachen, Germany (see Figures 1.1 and 1.2), preserved some of the formality of the divided chancel church but, by lowering the chancel and having a single, unified ceiling height, Schwarz mitigated the separation between people and clergy. Criticism of the divided chancel did not necessarily rule out an axial plan.

One way of thinking about worship space is as a spectrum from immanence/informality to transcendence/formality.[14] Immanence suggests a God who comes down to act in the midst of the ordinary; transcendence emphasizes the mystery of an awe-inspiring God who draws the worshipper toward glory. Although significant, it is important not to make too much of the differences between these theological and material polarities of worship space as far as they affected the worshipping congregation. The subjective experience of worshippers is dependent on far more than the architecture alone. Architects, moreover, might never have recognized a significant dichotomy between immanence and transcendence. Sövik believed that both were at play in his sanctuaries, where the gathered body of Christ celebrated the immanence of God and the simple beauty of the architecture shone with transcendence. He claimed that "the hardest but truest metaphor for transcendence is beauty" and maintained that even the most evidently "immanent" of his sanctuaries had this transcendent quality.[15] He held a democratic understanding of the sacred. For him, *all* art, *all* space was potentially religious—a beautiful barn could move him to a sense of wonder and awe.[16] The nature of the sanctuary was not simply a matter of the arrangement of the people around liturgical centers. Beauty conveyed by the use of materials and strategic application of ornament also contributed in important ways to the "atmosphere of worship," and for postwar church builders, beauty was definitely in the eye of the beholder.

At national meetings, conversations about worship space were frequent. In Minneapolis in 1960, participants at the National Conference on Church Architecture could attend a session titled "Building for Worship—with Purpose and Beauty." Speakers included Sövik and the liturgical consultant, Reverend A. R. Kretzmann. Their conversation reflected some of the chief concerns of contemporary church builders: participation, sense of community, and meaningful aesthetics. Kretzmann began by urging pastors in the audience to be creative and inventive in demanding worship spaces that encouraged participation. Sövik argued that there was much the church building could offer in support of worship, using lighting, seating, and acoustics to "awaken the awareness worshippers should have for each other as individuals" and enhance their participation.[17] Finally, an audience member raised the question of symbolism within the worship space, wondering how and in what sense symbols should be meaningful to worshippers. The response allowed that some symbols might not be immediately legible *as* symbols but argued that the observers "must learn to read the symbols, to grow in understanding."[18]

Concern for the symbolic aspects of worship space is evident in the work of Stade, Dart, and Sövik and in their interactions with congregations and the studio artists who were also very much a part of the international conversations on religion and the arts. Interest in the arts and contemporary culture developed vigorously on its own terms among the Catholics, and there were many fruitful points of contact with Protestants on matters of the arts.[19] Evangelicals were slower to engage contemporary arts, although the general secretary of the NCC, Edwin Espy, noted hopefully in 1966, when the evangelical publication *Christianity Today* devoted a substantial portion of a new issue to arts and culture, "Wouldn't it be something if we were to find that this area of concern were to constitute a meeting point with some of our brethren of that persuasion!"[20] Although ornamentation was streamlined and reduced in postwar churches, the visual arts remained integral to discussions of church design.

Art was an added expense for congregations that were already financially stretched by their building projects, but as much as possible architects such as Sövik, Stade, and Dart insisted on the importance of appropriate contemporary art and furnishings in their buildings, particularly in the sanctuaries, where they maintained more control of the design details. Although stock liturgical fittings were available from many manufacturers, experts argued that the furniture, especially the communion table, "should never be bought out of a catalog but should be designed and built specifically for the spot which it is to occupy. In a new church this is a job for the architect."[21] This was the common practice for Stade, Dart, and Sövik, who regularly designed altars, pulpits, and fonts or worked in collaboration with liturgical artists, using materials and ornament that corresponded with their buildings.

What the example of the A-frame type so clearly shows is that the application of a contemporary aesthetic and the adoption of a new form did not always move forward at the same pace. Well into the 1960s, as the popularity of the A-frame attests, the axial form of the sanctuary persisted, recast in modern materials with modern art as decoration. These churches had a characteristic elemental simplicity, old forms stripped down and given new clothes, worn lightly with limited and restrained ornament.

In the later 1960s and 1970s, much sanctuary design moved decisively away from traditional forms and toward what Richard Kieckhefer has called "modern communal" religious architecture.[22] Architects increasingly designed churches in the round, removed barriers such as the altar rail, and accelerated the trend toward informality. At the same time, however, church architecture often presented a face to the community outside that was more massive and angular, less readily approachable, less transparent. These later buildings have a weightiness not evident in many of the lighter and more open designs of the 1950s and early 1960s. It is tempting to interpret this new architecture as more closed to the outside world, the result of increased fears of social and political threat, a turning inward of the Christian community. This may well have been so in northern Europe, where this style originated. As editor William S. Clark observed, after a 1961 architects' tour of new European churches, "Height, together with massive clean walls, reflects the feeling of *Geborgenheit*, or the sense of security, which Europeans are trying to achieve in their church buildings."[23] Perhaps this was a match for a changing mood among suburban American church builders, too. Yet this new style of church, bare-walled buildings with massive bell towers, also coincided with an increased interest in urban outreach among suburban congregations and more socially conscious and culturally accommodating programming. Modern churches in the 1960s may have provided suburban worshippers with a refuge and respite from the outside world, but that does not necessarily mean that those congregations were turning their backs on that world.

The experience of the postwar suburban worshipper by and large took place in the pew (with the important exception, in some traditions, of an important pilgrimage to the altar for communion). For many worshippers, no material aspect of the sanctuary conveyed "church" as personally as their eighteen inches of space on a hard wooden bench. In 1956, Stade published an article, "The Business of Seating," in which he did not belittle the obsession with pews but acknowledged their importance. It was not a simple problem. "During recent years," he wrote, "many churches have begun to recognize the need for more comfortable seating," but they have been "reluctant to sacrifice any of the traditional dignity" of the solid wood pew. He advocated for pressed plywood pews that fit the contours of the human body.[24] Pew cushions were widely advertised in the religious press, but more often than not, for reasons of durability and tradition, solid wood pews were the choice of the congregation. In all the churches I visited, just a few had original pews with padded seats (including Stade's Villa Park Christian Church in Villa Park, Illinois). Stade's early churches typically have pews with closed ends, but throughout this period open-ended pews grew increasingly popular. In 1960, the pew committee of St. Peter Lutheran Church, Arlington Heights, Illinois, opted for full-backed, open-ended pews, noting that "many new, contemporary churches are using this style of seating."[25]

Enter a 1950s Midwestern sanctuary—one of Stade's A-frames, for instance—and certain physical features and atmospheric impressions tell you immediately where you are. Walls of brick and stone, large expanses of clear or colored glass, and an abundance of natural wood surfaces, reveal the true nature of their materials. Clean lines predominate, and there is little if any applied ornament. In most cases wooden pews are arranged in rows and often have a 1950s blond finish. Floor surfaces, such as asphalt tile or, for the well-heeled congregation, terrazzo or slate, document both material choices and taste and indicate acoustic qualities. A slightly raised platform, often at the end of a rectangular nave, but sometimes in a more central location, signifies the chancel where you find altar, pulpit, and possibly lectern and font or baptismal pool. Light filters in from side windows, and hidden sources near the altar bathe the ritual center in soft light. The mood is one of calm and unaffected simplicity, an "attitude of quiet" as requested by the building committee of First Baptist, Bloomington, Indiana.[26] Frequently, there is a rear choir balcony, accessible by a staircase in the narthex or the back of the sanctuary. And, as a practical necessity, many postwar sanctuaries had some accommodation for overflow seating.

Grasping the meaning of such modern worship spaces for the postwar congregation is difficult. To a degree, new churches looked like new houses, new schools, and new shopping centers. The advocates of contemporary church architecture went home after Sunday services to their contemporary suburban houses. And, whatever the unspoken material cues embedded in the architecture, how congregations were taught to understand these spaces might have been as significant as the architecture itself in informing their experience of it. Architects with theological sensitivity could shape the way congregations thought about the liturgy through their discussions of chancel design. Pastor Glennys Knutson in Austin, Minnesota, remembered that Sövik "spoke of it [the altar] as a communion table and not an altar," which, for Lutherans, was "kind of radical in the 1950s and 60s."[27] Through such lessons, Sövik instructed congregations to shed the trappings of centuries of Christian tradition and return to what he believed to be the pure and direct practices of the early church. At Stade's Holy Spirit Lutheran in Elk Grove Village, Illinois, members of the congregation were taught by pastor and congregation that their church's fresh and simple architecture "wasn't modern architecture" at all, but rather "the old tabernacle" expressed in contemporary materials.[28] Yet builders of contemporary sanctuaries, as dedication records show, certainly did not take contemporary architecture for granted. To them, modernism represented a vivid transformation of the nature and meaning of worship space. The adoption of contemporary design, however superficial, was a break from tradition and an effort to make religion relevant.

Suburban reminiscences of worshipping in these spaces, however, tend to center not on the communal significance of worship, the particularities of denominational practice, or even the effect of modernism, but on the atmosphere of peace and reassurance. Bob Stout, of First Baptist, Bloomington, had an active life, with four children born within six years and additional pressure from a busy workweek. He claimed he would come to church on Sunday mornings because it was the only calm hour of the week, a place where he could "get peace and quiet."[29] Lorraine

Hubley, longtime member of Salem United Church of Christ in Oak Lawn, Illinois, still loves the atmosphere of her church. "When I go inside," she says, it is "so quiet," and I "feel the Lord's arms come around me . . . I feel safe, peaceful."[30] Congregations respected the special qualities of sanctuary space, and "the atmosphere of worship" called for a reverent response.

The following examples of sanctuaries designed by Sövik, Dart, and Stade in the 1950s and 1960s illustrate the postwar progression of ideas about worship space as well as the persistence of certain practices and attitudes throughout this period. Although difficult to find in church records, evidence of the conversations between architect and congregation in the process of sanctuary design suggests that architects often tutored their clients in the meaning of worship space, and pushed them toward new and unfamiliar ideas. Enough stories of disagreement and division exist to say with certainty that this was a learning process with both theological and aesthetic dimensions. Those postwar congregations that were willing to engage contemporary design discovered new ways of thinking about their faith through the process of building worship spaces. As the experiences of these three architects and their clients indicate, this was a time of learning and change, curiosity and resistance. Ideas about sanctuary design, like the people of God, were "on the move."

## SÖVIK'S JOURNEY TOWARD THE "NONCHURCH"

Edward Sövik is best known for his church designs of the late 1960s on, when his idea of the "nonchurch" coalesced. Yet his early work is equally interesting, in part because his role as an advocate for modernism was more challenging at that time, and the relationship between his developing ideas and the expectations of his clients was so dynamic.

One of Sövik's first major commissions, when he was just thirty-two, was a new sanctuary for Trinity Lutheran Church in Moorhead, Minnesota, whose 1916 brick Gothic church had been destroyed by fire in 1950. This church is an excellent example of the leading edge of Saarinen-influenced parish church design in the early 1950s upper Midwest. The architect of Trinity's 1940s education wing, Thorvald Thorsen, handed the new design task to the young Sövik because he recognized, as Sövik recalled, "there is another way of doing things and it would be better to be modern."[31] Sövik was constrained by the congregation's wishes to build the new church on the foundations of the old, and the cautious building committee proceeded slowly and asked to see many potential plans, although overall it was sympathetic to modern design. The new church, dedicated in 1952, looks little like the old one in detail, although the footprint is basically the same, with a processional sanctuary sitting above a full basement (Figures 5.1 and 5.2). The rectangular shape, mostly unornamented exterior, relatively flat roof, and the tower show the influence of Saarinen's Christ Lutheran Church in Minneapolis, a church Sövik greatly admired and visited many times for inspiration. Inside, the sanctuary has a traditional axial orientation, with additional seating in a transept with balcony to the right of the chancel. The simple stone altar, subtly lit by windows at the clerestory level, is on a low rise, behind a wrought-iron altar rail. A lectern is placed in front to the left, the pulpit to the right.

Although critics later referred to this kind of design as "modern Gothic," to the congregation, it was anything but Gothic. Members' reactions to this forward-looking building were mixed. Jane Loeffler found the architecture exciting. "I was young and I was open to anything," she said.[32] She thought the sanctuary interior especially pleasing after her experiences in the former, relatively dark, Gothic church: "Oh light, it was light . . . there really was no color [the stained glass was added later] . . . everything was light and airy, of course, with the tall, tall ceiling." Loeffler recalled a congregational meeting regarding the building design: "Sövik was there showing slides and talked, explaining why different concepts were used . . . explaining what they wanted to do. The interior was definitely going to be different." Other members were less certain initially about the remarkable changes. One woman, for instance, remembered, "it didn't look like a church to me. [It was] very

FIGURE 5.1. Edward Sövik, Trinity Lutheran Church, Moorhead, Minnesota, 1952. Courtesy of Trinity Lutheran Church, Moorhead, Minnesota.

FIGURE 5.2. Trinity Lutheran Church, Moorhead, Minnesota, sanctuary. Courtesy of Trinity Lutheran Church, Moorhead, Minnesota.

modernistic" and lacked ". . . warmth isn't the word that I want . . . charm?" She remarked, "the lines were all so straight."[33] The difference between the old and new sanctuary, early in the 1950s, was quite striking to church members.

In Sövik's dedication notes for Trinity Church, Ellsworth, Iowa (1952–53), a design very similar to that of the Moorhead church, he made a comprehensive argument for the new architecture. On the one hand, good stewardship, he claimed, requires a building to be as efficient as possible, well-built and easy to maintain, and modern materials provided that efficiency. He also believed that it was the job of the architect to reflect the congregation's faith and ideals, and to strive for beauty. "To say that a church ought to be beautiful is a truism," he claimed, "but it really means that we believe in a God of order, and if the forms, colors and proportions of a building are pleasing it is a reflection of that faith in the order Creator." Sövik defended his use of the modern materials and forms: "We believe that the principle *[sic]* value of our faith is not that it is old but that it is alive . . . so we do not hesitate to build a church which proclaims by its appearance that it was built in the twentieth century, and not to a pattern of a preceding age."[34] He often wrote extensive explanatory notes for his buildings, teaching the congregation to see what *he* saw.

In the course of his early commissions, Sövik employed the language of symbolism as a way of convincing building committees to break from the old ways of building churches. For example, he asked the congregation of Zion Lutheran in the small town of Galesville, Wisconsin (where he built a church similar to the churches in Moorhead and Ellsworth), to recognize "outstanding features of the interior design" in their new sanctuary. These included "its natural lighting and loftiness, creating a spirit of uplift and reverent enthusiasm," and the "simple ruggedness and vigor of the design," which symbolized "the power of the Word to meet the fears and anxieties of this atomic age."[35] At the sanctuary's dedication, Sövik pointed to Lutheran themes such as "light, rather than dimness," "the priesthood of all believers," and a "sense of dignity," given expression in the high and open sanctuary with a chancel just barely raised above the nave. Strength, uplift, dignity, and light are symbols written into this architecture, ideas that appealed to these early postwar building committees.

Sövik was constantly in conversation with contemporary liturgical artists and encouraged his clients to include art in their building programs. His interest in Christian art is already evident in Trinity, Moorhead. The interior is rich in decorative, symbolic detail. Wrought-iron work designed by Sövik and fabricated by John Haider brings symbolism to the sanctuary doors and altar rail, which incorporated words and symbols of the liturgy. Arnold Flaten, who was Sövik's college mentor, designed and carved the dominant 8 × 35-foot oak reredos illustrating "I am the vine, you are the branches" (John 15:1–17). Flaten was the artist Sövik worked with most frequently, and his bold carving can be seen in many of Sövik's churches. Sövik designed the travertine marble altar and font (font not visible in photograph).

Jane Loeffler was fascinated by all the symbols and studied their meaning. She made out a study sheet and was frequently called on to give tours to members and visitors explaining the meaning of the decorative designs.[36] Trinity's church members found that the symbols, unfamiliar as they were, enriched their use of the space, although they did require education. These particular symbols were grounded in the extensive Christian visual tradition and were a way of connecting the modern church to the historical past. At Trinity, Ellsworth, Sövik collaborated with another artist, Cyrus Running, of Concordia College, Moorhead, who painted nine scenes from the life of Christ on the wall above the south aisle. Rather than a carved reredos, here Sövik used a more unusual (and less expensive) feature behind the altar, a floor-to-ceiling dossal curtain hung at an angle to the wall (green fabric originally, later a gold/orange color).

Most of Sövik's (and Stade's) clients were Lutheran, and required a strong liturgical center with altar and pulpit. Sövik's First Baptist, Bloomington, Indiana, illustrates how he applied his design ideas to a nonliturgical church (Figures 5.3 and 5.4). The sanctuary, with its low, oxbow roof profile, dominates the building complex, together with the tall bell tower at the corner of the courtyard framed by the sanctuary and wing. The high north wall of the sanctuary is pierced with narrow, clear glass windows floor to ceiling; the south wall (not visible in photograph), as is typical in this rectangular type of church, drops down to ceiling height and then opens into a broad side aisle lit with generous, clear-glass windows that reveal the courtyard. A delicate choir balcony extends from the back of the sanctuary in a narrow band along the north wall. The chancel area is spare, with its wood-paneled rear wall adorned by a simple cross and Bible verse. At the right rear is the immersion baptistery, hidden behind a low limestone wall and, later, a partial brass screen. Sövik designed a long communion table with matching low movable stools (the influence of Scandinavian modern design is apparent), and a low pulpit of a wood frame with textile panels. The sanctuary interior, with its rich wood tones (the trusses were originally painted an olive green) and simplicity, has a Japanese feel and, indeed, locals referred to First Baptist as "the pagoda church," also because of the yoke shape of the roof.[37] This was a remarkable southern Indiana church for 1956, one that met with both surprise and acclaim throughout the region. For all its plainness, critics did notice that it was a very *refined* sort of plain. "Though one of the congregation's aims was to produce a church of simplicity," wrote a reporter in a Louisville newspaper, "it turned out to be one of rather sumptuous plainness."[38] "Sumptuous plainness" is an excellent descriptor for much of Sövik's quietly elegant early work.

These Sövik churches, with their rectangular naves, slightly raised chancels, flat or nearly flat roofs with substantial, tall towers, share a common, 1950s way of

FIGURE 5.3. Edward Sövik, First Baptist Church, Bloomington, Indiana, 1957. Les Turnau for Michael Myers Studio. Courtesy of SMSQ Architects.

FIGURE 5.4. First Baptist Church, Bloomington, Indiana, interior. Courtesy of First United Church, Bloomington, Indiana.

thinking about sanctuary design. Sövik had not yet fully developed his theology of space that looked back to the earliest traditions of Christian architecture to break more cleanly with medieval tradition. Yet he was already thinking of these spaces as one "very clearly unified room" because, as he explained, the ceiling runs through in one plane, a canopy over the entire space underneath, bringing clergy and people together.[39] In the notes for Trinity, Moorhead, as well as celebrating its modern construction features such as its steel frame, Sövik recognized and lauded the continuity of the church's design: "Trinity has a great deal in common in its design with most of the other churches that have been built in the last thousand years. The relationships of the narthex, nave and chancel, transepts and choir loft, are all in the longest tradition, an arrangement which is most ideal for the Lutheran liturgy."[40] Sövik at the time understood the long nave as a "symbol of the Christian life in its passage through a sort of network of light and dark into the presence of God."[41] He believed that Trinity was informal and accessible, a warm and cheerful space, against the grain of some forms of modernism that "have about them an austerity which suggests the awful purity and justice of the God to whom they are dedicated."[42] In sum, in the 1950s, Sövik was reaching for a contemporary church architecture that conversed with tradition, a blending of old and new manifest in clean and direct forms and materials.

About fifty years after the dedication of Trinity, Moorhead, Sövik returned to visit the congregation.[43] His critique of his own church decades later shows how his thinking about worship space had changed. He found the division of church into nave and chancel inappropriate, and his former metaphor of pilgrimage was replaced by the idea of family gathering in a circle around the table. Rather than a separate lectern and pulpit, Sövik now argued, there should be just one place for the Word, and the cross should be placed among the people, not remote and above them. The communion rail, which he promoted in the early 1950s, now seemed to him an unnecessary barrier.

Such ideas were already altering his work by the later 1950s, although congregations might have been slow to embrace them. In Austin, Minnesota, he had designed, in 1954, a first-unit church and fellowship hall for an expansion congregation, Our Savior's Lutheran, and a Sunday school wing not long after. In 1959, with the debt already retired from the first two building units, the congregation began planning for a larger sanctuary to serve its two thousand members. After much deliberation about the shape of the new church, the building committee determined that it should be round. Sövik designed a sanctuary with a continuous ring of peaked gables radiating out from the center point of the roof. The building committee then took the drawings to the church members, who narrowly rejected the design, apparently because it was too unfamiliar. The discouraged building committee agreed to give Sövik one more chance. His subsequent Greek-cross design was unanimously accepted by committee and congregation, and the church was dedicated in 1962 (Figure 5.5).[44]

The eventual sanctuary and the congregation's interpretation of it say a great deal about how church design, and a congregation's understanding of worship space, was changing at this time. In a lengthy dedication brochure, the congregation made it plain that they desired "a unique combination of that which is old with that which is new," "the ageless Gospel" expressed in "the architectural language of our present day."[45] The shape of the sanctuary is a Greek cross with wide, shallow arms. The rear arm serves as the narthex, and the front arm the chancel area. Behind the altar is a row of arched brick openings, creating an ambulatory space, and giving the effect of open space beyond. In each of the side arms of the cross there is a narrow rank of pews slightly angled to better face the altar in this large, square space. In the core of the nave, a large central block of pews, divided by an aisle, is arranged axially. A rear choir balcony is accessible by stairs inside the sanctuary.

Although this might not appear to be a centralized plan, the congregation understood their sanctuary in this way. To their mind, principles expressed included "the church is a community of believers gathered for worship," and not "an audience attending a performance."[46] Because the width of the sanctuary exceeded the length, it seemed that no worshipper, no member of the "family of believers,"

FIGURE 5.5. Edward Sövik, Our Savior's Lutheran Church, Austin, Minnesota, 1962. Photograph by the author.

would be far from the altar. The light, freedom, sense of discipline, humility, and dignity of the sanctuary, the congregation believed, would remind them of God's presence both here and in the world, and of their mission to creation. By using the ambulatory, accessible through the arches, it was supposed that the people could, in fact, "gather around" the altar or cross if so inclined (no evidence suggests that the space was ordinarily used in this way). This example illustrates that simply moving from a rectangle to a square plan and increasing the sense of space behind the altar could be read as moving decisively toward the centralized space for the gathered congregation.

These same principles are evident at Westwood Lutheran Church in St. Louis Park, Minnesota, completed in 1963, one of the best known of Sövik's churches (Figures 5.6 and 5.7). Inside and out, the effect of the massive square brick box is lightened by contrasting concrete bands, a slight concave bend to each of the narthex end brick panels, and the verticality of the many windows. The sanctuary is a light, airy, and open space, with a terrazzo floor in gray tones, oak pews, and a cantilevered organ/choir gallery to the rear, accessed by two open staircases. The side

FIGURE 5.6. Edward Sövik, Westwood Lutheran Church, St. Louis Park, Minnesota, 1963. Les Turnau for Michael Myers Studio. Courtesy of SMSQ Architects.

FIGURE 5.7. Westwood Lutheran Church, St. Louis Park, Minnesota, sanctuary. Les Turnau for Michael Myers Studio. Courtesy of SMSQ Architects.

walls are pierced by a grille of tall, narrow windows of clear glass. Visible in this interior photograph is a front loft designed for antiphonal singing, sitting above a row of arched openings that create an arcade. The sanctuary is designed for singing. Westwood had a highly successful choir school, which operated for many years under the direction of Ronald Nelson, who arrived in 1955. Although, as Nelson reports, the "congregation on the whole was very forward looking," some compromises were made, hence the fixed chancel area, pews, and full basement, none of them features that Sövik wanted.[47] The original, table-like altar was also a compromise: Sövik wanted a table, the pastor a tomb, so the table was given panels that could be inserted during Lent to create a sealed box.[48] The arches leading to an ambulatory, the overall square shape of the sanctuary with its forward-facing pews, and the rear balcony are all features that Westwood shares with the Austin church.

A slightly later church, Olivet Lutheran in Fargo, North Dakota, dedicated in 1965, is similar to the churches in Austin and St. Louis Park, although there is no ambulatory behind the altar, which is raised several feet above the floor of the nave, a more conservative treatment of the chancel area. An interesting aspect of Olivet is Sövik's experimentation with the meaning of materials; its most unusual feature is the use of sewer pipe for the side wall windows (Figure 5.8). This was intended to convey a sense of light and joy, and does indeed bring in radiant sunshine through blue and orange glass. But it also is the reason locals refer to the church as the "Swiss cheese church." This newer congregation was growing rapidly in Fargo's south suburbs, and an enthusiastic pastor, Nelson Preus, together with the chair of the building committee, optometrist Clifford Wold, motivated the congregation to think boldly about modern church design and "really pushed and pushed and took people to Minneapolis to see churches."[49] Reverend Preus "thought he [Sövik] was one of the up and coming church architects" and the committee looked long and carefully at Sövik's Trinity Lutheran in Lisbon, North Dakota (1962), thirty miles southwest of Fargo.[50] Preus "kept emphasizing common ingredients: brick, mortar, common glass, and sewer pipe."[51] To some members of the building committee, "the idea of using sewer tiles in a church was a little revolting," and it was difficult to figure out how to seal the glass in the pipes, but the overall reception of the idea was positive.[52] This was about the same time Sövik

FIGURE 5.8. Edward Sövik, Olivet Lutheran Church, Fargo, North Dakota, 1965, sanctuary. David Hetland, *Tree of Life* sculpture on chancel wall, 2001. Photograph by the author.

experimented with folded concrete at Trinity Lutheran Church of Minnehaha Falls, Minneapolis, and found it to be more trouble than it was worth.

Just two years after Olivet, Sövik completed the Lutheran Church of the Good Shepherd, in Moorhead, Minnesota (1967; first-unit church 1954) (Figure 5.9). His eighty-thousand-dollar first unit for the congregation (on left in photograph) had been a simple open hall with a slight peak to the roof, divisible for Sunday school rooms. The 1967 church, a square auditorium with slightly raised platform, is like many of his 1960s churches, with bands of tall, narrow, clear windows, a hard, uniform floor surface (concrete), and a rear gallery. The slanting roofline, along with the asymmetrical massing and substantial bell tower with a shed roof, reflect later 1960s trends and the influence of European church design. Openness and asymmetry are evident in the sanctuary interior. At the same time, the space is more rectangular, and two ranks of forward-facing pews, seating five hundred, are divided by a central aisle in an axial manner. Furthermore, the altar is raised several steps in front of a brick wall, as at Olivet. Sövik asked the congregation to grasp the "sturdiness and strength" of the architecture and the celebration of creation found in the use of ordinary materials (brick, concrete, wood, glass, and iron). The asymmetry of the room he intended to lead to visual tension, indicating that the sanctuary was "a place for action."[53] An axial plan, and even a raised chancel, did not mean that architect and congregation were not responding creatively to current theological and design trends.

FIGURE 5.9. Edward Sövik, Lutheran Church of the Good Shepherd, Moorhead, Minnesota, 1967. Les Turnau for Michael Myers Studio. Courtesy of SMSQ Architects.

Sövik made this point very clear in an article he wrote for the congregation of Our Savior's, Austin, in 1959. He noted that many churches built around central altars had aroused comment and interest, yet maintained that "this concept of the community does not necessarily demand that an altar be in the center, or that the space be precisely round. The essential is that the space support, by its shape, the idea of a community gathered, not a moving procession."[54] This was achieved by a pastor who faced the congregation when celebrating communion, in a unified space. Whether that altar was at the front of a rectangle or the middle of a circle mattered less than the absence or presence of symbolic or physical barriers between the people and the clergy.

In 1973, Sövik's influential book *Architecture for Worship* articulated the mature formulation of his idea of the "nonchurch," a flexible, multipurpose worship space he called a "centrum," rendered in a quiet beauty that he believed was the best witness to Christian faith. This is initially expressed in mid-1960s buildings such as Westwood and Good Shepherd, although not fully developed. Once he arrived at his idea of the nonchurch, he was convinced of its universal fitness for Christian worship and maintained that principle in his future work. His churches evolved stylistically in keeping with architectural trends, but without a fundamental conceptual change. In the 1950s and early 1960s, however, these ideas were in process. Watching as this highly influential architect experimented and found his way to what he believed to be a correct expression of Christianity in contemporary form gives insight into the dynamics of this period in sanctuary design. Although he worked with many progressive congregations, Sövik's design impulses were all the while tempered by building committees (or factions within them, or even a persistent pastor) that insisted on attributes such as fixed pews and basements that ran counter to his vision.

## STADE'S SANCTUARIES: SPEAKING THE LANGUAGE OF MODERN FAITH WITH DIGNITY AND REMEMBRANCE

Charles Stade's go-to church design of the 1950s was the small to medium-sized A-frame, considered in detail in chapter 4. Like Sövik's Saarinenesque sanctuaries, these A-frames were a blend of traditional and modern acceptable to 1950s congregations and their architects. Among Stade's early churches, however, there are significant buildings of different configurations, and it probably was his clients who kept insisting on the popular, simple, and familiar A-frame. Stade had a good sense of what a congregation needed in a church building. He referred to the "personality of a congregation" as one of the determining factors of church design, and he worked closely with congregations to understand what made them distinctive. He felt the architect should consider regional practice when choosing materials and form without making them "overly determinant." Liturgical requirements and denominational memory were equally important factors.[55]

The popularity of Stade's A-frame churches among suburban Chicago building committees limited the variety of his output through the 1950s, but he did find ways to individualize the A-frame form. St. Andrews Lutheran in Park Ridge (see Figure 4.15) won a citation from the Chicago chapter of the AIA in 1956, and, according to Stade, was "responsible for seventy additional commissions for churches."[56] In many ways, St. Andrew's is simply a larger version of his smaller A-frames, yet the four rectangular gables on each side of the sanctuary are a unique feature.

As the traditional axial plan increasingly drew criticism, architects managed to maintain the advantages of the A-frame by adding transepts, creating a cross or T-shaped sanctuary with the altar at the crossing. Stade's St. Paul Lutheran Church, Mount Prospect, Illinois (dedicated 1961), was one such example (Figures 5.10 and 5.11). This half-million-dollar project, while contemporary, evokes the prewar Gothic church, in part because the building is clad in Lannon stone (a strong and dense limestone found in southeastern Wisconsin), a building material often used by wealthier congregations to distinguish their modern buildings. After

FIGURE 5.10. Charles Stade, St. Paul Lutheran Church, Mount Prospect, Illinois, 1961, interior. Hubert Henry for Hedrich-Blessing, HB-24719-E, Chicago History Museum.

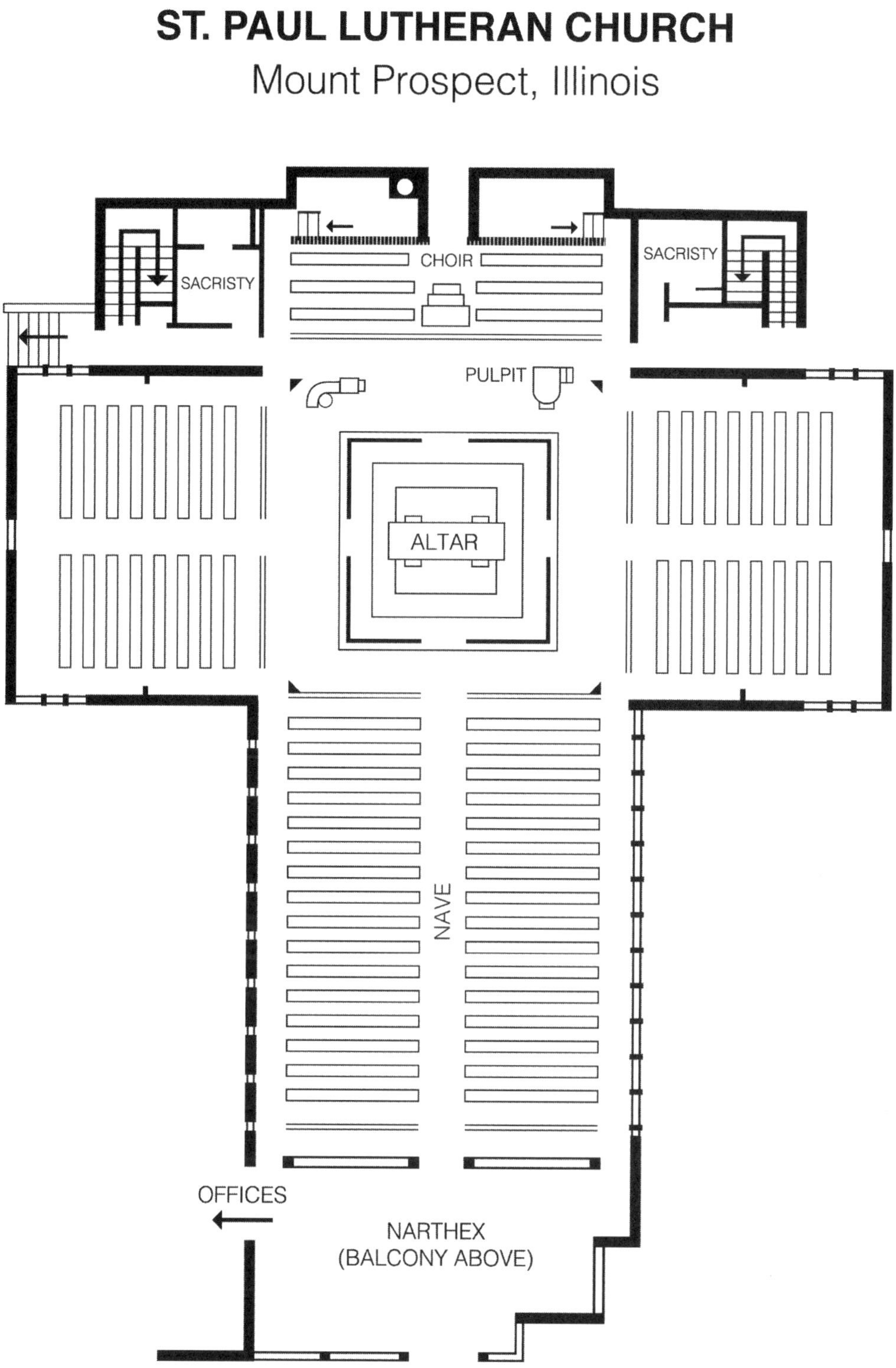


FIGURE 5.11. St. Paul Lutheran Church, Mount Prospect, Illinois, plan from 1953 fund-raising brochure in church archives. Redrawn by Jacob M. Just.

viewing some of Stade's churches, the building committee selected him, albeit with some reservation. "Most of the churches designed by Mr. Stade," they noted, "have been 'modern' churches and the Building Committee was a little concerned about this."[57] The committee feared that many in the congregation would prefer a traditional church, but Stade assured them that "he would design a church that St. Paul's congregation would be proud of."

Stade's answer was, not surprisingly, a blend of past and present: an aesthetically modern church, structurally composed of two crossed A-frames, with the chancel at the center. Four divided rows of pews surround a low, square platform, at the center of which sits the altar. Formality is preserved by an altar rail that frames this platform, and also by the overall rectilinear arrangement of pews, with the choir occupying the pews behind the altar. The interior of this sanctuary, with its nave and transepts and angular crossing, does not appear terribly modern, although the members of the congregation did face each other, and came closer to the altar than a fully axial plan would have allowed.

The tightrope of opinion Stade and his client walked is evident in a 1963 article about the design:

> At first sight, one may receive the impression that this building was romantically conceived, that it is "a church that looks like a church" in the nineteenth-century sense. Its cruciform floor plan and its familiar roof pitch seem to lend strength to this impression and to verify it. However, when the building is studied and the theological reasonings related to it are understood, it is recognized that the plan and elevation are a natural outgrowth of function and are not imposed by previously conceived ideas.[58]

The author (most likely Stade) explained how the design reflected current thought about the "faithful community of believers" gathered around the altar on four sides. All features of the sanctuary emphasized the centrality of the altar in the liturgy as well as the "strong placement of the pulpit." Reverend E. A. Zeile declared, "the theological idea that portrays the church as people gathered about the Word and Sacraments is honestly and openly lived here."[59] This building was intended to be dignified and "quiet"; St. Paul, the pastor claimed, "reveals itself slowly." This example shows how, in 1961, architect and client combined an interest in modernism, the need for a sanctuary to support the "gathered" community, a hope for tradition and dignity, and a common church form into a worship space that matched the congregation's needs. Other Stade churches from the early to mid-1960s place a multigabled roof over a sanctuary that is even more circular in shape, responding to this desire for a worship space that configured the "gathered congregation." St. Paul Lutheran in Peoria, Illinois (1966), and St. Peter Lutheran in Arlington Heights, Illinois (1961) (see Figure 3.2), display this tendency.

By the early 1960s, Stade was designing numerous non-A-frame churches. Salem United Church of Christ in Oak Lawn, Illinois (1961–62), shows both Stade's break from the A-frame and the influence of the Valparaiso University Chapel on his later designs and commissions (Figures 5.12 and 5.13). The one-hundred-year-old Englewood congregation was struggling to remain in a neighborhood with an increasingly transient population. In 1956, a new pastor encouraged the church to relocate to the southwestern suburbs, a region to which many of the younger church members were moving. Although the sides of the rectangular nave are straight, a series of gables at the roof line gives the impression of a sawtooth wall. Typical Stade decorative features include aqua and tan rectangular glass windows all over the building (including panels in the interior hallway doors) and brick planters. The most striking feature of the Salem sanctuary is the stained glass. The pioneering Willet studio of Philadelphia designed a full-length chancel window of strongly colored thick chunks of "faceted" glass set in epoxy, which dominates the sanctuary. One long-standing member of the church says she hopes to "look down from heaven" and see that stunning window.[60] Ten diamond-shaped, leaded stained-glass windows, also by Willet, fill the gables at the clerestory level, and a final window graces the rear wall. Stade's collaborator, artist Ernst Schwidder, designed the bronze and walnut chancel furnishings. Schwidder's wood carvings are found in many Stade churches, as wall panels or on liturgical furniture.[61]

FIGURE 5.12. Charles Stade, Salem United Church of Christ, Oak Lawn, Illinois, 1962. Photograph by the author.

FIGURE 5.13. Salem United Church of Christ, Oak Lawn, Illinois, sanctuary. Photograph by the author.

A church in Burlington, Iowa, and a synagogue in Joliet, Illinois, demonstrate Stade's interest in using the circle as a motif. He designed Messiah Lutheran in Burlington (1961) around a central point, with rays from this center lining up with major walls of sanctuary and wings (Figures 5.14, 8.6–8.8). At this center he placed a tall cross, the shadow of which falls on different parts of the building throughout the course of a day. In 1967, after many meetings with the Joliet Jewish Congregation in which he "relentlessly sought from them their meaning of God, of life, and of their faith," he returned to this idea of a central point (Figure 5.15).[62] Here the center is a courtyard sculpture of a burning bush. The angular front of the sanctuary represents the two stone tablets of the Ten Commandments, and the sides are arranged in six panels each, representing the twelve tribes. Clear windows between the side walls and the roof evoke the unattached roof of the traditional sukkah, designed to allow sight of the heavens.[63]

Stade's sanctuary for Good Shepherd Methodist Church (1963) in his hometown of Park Ridge was a full circle, marked on the exterior by the cone-shaped roof over the space (Figures 5.16 and 5.17). When working with this congregation, an emphasis on community worship and the Methodist tradition led Stade to eliminate any barriers between people and communion table, use chairs rather than pews, and avoid most traditional, ecclesiastical decorative features. Stade did

FIGURE 5.14. Charles Stade, concept for Messiah Lutheran Church, Burlington, Iowa, 1961. Courtesy of Messiah Lutheran Church, Burlington, Iowa.

FIGURE 5.15. Charles Stade, Joliet Jewish Congregation, Joliet, Illinois, 1968. Photograph by the author.

not, however, move the table to the center of the congregation, but it remained at the front of the sanctuary on a low platform (see Figure 8.5), with the lectern behind.[64] This was the most futuristic of Stade's sanctuaries, with unusual large triangle shapes dominating the interior, perhaps showing the influence of Frank Lloyd Wright's Beth Sholom synagogue (1959). Good Shepherd won Stade an award from the Chicago chapter of the AIA, an honor award from the National Conference on Church Architecture, and appeared on the cover of *Your Church*. It was a compelling building that illustrated Stade's increasing interest in revolutionary forms and departure from his common A-frame.

Other 1960s Stade churches reflect experimentation with form and contemporary decorative features. He designed a few parish churches with a rectangular box chancel, including Our Savior Lutheran in Joliet (1961) and Lake View Lutheran in Chicago (1961). Another award-winning Stade church, St. John's Lutheran in Lincolnwood, Illinois (1962), makes use of a clerestory to construct a tall, nearly flat-roofed sanctuary of soaring height (see Figure 8.1). This four hundred thousand–dollar project included an extensive sculptural program by Ernst Schwidder; the congregation made a commitment to the arts and for many years hosted art exhibitions.

FIGURE 5.16. Stade, Dolan, and Anderson, Architects, Good Shepherd Methodist Church, Park Ridge, Illinois, 1963, on the cover of *Your Church* (May–June 1965).

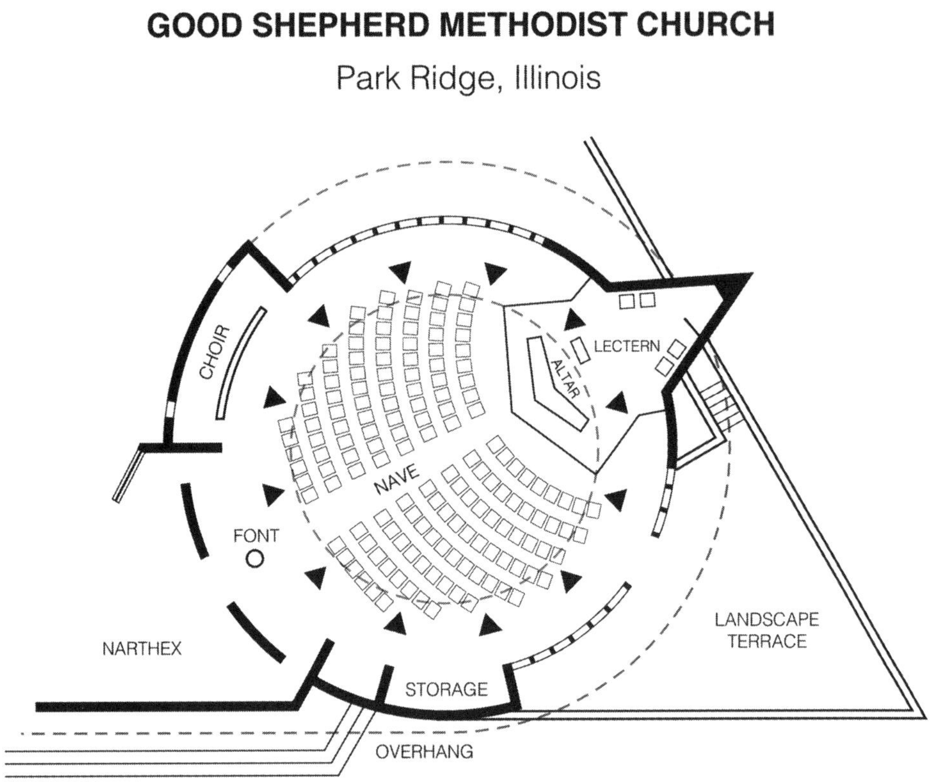


FIGURE 5.17. Good Shepherd Methodist Church, Park Ridge, Illinois, plan from *Your Church* (May–June 1965): 13. Redrawn by Jacob M. Just.

A church complex from the later 1960s illustrates how Stade's designs evolved toward the blockier, shed-roof type of the 1960s. St. John's Lutheran in La Grange, Illinois, razed its historic 1894 building in 1967 in order to make room for Stade's new red-brick sanctuary (Figure 5.18). Here Stade used the impressive height of the sanctuary roof for effect. Starting in a low-ceilinged narthex, one passes the baptistery and enters unimpeded into the nave. A single source of light dramatically illuminates the sanctuary. An open bell tower with an asymmetrical shed roof is integrated into the sanctuary building. Overall, St. John's is rather fortresslike and heavily massed (similar to Sövik's Good Shepherd in Moorhead and much of Dart's work from the 1960s).

Pages flagged in Stade's books (for instance, *Kirchen: Handbuch für den Kirchenbau*) show European examples from the 1950s with simple forms, solid massing, and a tall tower with shed roof.[65] St. John's is by no means an exact copy of a European church, but the overall impression these buildings produce is similar. Leafing through this German book, it becomes clear that Stade looked to these sources for inspiration. Another flagged page in *Kirchen* illustrates two Fritz Schaller churches

FIGURE 5.18. Charles Stade, St. John's Lutheran Church, La Grange, Illinois, 1968. Photograph by the author.

in Cologne with upper-level clerestory features that echo those of Stade's St. John's, Lincolnwood. European church design had a profound impact on the ideas of these three Midwestern church architects. Stade, more than Dart and Sövik, appears to have consciously incorporated European influence into his own work. I have found no evidence that the congregations that employed these architects thought or even knew about the connections their architects were making with emerging European church design, although the possibility cannot be ruled out. But the architects themselves certainly understood their work in this international context, and it was their burden to package those ideas in ways that were appealing to American building committees.

## DART'S PLACES OF WORSHIP: HISTORICAL RESONANCE IN CRISP, MODERN SPACES

Edward Dart designed far fewer churches than either Sövik or Stade, but his thoughtful sanctuaries document his engagement in the church architecture conversations of his time. While often constrained by small budgets for first-unit buildings, Dart preserved the individuality of each commission. He thought carefully about the way people experience worship, and especially about their procession into the sanctuary, the successive stages of movement that bring one into the presence of God.

Dart worked with clients who had a sense of their uniqueness and were clear and intentional about their theology. Many of his churches (the lesser-known ones) were small, personal spaces, with atypical details and often something of the romantic—swooping, curved lines; dark, low entrances; or small, enclosed gardens. Most of Dart's church work falls later than the 1950s, so his designs reflect the 1960s emphasis on more solid and irregular massing, darker interiors, and rough surfaces. His sanctuaries typically convey an idea of sacred shelter rather than transparency. Although there can be an intimacy and thus a warmth to his smaller-scale sanctuaries, they tend to be sober and cool, the result of their formality and his choice of rough concrete and brick finishes.

Two of Dart's buildings from the early 1960s, the Episcopal Church of the Resurrection (1963) in the suburb of West Chicago (Figure 5.19) and his last family house in Barrington (1964), exhibit a notable feature of his work: attention to place and history. Both buildings evoke barns or mills, a nod to local vernacular sources. Inside, exposed beams reveal the structure, creating lofty ceiling spaces. In the case of Resurrection, a mission congregation established in 1954 and located in an undeveloped suburban area, the architecture referenced the old sawmill and watercourses originally on the site. In an article for *Building Stone News*, published in February 1964, Dart expressed concern for history and tradition. Modern architecture, he claimed, was often "a rather sterile, chaotic, in large part inhuman,

FIGURE 5.19. Edward Dart, Episcopal Church of the Resurrection, West Chicago, Illinois, 1963. Photograph by the author.

orderless and thus meaningless architecture" having "no meaningful historical relationship between past and present." He understood that design for its own sake was shallow, and that his clients needed something with richer resonances. "If our architecture is to survive beyond a mere estheticism," he argued, "we must search for these fundamental qualities in our programming and try to find fulfillment for them in the finished building."[66] His sanctuaries offer a special blend of tradition, stark and forceful expressions of modernity, and humanity.

Dart brought these concerns to an award-winning 1963 church for a young Presbyterian congregation in Lansing, Illinois, a southern suburb of Chicago (Figures 5.20 and 5.21). Organized in 1954, this small but growing congregation had a clear vision for what it wanted the building to express: "man's vertical relationship to God and man's horizontal relationship to his fellowman."[67] The church plan is a series of intersecting triangles with an asymmetrical angularity, sloping roofline, and a dominant tower situated directly above the altar. The pastor believed that Dart's church gave "physical expression to this double relationship . . . the massive tower unavoidably confronts us with God's downward thrust in Jesus Christ . . . how fitting that this . . . should be centered on the Table of our Lord!" The congregation found that this building was a perfect match for their Reformed faith and their particular character in its "compactness," leading to a "feeling of family

FIGURE 5.20. Edward Dart, Lansing Presbyterian Church, Lansing, Illinois, 1963. Photograph by the author.

intimacy."[68] The procession to worship begins in the sheltered courtyard, passes through the narrowing narthex, and turns around a corner into the small sanctuary. The dynamic chancel and nave display nonparallel walls that compress the space toward the chancel, and hard surfaces (concrete and rough stone), dark, rugged pews, and indirect side lighting, create a dramatic sanctuary. The congregation asked for the choir to be incorporated into the worshipping body, so Dart placed their seats, facing forward, at the front of the congregational pews. He planned for eventual expansion at the back to provide more seating, and a small addition was indeed constructed, although it remains a modest church. One Lansing parishioner appreciated the fortresslike aspects of her church, stating that it "was like a cave" that "put me in mind of how the first Christians had to go underground . . . they couldn't be open about their religion."[69] This intriguing memory may suggest a connection to William Clark's observation that the similar European churches of this era promoted a "sense of security." Other Dart churches share many of the same features. Dart's first unit for St. Matthew United Church of Christ in Wheaton, Illinois (1964), was another small church with unusual geometry, in this case a long, curving sanctuary wall. A similar church from this period, Dart's Emmanuel Presbyterian (1963) in the Pilsen neighborhood of Chicago (demolished 2007), looked much like the Lansing church with its sheltered entrance, asymmetry, and bell tower with shed roof.

FIGURE 5.21. Lansing Presbyterian Church, Lansing, Illinois, sanctuary. Photograph by the author.

A suburban example that represents the heart of Dart's 1960s sanctuary design is St. Luke's Methodist in Indianapolis (Figures 5.22, 3.10–3.11). Although the worship space is rectangular, the main axis is on the diagonal, with pews angled in (and down, on a sloping floor) toward the corner altar. A low wall defines the choir area and also points to the chancel. This geometry, very common in Dart sanctuaries, enhances the further momentum toward the altar and pulpit. Massive trusses spring up from the north to the south wall. The walls rest on substantial, heavy concrete posts with integrated capitals and architrave, creating an ambulatory space on each side, lighted on the south side by deeply set stained-glass windows. In both

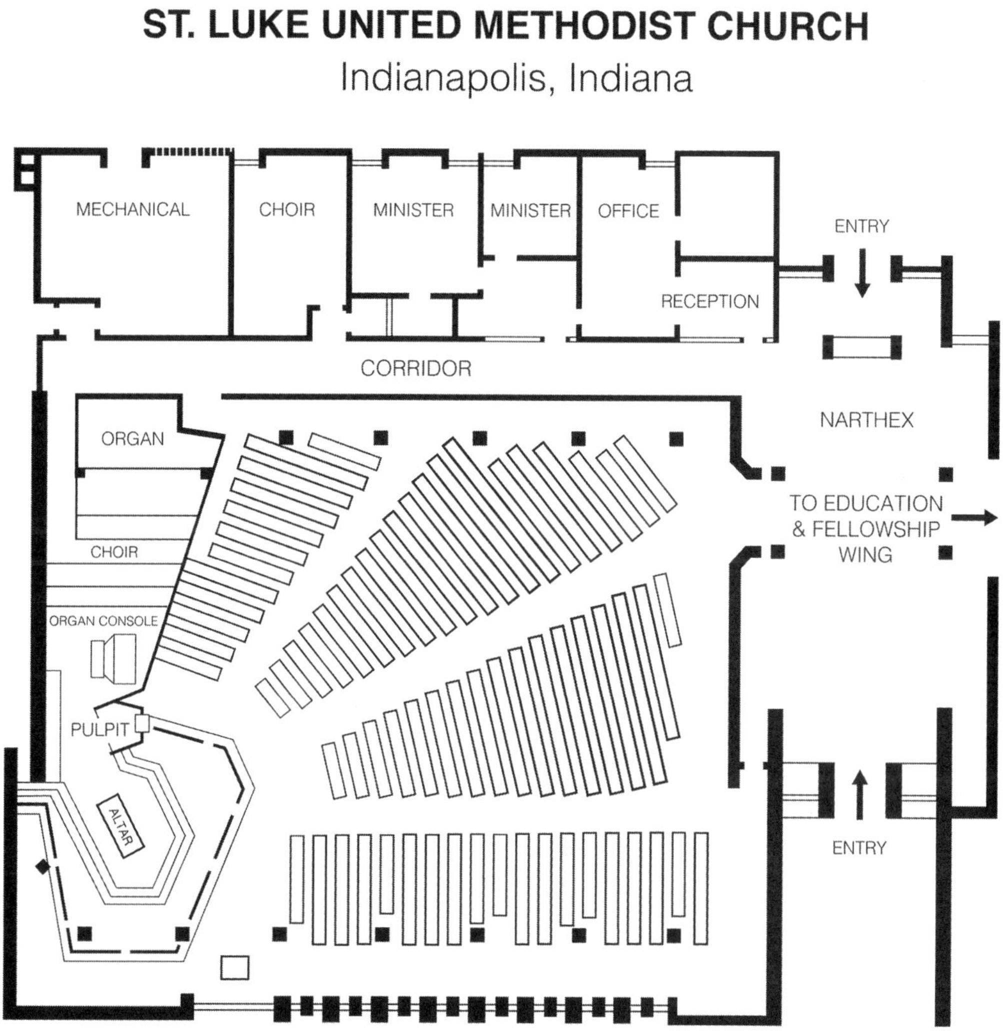


FIGURE 5.22. Edward Dart, St. Luke's Methodist Church, Indianapolis, Indiana, plan in brochure ca. 1967, St. Luke's United Methodist Church Archives. Redrawn by Jacob M. Just.

Dart's and Sövik's sanctuaries, this use of arched openings along an ambulatory is unmistakably a historical quotation that blends seamlessly with the contemporary architecture. The long, narrow windows on the south wall, the tall clerestory windows on the north, the brick and stone, and the soft lighting—these features, too, give Dart's sanctuary a medieval sensibility. St. Luke's was the progressive congregation that told Dart it wanted "a sanctuary that would be a true sanctuary," and the result was certainly that (see chapter 3). Reverend Richard Hamilton, the pastor at the time of construction, was enthusiastic about the adventurous spirit of the building committee. Hamilton particularly admired the "almost cloistered effect of the side aisles" and "the way he [Dart] gave the choir some visible presence," integrating them into the sanctuary rather than placing them in a back gallery.[70]

One of Dart's last suburban churches, completed in 1968, was the Presbyterian Church of La Porte, Indiana (Figure 5.23). Unlike many of Dart's clients, La Porte Presbyterian was a long-established congregation, with nearly eight hundred members and a beloved historic building downtown. After purchasing land on the outskirts of the city, a two hundred thousand–dollar education building was designed by William Cooley, former architectural partner of Charles Stade, and opened in 1958. For several years, church activities were split between the two sites. Cooley had sketched out an A-frame church to go with the education building, but by 1964, when the congregation revisited the idea of building a new church, this design no longer generated enthusiasm. John Hupp, a member of the building committee who was an engineer with Loebl, Schlossman, and Bennett, brought Dart to the committee's attention.

FIGURE 5.23. Edward Dart, Presbyterian Church of La Porte, La Porte, Indiana, 1968, sanctuary. Courtesy of Presbyterian Church of La Porte, Indiana.

As in the Lansing Presbyterian church, from a dark and narrow narthex one emerges into the openness of the sanctuary. Dart insisted on hard floor surfaces for the aisles because he felt that it was important that people in the pews heard others coming in. The day the concrete floor of the main building was poured was memorable for Daniel Lewis Jr., chair of the building committee. The walls were already in place, and each of the three planes of the floor had to be filled in one pour, requiring well-coordinated, furious activity. "You never saw men working so hard in your life," Lewis recalled.[71] Dart and his client chose as focal point a plain stone communion table. His altar fittings were also spare, as the congregation originally was served communion in the pews. Lewis remembers some suspicion among members of the congregation as they watched this building—"not like anything they'd seen before"—take shape. To some, it seemed dark and cold, but it was also an extremely peaceful space. Excellent acoustics contribute to the sense of congregational unity. And here, as at St. Luke's, Indianapolis, Dart's use of modern forms and materials is complemented by a historical sensibility. Although having "little resemblance to traditional sanctuaries," the pastor noted, "its use of inside columns and simple lines invokes classical forms."[72] Unlike most of his other churches, the walls are a stark white, contrasting with dark pillars, possibly evoking a New England meetinghouse, an antecedent for this Presbyterian congregation.

### PROTESTANT ARCHITECTS DESIGNING FOR ROMAN CATHOLIC CLIENTS

Sövik, Stade, and Dart each worked for some Catholic clients, and these churches provide a counterpoint to their designs for Protestants. The buildings followed the reforms of the Second Vatican Council (1962–65), so are somewhat later work for these architects. All exhibit the 1960s trends in church design noted earlier. These buildings are a good place to take stock of what we might call the architect's individual "style," for although the three continued to change and develop as designers, it is very clear which architect designed each building. The Catholic churches of Dart and Stade were large, auditorium-style sanctuaries, often with rooflines rising significantly to the front, and light coming into the chancel from hidden windows. Sövik's Catholic churches are much like his 1960s "nonchurch" with details suited to Catholic worship. With his strong interest in ecumenism, this is not surprising. He stated, "It seems to me to be an obligation of church builders nowadays, that they leave behind the patterns and habits of denominationalism, which are almost all accidents of history."[73]

Stade designed at least three Roman Catholic churches: St. Joseph, Summit (1970), St. Mary, Des Plaines (1971), and Holy Family, Rockford (1973–75), all in Illinois. The large sanctuaries of both St. Joseph and Holy Family reflect Stade's accumulated experience with institutional architecture, including theaters and student centers, managing large quantities of space for audiences of significant size. Lacking the decorative detail of his churches from the late 1950s and early 1960s, they are less definitively ecclesiastical. From the outside, St. Joseph is unlike other Stade churches, almost a cave or fortress in appearance (Figures 5.24 and 5.25). The congregation walks through simple, low-arched doorways into the narthex area; the only sign that this is a church is the simple cross rising from the small patch of lawn outside. Inside the sanctuary, light flows from an upper tier of windows, invisible to the congregation (the dormer-like gridded area atop the sanctuary exterior), and softly illuminates the sanctuary. The combination of the fan-shaped seating arrangement, with each rank pointing toward the relatively small, low chancel, and the massive laminated roof trusses rising up from the back of the pews, create a dynamic sense of movement toward the altar and give a sense of unity to the cavernous space required to accommodate this large suburban parish.

Dart designed two Roman Catholic parish churches in Illinois, Holy Ghost in South Holland (1971) and St. John of the Cross in Western Springs (1977, posthumous). Holy Ghost was an inexpensive design for a new parish in the rapidly growing Chicago suburb of South Holland (Figure 5.26). The church has features of many of Dart's other ecclesiastical designs: angular geometry; vast, unadorned

FIGURE 5.24. Charles Stade, St. Joseph Catholic Church, Summit, Illinois, 1970. William S. Engdahl for Hedrich-Blessing, HB-34697-J, Chicago History Museum.

FIGURE 5.25. St. Joseph Catholic Church, Summit, Illinois, sanctuary. William S. Engdahl for Hedrich-Blessing, HB-34697-E, Chicago History Museum.

and flat wall surfaces gashed with clear windows (the vivid pattern of light from the rear window is evident on the altar wall in this photograph); the almost exclusive use of simple brick and natural wood; a gently downward sloping floor leading to a slightly raised altar platform placed near a corner. At the 1971 dedication, the architect took the opportunity to explain modern church architecture to the parish, an iteration of what Protestants had been hearing from their architects for fifteen years. "Most of us think of a church in terms of a cathedral of ornate design," he wrote. "These majestic structures stand in glory in all parts of the world as monuments to the past . . . now think of a contemporary church building, designed for a modern community."[74] He explained the space in terms of the new liturgy and drew on themes of simplicity, spaciousness, unity, and an absence of barriers.

Edward Sövik's ideas have had a significant effect on American Catholic architecture since the publication of *Architecture for Worship* in 1973. Even before then, Sövik had collaborated successfully with the clergy and congregation of St. Leo's in Pipestone, Minnesota, his first and probably best-known Catholic commission

FIGURE 5.26. Edward Dart, Holy Ghost Catholic Church, South Holland, Illinois, 1971, sanctuary. Photograph by the author.

(see Figure 2.1). St. Leo's has a nearly square, brick-floored worship space without a nave-chancel separation (Figure 5.27) to allow for movement and flexibility. Brick steps lead up to a low central platform with an altar table. Walls of contrasting solid and open brickwork mask acoustical panels. A wooden screen behind the altar creates an arcade between altar and rear wall that houses the Stations of the Cross.[75] As you enter the sanctuary from the narthex, you pass the font, a square of dark gray granite signifying entrance into the community of believers—open, with water running.[76] The asymmetrical arrangement of pews—two primary ranks with a central aisle leading to the altar, but with facing pews on the side—means that there is no one center to dominate the worshipper's attention; the changing action of the people becomes the focal point. Twelve pillars form a circle around the congregation. On each pillar is a feature unique to this church, a square of local red pipestone with a candle above.[77] At the time, Sövik spoke of the Japanese tearoom as the best analogue for worship space, a place not for private meditation but "for a dialogue and for certain actions in which human relationships are established."[78] Sövik's sketches of such a room show not just the symbolic connections but the visual relationship between the sliding screens in such a traditional Japanese room and the strong horizontal and vertical elements in the walls of this sanctuary.

FIGURE 5.27. Edward Sövik, St. Leo Catholic Church, Pipestone, Minnesota, 1969, interior. Les Turnau for Michael Myers Studio. Courtesy of SMSQ Architects.

Father Brian Willette believed that there was very little resistance to St. Leo's revolutionary design because "there was a lot of education and experiential learning" along the way. As the congregation met in its auditorium, for instance, while planning the new sanctuary, they were able to experiment with the arrangement of seats, and discovered that they enjoyed being able to see one another's faces. That is not to say that there was *no* resistance. One well-heeled donor, a traditionalist, pulled back on his contributions. But for the most part the response was positive. Patt Johnson, a parishioner who arrived in August 1969 was delighted with the building from the start, finding it "a very community-centered church" that speaks of "God-centered" worship, "so conducive to many things," including plays, concerts, and seasonal decorating.[79] Parishioners tend to agree with Johnson that "it is huge and massive to bring us all in—but we can hear everyone sing, everyone speak." Sövik said, "You have to be fairly open-minded to understand that room . . . strong, serious, coherent . . . I think it quite beautiful."[80] Sövik confidently persuaded his clients, such as St. Leo's priests and congregation, to come around to his way of thinking about worship space.

## THE INTIMATE WORSHIP SPACE OF THE SUBURBAN CHURCH CHAPEL

Although the primary sanctuary was by far the most important worship space in the suburban church, a consideration of the architecture for suburban worship would not be complete without recognition that congregations believed that worship was an activity that did not need to be—indeed, should not be—confined to the space of the sanctuary. Worship was a practice, a way of being, that could be experienced by Sunday school children in their classrooms, teens sitting around the fire pit in the youth lounge, a congregation gathered outside at a ground breaking or for an informal outdoor service. Architecturally, the expression of worship is, of course, primarily in the sanctuary. But the presence of small chapels, a feature of more substantial church building projects, demonstrates that other types of worship and meditation also required specially designated spaces. These chapels, typically at a remove from the more active areas of the church plant, seated a few dozen worshippers comfortably. Records indicate that they were used for individual meditation and smaller, family-oriented services such as small weddings or funerals, as well as more intimate services.

Some of the larger Sövik churches of this era, such as First Baptist, Bloomington, St. Paul's, La Crosse, Wisconsin, and the Evangelical Lutheran Church in Mt. Horeb, Wisconsin, have such intimate chapels. Sövik's chapel for First Baptist was a shadowy space lit only by skylights along one side of the roof and a side window lighting the chancel from behind a bend in the side wall—very different from the airy sanctuary. Stade designed a few chapels, including one for the Joliet Jewish congregation. Smaller suburban congregations did not have the means for such additional worship space, although first-unit churches were sometimes refitted as chapels, such as at Stade's Hope Lutheran in Park Forest. Also, the overflow space for a typical rectangular sanctuary, such as commonly appeared in Stade's A-frames, could be closed off and used as a chapel. The fact that a chapel was often one of the last elements of a full building plan to be completed argues for their minimal importance relative to other aspects of the church building program. On the other hand, that they were often desired by congregations, and were a component of the long-range plan, is clear. Sanctuaries worked well for Sunday worship and large congregational gatherings. The presence of chapels, on the other hand, is one more indication that quiet and intimate worship was an important part of spiritual life as understood by suburbanites, and that these church buildings accommodated the private as well as the public experience of faith.

The "gathered church" was the commonly understood motif of the postwar sanctuary, but as these examples show, that idea could take physical shape in a variety of ways. Although the plan of the worship space was, for experts, a critical marker of congregational unity in worship, there were other ways to mark the progress of the gathered church. For instance, whether axial or centralized, the visual clarity and simplicity of contemporary sanctuary space mitigated distraction and encouraged the people to focus on God and each other. Sövik's idea of "under one roof" is a helpful way of understanding how the idea of the "family of God" was manifest in the religious architecture of the postwar decades. Architecture that minimized barriers between people and functions, with spaces that flowed easily into one another, promoted a sense of togetherness, not only in sanctuaries but in the entire church building. In social and educational rooms as well, the architecture of the postwar church, "under one roof," drew people together for their common work, while still preserving and encouraging individual growth.

CHAPTER 6

# Living and Learning as a Suburban Church Family

## *Modern Spaces for Education and Fellowship*

Worship was the central focus of suburban congregations, but it was hardly their only activity. Beyond the sanctuary, churches buzzed with life. Inside and out, the architecture of the new churches announced the multiple roles that suburban congregations were ready to play in their communities. Attached to the architecturally dominant sanctuaries were informal, sprawling wings that contained classrooms, offices, recreational spaces, and community meeting places. Charles Stade noted the impact of diverse programming on the demeanor and plan of churches. "One of the important community influences on church construction and design," he wrote, "is a turn toward less stately, less formal buildings. It is now necessary for a church to be far more than a one hour a week sanctuary. It must also give service during the full week through meeting rooms, Sunday schools, auditoriums, etc."[1] Roughly half of the money spent on churches during this era paid for the education and fellowship facilities that often preceded sanctuaries in construction.[2] In addition to worship and Sunday school, postwar suburban churches desired facilities to support youth organizations, choir practice, vacation schools, preschool and kindergarten classes, scouts, women's and men's associations, and a host of other clubs and meetings each week. These were busy places.

A broad range of educational and social activity distinguished the American church. As Chicago architect William Cooley observed in 1962, "A notable difference between European and American churches is the many more diverse activities found in the latter. We are concerned here not only with the spiritual progress of the church, but also with its educational and social responsibilities."[3] Cooley predicted that "the shape of new church buildings will be different than anything we have seen before. A complex of buildings designed for religious living will offer a great variety of activities for all age groups."[4] "Educational and social responsibilities" and "religious living" are telling phrases that indicate the earnestness and all-encompassing scope of this postwar vision of religious community.

Architecturally and conceptually, this language indicated a new way of imagining the function of the church in its community. Although prewar congregations had numerous programs and events, also calling themselves "seven-day-a-week" churches, their activities and the spaces in which they took place were more formal and less deliberately integrated into a total program for "religious living." Larger congregations had housed social and educational programs in ample, multistoried parish halls, notably distinct from the church proper, and gymnasiums and other recreational facilities were likewise common in these bigger churches. These buildings had many smaller rooms designed for specific functions (such as the ladies' parlor) arranged along often meandering hallways in multiple-floor buildings. Smaller prewar congregations would have typically pursued their nonworship activities in an ancillary church hall or simply a multipurpose basement below the sanctuary. Postwar Christians desired a degree of integration, informality, and flexibility not easily accommodated by these older facilities. Moreover, they wanted to escape the cramped and dark church spaces of their childhood parish hall, the "dingy, dark brown gloom factory with its musty odor, flaking paint, and forbidding, battered interior and bad acoustics."[5] "The whole trend of modern life," said the author of one of the *Briefs for Church Builders* in 1956, "is towards sunshine and fresh air."[6] Even in modest first units, architects and congregations strove to bring in light and air and create a feeling of openness.

On tracts of suburban land, postwar congregations crafted a new, integrated version of the seven-day-a-week church plant that centered on a postwar idea of family. Suburban churches, as the building committee of St. Augustine's Episcopal Church in Benton Harbor, Michigan, recorded, were designed around the "family-at-worship" theme.[7] Pastor Norman Hjelm of Orland Park, Illinois, told Edward Dart in a memo containing instructions from his building committee, "the prime witness of parish (especially in suburban America) life ought to be in terms of family life."[8] The complex and confusing world suburbanites confronted in the 1950s led many to seek answers and stability at church, and Pastor Hjelm and his peers thought of the church as example and witness in their communities. In 1959, Sövik told a Minnesota congregation, "it seems to me that the idea of THE FAMILY GATHERED has particular significance in our day." The challenges of the age were many: the "shrinking world and the problems of world peace, the world-wide issues of race prejudice and social status, the concern of sociologists and psychologists with the fracturing of society and its effects on individuals,—all these things are on our minds in this generation and promise to be continually so."[9] Such perplexities followed Christians to the suburbs, places that contributed their own versions of isolation and loneliness. The churches felt called to serve as a resource for suburban families as they navigated the postwar world looking for purpose, direction, and community as the "family gathered."

Christian parenting took on new meaning for postwar suburbanites. Since the mid-nineteenth century, many middle-class Americans had aimed to provide a stable and nurturing Christian home centered on the material, social, and spiritual needs of children. In the late-nineteenth-century Gilded Age, the middle class further fastened on domestic, family-centered morality as a way to distinguish itself from the excesses of both the amoral rich and the wayward poor.[10] The economic, social, and political disruptions of the first half of the twentieth century seemed to upend these norms and bring chaos to the family hearth. Postwar Americans, however, enjoyed a "reinvigorated and more stable family life," and looked to the family to right the ship of society.[11]

Historians argue that what it meant to be "child-centered," however, took a different turn in this period, one that put children more in the driver's seat. With the rise of the developmental paradigm in the twentieth century, parents understood their children's growth as a sequenced process of maturation. They waited anxiously for their children to reach the markers of each stage of development, instructed by experts to let children explore on their own while they themselves perched attentively on the side, acutely tuned to their children's needs. Parents were concerned about their children's progress toward productive work, responsible citizenship, and moral character in what seemed to be an increasingly complex world. Even the most relaxed parents could not miss the news about the critical importance of their children's many-dimensioned development in a society fraught with danger and temptation. As concerns about the rising generation mounted in the popular press, this unusually well-educated generation of parents had shrinking faith in their ability to rear their own children.[12] Americans placed their confidence in institutions designed to help themselves and their children reach a healthy maturity, and this had implications for the church. Integrating the nurture, authority, and tradition of the church into family life could be an important component of postwar "family building."[13]

Although the nuclear family was its essential building block, congregations as a whole thought and spoke of themselves as extended families. Especially for young couples living away from their kin, the church community could provide important support and a network of friends. Helen and Gil Reinkensmeyer, for instance, came to Kalamazoo, Michigan, in the mid-1950s, soon after Zion Lutheran had moved outside of the center of town into a new Stade church. For them, busy young parents, Zion was an anchor for their lives. "It was family. It was all family," Helen remembers. The congregation formed the core of their friendships, was associated with all major life events, and was a site of "plain, old-fashioned, Christ-centered fellowship," which sometimes included spontaneous trips to Lake Michigan for a picnic after Sunday worship.[14] This social need for a close community of friends corresponded with the idea of worship as the family of God gathered around the altar. Sövik noted that as architects broke away from the traditional, formal church-with-a-tower concept there was instead "the perception of the church building as an image of community . . . shelter for a Christian family" gathered around the table or the hearth.[15] The church would, literally, provide a new foundation for the Christian family.

A frequent criticism of the postwar suburban church stems from its complex social nature. When the cynicism of the 1960s gathered steam, it is no wonder that a stereotypical prosperous and comfortable suburban church rang false. Suburban church complexes could seem impossibly ill-suited for the spiritual and social transformation the revolutionary 1960s generation championed. But that suburban model was precisely what the immediate postwar generation—a generation formed largely in cities and small towns, not the suburbs to which they were moving—found revolutionary in its own time. This generation found solace and spiritual significance in church-related work—raising money, raising a church, raising Christian children. That is how these Christians experienced community and felt their individual value. As they aged, many looked back fondly on this time as one of "fun, fellowship, food and laughter" within the congregation.[16]

Church members recall the excitement of joining a new congregation in a new place. After Eleanor Vickers and her husband moved from Harvey to Lansing, Illinois, in 1947, their next-door neighbors, charter members of Our Saviour Lutheran Church, encouraged them to attend. Eleanor belonged to the woman's guild (Lutheran Church Women, or LCW) and participated in the service-oriented Martha Unit, and also social events such as the mother–daughter banquet and the annual ladies' Christmas dinner. The LCW, she remembers, had a goal of serving the whole community, giving Thanksgiving baskets and welcoming new people. When a newcomer joined the church, she recalled, the pastor, who was very successful at bringing in young people, would ask them to serve on the altar guild as a way of giving newcomers a sense of the traditions and liturgy of the church. Pastors found that a "worthy project affords the church the best means for integrating them [newcomers] into the life and work of the church."[17] In an era of do-it-yourself projects—pastimes that could serve as an antidote to sedentary, white-collar day jobs—suburbanites found that churches welcomed their craft skills. Vickers's husband Charles "didn't like to go to meetings but he liked to work," so he contributed his skills and energy around the church.[18] Starting in 1962, the family helped out when their congregation used its fellowship hall to hold morning summer school for children of migrant workers. As the experience of the Vickers family illustrates, belonging to a congregation provided a diverse mix of opportunities for worship, education, service, and sociability.

Church leaders, architects, and their clients believed that the architectural setting for these multiple facets of congregational life would have a significant impact on spiritual formation. Classrooms, fellowship spaces such as social halls, kitchens, and lounges, and even work areas all played a formative role. In contrast to sanctuaries with their unique qualities, these spaces were much like their secular counterparts, and this was by design. Favorable comparisons to cutting-edge school facilities and offices stoked pride but also reassured congregations that they were offering their communities buildings designed and equipped according to the best new knowledge. An emphasis on efficiency, practicality, and warmth or "friendliness" permeated the advice literature. Set next to comparable architecture of the day, one sees the modernity of these spaces, with their crisp lines, plain surfaces, and abundant light. They bustled with noise and activity: children playing, choirs practicing, mimeograph machines churning out the weekly bulletin.

In the midst of impassioned building campaigns and weeks densely packed with activity, suburban Christians often reaffirmed that the church was about people, not architecture. A church did not exist for its own sake, but had a responsibility to serve a complex and troubled society. Martin Marty, speaking to an audience of church leaders and architects in 1963, cited Dietrich Bonhoeffer's plea that the church must "take part in the social life of the world, not lording over men, but helping and serving them. She must tell men, whatever their calling, what it means to live in Christ, to exist for others."[19] "Helping and serving" in a manner that communicated a "religious understanding" drove the planning of nonworship spaces. Church buildings were not to be grand monuments or sacred enclaves, but generous, open buildings that represented the nature of Christian community and its relationship to the broader world—comfortable and welcoming places where "the undisciplined possibilities of human personalities" would come into contact with "the transforming influence of the person of Jesus Christ."[20]

## THE FLEXIBLE AND INTEGRATED SUBURBAN CHURCH PLAN

Congregations desired informal, flexible, and integrated spaces. In these multifaceted buildings, functions needed to be separate enough to prevent one from impeding the other (ensuring noise barriers, for example, between social spaces and sanctuaries). Yet, at the same time, activity required integration, so as not to isolate one function or one group of people from the whole. Worship, education, and fellowship were hardly mutually exclusive activities but were intertwined, intentionally, in the weekly activities of the church. The typical suburban church, whether a small first unit or a more extensive suburban complex, communicates this balance.

In 1953, church building consultant William Leach made an architectural connection between homes and churches. "What other age has built for family use and general utility as the modern American churches are now doing?" he asked. He suggested that "a congregation plan its building as a family plans its home. There must be facilities for all age groups and many kinds of social activities."[21] Indeed, middle-class houses and ordinary suburban churches did have much in common. Both were typically one-story buildings with a primary central entrance into a welcoming social space. Postwar houses often combined a large, open living/dining/kitchen area with smaller, more private rooms for children and parents. Churches likewise divided space between open, flexible rooms for large gatherings and smaller spaces for the more particular needs of age and interest groups. Both demonstrated a negotiated balance between a desire for spaciousness and togetherness and the need for containment, order, and the fostering of individuality.[22]

Three postwar plans illustrate the commonalities of spatial organization in two small churches and one larger suburban plant. Stade's streamlined first-unit plan for St. Paul Lutheran, Oak Lawn, Illinois, typified the organization of a small postwar church around worship, education, work, dining, and storage functions (Figures 2.7 and 6.1). One wing of the L-shaped building is the sanctuary. The slightly raised chancel area, with the sacristy off to one side, was the furthest from the social and education spaces, at some distance from the rest of the building and its bustle of activity. The rear of the nave was partially open to the narthex (via large interior windows and doorways) and another large room behind, also designated

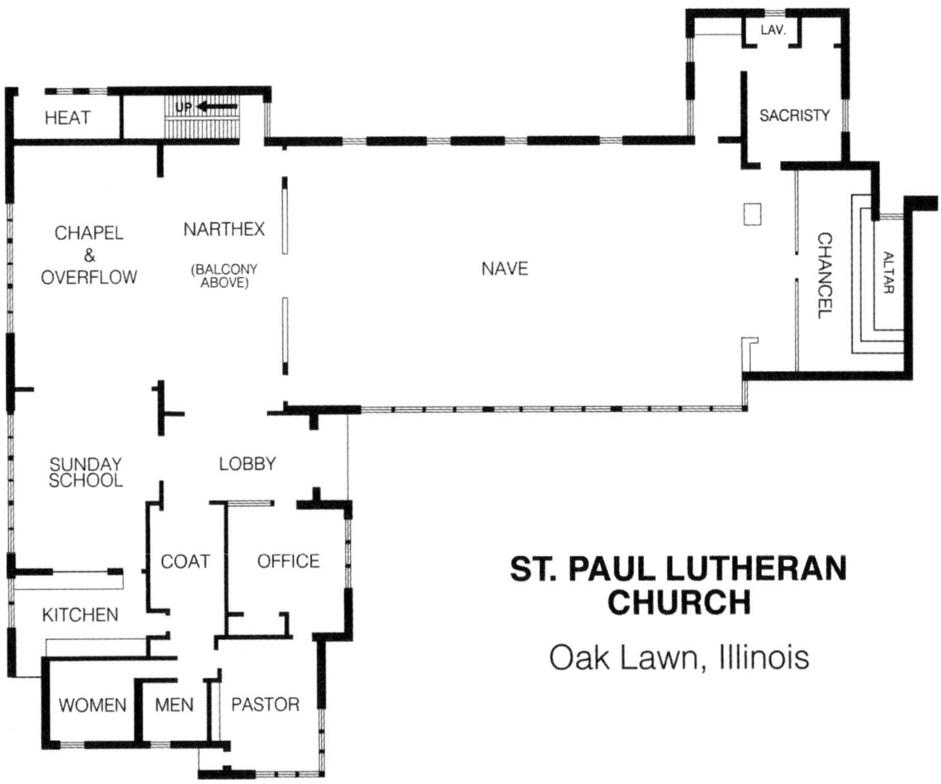


FIGURE 6.1. Charles Stade, St. Paul Lutheran Church, Oak Lawn, Illinois, proposed plan in fund-raising brochure, 1953. St. Paul Lutheran Church Archives. Redrawn by Jacob M. Just.

as a "chapel." When combined with the open Sunday school area, the congregation had a large and flexible L-shaped space that could be used for worship overflow, and for social and educational purposes. Furthest from the chancel were the kitchen, restrooms, pastor's study, and office. The entrance lobby and coatroom were nestled in the entrance at the bend of the L. There are no narrow hallways, and windows are generous throughout the public areas of the building, with the exception of the chancel area, lit indirectly by a small side window. Education space was slight in the first unit because that was an important second phase of the building campaign. By 1959, St. Paul's congregation had added another classroom wing (the first phase of a weekday school building), turning the L into a T. This was typical; as building progressed, with second and third units added to the first, original L-shaped plans often became U- or T-shaped.[23] The first wing, then, became primarily social space. Even typically modest 1950s suburban churches of the new suburbs, such as this Stade design, reflect the values of integration, informality, and flexibility.

Dart's Lansing, Illinois, Presbyterian Church is another small suburban church, even more modest than Stade's St. Paul (Figure 6.2). The butterfly-like plan demonstrates Dart's interest in unusual geometry—common for Dart but not the suburban norm. The congregation accepted Dart's preference for processional drama into worship, and the triangular narthex is a fairly dark space. The minimal education and social spaces are separated by two small offices just off the back entrance from the parking lot. A skylight lets daylight into the interior meeting room. The original multipurpose room that took up the majority of the opposite wing, as shown in the plan, had limited kitchen facilities along one wall. Lansing Presbyterian's congregation embraced this uncommon plan because Dart offered an affordable yet striking design with an artistry that appealed to them. The building enchanted architectural critics, who deemed it one of the best small churches of its day. Despite its charms, this is not an altogether workable plan, and the congregation did eventually make a significant addition to the multipurpose area. Although certainly not cookie-cutter suburban fare, even here we see the principles that characterized the majority of these small churches: a coherent, integrated plan; primary central access at the intersection of social, educational, and worship spaces; open and flexible social space; self-contained classrooms with large windows; and a domestic scale overall.

An example of a larger suburban church plant is Sövik's First Baptist, Bloomington, Indiana. Sövik designed this church in the form of a T (Figures 6.3, 5.3–5.4). The broad and brightly lit left side aisle of the sanctuary serves as an open passage between the worship and education/fellowship areas. One long, wide hall runs the length of the cross of the T, from the spacious fellowship hall (with fireplace, divisible into two rooms by accordion screens) and kitchen at one end, to the youth lounge, choir room (with sanctuary access), and eighty-seat chapel at

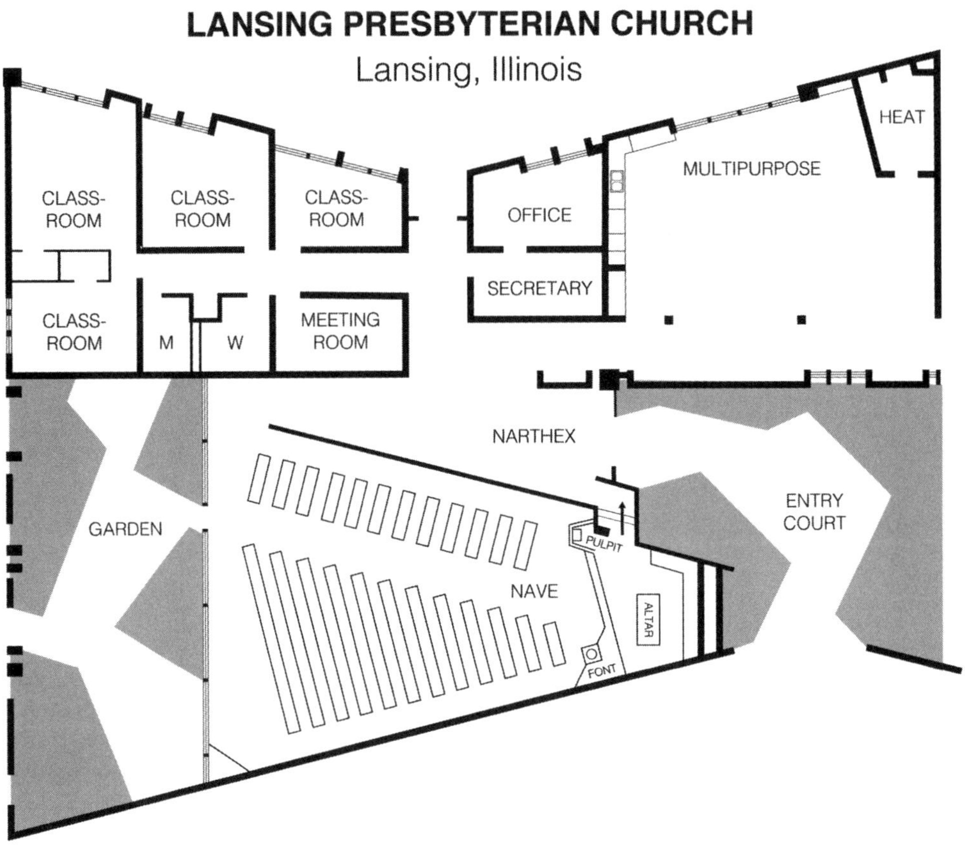


FIGURE 6.2. Edward Dart, Lansing Presbyterian Church, Lansing, Illinois, plan. *Your Church* (January–March 1964): 15. Redrawn by Jacob M. Just.

the opposite end. Well-lit classrooms are situated along the far, outer wall (away from the sanctuary). Administrative offices line up on the other side of the hallway, where they would be immediately visible to persons entering the church from the automobile turnaround next to the courtyard. Ample space was provided for the youngest members of the congregation in the specifically designated crib, toddler, nursery, and kindergarten rooms. Older children, grades 1–6, were assigned combined classrooms. Sövik designed the youth lounge, with a large, open, hooded fire pit and small kitchen, as the home of grades 7 through college-age church members. Welcome areas included the narthex off the back of the sanctuary and also a spacious lobby outside of the kitchen and hall. As recommended by the experts, access to each space was possible without interrupting activities in other rooms.

Despite their differences, these plans all reflect the same general principles of flexibility and integration. Even worship was not an activity relegated to just one space in the building. Yet flexibility did not mean uniformity. A considerable degree

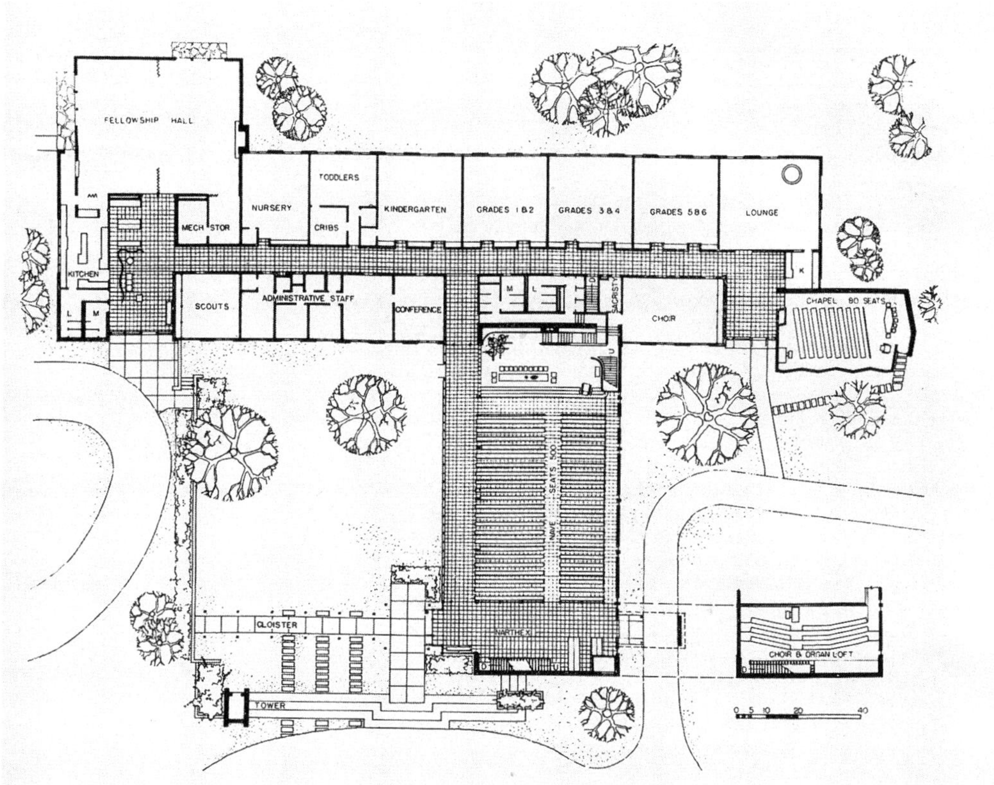


FIGURE 6.3. Edward Sövik, First Baptist Church, Bloomington, Indiana, plan. From Albert Christ-Janer and Mary Mix Foley, *Modern Church Architecture*, 247.

of thought and effort went into shaping the spaces according to the particular needs of each congregation. The following chapter sections consider education and fellowship spaces in turn. As this analysis will show, however, it is impossible to draw the lines clearly between those functions. Social and educational purposes were entwined, both integrated in the practice of "religious living." Both were essential to the mission of the suburban church. In these spaces, the simplicity that was a theme of the postwar sanctuary took the form of friendly informality, a casual but calculated approach to architecture and interior design meant to convey welcome and to encourage Christian growth and belonging.

## SHAPING CHRISTIAN LIVES IN THE SUBURBAN CHURCH CLASSROOM

As C. Harry Atkinson, the executive director of the National Council of Churches' Bureau of Church Building and Architecture, claimed, "The religious life and the hope of a better world are largely in the keeping of those who teach within the church. No other human institution can be expected to meet this solemn responsibility."[24] The stakes were high.

By the mid-twentieth century, a professionalized cadre of directors of Christian education significantly expanded educational activities for the average congregation. Reverend J. Gordon Chamberlain, professor of Christian Education at Pittsburgh Theological Seminary, claimed that in recent decades "the educational program of the church has proliferated with weekday schools, released-time classes, extended sessions of Sunday morning church school from two to three hours, Sunday evening programs for young adults, new weekday programs of religious education, and the growth of religious libraries."[25] Many suburban churches also ran kindergartens before the public schools took over that role.

The Sunday school program encompassed learners of all ages, from toddlers to the elderly, but especially in the new suburbs spilling over with youngsters, the education of children took priority. Thirty-two million American children were born in the 1940s, and more than forty million in the 1950s. Church planners enthusiastically accepted the newest thought about how children learn as well as innovative public-school design intended to serve them. Most believed that keeping up with the public schools was essential for the success of the Sunday school. Atkinson wrote in his widely circulated 1956 book *Building and Equipping for Christian Education* that "the attractive surroundings with which our children are environed while in public school, and the great variety of interesting activities which make up the curricula of these institutions, lend further incentives to the church to provide facilities and procedures which do not suffer by comparison." "Failure to meet this challenge," he warned, "puts religious teaching at a serious disadvantage."[26]

Hallmarks of the new public education matched those of the suburban church: flexibility, informality, and comfort—a cheerful, student-centered approach to instruction and a curriculum and environment that recognized that children learn by doing. Educators favored the age-specific "self-contained" classroom: a larger room with movable furniture, zones for creative discovery and quiet reflection, individual student storage areas, and a sink/restroom facility. Lessons from physics and psychology contributed to a richer understanding of how light, color, and the movement of air affected learners. Building manuals covered topics such as the practical arrangement of space, the use of color according to age group, the appropriate height of windows and width of hallways, planning for convenient circulation of air and people, and effective sanitation. Progressive new school buildings tended to be one-story facilities with ample windows and access to the outdoors.[27]

Church leaders turned to secular experts but insisted that "sound psychological, educational, and sociological principles must be combined with our theological base to determine our Christian education philosophy and the methods which derive from it."[28] Ideal classrooms would be large and informal, with more freedom leading to greater student engagement. This approach promised to convey a more holistic understanding of Christian faith, conduct, and community. Atkinson claimed that by employing adaptable space and curricula, "the group learns to live the Christian life by living and working together within the classroom."[29] Christian educators geared the program to the development of the whole child—body, mind, and spirit.

An illustration in Atkinson's book conveys a midcentury ideal: small groups of engaged children, multiple and individualized activities in a large, comfortable, and well-lit space, with one male and one female teacher guiding, rather than talking at, the children (Figure 6.4). Children are painting at an easel or sitting at tables; to the left is a small worship area and a library corner. Sunday school experts recommended that "large self-contained classrooms where groups remain for the entire learning period (in contrast to assembly rooms and adjoining tiny cubbyhole classrooms) furnish a setting for almost unlimited flexibility in the program."[30] Staffed by instructional teams, these hypothetical classrooms would enable teachers to experiment with new teaching techniques and respond to the needs of students rather than herding them into rigid patterns of teacher-centered instruction. This new approach was poles apart from the nineteenth-century "Akron Plan," which organized small classrooms radially around a large central gathering area overseen by a superintendent. Sanctuaries and fellowship halls were shared spaces where the

FIGURE 6.4. Design for primary class, from C. Harry Atkinson, *Building and Equipping for Christian Education* (New York: Bureau of Church Building of the National Council of Churches of Christ, 1956). Courtesy Presbyterian Historical Society, Presbyterian Church (U.S.A.) (Philadelphia, Pennsylvania).

entire congregation was expected to mingle. Classroom areas, on the other hand, addressed the individual's need to grow in his or her own age-specific fashion.

In Eero Saarinen's state-of-the-art addition to his father's Christ Lutheran Church, Minneapolis (1962), the school area, finished in bright colors, is capacious and light-filled. Six roomy classrooms open into wide, skylit hallways. A large kindergarten room accommodates eighty children, and all classrooms were equipped with the recommended blackboards and tackboards, sinks, built-in storage, and worship centers, approaching the idea recommended by the experts (Figure 6.5). More typically, suburban churches held Sunday school classes in smaller rooms lined up on one or both sides of long hallways that did not have all the features of Christ Church's state-of-the-art building.

The advantages of the new architecture, such as ample light, clean lines, and a fresh aesthetic, could also be had in a less expensive building. Charles Stade's 1963 addition to Lutheran Church of the Holy Spirit in Elk Grove Village, Illinois, was an education wing consisting of five classrooms, restrooms, and offices finished in dark wood, with wide connecting hallways (Figure 6.6). Despite the modest size

FIGURE 6.5. Sunday school class at Christ Church Lutheran, primary Sunday school room, 1960s. Photograph copyright Christ Church Lutheran, Minneapolis, Minnesota. All rights reserved; reprinted by permission.

FIGURE 6.6. Charles Stade, Lutheran Church of the Holy Spirit, Elk Grove Village, Illinois, education unit. Photograph by the author.

of many of Stade's suburban churches, he would, if possible, insist on brick and wood interior walls and fine finishes, as seen in this image. He did not like using concrete block as an interior surface, which would create "anything but a religious atmosphere."[31] Concrete block, nonetheless, was an affordable means of construction left exposed in some areas of most suburban churches. This image of Stade's addition illustrates another common technique: the use of large laminated beams to bridge the space between the top of the corridor wall and the roof, allowing a ribbon of clear windows to sit at the top of the wall and permit daylight to pass through. The wooden ceilings preferred by Stade and seen here added substantial warmth to the corridor as well. These features carried over into his classrooms.

Church educators believed that classrooms should be designed for the particular age group that would use them. For instance, Atkinson informed his readers that "Kindergarten children grow spiritually in an environment which carries intimations of God." His suggested floor plan included a number of "interest stations [that would] stimulate attention, moments of worship, and conversation between teacher and child" with places designated for reading, doll play, kitchen play, music, and group story time. Rooms such as these anticipated that "spontaneous worship arising under guidance out of situations meaningful to the child will make God more real than a so called 'worship period' imposed upon him as a routine procedure."[32] These prescriptions define a multivalent architecture where ideas of God were to be *discovered* by active learners, never forced. In Figure 6.7, a small cluster of young children and their Sunday school teachers in suburban La Porte, Indiana, investigate God's growing things at a table placed next to large windows that looked out to nature.

Some churches in the 1950s continued to plan for the "departmental assembly," which necessitated a larger area, sometimes with a special altar and liturgical objects for use in children's worship or even an actual children's chapel. Professional educators, however, increasingly deemed this practice inappropriate and false. Children's worship, they believed, "is more meaningful when it takes place in

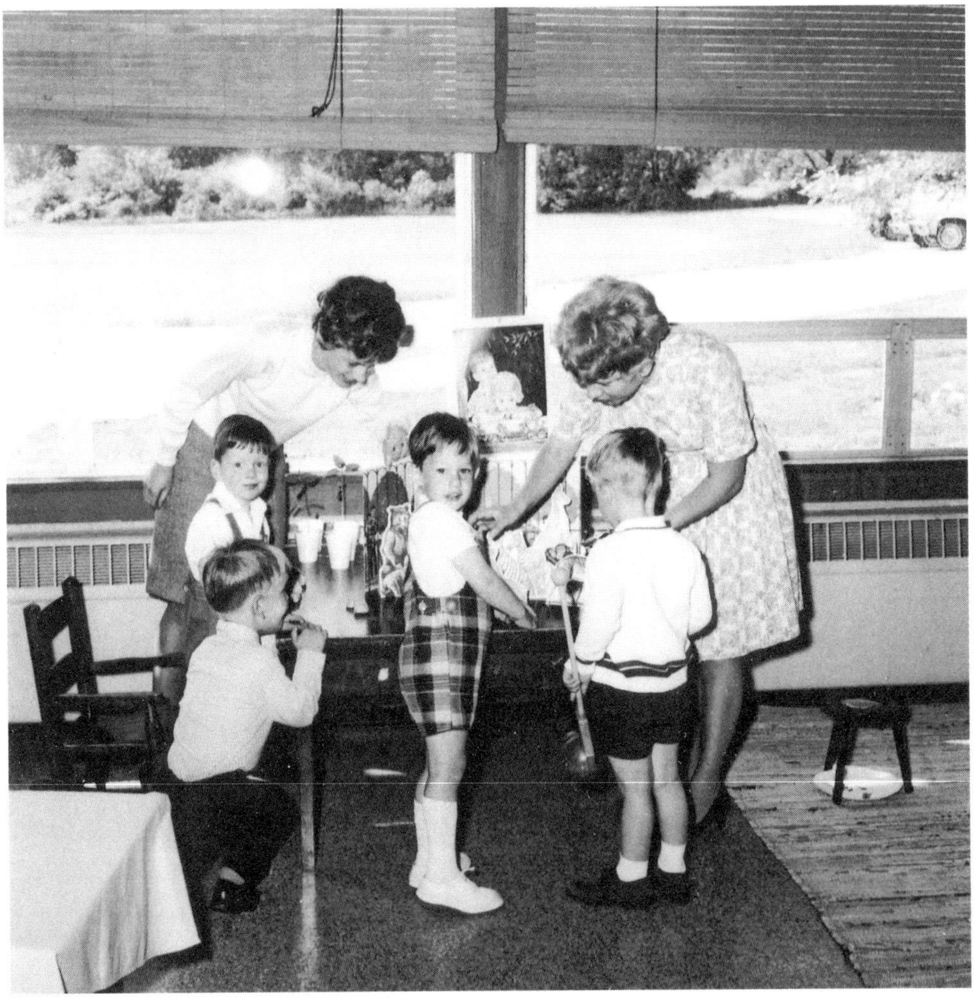

FIGURE 6.7. Sunday school class at Presbyterian Church of La Porte, Indiana, 1960s: children learn about God's world by growing plants in the sunlit classroom. Building by William Cooley, 1958. Courtesy of Presbyterian Church of La Porte, Indiana.

the classroom to 'celebrate' the fact that the Holy Spirit can make himself real through the learning experience."[33] By allowing that worship could take place as the children learned about God's world in their classrooms, churches lessened the distinction between the sanctuary and the Sunday school.

In the early 1950s, rooms designated for teens were nonexistent in many first-unit churches, as congregations assumed that teens could share the adult spaces and that they would worship in church with their parents. John Scotford advised building committees in 1955 that teens "need large rooms, but it does not follow that these should be class rooms. Church parlors and the minister's study can serve them well."[34] By the later 1950s, the literature reflects a marked increase in concern over the place of teenagers in the congregation. Adults believed teens to be especially susceptible to attractive elements of the wayward culture; the church needed to present a compelling alternative in order to keep teens under the influence of the Christian community.

Designers noted the importance of drawing teens in by means of visual and material informality. They recognized that young people had a very different sense of order, and would "often discuss serious religious problems . . . with the record player or television or radio going full blast."[35] Understanding the interests and tastes of teens was important: "Rooms for older young people should be conducive to group study, discussion, and related activities . . . it is psychologically important that the rooms be fresh and modern in their colors, furnishings, uses of light, and arrangements. Nothing inhibits the use of a room more than an impression of overall unimaginative dullness."[36] All areas of the church needed to be up-to-date, but church planners recognized that this was especially critical for teens.

Historian Jon Pahl describes the nature of youth ministry in the mid-twentieth century as an evolving shift in emphasis from *purity*, efforts to keep youth safe from the negative effects of the secular culture, toward *practices*, opportunities for youth to experiment "with adult roles and responsibilities" within that troubled culture.[37] While Christian purity remained an important concern, according to Pahl, congregations eased up on doctrinal education and increasingly called on youth to practice God-centered living that engaged the wider world and its social and political problems. The "youth group," a teen fellowship organization centered in the local congregation, also grew in popularity, often meeting on Sunday nights. And, answering a need for ministry specifically directed to youth, congregations increasingly hired youth directors, a position that became a suburban church standard by the 1970s.

Evidence suggests that transforming attitudes toward youth was a slow and uneven process. Initially, model youth rooms looked very much like a sprightly version of the suburban living room, with teenagers acting as proto-adults in definite midcentury gender roles. Adults imagined that teens would enjoy the same kind of social spaces as their parents, albeit pitched for a younger crowd. Atkinson's book illustrated one such scene, with an aproned girl at the kitchenette, a young man in a club chair perusing a newspaper, a girl reading at a library table, another boy at the stereo (Figure 6.8). The fire blazing in the fireplace and a boy and girl chatting on the sofa accentuate the domestic nature of the scene. Although this image is an unrealized, perhaps even amusing ideal, postwar congregations did want to provide sophisticated spaces for their teenagers and young adults. The congregation of First Baptist, Bloomington, for instance, desired an attractive youth space as early as the mid-1950s, rooms that would have a "club room informality" centered on a capacious fire pit, kitchenette, and Ping-Pong table, and Sövik's youth "lounge" did in fact have all those features.[38] Without extensive athletic facilities and leagues to draw teens, most suburban churches found a solution in the youth room, with comfortable seating and some recreational accoutrements (shuffleboard or Ping-Pong, radio or record player).[39] More structured, adult-style learning situations did continue for teens, especially when Sunday morning classes were held in classrooms or adult spaces such as a library (Figure 6.9). In later decades, adults would abandon their teens to youth rooms with mismatched, cast-off couches and do-it-yourself

FIGURE 6.8. Design for youth room, from C. Harry Atkinson, *Building and Equipping for Christian Education* (New York: Bureau of Church Building of the National Council of Churches of Christ, 1956). Courtesy Presbyterian Historical Society, Presbyterian Church (U.S.A.) (Philadelphia, Pennsylvania).

DayGlo wall murals. But in the 1950s and early 1960s, adults had not yet resigned themselves to a drastically different youth culture in the churches and elsewhere. Historians have noted that 1950s Americans valued maturity as defined by marriage and parenthood, and these postwar youth rooms were spaces parents designed for their teenagers with that goal in mind.[40]

The informality shaping many of the spaces for children and teenagers also affected adult rooms. Atkinson noted that "the tendency today is to make the adult classroom far less formal."[41] Spacious rooms with comfortable furniture provided a homelike atmosphere and encouraged informal group participation. Such multifunctional rooms, more likely to be used many times during the week, afforded the

FIGURE 6.9. High-school class in the library of the Presbyterian Church of La Porte, Indiana, 1960s. Education wing built by William Cooley, 1958. Courtesy of Presbyterian Church of La Porte, Indiana.

most practical use of space. Although architects and congregations differentiated children's spaces more than those for adults, that does not mean they viewed all adults as having the same social and spiritual interests or requirements. Advice literature suggested a consideration of the particular needs of young adults, parents of small children, midlife members, and seniors, needs that differed not just according to stage of life but according to personality and interests. Seniors, for instance, required space "to enjoy each other's company and to engage in creative activities suitable to their ages," such as craft work.[42] Physical needs were also important; one of the expressed reasons for the one-story church complex was that stairs could prove difficult for both the very young and the elderly, limiting their ability to circulate through the building.

The literature of the 1950s indicates the continued use of the term "Ladies Parlor," although suburban congregations rarely included such narrowly defined spaces in their new, modern churches. Instead, something more like a postwar living room found a place in the church, a multipurpose, comfortable, and casual space used for adult discussion, meetings of older youth, family gatherings at weddings and funerals, Sunday morning discussions, or new member classes—both education and fellowship space. This church parlor, or lounge, "can become the most used room in the church," wrote John Morse, particularly if it was an accessible, inviting room where "people can communicate easily with others and feel welcome and part of a group."[43] Sövik's adult lounge at Olivet Lutheran in Fargo, North Dakota, is crisp midcentury modernism, with a low, natural wood ceiling and Scandinavian-inspired comfortable seating furniture (Figure 6.10). Note the grand piano in the upper corner of the photograph. In many churches, this lounge or parlor doubled as a library, with comfortable chairs and a suburban living-room atmosphere. Perhaps this domestic way of thinking is behind the success of many of Sövik's (and Stade's) social and education rooms. Less successful wings, he claimed, were the product of architects who "thought of them as another structure" rather than an integral part of the plan.[44]

## IN BELONGING, BELIEF IS STRENGTHENED: FELLOWSHIP IN THE SUBURBAN CHURCH

As these casual spaces for youth and adults demonstrate, there was often no clear demarcation between educational and social spaces and activities. Suburban churches stated practical, educational, even theological motives for their interest in social activities. America's postwar secular culture appeared seductively attractive to people of *all* ages, the churches reasoned, and they saw the danger in a Christianity that consisted only of attendance on Sunday mornings. A deep integration of faith into all of life's activities seemed all the more urgent because communities of newcomers did not have the generational influences and structures of accountability they had left behind. A social appeal was not intended to be an end in itself,

FIGURE 6.10. Edward Sövik, Olivet Lutheran Church, Fargo, North Dakota, ca. 1965, lounge. Courtesy of Olivet Lutheran Church, Fargo, North Dakota.

but a strategy to get people in the door. Persis Smith, writing in 1958, noted, "It is widely accepted that today's churches in the Western World count heavily upon the social side of church life as an appeal to many who need urging to come to church, and as a means of holding them there."[45] Smith argued for a carefully planned social program that constantly and deliberately integrated religious content, "so that in belonging, our beliefs are strengthened."[46] This presumed connection between *belonging* and *belief* promoted the church's social world as a partner in the development of Christian character. Congregations desired to project a spirit of warmth and welcome that would draw newcomers into meaningful, shared activity and spiritual growth. Fellowship areas called for "welcoming" architectural features in inviting rooms where one could fall into a comfortable chair, talk with friends, and feel at home.

A sense of welcome began with the outward appearance of the church as potential visitors drove and walked through their suburban neighborhoods. When congregations and church consultants encouraged churches to "cultivate the atmosphere of a home," to think of their spaces as "not stiff and institutional but informal and human," they were thinking principally about the entrance and social spaces.[47] Pleasant, curved walkways, trimmed shrubs, and beautiful flowers should lead to an obvious and transparent entrance close to parking (Figure 6.11). Particularly once the plantings around these entrances grew up, as in this image of Lutheran Church of the Holy Spirit in Elk Grove Village, Illinois, these casual and inviting doorways communicated welcome. The architecture is softened by planting beds at ground level, and the sheltering eaves, walkway, and lawn resemble the yards of the neighborhood's houses. Church builders wanted the narthex to say, "We're glad to see you. Relax and feel at home."[48] The author of the NCC's leaflet "Making the Church Homelike" suggested that a comfortable friendliness in church spaces could counter the increasingly impersonal nature of the workaday world. Social events that involved eating and drinking appealed to suburbanites who found "the quickest and easiest place to make friends in most communities is the church."[49] Social spaces were called upon to "dramatize friendliness."[50] Sövik, and occasionally Stade, would, if possible, incorporate a hearth, as fireplace or hooded fire pit, into one of the fellowship areas, offering an especially potent symbol of warmth and friendliness in the Midwest.

FIGURE 6.11. Charles Stade, Lutheran Church of the Holy Spirit, Elk Grove Village, Illinois, 1960, entrance from parking lot. Photograph by the author.

Much thought went into creating a welcoming entrance, called the narthex, although many now seem small by today's standards. Conceptually, these were active spaces where important work was done, not simply a pass-through to the sanctuary. Centrally placed between the wings of the church, they served as a collection site and traffic hub, offering a direct path and open view to worship, fellowship, and education areas. Several common features stand out: few or no steps to the wide main doors; large, clear windows that let copious light into the space; plentiful hooks or hangers to receive the coats and hats; and a prominent guest book and information station for newcomers. These spaces read as transparent and accessible. Often the ceiling of the narthex was at the lower height of the education wing, rendering the entrance into the high-ceilinged sanctuary more impressive. Dart explicitly thought of this compression-release aspect of approach to the sanctuary, and there is less of the community and more of the individual journey in the path to the sanctuary in his buildings. Stade and Sövik created narthex areas that often seem airy and light despite their lower ceilings. On several occasions, Stade created a loftier narthex space, such as at Hillside Methodist in Evanston, and Zion Lutheran, Kalamazoo, where an open upper-loft area provided access to the choir balcony (and, at Zion, served as the congregation's first library). In his light-filled narthex of Immanuel, Des Plaines, a built-in platform provided a setting for the visitor's book and a brochure rack (Figure 6.12). In this early photo, Stade's common practice of incorporating planters and plantings in his buildings, most frequently in the narthex or chancel, is evident in the extreme. Stade was very concerned with mitigating the separation between outside and inside, in this practice following the example of both Wright and Dow. (Today, these planters in Stade churches are mostly empty or filled with artificial plants.) At the Evangelical Lutheran Church in Mt. Horeb, Wisconsin (1962), Sövik created a library niche in the long, narrow narthex, inviting contemplation as well as sociability and passage. First Baptist, Bloomington, looked forward to Sövik's "large and spacious, warm and welcoming lobby" as a sure sign that the congregation made hospitality a priority.[51]

Commentators and homeowners both noted that because contemporary houses seemed smaller than they had been in the past, opportunities for large social gatherings at home were restricted. Scotford wrote: "The American home is getting smaller. The trend is to omit the dining room and eat in either a nook off the kitchen or in a corner of the living room. We no longer have room for much company."[52] Churches with expansive social facilities could serve the community at large. The weekday use of churches was growing, and in new ways. Rather than formal lectures or midweek prayer meetings, weekday events brought small groups and committees for projects and functions. These events required pleasant and useful spaces where attendees could feel at home, and this was the primary purpose of the church fellowship hall. Stade's Salem United Church of Christ, Oak Lawn, Illinois (1962), was one of his larger commissions, an example of an older

FIGURE 6.12. Charles Stade, Immanuel Lutheran Church, Des Plaines, Illinois, 1957, narthex. Photograph by Herrlin Studio, Barrington, Illinois. Courtesy of Immanuel Lutheran Church, Des Plaines, Illinois.

congregation moving from the city to a new suburban location. The cost of Salem's entire complex was close to half a million dollars, including the 430-seat sanctuary (see Figures 5.12 and 5.13). Salem's fellowship hall is an example of the more elegant of these social spaces, with warm wood beams, a long wall of stained glass, and the ubiquitous postwar church kitchen pass-through (Figure 6.13). This room could be dressed up for a congregational dinner, but it was also a comfortable place to drink Sunday morning coffee. As this hall illustrates, in many of Stade's education and fellowship wings, he used blocks of colored glass in windows and doors to tie the spaces back to the sanctuary. Many congregations managed for years with one multipurpose fellowship hall such as this.

The smaller fellowship hall at Lutheran Church of the Holy Spirit in Elk Grove Village, the church of Reverend Marty and his young congregation, is even less formal, not simply because of the congregation's limited budget and smaller size but because of the intended use of the space. An accordion wall at the rear of the church separates the sanctuary from the social hall, which could thus be used either for

FIGURE 6.13. Charles Stade, Salem United Church of Christ, Oak Lawn, Illinois, 1962, fellowship hall. Photograph by the author.

sanctuary overflow or for social or educational purposes (Figure 6.14). Another accordion wall could divide the space in two. The full kitchen is off to the left in the photograph, a space roomy enough to prepare a meal for the congregation. To the right in the photograph is a stage with curtain, which could also be used as a classroom. By the 1960s, stages were becoming less common in suburban churches, but in the 1950s congregations still often chose to place a stage at one end of the fellowship hall. These stages signify a type of group activity—such as a play or a fashion show—that was part of the 1950s congregation's social world.

The more attractive the space, congregations logically reasoned, the more likely parents and children would want to be there. "With many families the church is just an extension of the home," proclaimed a popular guide for church builders. "This means that our faith is touching our lives in more ways than ever before. For this we should be grateful."[53] Casual sociability thrived in the newly popular after-service coffee hour, which became very important in the weekly rhythm of activity.[54] With the decline of the gymnasium, the fellowship hall became a recreational facility as well. A chief reason for the often generic nature of these fellowship rooms is that they had to serve multiple purposes; congregants attending the after-church coffee hour often stepped on a shuffleboard grid.

FIGURE 6.14. Charles Stade, Lutheran Church of the Holy Spirit, Elk Grove Village, Illinois, 1960, multipurpose room. Photograph by the author.

Churches were aware that they could be criticized for an overemphasis on social activities, and they resisted this characterization. For example, in a pamphlet for its new church, the congregation of Our Savior's Lutheran in Austin, Minnesota, insisted, "Our Savior is not a social club, although we will have many social functions. We are not a service group, although we perform many services in the community and the world. We are part of the Kingdom of God, a part of the living body of Jesus Christ."[55] The urge to know God and the urge to know fellow human beings mingled in all the spaces of the church where bonds of fellowship were formed, an integration of faith and community that resonated both with liturgical reform and the spirit of contemporary church architecture. Certainly, much of the social activity in the postwar congregation had a secular component, but suburbanites did hope to distinguish activities that took place in the church from those of a purely secular nature.

The flexible and comfortable character of the postwar church building might have made this challenging. Many parts of church buildings had overlapping functions. Worship might be held in a gym for several years, and the social hall or narthex often doubled as overflow space for the sanctuary. Harold Wagoner's 1956 first-unit multipurpose sanctuary/social hall for St. Luke's Methodist, Indianapolis, was used for both worship and fellowship until 1967. Figure 6.15 shows a

FIGURE 6.15. St. Luke's Methodist Church, Indianapolis, Indiana, congregational dinner in combination sanctuary/social hall, ca. 1965. Courtesy of St. Luke's United Methodist Church, Indianapolis, Indiana.

father–son meal being served in this space, with plates and coffee cups just a few yards from the altar. But this interplay of function might just as well have brought a spiritual character into recreation and education areas. The Cub Scouts and Cradle Club met in rooms with Christian images, such as Warner Sallman's popular *Head of Christ* on the walls. And where else but a church hall would a suburbanite, dressed in her Sunday best and fresh from worship, accept a cup of coffee from a friend across a kitchen pass-through?

## FRIENDLY AND EFFICIENT SPACES FOR THE WORK OF THE POSTWAR CHURCH: KITCHENS AND OFFICES

Two practically and symbolically critical areas of the suburban church—kitchens and offices—supported the work that was absolutely essential to the modern, suburban congregation. Church leaders frequently noted the attention lavished on the kitchens in suburban churches, well-equipped rooms directly adjacent to the fellowship hall. In 1959, Edward Frey lamented, "I regret to say that I have visited many buildings in which the kitchen is the best planned room and the most adequate and best equipped for its function of any in the whole building complex. What can one believe about this other than that the congregation understands better what goes on in the kitchen than what is meant to happen in the sanctuary or in the classroom?"[56] The material evidence in suburban churches proves the validity of Frey's impression, and this certainly makes sense in light of suburban culture. If these churches were to be "homelike" and "friendly," then a great deal of importance would be assigned the "heart of the home," the kitchen, which provided "a commendable means of furthering the friendship and the functioning of the church."[57] Similar careful attention was poured into the kitchens of suburban homes, often sites for the newest technology and ideas about modern living.

John Scotford's church building manual often betrays his sexism, but never more blatantly than here: "the ideal church kitchen should inspire every woman who sees it to want to feed a man."[58] Not surprisingly, this does not appear to have been the motivation for the women who served on the postwar kitchen committee (although Figure 6.15 shows this principle in action). Women were serious about the business of cooking and carefully considered organization, sanitation, and safety when choosing the most up-to-date equipment the congregation could afford. Work in the church kitchen could undoubtedly be a chore, but it was also an outlet where suburban homemakers might take a public, professional approach to the labor that often defined them. Kitchen committees took note of best practices, especially with regard to handling dirty dishes and utensils. Stainless-steel surfaces and commercial dishwashers were the gold standard. The suburban church kitchen (for a sanctuary seating a few hundred) was organized around a central preparation area, often a stainless-steel table, with sinks, ovens, stove tops, and dishwashers around the edges of a room lined with cabinets and a maximum of counter space.

Betty Ackerman of First Presbyterian, La Grange, Illinois, recalled visiting many church kitchens with several other women on the kitchen committee, gathering ideas to help them design the most up-to-date kitchen possible. Carol Ferguson remembered with pride the state-of-the-art kitchen at her church in Fargo. She noted, "the big thing in the kitchen was the commercial dishwasher . . . it was a fabulous kitchen for the time."[59] First Presbyterian's kitchen was in constant use during the 1960s, for men's breakfasts, women's lunches, and family dinners. Cooking, Ackerman claimed, was the best way to get to know other women in the congregation, as they worked and talked together.[60] Even though the kitchens in many of these churches lack many of the amenities a congregation would want today (and most have undergone numerous renovations), they elicit happy memories for the people who found them fresh and new in the 1950s, particularly for the fellowship they fostered, as sites of meaningful common labor and good conversation.

Like other social spaces, the kitchen and its use changed during this period, and most kitchens were not as extensive or extravagant as the criticism would indicate.

Rather than supporting large banquets or fund-raising dinners, suburban church kitchens increasingly served as preparation and serving centers for frequent but smaller, more informal meals.[61] Kitchen volunteers became less interested in sequestering themselves in the kitchen, cooking and serving, but desired to be full participants in social events—one reason the informal potluck became more common as the sit-down prepared meal grew out of favor. In the larger suburban churches, the kitchens could still be quite large and therefore feel more industrial, and several of the kitchens in this study, such as the kitchen at Faith United Protestant Church in Park Forest, Illinois, are truly of commercial proportions. Many congregations managed to fit in the most up-to-date equipment in moderately sized spaces. But most suburban, particularly first-unit, churches had kitchens that appeared just as a larger version of a domestic example, such as Stade's kitchen for Salem United Church of Christ (Figure 6.16). A large, hooded range, a double sink, a central island work surface, and the stainless-steel serving cart were staples of the suburban church kitchen. Dart's early churches, in particular, tend to have small kitchens tucked into a back corner, such as the galley kitchen in the multipurpose room of the Lansing Presbyterian Church (see Figure 6.2).

Just as kitchens displayed flashy and efficient new technology, office spaces became increasingly professionalized and specialized. "Too many times in the past,

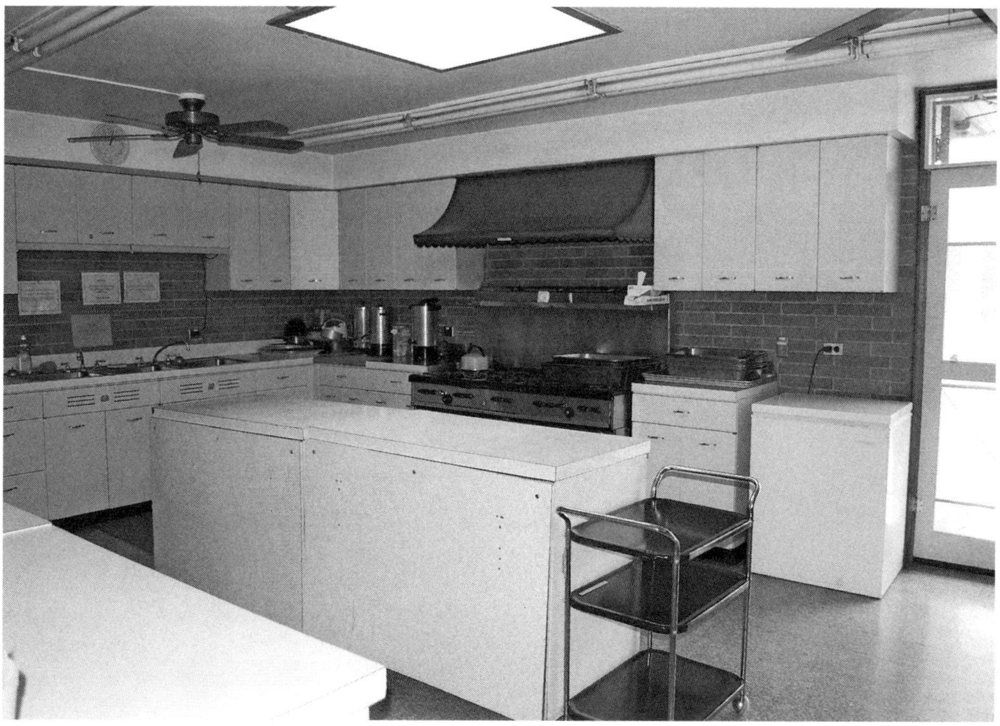

FIGURE 6.16. Charles Stade, Salem United Church of Christ, Oak Lawn, Illinois, 1962, kitchen. Photograph by the author.

the 'Church Office' was a left-over room, squeezed-in, adjacent to an entrance; at the top of a stairway; even an unused room in the parsonage."[62] A desire to professionalize the work and work space of the pastor and his staff is reflected in the office areas of the suburban churches. Figure 6.17 shows a delighted young pastor at his midcentury modern desk in his new office at St. Peter Lutheran Church, Arlington Heights, Illinois, the "smile" reminder on his desk putting an exclamation point on his enthusiasm. Pastor Bartz's clerical collar, nameplate, and Bible are the only things in the picture that suggest it is not the office of a rising young executive, complete with pen set, picture of wife and children, and wood paneling. William Clark's editorial in one of the first issues of the church building journal *Your Church* called for a new generation of church administration professionals capable of handling the more complex affairs of contemporary churches. He suggested that these employees should have a wide range of education in "*Psychology, Personnel Management, Accounting, Office Management, Purchasing, Publicity* and *Public Relations, Fund Raising, Recreational Programming and Direction,* as well as

FIGURE 6.17. Pastor Robert O. Bartz in his new office in St. Peter Lutheran Church, Arlington Heights, Illinois, ca. 1961. Courtesy of St. Peter Lutheran Church, Arlington Heights, Illinois.

*Educational Philosophy and Methods*."[63] That was no small feat, and the work spaces had to support this increasingly complex labor.

Office areas were the most consistently used spaces in the church, occupied six days a week. For convenience and also for surveillance, offices were typically located just off the main entrance, easily accessible and visible (Figure 6.18). Large windows enabled the office staff to keep watch over who entered and exited the building. Clergy were true professionals and required modern work spaces: a well-equipped office in a quiet corner that was *not* in one's own home, comfortable spaces for counseling, and technically efficient adjacent spaces for support staff. The work of filing membership and financial data, copying bulletins and newsletters, and preparing documents for mailing was ideally relegated to a separate workroom where unruly piles of paperwork would be less visible and disruptive. As churches grew and their staffs specialized, they required more task-specific offices, such as a library, music office, or Christian education office. Office spaces in the Stade, Dart, and Sövik churches are generally centrally located and equipped with an eye to efficiency. As in his houses, Stade used extensive built-in cabinets in office areas and frequently maintained an ecclesiastical sensibility by installing stained glass or large panels of colored glass, as at Hillside Methodist in Evanston, Illinois, or Messiah Lutheran, in Burlington, Iowa.

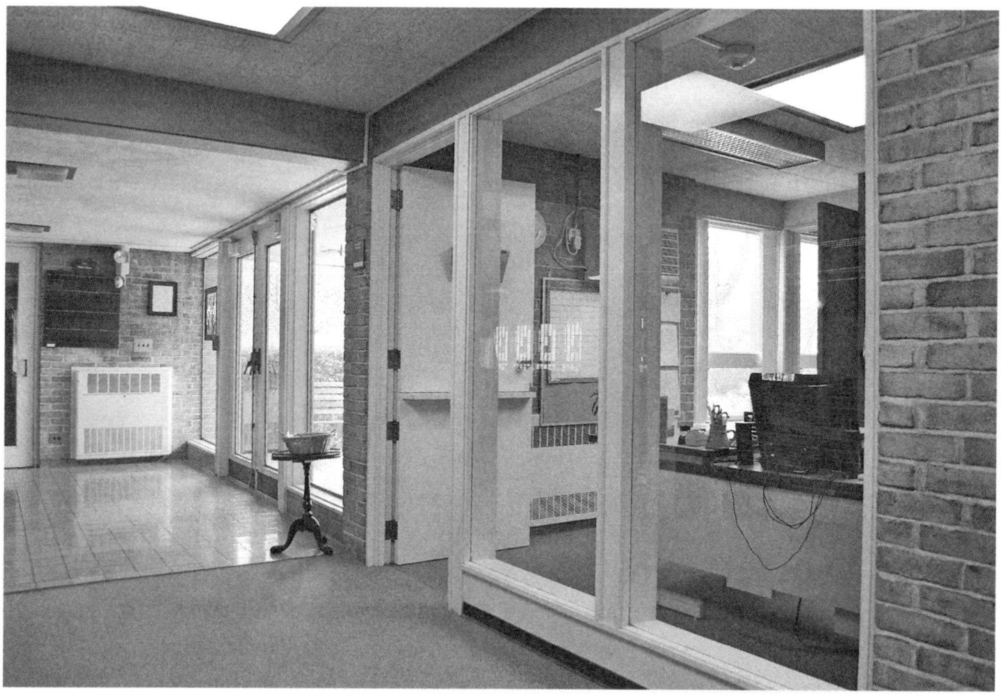

FIGURE 6.18. Charles Stade, Northbrook Methodist Church, Northbrook, Illinois, 1960, showing narthex with offices behind large glass windows. Photograph by the author.

## POSTWAR EDUCATION AND SOCIAL SPACES IN PERSPECTIVE

Practical necessity often limited the extent to which new ideas were applied to suburban church architecture, particularly in nonworship areas. For example, although the experts prescribed one-story education units, Midwestern churches often built two-story structures with double-loaded corridors, an efficient solution to the problem of organizing many small rooms conveniently. Furthermore, teachers often had to navigate shared space that was a far cry from what the experts recommended, conducting Sunday school in a basement or fellowship area that served double duty as classroom space, divided by curtains or the accordion walls so common in the churches of this era. Edward Dart, in particular, designed very few substantial education or social facilities for suburban churches because his churches were simply smaller overall, and a multipurpose basement, far from ideal, was the inexpensive solution at Dart churches such as St. Augustine of Canterbury, Benton Harbor, Michigan, or St. Augustine's in Gary, Indiana. It is clear that the quality of education and social spaces in suburban churches depended on the intention and skills of the architect, but even more so, on the resources of the congregation.

Small, multipurpose spaces, on the other hand, did avoid one criticism that larger, sprawling suburban churches attracted: the increasing isolation of church members and functions from one another. The "education wing" concept itself was of concern to some critics. This type of plan, they argued, "can cause young people and older ones as well, to think of education as divorced from the main life and principal activity of the church. Young people especially begin to think of 'their place' as opposed to adult areas."[64] It seemed to some that compartmentalization of grade-specific classes missed the big picture of the family of God worshipping and serving together. "What view of the church does a child have," questioned one church leader, "if he is dropped off at the parking lot and makes his way on a campus plan to a rabbit hutch cubicle in a hallway where he meets three other children and a well-meaning teacher; talks and reads and sings with them; turns out and follows the map to the parking lot?"[65]

The close relationship between churches and schools was both asset and liability. The architect Abraham Eastwood Jr. wrote in 1962 that "in most cases, where a photograph shows the worship unit and education unit together, if one covers the worship unit with any convenient piece of opaque paper, it is found that the education unit remaining appears as a typical public school."[66] Church leaders handed building committees and their architects a difficult task by asking them to convey a religious ethos and create spaces of transformation, but in buildings that "fit in" with the architecture of the day, were as up-to-date as the new model public schools, and facilitated the sorting of hundreds, if not thousands, of suburbanites through multiple Sunday morning sessions.

Religious leaders were, of course, aware that Sunday school had to be something more than a carbon copy of weekday public school. Architects and planners talked at length about building explicitly for Christian formation, yet it was difficult to materially distinguish these classrooms from those of the schools. Building fabric or details rarely provide clues that the structures were intended for religious purposes. Worship "centers," if they did exist in individual classrooms, might be temporary and undistinguished. Some educators suggested that Christian art and symbol would define these spaces. Others advocated displaying evidence of God's handiwork in the form of greenery. More often, a creative and open spirit and the skills of the teachers, rather than any distinctive material difference, established the character of the spaces. "How can Christian education buildings help create a climate of expectancy of the Holy Spirit?" asked one church educator. "Not by the use of children's chapels or stained glass windows in mysteriously darkened rooms. If the building facilitates a creative program, the teachers and learners can establish the climate of freedom and openness."[67]

As these experts suggested, both belonging and belief formed in the interplay of space and action. Jean Utes, a young member of the Church of the Holy Family in Park Forest, Illinois, with a salesman husband and a three-year-old daughter, claimed that her mother had wanted her to "center her life around the church . . . and that is what I've tried to do." She found the most important part of Christian fellowship to be not her attendance at meetings or social events but her participation in the shared work of the congregation. "Women could go to church every day of the week," she claimed, yet "not get to know other women intimately until they work as a group together."[68] For suburbanites like Jean Utes, Christian faith was most meaningful when the secular and the spiritual came together in shared community experiences, and those experiences were mediated by suburban church architecture.

Buildings fall into what David Morgan calls "the conditions that shape the feeling, emotions, senses, spaces, and performances of belief."[69] Sanctuaries, classrooms, fellowship halls, and kitchens—their stature, their relationships to each other, their textures, contours, and colors, even the way sounds echoed against their plain walls—inflected the religious experiences of millions of postwar Americans, week after week. As the culture moved into the 1960s and 1970s, the clearly defined social roles and middle-class, suburban "homeyness" that these buildings proclaimed no longer drew newcomers in the same way. Yet, in their heyday they supported the various church-based needs of the suburban Christian family and provided an effective setting for the shared time and work that created congregations out of crowds of newcomers.

These spaces today, particularly classrooms and fellowship areas, often appear worn and dated, testifying to the heavy use they have supported over the decades.

Although not the "dingy, dark brown gloom factory" of the prewar parish hall, they nonetheless do not easily communicate, at first glance, the excitement and appreciation of a generation of parents and children who encountered these spaces as modern and new. But the intention to be open and informal, the expectation of friendly and easy interaction among family members of all ages pursuing a multitude of church-related activities—this remains visible in the buildings.

CHAPTER 7

# Religion, Architecture, and Community in the Celebrated Suburb of Park Forest, Illinois

In the fall of 1948, thirty miles south of Chicago, the newly organized American Community Builders Corporation (ACB) began transforming twenty-four hundred acres of farmland into one of the first extensively planned postwar suburbs in America: Park Forest, Illinois. The investors and planners who created this community shared a vision for a new suburban experience. "We aren't interested in houses alone," claimed ACB president Philip Klutznik. "We are trying to create a better life for people."[1] By 1958, Park Forest was home to twenty-eight thousand people, many of them veterans with growing families (Figure 7.1). Park Forest was a complete community, an independent political unit with rental units and single-family houses, a central pedestrian shopping plaza, schools, municipal services, recreation areas, churches, and synagogues.

Park Forest is perhaps best known as William Whyte's primary research lab for his influential 1956 book *The Organization Man*.[2] Whyte's book, based on a series of *Fortune* articles about the character of the new white-collar worker and his family, hit a nerve with Americans suspicious of the social world of the new suburbs. Whyte identified a "social ethic" that valued "belongingness," a need that conflicted with expressive individuality. He believed that this social ethic, learned in the corporation, animated new suburbanites looking for a sense of home. This "secular faith," a largely unarticulated ideology about the individual's relationship to the group, required that conflict be minimized. Whyte did not claim that Park Forest was a typical suburb, and indeed it was not, but he did believe it threw American social and cultural trends into relief. With its uniform houses, tot lots, kaffeeklatsches, and proliferating clubs and social expectations, Park Forest was a harbinger of things to come. Whyte observed: "The schools are a little more modern than elsewhere, the politics a little more intense, and most certainly the social life is a lot more social. Abnormal? Or the new normality? Park Forest, one gets the feeling, is the way a lot of places are going to be."[3]

FIGURE 7.1. Aerial view of Park Forest, Illinois, showing the courts under construction, 1948–50. Courtesy of Park Forest Historical Society.

Through a close study of Park Forest's postwar architecture and institutions, this chapter examines a multidimensional, physical, and social context for modern suburban churches. A July 1953 article in the *Christian Science Monitor*, titled "Park Forest, Ill., Built to Order as Model for Future Community Growth," provided this glossy snapshot of the community: "Slums and uninvited industry kept out. Its schools are modern. Its streets are friendly and homelike. Its churches are modern."[4] Park Forest's "friendly" and "homelike" streets promised that Midwestern neighborliness would persist. Claims of modernism, on the other hand, indicated that the new town—including its churches—would take shape in conscious opposition to the past. What did the simple phrase "modern church" signify in Park Forest?

Park Forest's architects and planners designed the houses, central shopping area, and many of the schools and churches according to a coherent, contemporary aesthetic mapped onto long-standing ideals of American community. In wanting their churches to be fresh and relevant, religious congregations were no different from the builders of other Park Forest buildings. There were significant and meaningful architectural relationships among Park Forest's houses, schools, churches, stores, and offices. Inexpensive church education buildings, for instance, displayed a strong connection to the ideology and design of public schools. Similarities between shops, theater, and churches indicated a comfortable blending of middle-class consumerism and religious practice. Church building committees often used the language of "fitting in" to describe their architectural goals. As architect T. Norman Mansell wrote in 1953, "To have a church building contrast with the community's character and stand out like a sore thumb is no advantage."[5] But all was not conformity and capitulation. Hidden behind a shared Midwestern modernism, features of church architecture express the specific character of religious organizations. Church architecture proclaimed both ecumenical cooperation *and* the insistence on unique religious identities and practices within the broader religious community. Altogether, aspects of Park Forest's religious buildings suggest tensions between secular and religious life, economy and aspiration, and individuality and conformity that marked the postwar suburbs.

## A PLANNED COMMUNITY

Park Forest's Chicago investors recruited Philip M. Klutznick, an Omaha lawyer who had successfully worked in government housing development and reform during the war, to direct the project.[6] The Chicago architecture firm of Loebl, Schlossman, and Bennett served as community designers. The first housing consisted of 3,010 low-density rental units organized into "courts" grouped around parking lots, with shared green space (Figure 7.2). One- or two-bedroom units typically rented for between seventy-five and one hundred dollars per month, a bargain relative to Chicago prices.[7] By November 1949, there were already two thousand families renting these court units. Additional rental housing for a total of twelve thousand people was completed by 1951, and single-family houses soon followed. The modern, flexible, and safe spaces of the community's architecture and landscape responded primarily to the needs of these young parents and their active children. Under the direction of landscape architect Elbert Peets, a skilled designer known for his work on the New Deal–sponsored greenbelt town of Greendale, Wisconsin, the planners sought to enhance beauty and value by drawing from the picturesque tradition to create a landscape of open spaces and broad, winding streets. ACB's total investment in Park Forest eventually topped $60 million.[8]

Park Forest was for many a short-term home; the rental units had a 20–25 percent annual turnover in the early years.[9] Typical residents were young married couples with a child or two and more on the way. They possessed relatively educated and sophisticated tastes and, although not wealthy, anticipated a growing income. They were executive trainees, research chemists, army officers from the nearby base, pilots, editors, salesmen, and teachers.[10] Many residents came to Park Forest because it was affordable and within commuting distance of good jobs. It

FIGURE 7.2. Children on bikes in courts area of Park Forest. Vehicular traffic in these alleys was restricted to delivery trucks and fathers commuting to and from work. Courtesy of Park Forest Historical Society.

was difficult to find rental housing in Chicago that allowed children, and here was a safe community that welcomed families. The number of people who passed through the city is astounding; one member of Trinity Church claims that today "you can go anywhere in the world and meet someone who lived in Park Forest, or knew someone who did."[11]

Advertisements for the community stressed its social advantages. "You *Belong* in PARK FOREST!" claimed one ad. "The moment you come to our town you know: You're welcome. You're part of a big group. You can live in a friendly small town instead of a lonely big city. You can have friends who want you—and you can enjoy being with them."[12] Although such promotional materials promised a community with open arms, housing reflected the monolithic expectation that the building blocks of the community would be single-family units. Park Forest was less restrictive than many postwar suburbs (there were never legal race barriers, although FHA mortgage policies made racial integration nearly impossible, and there were tensions in 1959 when the first black family moved in), yet no rentals were offered to singles until 1956.[13] The young pastor of Trinity Lutheran Church, for instance, could not find housing in Park Forest until he married.

The first houses were the "Cape Cod" type, a ubiquitous form since the late 1930s (Figure 7.3). Although modern in plan, they had a traditional aspect, with peaked roofs and decorative shutters. By 1953, buyers could purchase the more contemporary "Futura" model, and split-levels were available by 1957. Park Forest's public buildings were distinctly modern from the outset. The commercial center, the Plaza, was near the geographic center of the village. Architect Richard Bennett laid out more than two hundred thousand square feet of retail space around an open, pedestrian courtyard (Figure 7.4).[14] At the edge of the mall was the 1,100-seat Holiday Theater, which opened in October 1950. With an eye to the needs of young families, it contained a "cry room," a soundproof room where parents and active young children could hear but not be heard, a space more commonly found in churches.[15] Many religious groups used this theater for worship and other church functions while they waited for their churches to be built, and some congregations continued to use the theater for special functions long after (Figure 7.5). It

FIGURE 7.3. New, single-family homes in Park Forest, showing winding street and preservation of old-growth trees. Courtesy of Park Forest Historical Society.

FIGURE 7.4. Holiday Theater and shopping center in Park Forest. Courtesy of Park Forest Historical Society.

FIGURE 7.5. United Protestant Church worshipping in Holiday Theater, 1950s. Courtesy of Park Forest Historical Society.

functioned as the chief public gathering place of the community, serving both sacred and secular purposes.

Whyte found a high degree of civic engagement among Park Foresters, particularly regarding education. Residents elected a school board in March 1949, and the board turned immediately to the problem of school buildings. ACB underwrote the nonprofit Park Forest School Building Corporation, and the first Park Forest school, Lakewood Elementary, designed by Loebl, Schlossman, and Bennett, opened in the fall of 1951 (Figure 7.6). Lakewood exemplified a common type of postwar elementary school: one level, two classrooms per grade, with administrative and classroom wings separated by a cafeteria/multipurpose room. By 1954 the same firm had designed four "modern and cheerful" Park Forest elementary schools: Lakewood, Sauk Trail, Dogwood, and Mohawk.[16]

A state-of-the-art high school opened in the fall of 1953. This bi-level building contained twenty-four classrooms plus a library, gym, shops, cafeteria, clubrooms, and music and activity rooms. Whyte described it as the "the new $1,600,000 'learning laboratory'" that would be "one of the most modern in the country."[17] A large part of the building was devoted to vocational training, and in general Park Forest's schools reflected a national trend away from traditional subjects and methods and toward practical knowledge supporting the "total growth of the child." The high school's "fine homemaking department" was notable for creating

FIGURE 7.6. Loebl, Schlossman, and Bennett, Lakewood Elementary School, Park Forest, Illinois, 1951. Courtesy of Park Forest Historical Society.

"the same surroundings that may be found in a beautiful home," including a "living-dining area, which is furnished like a model home, and which features a screened or glassed-in porch overlooking the landscaped lawn." The "light, airy, and comfortable" industrial arts area was designed to "provide boys and girls with exploratory learning experiences" and residents expected "full community use of special facilities."[18] Park Forest's school superintendent claimed that "ours is an age of group action" and believed that schools should encourage that trend.[19] These school buildings emphasized the comfortable and the domestic. Architectural boundaries between home and school were meant to recede in line with a holistic approach to the rearing of citizen-children. These emphases on domesticity, practicality, and "group action" shaped the architecture of Park Forest's churches as well.

## A PLAN FOR RELIGION IN PARK FOREST

Park Forest has a dynamic religious history, the story of booming, cooperating, and, at times, competing institutions. The developers believed their village needed to be anchored in religion in order to build a positive sense of community; they also knew that moral stability, demonstrated by the presence of churches and synagogues, was a selling point for their investment. "Any pattern for community living must include plans for a vital religious life," declared a promotional brochure.[20] Indeed, the "Prospectus for the Community" from July 25, 1946, specified that "areas are being set aside for churches. Any denomination will be provided with required land at little or no cost, but its plans for a structure will be subject to the approval of the town's architectural advisors. The aim, of course, is to maintain reasonable architectural standards."[21] ACB provided building sites to congregations and encouraged ecumenical activity. In their outlook, the developers reflected a pervasive sentiment best expressed in Will Herberg's 1955 book *Protestant—Catholic—Jew,* a sociological work that described an American religious life rooted in friendly relations between three separate faiths of the Judeo-Christian tradition, united by common social and ethical values.[22]

By 1960, a variety of religious groups were active in town, and ten had their own ecclesiastical buildings, distributed around the neighborhoods (Figures 7.7 and 7.8).[23] As this map indicates, churches were placed near major intersections, often bordered by schools and parks, indicating that they were conceptualized as part of the public landscape of the community. A 1963 register of ministers of all religious groups in Park Forest and the near vicinity also included the Institute for Research in Psychology and Religion, a Christian Science society, Village Bible Church, Friends meeting, a Unitarian congregation, and another Catholic parish, St. Mary's. More than fifty years later the casual observer sees about a dozen religious buildings that blend in with Park Forest's postwar, Midwestern, suburban character. Looking closely, we discover difference as well. A study of the original Catholic parish, five original Protestant congregations, and the Jewish community

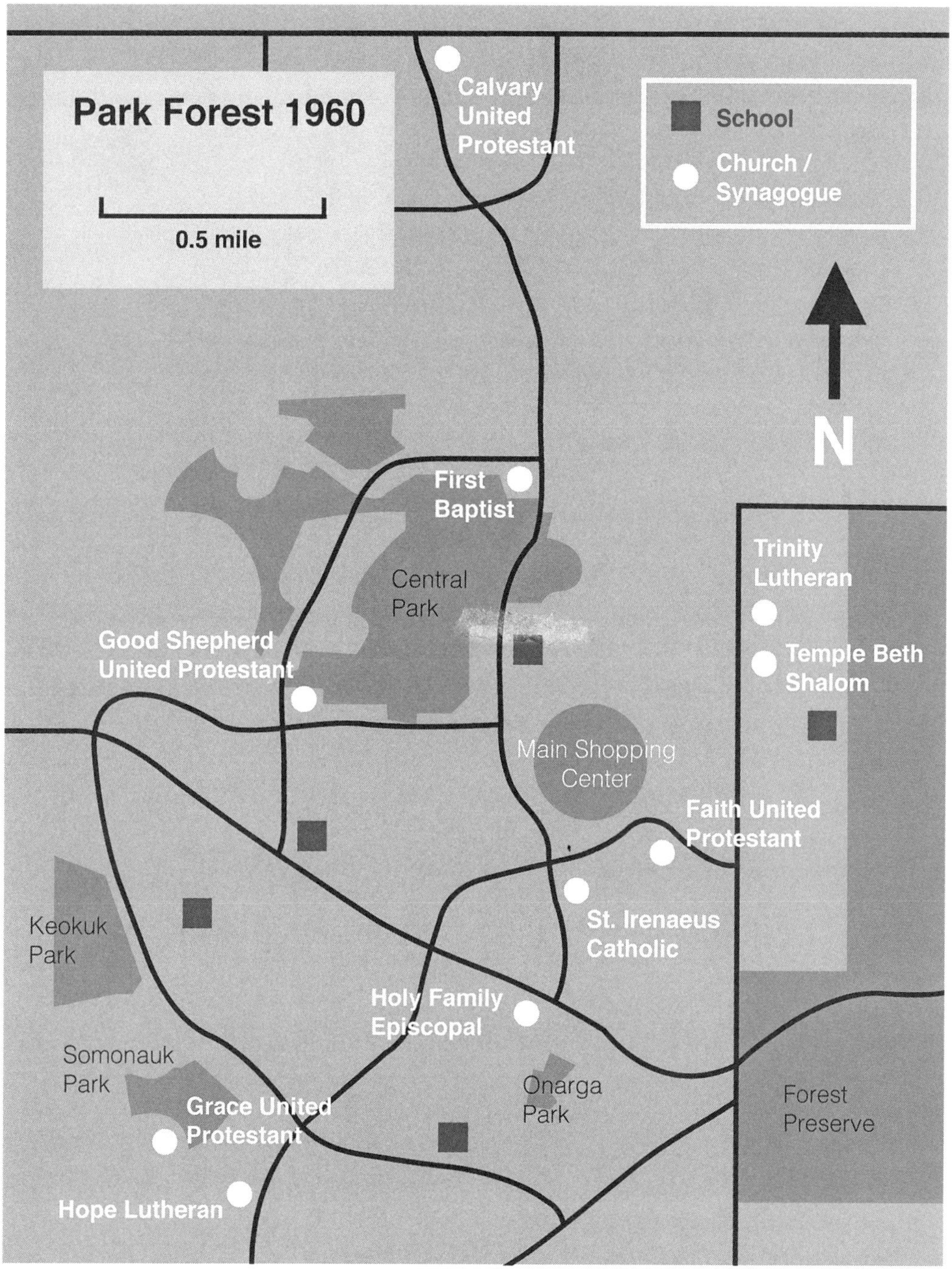


FIGURE 7.7. Churches in Park Forest, ca. 1960. Drawing by Jacob M. Just.

St. Irenaeus Roman Catholic Church, established 1948; school 1952, church 1964
Trinity Lutheran Church (Evangelical Synod), established 1949; first unit 1950, dedicated 1951; new church 1964
Faith United Protestant Church, established 1949; education building 1952, church 1958
Church of the Holy Family (Episcopal), established 1949; first unit 1954, church 1959
Hope Lutheran Church (Missouri Synod), established 1952; first unit 1954, school 1960, church 1967
Unitarian Fellowship, established 1952; meeting in schools during this period
Grace United Protestant Church, established 1953–54; church 1959, education building 1964
Congregation Beth Sholom (Reformed), established 1954; temple 1954
First Baptist Church, established 1954; education building 1958, church 1965
Good Shepherd United Protestant Church, established 1956; church 1959, education building 1962
Calvary United Protestant Church, established 1958; first unit 1958–59, church 1963

FIGURE 7.8. Park Forest churches and temple established in the 1940s and 1950s.

reveals an innovative, diverse, and assertive religious community. Churches had an undeniable social function, but for many residents, their religious affiliations signified considerably more than a social identity or a need for "belongingness."

The oldest congregation in Park Forest is the Catholic parish, St. Irenaeus, founded in 1948 by Chicago Cardinal Samuel Strich "to serve the people of a yet unnamed and unpopulated new village in the southern extreme of Cook County."[24] The congregation first celebrated mass at St. Anne's Chapel on Sauk Trail, a wood-frame church built originally for another local parish. When more space was necessary, the parish worshipped in the Holiday Theater. ACB gave St. Irenaeus a seven-and-a-half-acre parcel of swampy land at the intersection of Indianwood and Orchard, at the southern end of the plot designated for the central shopping center.

The parish made educational needs a priority and in 1950 broke ground for a large school. The parish education building and rectory opened in 1952, and mass was held in the school auditorium where, according to one church member, "you did your penance every Sunday" on the hard chairs and kneelers.[25] With 30 percent of Park Forest's population Catholic, St. Irenaeus had a ready congregation, although financial resources were limited. Members of the parish contributed much of the labor for construction and furnishing of the new buildings. Irene Hickey, who came from Peoria in 1952, remembers that when the priest dropped hints such as "don't you think we need some bookcases?" parishioners obediently set to work.[26]

However limited its financial means, the parish was rich in children. The school had a peak enrollment of 850 in 1960, with one hundred students in two classrooms per grade. Parishioners slept out on the lawn the night before school registration in order to secure a place for their children.[27] St. Irenaeus was very much a modern suburban congregation, well suited for a place like Park Forest. The parish quickly established a "tradition of involvement in the life of the community and in the advancement of ecumenical relations."[28] It was also the social world of many residents. For Park Forest's Catholics in these early years, who "didn't have any money to go out," life centered on the church. One couple, having moved from a very conservative church in New York, found St. Irenaeus "much more liberal," the congregation more active, and "priests very casual about coming to your house."[29] No one Catholic ethnic group predominated in this new suburban parish.[30]

The Catholic diocese was strong enough to foster the growth of the new parish. For Protestants and Jews, however, establishing a permanent presence in the community was more difficult. Klutznick, a Reform Jew, had been concerned about Park Forest's religious life as soon as the community was under consideration. In 1948 he sought advice from the Church Federation of Greater Chicago, a consortium of twenty-three Protestant denominations interested in planting congregations in the growing Chicago suburbs. The federation's director, John Harms, invited all denominations to send a representative to the newly formed Park Forest Council of Cooperating Denominations. Nine denominations responded. The council created a position of "Village Chaplain" and called Reverend Hugo Leinberger to the post in October 1948.[31] Leinberger "quickly became the most influential person in this new community."[32] Harms suggested that the chaplain serve the entire population while technically working for the sponsoring denominations.[33] Leinberger, a graduate of Union Seminary ordained in the Evangelical and Reformed Church, had been a navy chaplain in the Pacific. He went about his work with gusto, first taking account of the residents' religious leanings. Early surveys indicated that nearly half of the residents (49 percent) were Protestant, 29 percent Roman Catholic, 10 percent Jewish, and the rest had another or no affiliation.[34] Leinberger turned his attention primarily to the Protestants.

Church planning, organized by the council, a separate Layman's Group, and the chaplain, progressed in an original fashion. Thinking in terms of practice more than doctrine, the council recognized the "uniqueness of the Lutheran and Episcopalian faiths" but "urged that the minor differences among the other Protestant denominations do not justify the establishment of several separate denominational churches."[35] The second congregation in Park Forest, Trinity Lutheran (Evangelical Lutheran Church), organized with the ACB's blessing in 1949. Soon after, an Episcopal Congregation (Holy Family) established a core membership. These two congregations were to be *the* liturgical Protestant churches in town. Beyond this point, the array of diverse, struggling Protestant groups perplexed community leaders. Both the disorganization and the potential divisiveness of having many competing denominations threatened the establishment of viable churches and community cohesiveness. With limited capital all around, it was important that the denominations work together "to help us get started rather than struggling along for several years with inadequate church plans and programs."[36] The most efficient way to proceed, it seemed, was to unite forces to organize and build one Protestant church at a time.

Leinberger and volunteer laymen completed more extensive surveys of the residents and found that although about half of the Protestants identified themselves as Methodists or Presbyterians, denominational affiliation was less important to them than other factors, such as the quality of the minister, the location of the church, and educational programming. Many people were interested in the idea of a pan-Protestant congregation, encouraged by their recent experience with college fellowship groups and military chaplaincies. One resident recalls that Leinberger came to her house and said, "Well, you've both been in the service, how did it work for you to be in religious groups?" When she replied "Great, just fine," Leinberger asked, "Would you like to have that kind of church established here?"[37] Residents hoped to gather enough Protestants to hire both a senior pastor and a pastor of Christian education. Furthermore, "because at present we have no community center, school, auditorium, public library or other large meeting place," they reasoned, "we have urged the immediate building of a church which will be large enough to fill these needs and become the real center of every-day life of our community."[38] Even before construction, Park Foresters anticipated that their church buildings would serve wide and diverse roles in the community.

Religious life in Park Forest attracted broad attention in November 1949 when a controversial article appeared in *Christian Century* describing the state of Park Forest's Protestant churches. The author claimed that "denomination competition has brought to a stage of complete paralysis an intelligent and determined effort to meet the religious needs of a community."[39] Striking a foreboding tone, the author suggested that "the story of Park Forest raises some of the most important questions which must be answered if Protestantism is not to become a factor of dwindling significance in the urban development of America."[40] According to the author, the blame rested on church leadership, not the people of Park Forest, who were eager to have healthy religious institutions in their midst. The author noted that "families of all faiths have indicated a decided preference for community-type churches," not because they had no interest in maintaining denominational ties, but because they desired to "maintain the integrity of the community at all costs."[41] In large part, it was a financial problem: the Protestant residents did not have enough money to build their own churches and they wanted the denominations to provide start-up funds and loans. To be fair, the resources of the denominations were pulled in many directions as new congregations formed all over the region. Park Forest was just one of many communities in this predicament.

With their pioneering spirit and Leinberger's assistance, Park Foresters responded to this crisis by creating a "United Protestant Church." Five denominations (Methodist, Evangelical and Reformed, American Baptist, Presbyterians, and United Presbyterians) originally supported this umbrella organization.[42] By 1959, four such United Protestant (UPC) congregations had formed in Park Forest, distributed geographically within the village (see Figure 7.7).

William Whyte focused his discussion of Park Forest's Protestants on the first of these congregations (later named Faith UPC), the religious organization that most directly proved his point about the Organization Man. True, many residents were pleased with the UPC churches. Yet, other congregations chose to form as distinct Protestant bodies. Stan Boie and his wife Virginia, who moved into a Park Forest house in 1952, were founding members of Park Forest's Hope Lutheran Church–Missouri Synod (LCMS). Boie remembers the "Dutch Reformed Village chaplain" whose "dream was to have an ecumenical community."[43] As he recalled, Leinberger "rigged it so we couldn't find a place to worship" because he did not think Park Forest needed another Lutheran church (Trinity Lutheran had already been formed), and it was Boie's impression that Leinberger pressured the school district to refuse to rent the LCMS congregation a place for its services. Members of the Hope congregation went to Klutznick, Boie remembered, and Klutznick worked things out. Boie believed his wife infuriated the chaplain when he came calling and she said she would belong only to an LCMS church; he slammed the door and left. It was a point of pride and identity for these Lutherans, as well as some others in the community, that they did not melt into an undifferentiated Protestant mix but held to their unique traditions.[44]

The UPC advocates expected their innovation to spread like wildfire across America as "a pacesetter for other communities and a model for the future of church life in America."[45] By 1960, the four active UPC congregations were working together under the collaborative United Protestant Council. But many residents had no intention of washing out their denominational identity. One young member of Trinity Lutheran claimed that this was a pure and simple issue of religious freedom, and he felt "a revulsion from any plan of herding citizens of varied religious backgrounds and sentiments into a conglomerate religious organization without any freedom of choice."[46] While the United Protestant movement had a tremendous impact in the community and an ecumenical spirit largely prevailed, it remained a local phenomenon. By 1960, religious life in Park Forest was much as it was in other postwar suburbs.[47]

Many of the same social and financial forces shaping the Christian denominations came to bear on Park Forest's Jews. Sociologist Herbert Gans critiqued this community in two articles he published in *Commentary*, the first in 1951 and the second in 1957.[48] Like Whyte, Gans claimed the Park Forest experience was a sign of what was coming nationwide, an indication of how an American-born generation of Jews would navigate the postwar world. Gans's initial findings (based on research from 1949) were controversial, and Park Forest's Jews themselves contested some of his conclusions.[49] He studied about 150 Jewish families, and found that they tended to be liberal and nonobservant, although inclined to make friends with others of their faith in the community despite being geographically scattered. Jewish organizations formed rapidly, including a B'nai B'rith lodge, a chapter of the National Council of Jewish Women, a Board of Jewish Education, and a Sunday school.[50] Significantly for Gans, the Jews did *not* immediately found a temple, and he saw the Jewish Sunday school not as Hebrew school but as an American response to Christian Sunday school.[51] Although a young Chicago rabbi had encouraged the Sunday school as a way to train children and prepare them for an eventual synagogue, Gans found that the parents were mostly opposed to anything that would "put pressure on [them] to *observe* these traditions in the home" and preferred a secular curriculum.[52] He believed Park Forest's Jews wanted their children to learn about Jewish identity to prepare them for prejudice they would inevitably face, but did not want to change their mainstream, middle-class American lifestyles at home. Park Forest's lack of an older generation, traditionally the bearers of Jewish practices, was particularly disruptive; lacking example and momentum, a secular lifestyle seemed to come easily.[53] Gans argued that there was a tension between "adult-centered" Jews, primarily well-heeled men desiring the establishment of congregations and ritual practices, and Jews who were "children-centered," middle-class women advocating a nondenominational Sunday school for Jewish children.

When he revisited Park Forest in 1955, Gans found a Jewish community that had grown to nearly seven hundred families and supported a Reform congregation, Beth Sholom, with a full-time rabbi. Beth Sholom dated from January 1951 when twenty-two families began meeting in a variety of locations, including the Sauk Trail School, ACB headquarters, and the fellowship hall of Trinity Lutheran Church, where they met for Friday night Sabbath services (covering up the cross and prominently displaying the Torah).[54] At first they seemed to take a page from the United Protestant movement and recommended "a United congregation designed to serve orthodox, conservative and reform groups."[55] This idea ultimately fell flat; Congregation Beth Sholom was Reform, and a Conservative congregation, South Suburban, organized in 1956. At the time of Gans's return, the Sunday school was still going strong, but Beth Sholom had recently dedicated its synagogue, "and all the evidence suggested that it was now the Jewish community's central institution."[56] Membership in 1955 was about 35–40 percent of Park Forest's total Jewish population, and the religious tone of the organization "combined Reform permissiveness about religious practices in the home with a quasi-Conservative array of ceremonials, Hebrew reading, and responsive singing at services."[57] In 1955, Congregation Beth Sholom started its own Sunday school and was teaching a smaller number of children in weekday Hebrew/religious school. In a printed response to Gans's article, Beth Sholom's rabbi and congregational president insisted that the community was neither adult- nor child-oriented but "a *family*-oriented institution with a program of activities established to meet the religious, social, and educational needs of both child and parent."[58]

## PARK FOREST'S RELIGIOUS ORGANIZATIONS AND THEIR ARCHITECTURE

The primacy of religious education, an emphasis on the family and family programming, an overwhelming social function, a lack of deep-rooted faith commitment, and a thin religious identity—this characterization of the new suburban churches began in the 1950s with critics such as Gans and Whyte. To this day, the blandness and ineffectiveness of religious life in the suburbs is a long-standing shibboleth invoked by urbanites, suburbanites themselves, church leaders, and even rock musicians. What can these Park Forest organizations and their architecture tell us about the truth of these accusations?

### *Trinity Lutheran Church*

In the fall of 1949, members of what would become Trinity Lutheran congregation began meeting in one of the rental units. The Evangelical Lutheran Church approved a fifty thousand–dollar building loan, and by the end of 1950 the congregation was worshipping in its new church, the first religious structure in Park Forest (Figure 7.9).[59] The architect of this first-unit structure was the chief designer for the town, Richard M. Bennett. A Harvard Architecture School graduate,

FIGURE 7.9. Pastor Neal S. Johnson standing in front of Richard Bennett's first Trinity Lutheran Church (dedicated in 1951), Park Forest, Illinois, 1950. Postcard in author's collection.

Bennett was chair of the architecture department at Yale when Sövik and Dart were students, and was well known for his suburban designs, especially houses and shopping centers. But he was also very interested in church and temple architecture, and published a book on the subject with Paul Thiry and Henry L. Kamphoefner in 1953, for which he wrote the section on Jewish temples.[60] Bennett's first Trinity Church was a simple, thirty-five-thousand–dollar California redwood structure designed as an adaptable, two-story building housing classrooms and offices, with a chapel area seating 168 on the southern end of the second floor. A three-bedroom parsonage was connected by a covered walkway.[61] Casual aesthetics and mixed functions gave the church complex a domestic feel, and it appeared like a modified cape house, with its entrance on the long side, pitched roof, and large clear windows. Inside and out, rough wood paneling covered the walls. A large white cross, formed by one post of the entry canopy, marked the building as a church. The church thanked the architect for a church building that "captured the spiritual tone which a church should stand for in the community."[62]

By 1953, with 250 confirmed members and four hundred Sunday school children, the small church was packed with people, and activities spilled over into classrooms at Dogwood School. Proximity to the courts might have helped draw members. Marge Roeder recalls that she lived very close to the church and first came for a potluck supper.[63] In 1956, the congregation authorized plans for a new building and again chose Bennett as architect. The new sanctuary (1958) was bigger and more adventurous than the first unit, reflecting both the expanded financial base of the congregation and the increasingly experimental tone of church architecture (Figure 7.10). Its distinctive saddleback ("hyperbolic paraboloid") roof, constructed, as the press noted, on eighteen-inch concrete walls, sheltered a cave-like worship space that seated 450.[64] The emphasis was on natural materials: wood, brick, concrete floors, pine paneling, and limed oak pews. Along with the worship space, the addition included offices, a new kitchen, fellowship hall, and nursery. The old church was transformed into an education wing. A brochure noted that the "completely functional" new building combined "old and new," and the "emphasis on natural materials has produced an overall warmth, and yet a dignified, reverent feeling within the sanctuary."[65] Trinity housed many activities beyond the Sunday morning program: preschool, scouts, Vacation Bible School, Kiwanis, Luther League, Women's and Men's clubs, banquets, and bazaars. The dedication book for the second sanctuary claimed that the building provided a space for "translating the Christian faith into a compelling seven-day-a-week outreach into the common life."[66]

Trinity built this outreach program from the village chaplain's survey results (targeting those who self-identified as Lutheran) as well as its own guest book and Sunday school records. The church mailed an informative leaflet and invitation to every contact, followed up by a phone call and a personal visit. The congregation

FIGURE 7.10. Richard Bennett, Trinity Lutheran Church, Park Forest, Illinois, new sanctuary, 1958. Photograph by the author.

was healthy but never wealthy, and this is evident in the practicality of the building. Nonetheless, the church served its purpose, and a stall in membership gains was attributed by the congregation not to the facilities but to a lack of "friendliness" (persons were "sometimes overlooked for three or four Sundays") or the fact that newcomers "lost interest because they were not put to work" fast enough.[67]

### *Faith United Protestant Church*

Surely the most striking of Park Forest's postwar churches, in terms of both organization and architecture, was the first United Protestant Church (after 1955 called Faith UPC), the first congregation to arise from Park Forest's ecumenical Protestant movement. Many new residents of Park Forest gravitated to (or were steered toward) this active, ecumenical church. Membership did not require relinquishing one's denominational affiliation, and each UPC congregation was sponsored by one denomination that provided financial support and pastoral staff.[68] Faith was affiliated with the Evangelical and Reformed Church initially, and after a 1957 merger with the Congregationalists, the United Church of Christ (UCC). In 1951, Reverend Gerson Englemann, who, like Leinberger, had a Dutch Reformed background, arrived as minister and stayed for nearly twenty-five years.

The congregation initially met in a nursery school and later the Holiday Theater. It rapidly drew members, most of them with young children. The first building project was a badly needed education facility. By 1951, when the congregation broke ground for construction, there were more than five hundred members representing thirty-five different Protestant denominations, but money was scarce. Reverend Englemann told a *Christian Science Monitor* reporter, "It's a community of people with income, but not with capital . . . They can buy Cadillacs on time, but most of them do not have ready cash for a pair of shoes."[69] Together with a one hundred thousand-dollar loan from the Evangelical and Reformed Church, the mostly lay-led congregation managed a building campaign without a pledge drive.[70] The leadership felt it was not appropriate to solicit the members for a multiple-year building fund commitment because of the instability of the population. Instead, each member was asked to make one annual pledge to the general church fund. An additional ten thousand dollars was raised by the sale of twenty-five-dollar bonds, a good strategy for gathering financial assistance from nonchurch members; according to two longtime members, "most of our fathers bought them."[71] A mid-1950s brochure, *Your Church in Park Forest,* suggests that one of the potential objections to giving was that the residents knew their stay in Park Forest would likely be temporary, and they were thus unsure about investing in big projects. This highlights the financial difficulty of building churches among suburban transients. Churches responded by representing church building as an activity with ramifications beyond one's particular congregation—not just a payment for a service, but a gift to the present and future congregation.

Architects Paul Schweikher and Wilson Elting, well-established Chicago modernists who had designed a small number of notable churches, created the UPC's education wing as the first phase of a projected three-unit project.[72] The $155,000, twenty-three classroom building, dedicated in April 1952, proved a good match for the needs of the congregation and community (Figure 7.11). Frank Klein, chairman of the building committee and structural engineer for the project, called the building "a modern functional building that embodies simplicity, utility, integrity, and dignity; one that is designed to meet our needs and scaled to fit our community."[73] Its wood construction contrasts with rugged end walls of granite embedded in concrete. The building served many purposes in Park Forest and saw heavy use from the day it opened. By 1952, nearly one thousand children were enrolled in two sessions of Sunday school, and the building instantly became a center for all kinds of civic activity. The very first event it hosted was the bar mitzvah luncheon of the eldest Klutznick boy, and it briefly served as the community's first high school, housing the ninth grade in 1952–53. *Newsweek* called the "sunny building" a "living example of interdenominational friendship."[74]

Whyte, commenting on the structure in 1953, recognized that "a good part of the physical plant represents evening and weekend hours given up by many a weary young executive."[75] In fact, swinging a hammer on such a building project might have been exactly what those "weary young executives" needed. Lucy Klein, Frank's

FIGURE 7.11. Schweikher and Elting, Faith United Protestant Church, Park Forest, Illinois, education wing, 1952. Paul Schweikher Collection, Archives and Special Collections, Architecture and Environmental Design Library, University Libraries, Arizona State University.

wife, believed it was the work of church building and the experimental nature of the UPC project that drew Frank, a disinterested former Catholic, into the church. For Frank, these projects set the pattern for a lifetime of faithful involvement.[76]

In 1958, the congregation dedicated its Schweikher–Elting six-hundred-seat sanctuary building that included a two-story fellowship area. At this time, Faith had 1,400 members and a whopping 1,500 children in Sunday school. The four hundred thousand–dollar structure, built in a blocky, austere manner reflected, according to Elting, the "idea of the church as a rock" (Figures 7.12 and 7.13).[77] Klein promoted its stark modernism to a congregation that was uneasy with the design; some said it looked like a warehouse, and many raised the understandable objection that it did not "look like a church."[78] From the north entrance, the building appears like a massive fort, but the east and west glass walls suggest openness. A pipe organ was intended for the west wall, behind the altar, but the cost was prohibitive, so the congregation chose a less expensive alternative, a chancel screen designed by Chicago artist Angelo Testa, containing hundreds of colored, translucent Fiberglass discs.[79] In the sanctuary, surfaces are industrial: bent plywood pews on metal legs,

FIGURE 7.12. Schweikher and Elting, Faith United Protestant Church, Park Forest, Illinois, 1958. Paul Schweikher Collection, Archives and Special Collections, Architecture and Environmental Design Library, University Libraries, Arizona State University.

FIGURE 7.13. Faith United Protestant Church, Park Forest, Illinois, sanctuary. Paul Schweikher Collection, Archives and Special Collections, Architecture and Environmental Design Library, University Libraries, Arizona State University.

rough concrete walls and floors. The clear glass in the east wall appears to proclaim transparency, but it was intended to be opaque stained glass. For several years curtains hung down to block the sun, and the intense light soon degraded the fabric. Lucy Klein states, "We wished we had the money to follow the designs exactly."[80] Such accounts illustrate how economy often shaped aesthetic choices.

The architecture of Faith UPC matches its ecumenical and pioneering vision. There is less of the traditional church in this structure than in any other of Park Forest's religious buildings, and perhaps more of the corporation. It is the least harmonious with other community architecture, especially its massive sanctuary, which is similar to other Schweikher and Elting churches. The language used by the congregation and the architects to describe Faith Church is intriguing. Elting, writing at the dedication of the Bell Tower, finally completed in 1963, reiterated the fit between building and the community. "These buildings," he claimed, "would not be possible in some communities. They are not sufficiently smug, self-satisfied, pretentious."[81] Did claims such as these truly reflect design intention, or did they merely gild a necessary economy? As these congregations marked themselves as different from both the urban churches many of their members left behind and more established and wealthier suburban churches, it is likely that both dynamics—aspiration and necessity—came into play.[82]

### *Hope Lutheran Church*

By May 1952 the Lutheran Church–Missouri Synod had identified about seventy LCMS families in Park Forest and sent Luther Bekemeier, a graduating seminarian, to start a church. Stan Boie, a Hope founding member who moved to Park Forest in 1952, recalled: "we were typical early Park Foresters—I was a veteran, I was married, I had three kids."[83] Boie was living in an apartment on the South Side and working in publishing. The appeal of an affordable single-family home, a good-sized yard, and good schools drew his family to Park Forest, and he commuted by train to his publishing job in Chicago. It was "miraculous in some ways, what [Park Forest] did for the postwar GIs," he recalled. There were "kids all over the place."[84] Although young, he had worked for four years for synod youth organizations, and the congregation elected him its first president. The first thing they did, he remembered, was to "knock out a constitution" and begin a Sunday school for the "wall-to-wall kids."[85]

While meeting in local schools the congregation obtained, as a donation from ACB, a deed for property near the center of the new single-family homes area.[86] They were enthusiastic about the location, noting that "90 percent of Park Forest's home owners will live within a mile of the church, and 75 percent of church members are home owners."[87] Homeowner members, rather than renters, were the key to congregational stability, and the time was ripe to build a church. School buildings did not offer "an appropriate atmosphere for proper worship," and were inadequate for "good Christian training of our Sunday school children." Furthermore, these public buildings could not provide "for the many other important aspects of congregational life—choir, society activities, opportunities for Christian fellowship."[88] Members of the congregation met with Charles Stade in November 1952, and construction began late in 1953.

Boie remembers that the congregation had to fight with the denomination to get Hope enough money to build a decent church. He claimed that "they thought a mission church was a little white church in the middle of a cornfield," but Park Forest residents were a "different breed of cat . . . young, upwardly mobile, moved around," and these bold young residents told the district they would look elsewhere if they did not get the support they needed.[89] The kind of conversations Boie describes between denomination, congregation, and architect set the tone for the decade of church building to follow. What Boie noted about the modern taste of the young Park Foresters was also remarked upon by Whyte and others; they were young, but they were educated and savvy about contemporary design, and a cheap, traditional structure did not fit their idea of community or mission.

Stade designed Hope's first unit as a small sanctuary and service education wing (Figure 7.14). He later designed Hope's parochial school of 1960 and a much larger 1967 sanctuary (Figure 7.15). The original church seated two hundred in a rectangular nave, with a meeting room to the back that could open into overflow seating for an additional hundred. The basement consisted primarily of a social hall, divisible into smaller rooms, with a stage and a kitchen. By building into a hillside, Stade created a walkout basement with plentiful natural light. This church displays all the material and symbolic advantages of the suburban A-frame: its "happy combination of beauty and utility . . . must lift the hearts and minds of men above the earthbound," stated the fund-raising brochure. The language of fitting in also appears: designed to be "contemporary," the church is "in harmony with the theme of the community."[90]

Boie remembers telling the district leadership that "every church that's built out here [Park Forest] was built too small," and indeed, Hope's congregation "outgrew that church in about a year, to the point where we had three sessions of Sunday school and used the school buses as classrooms."[91] Hope quickly became a large and complex parish, with Vacation Bible Schools, a kindergarten, many clubs, scouts, and bowling groups. As Boie recalls, "we even tried our hand at flooding part of the church property for an ice-skating rink during the winter of 1955."[92] Mixed in with serious conversations about furthering the Lord's work in Park Forest, the congregation exercised a wry sensibility about suburbia. A 1955 Advent event adopted the theme "Suburban Christmas Carols" and the congregation sang "O Little Town of Worn-Out Men," "Behold a Ranch-House Growing," and "Hark, the Herald Ad-Men Sing."[93]

FIGURE 7.14. Charles Stade, Hope Lutheran Church, Park Forest, Illinois, 1954, first-unit church. Courtesy of Park Forest Historical Society.

FIGURE 7.15. Charles Stade, Hope Lutheran Church, Park Forest, Illinois, 1967, second church. Photograph by the author.

In 1962, when the congregation began planning ambitiously for a large addition, including a new sanctuary, Stade was called in again. The second church, dedicated in 1967, shows Stade in a later, less traditional phase, with a substantial, open bell tower. This second church no longer expresses the "tent for the people of God on the move" lightness of the earlier church but is more fortresslike, firmly planted on its site.

### *Church of the Holy Family (Episcopal)*

Like Hope Lutheran, the Church of the Holy Family (Episcopal) possessed a sense of its unique role in the religious life of Park Forest. It began as a mission congregation of the diocese in 1949, first meeting in the basement of the ACB office and Lakewood Elementary School. The number of Episcopalians in Park Forest never reached that of the other major denominations and the finances of the congregation were occasionally precarious, which was frustrating when combined with the high expectations of the diocese. Despite its internal financial struggles, for instance, the congregation received a letter from the bishop in 1953 reprimanding them for not giving outside their local mission.[94] Put into the context of such financial pressures, the cheapness of many of these 1950s churches is understandable.

Before building its first church, the congregation investigated requirements of the ACB regarding cost and such matters as "physical appearance, type, size, etc."[95] In 1952, ACB gave the congregation a two-bedroom house and lot at the corner of Orchard Drive and Sauk Trail. The original, thirty thousand–dollar 1954 church was a very small, inexpensive structure, although not without architectural character.[96] The twenty-four-year-old vicar, John Ruef, wanted an architecture that would "fit in with the prevailing architecture of the neighborhood" and consequently the multipurpose building had a redwood and Lannon stone exterior. Parishioners themselves built a small addition with kitchen, office, and restroom.[97]

In 1954, a new vicar, Robert Ruffie, arrived. Father Ruffie was an Anglo-Catholic who, together with the bishop, wanted Holy Family to promote traditional and formal liturgy with extensive symbolism, Stations of the Cross, shrines, votives, and incense. Holy Family thus had the most formal Christian worship in Park Forest during these decades, and one senses in the records and the architecture a conscious declaration of difference. Through a 1955 canvass, the parish learned that many of the church's families had "mixed religious backgrounds" and had chosen the Episcopal church as a means of bringing "religious solidarity in their families." The parish felt that allegiance to tradition and formality was an advantage; with competition for distinctive and traditional worship narrowed by the large pan-Protestant churches, its own prospect for growth was greater, and it sanguinely expected Holy Family to grow to be the largest Episcopal parish in the diocese outside of Chicago.

When the need for a larger building became urgent, Holy Family's building committee interviewed six architects and chose Edward Dart, whose work they no doubt knew through Episcopal circles.[98] His $130,000 church, with its solid, cut-stone wall, high-pitched roof, and cruciform roof plan with the altar on a dais at the crossing, evokes both tradition and "religious solidarity" (Figures 7.16 and 7.17). A letter from the building committee to the Episcopal bishop of Chicago in 1957 described the plans: "The contemporary structure will combine the classical feature of cruciform roof on a rectangular floor plan . . . The windowless stone wall surrounding the church will symbolize the Christian principle that Christians, though living in the world are not to be of the world, but rather, set apart."[99] Thus, the Holy Family parish consciously matched its building with a theological idea.

The congregation's relationship with Dart was uneven. The building committee complained of inadequate supervision, poor quality of the laminated beams and trusses, and cracks in foundation walls (which were also bowing).[100] Symptomatic of the building's failings, the two peaks of the roof were misaligned, leading to an eighteen-inch discrepancy that still shows. Dart, at the time stretched between several projects, was not on-site to witness this disaster, and he wrote to the builders accusing them of not following the specifications.[101] The cracks in the foundation led to a wet basement, where the primary grades met in a large multipurpose space, with movable partitions separating their classes. Although an

FIGURE 7.16. Edward Dart, Church of the Holy Family (Episcopal), Park Forest, Illinois, 1959. Photograph by the author.

FIGURE 7.17. Church of the Holy Family (Episcopal), Park Forest, Illinois, sanctuary. Photograph by the author.

improvement over the previous, crowded arrangement, and perhaps a necessity given the small lot, the basement reflects very little of the advice of church leaders regarding education spaces in the new churches.

Despite these problems, the congregation was satisfied with the design. The dedication bulletin highlighted the symbolism of the form, which showed "the world the redemption offered to all by Jesus Christ and his Church." The sanctuary fits about two hundred, not large enough for the congregation at its peak membership during the 1960s; until the 1970s, there were folding chairs in the aisles and the children sometimes had a separate worship service in the parish hall (the old sanctuary).[102] Father Ruffie insisted on effective artwork, and worked with the St. Gregory art studio to acquire new furnishings and vestments. A new limestone altar and font created by Dom Francis Bacon, an Anglican Benedictine Monk, arrived in 1961. Behind the altar hangs a reredos consisting of five wrought-iron figures covered with silver leaf, with mosaic tile halos. On the exterior of the chancel wall, a black redwood distressed cross holds a "suffering Christ," designed by the Philadelphia artist Odell Prather to show "Christ emptying himself completely for love of humanity." Some in the parish found this graphic depiction, with Christ's "flayed flesh and gutted anatomy," ultramodern and distasteful, not exactly a match for Park Forest's cheerful outlook, but the will of the rector prevailed.[103]

### *First Baptist Church*

Tradition was also crucially significant for Park Forest's Baptists, who began meeting in the summer of 1953 with the guidance of a professor from Northern Baptist Theological Seminary. The group formally organized in 1954 with help from the Chicago Baptist Association. By this time Park Forest's developers had already assigned their allotted land to religious groups and, as one Baptist remembers, they "encouraged us to affiliate with the United Protestant Church, but we felt we wanted to be our own entity."[104] The group, holding services in the high school, accepted the fact that the free plots were taken, but "at first we were upset because at that time there was still a lot of vacant land" and no independent Baptist church. By 1955, ACB claimed it had already given nine sites—four UPC, two Lutheran, one Catholic, one Episcopal, and one Jewish, and "felt they had fulfilled their commitment to the village and Council of Cooperating Denominations."[105] But it did offer to sell additional land at cost, and in 1956 the Baptists were able to buy 3.3 acres in the northern part of Park Forest, at the corner of Westwood and Orchard. Although officially an American Baptist congregation, a large number of members of this group were former Southern Baptists, who tended to be more conservative and not likely to merge with the UPC of Park Forest. This congregation became the place, for instance, for those who wanted full immersion baptism.

With a strong tradition of tithing, the Baptists were able to build quickly. Their first objective was an education wing. Architects Robert Taylor and Derald West of Oak Park, Illinois, designed the $110,000 first unit as a utilitarian building, its downstairs assembly room used temporarily for worship (Figure 7.18). This building type is typical of the extremely common, rectangular, unadorned, inexpensive education wings of the era. Construction was bare-bones: face brick, concrete floors, laminated wood beams, and acoustical tile ceilings in the classrooms, with "color schemes specifically designed for each age group" and "movable partitions . . . to permit flexible use of various rooms."[106]

By 1964, more than six hundred children filled the Sunday school and the congregation was pressured to increase the size of the facility. Although Taylor and West had planned a sanctuary and chapel at the time of the construction of the education wing, the congregation now turned to William Cooley, Stade's former partner (Figure 7.19). This 1965 sanctuary is a typical A-frame on the outside, with a large chancel window, but inside the arrangement is distinctive. Whereas many churches at this time were minimizing the visibility of the choir, here it is showcased by the tiered choir seats behind the raised pulpit, with a choir room under the chancel. A former member notes that "some churches were having choir lofts to the rear of the church but we chose and liked the fact that the choir was up and back of the pulpit."[107]

Members recall that "people felt a part of the church and it was easy to donate your time."[108] As with all the congregations in Park Forest, the Baptists had to

FIGURE 7.18. Robert Taylor and Derald West, First Baptist Church, Park Forest, Illinois, 1958, education building. Photograph by the author.

FIGURE 7.19. William Cooley, First Baptist Church, Park Forest, Illinois, 1965. The church originally had a slender white steeple over the front, chancel end of the sanctuary. Photograph by the author.

contend with a revolving membership: "You came in, you got elected to a board, and you were transferred out."[109] First Baptist was a busy, racially integrated congregation (by the 1960s) of independent-minded souls. This was the nature of Baptists: independent, determined to exercise freedom of conscience and to emphasize the priesthood of all believers. Like the Episcopalians, denominational identity had a cherished meaning for this congregation with a keen sense of its particular mission in the community. At the dedication of the new church the pastor declared, "God really built this church! He brought a dream to the hearts of the organizing families. He led as men, women, boys, and girls from many different backgrounds and every section of our country moved to this area and came to our church . . . how much more is there to be done for the glory of God . . . how wonderful it is to have a church such as this as a help to carry out his plan!"[110]

These five congregations set the tone for the Christian churches in Park Forest. They were soon followed by three more United Protestant Churches: Grace (1954), Good Shepherd (1956), and Calvary (1958). Calvary, in partnership with the Presbyterian church, was the first Protestant church in Park Forest to begin with stock church plans provided by the denomination. Like Presbyterian churches elsewhere, its design was modern in concept with the red brick and white trim typical of a Colonial Revival building, demonstrating the strength of the American Presbyterian church's cultural ties to its early American past. The first unit was an intriguing split-level design, echoing the increasing popularity of that house type, with a second-story loft that could be closed off by a folding screen or open to the hall below (Figure 7.20). This building was repurposed in 1963 after the construction of a larger A-frame sanctuary.

Albert Ramp's Christian Science Church of 1962 is one of the most nonchurch-like of Park Forest's religious buildings, yet it, too, demonstrates the prevailing suburban aesthetic and the nature of suburban congregational life. Reflecting contemporary Christian Science practice, the original building had a lecture hall, small side rooms, and bathrooms. Sunday school met in a nearby recreation center and school, where the church also held social events. In the 1970s the church built an addition and renovated according to suburban norms. Changes included an updated auditorium with pews and carpet, new common space, and additional rooms for the large Sunday school.[111]

### *St. Irenaeus Catholic Church*

St. Irenaeus, Park Forest's oldest congregation, took longest to build its sanctuary. For fifteen years the parish experienced the full range of church activities in a building that was solidly institutional—a school, indistinguishable from secular buildings except for the statuary in the front garden (Figure 7.21). In 1964, something of

FIGURE 7.20. Calvary United Protestant Church, Park Forest, Illinois, 1958–59, 1963. The small building to the right is the first unit; to the left is the larger A-frame sanctuary of 1963. Photograph by the author.

the rich Catholic visual tradition showed up in the form of the arches and buttresses on the new sanctuary (Figure 7.22). The building displays the customary mix of new and old evident in most 1960s suburban parish churches. Architect James R. Cronin designed the $450,000 church, describing the brick building as "contemporary design, incorporating characteristics of the Gothic style."[112] This vast A-frame intended to serve 1,300 families had a rectangular plan with a raised chancel. Gothic features include the pointed arches set into the front and side gables and a pair of buttresses on either side of the nave entrance; the chancel furniture is Gothic revival in light oak. A tall, narrow steeple crowns the exterior, which is clad in a mix of brick and limestone. St. Irenaeus Catholic has one of largest sanctuaries in Park Forest, seating 1,000–1,200, but even so, in 1964 the membership was too large to sit together for one Sunday mass.

The architecture of St. Irenaeus demonstrates a traditionalism not seen in the slightly later Catholic churches of Sövik, Dart, and Stade. The A-frame was already out of favor with many architects by 1964, and the applied Gothic details on St. Irenaeus ask the 1950s form to look even further backward. But that was clearly intentional, perhaps in order to reestablish a sense of presence and authority lacking in the school building. It is likely that, had the parish waited just a few more years to build, following Vatican II, the sanctuary would have taken shape much differently.

FIGURE 7.21. St. Irenaeus Catholic School and Parish Hall, Park Forest, Illinois, 1952. Photograph by the author.

FIGURE 7.22. James R. Cronin, St. Irenaeus Catholic Church, Park Forest, Illinois, 1964. Photograph by the author.

*Congregation Beth Sholom*

Park Forest's Christian buildings all reflect adaptability, economy, and an emphasis on educational and fellowship spaces, and this was true for Jewish spaces as well. Beth Sholom built its 1955 synagogue on the main north–south thoroughfare of Western Avenue, with the help of ACB and a large mortgage (Figure 7.23). The fifth religious building erected in Park Forest, it included five classrooms, offices, a kitchen, and a full basement that served as a large social hall. A religious school wing was added in 1964. Beth Sholom was another of Richard Bennett's Park Forest buildings. Early concept drawings for the temple appear in his book *Churches and Temples* (1953), with a Quonset hut-like assembly room.[113] Although closed along its length except for a narrow skylight running along the ridge, Bennett's earlier design has a full wall of clear glass at the ark and pulpit end, opening into a garden courtyard enclosed by a stone wall. At the entrance, "a large menorah combines symbolic identification with actual lighting for the entrance terrace of the wing."[114]

Bennett wrote that "from earliest times the synagogue has been a neighborhood institution, related to daily life and domestic forms, warm and friendly," and this initial design displays that attitude, with a frank openness to the community.[115] The eventual building is much more closed, the sanctuary having a solid, curved wall presented to the street. It could be that the original design felt unfinished or that the congregation was uncomfortable with the amount of light and exposure in the sanctuary; on the other hand, it might simply be a change motivated by

FIGURE 7.23. Richard Bennett, Congregation Beth Sholom, Park Forest, Illinois, 1955. Photograph by Bernard Klein. Courtesy of Park Forest Historical Society.

aesthetics. We know that Bennett was interested in Eero Saarinen's MIT chapel (1955) because he lauded it as "one of the most inspiring chapels of our time," noting the beauty of the material and the grace of the solid, curved wall.[116] Just such a curved, red brick wall appears in Beth Sholom synagogue, a ninety-thousand-dollar structure "of advanced modern design."[117]

Conversations about temple architecture in the postwar period echo those surrounding Christian architecture: a desire to break with "imitative" architecture in order to forge something timely, and a critique of the "false" use and treatment of materials. In *Churches and Temples,* Bennett noted that there was no single model for synagogue design. American contributions, he claimed, were the development of a mechanical plant, increased specialization of rooms, and more elaborate and complex planning. Because the Torah was the most important element in the worship space, an ark, sometimes just a curtained niche, needed to be accentuated. Beyond the worship space, these postwar synagogues had spaces similar to Protestant and Catholic churches: a narthex or vestibule for visiting, a banquet/social hall, classrooms and hobby/club rooms, offices, restrooms, and a kitchen. One of the challenges of synagogue design was the typically huge discrepancy between ordinary Friday attendance and attendance for High Holy Days. Architects provided for overflow in a variety of ways, most commonly a large meeting room that could be opened as an annex, not unlike the narthex overflow spaces of many suburban Protestant churches.

Alice Friedman has argued that "glamour" characterized the synagogues of the postwar years, based in large part on her careful study of Frank Lloyd Wright's Beth Sholom in suburban Philadelphia.[118] Jews, she claimed, used religious architecture to mark a sophisticated, upwardly mobile class status. This argument has merit at the high end, but it does not apply to the earlier Park Forest congregations. Jews did, as a whole, confidently embrace the modern architecture after the war, and there are certain class and cultural meanings attached to this choice. But other factors were at play as well—sometimes aspiration and means were in conflict. In Park Forest, comfortably and unpretentiously "fitting in" was important for both Jews and Christians.

## FITTING IN AND STANDING OUT: THE PLACE OF PARK FOREST'S CHURCHES

Given the interconnectedness of the architects and their shared design convictions, the sameness of Park Forest's religious architecture is understandable. Architects and building committees preferred red or tan brick mixed with light gray or tan stone. They used inexpensive contemporary materials in "honest" and practical ways, with minimal decorative finishes or flourishes. When deciphering the messages of these architectural spaces, two contrasting arguments arise. The first relates to the education and fellowship rooms so important to the life of the community. Here, one would be hard pressed to find significant differences in design or plan according to religion or denomination. In these spaces we can read conformity and the accommodation, to a large degree deliberate, of secular ideas and influences. In congregational worship spaces, however, design choices could be significant markers of difference that reveal the persistence of particular faith practices and the assertion of religious identity.

The first buildings of many of Park Forest's congregations were education and administration wings, a common pattern nationwide. As one Park Forest resident claimed, "we wanted to get our children started in religion."[119] These workaday spaces housed a great variety of activities, both sacred and secular. In Park Forest there was an especially tight relationship between public schools and churches. Local church leaders encouraged congregations to build education facilities that echoed the current thought about public-school buildings. The congregation of St. Irenaeus reported that its education wing would be "an attractive building which will serve our needs and will be in keeping with the up-to-date attitude of this community . . . the structure will be expressive of the latest developments in church-school architecture."[120] Faith UPC's first-unit education building was similarly functional, with offices and classrooms for the youngest children on the first floor, and classrooms for children aged six to high school on the second. Building committee chairman Frank Klein reported, "The Sunday school plan follows the modern ideas of a good school building."[121] With the same architects designing schools and church education wings, it is no wonder that the buildings are largely interchangeable, although Sunday school classrooms are smaller and, with limited budgets, church education buildings boast fewer amenities. But the hallways, floor plans, bathroom tile, drinking fountains, acoustical ceilings, light fixtures, and large picture windows of public schools and Sunday school buildings were largely the same.

New education facilities, however practical and well used, never erased a congregation's desire for dedicated worship space, and this is where distinctiveness took hold. In part, sanctuary design responded to the demands of denominational custom and ritual practice, although this could be subtle and relatively insignificant. Episcopalians, for example, placed certain specific liturgical demands on their worship spaces, whereas the United Protestant churches could be large, flexible auditoriums. But not all design differences are attributable to the needs of ritual or the dictates of doctrine; they also reflect a congregation's character, as seen in both the buildings themselves and the way congregations talked about them. Trinity Lutheran was defined by its big white cross, tentlike structure, and organic, domestic form; members emphasized the building's "warmth and dignity." Faith, in contrast, is vast, confident, and symmetrical. While its volumes suggest magnificence, the materials suggest the ordinary. William Whyte believed that Faith best expressed the "temper of the organization man," for which doctrine was far less important than a "sense of community." If any of these congregations had a corporate architecture, it was Faith.

Holy Family Episcopal deliberately showcased a different tradition. The dedication bulletin noted that "a church building should do two things: first, its exterior and appearance should be such as to welcome and invite all who pass by and enter its portals. Second, the interior of the church should be of such character and design as to make us kneel in prayer, praise and thanksgiving to Almighty God."[122] This church is full of symbolism, with an exterior wall serving as barrier between sacred and secular, a building in the form of a cross, a sanctuary interior that is not for oblique "searching" but specifically designed to point in one direction . . . to "make us kneel in prayer." There is a stillness to the sanctuary; its smooth wood and brick surfaces and soaring roofline draw one inward and upward. The sanctuary is dark, closed, hidden behind a high wall. Denominational and congregational identity does seem to be consciously and deliberately written into these building programs. Congregations expressed difference primarily in their sanctuaries, the spaces that most defined them as religious people.

When Whyte imagined the "Church of Suburbia," he drew primarily from his study of Park Forest's United Protestant Church. Some of Whyte's observations do hold true for all Park Forest's congregations: they replicated the structure of business organizations, emphasized growth as an important measure of success, and were actively social, appealing to transient residents looking for a group of friends. In light of the diversity of religion in Park Forest, however, this focus on the United Protestant Church is misleading. Whyte's reading of the United Protestant Church itself was shaped by what he was looking for—a church that expressed the temper of the Organization Man. Residents of Park Forest acknowledged the social utility of their church affiliations. As one member of Trinity Lutheran admitted, "it was a way of meeting people—let's face it, a lot of it was social,"[123] But church attendance was not *only* social. Amy Hensold, a long-term member of Faith UPC, insists that the church was "really the center of our lives, and always was."[124] One member of Faith UPC claimed that her pastor realized "how terribly important church work is for young couples like us . . . If you're going to have any stability in our kind of life, you have to get involved with other people in things that really count."[125]

Was a doctrinal Christian faith becoming irrelevant to church life in Park Forest? Leinberger told Whyte, sounding both soundly practical and theologically indiscriminating, "This business of doctrine should come later." "Very few people, after all," he claimed, "are concerned with the ultimate implications of their beliefs . . . We try not to offend anybody."[126] One can see why Whyte would have been fascinated by the UPC idea. But did Leinberger fairly represent the faith commitments of clergy and people? Martin Marty, curious about the religious life in Park Forest, went down to the south suburb to see for himself, and he found that there was more authentic religion there than the sociologists had recorded. After speaking with the leaders of the United Protestant Church, he "retained one clear and consistent impression: the ministers resent Whyte's description of their lack of theology." Marty wrote that one church leader asked him to record this response word for word: "I object strenuously to that part of the picture."[127] Nor was Protestantism in Park Forest all consensus. Reverend Englemann strongly contested Whyte's contention that Park Forest's churchgoers replicated the self-suppressing behavioral patterns of the ambitious businessman. "I insisted that that was exactly what he did not do," Englemann recalled. "That the man who worked for *Life, Time, Fortune* and so forth, when he came home to the village he could really let loose all the frustrations that he felt when he was confined by the ideas of the organization, and that it was in this community that he expressed his individualism." Englemann remembered thinking at the time, "I wish my board of directors of the church once in a while would act like organization men."[128]

Traditionalism and conformity were two great threats to a vital contemporary faith. The young congregations of Park Forest were susceptible to both, but only to a degree. Tradition showed in sanctuaries that did still "look like churches." Even Faith UPC is unmistakably a religious structure. Conformity is evident in the often expressed desire for buildings to "fit in." Yet, what these congregations were fitting into, through their architecture and programs, was a modern community with a strong sense of itself as visionary and new. They were experimenting, not replicating the past. Moreover, church membership, as revealed in architecture, offered both a sense of belonging *and* an opportunity to assert difference within the community.

Park Forest's church buildings thus did three things at once: they fit in to the community and its inexpensive contemporary architecture; they facilitated a busy schedule of worship and fellowship activities, a multidimensional expression of faith common to all denominations; and they allowed congregations to express and experience particular religious identity claims. Underneath a veneer of workaday Midwestern modernism, these religious buildings reveal a dynamic and diverse religious community.

The experience of religious life in postwar Park Forest was not the ideal promoted by the religious press, nor was it the self-sacrificial, antimaterialistic standard that liberal critics somehow thought possible. Conflict, tension, and worldly concerns found their way into church social halls, classrooms, and sanctuaries. With their members swept up by the concerns of building a career, raising a family, and creating a community where there had been cornfields, the churches centered their work on the needs of their suburban members. This was important for families seeking purpose and stability while facing physical and social dislocation, the temptations of material abundance, and a full range of joys and heartaches. In Park Forest and elsewhere, suburban church buildings grounded and shaped this work. Beyond tradition and conformity, in these places, suburbanites aimed for something new, and "something greater."

CHAPTER 8

# The Afterlife of the Postwar Suburban Church

Postwar suburban communities like Park Forest are today very different from what they were in the 1950s. Although research for this book centered on the experience of the suburban churches in the 1950s and 1960s, my visits to these places inevitably included conversations about what was happening there in the early twenty-first century. The people I met wanted to tell me not only about the past, but to reflect on the past's relationship to the present. The ongoing lives of these buildings and the way they continue to shape congregational life drew my interest. This chapter is about the present and possible futures of postwar churches and their communities and how the histories of buildings and people are entwined.

## AFTER THE CHURCH BUILDING BOOM

Suburbanites read William Whyte's *Organization Man*. They watched movies such as *No Down Payment*, a 1957 depiction of a California suburb riddled with alcoholism, alienation, and racism.[1] To a certain extent they internalized the critique of the suburbs, even at a young age. In 1968, for example, *McCall's* magazine published "The Suburb That Turned Its Back," a new look at Park Forest. The author interviewed teenagers such as seventeen-year-old Sharon who sighed, "Oh I feel so sheltered . . . and I just hate it. I don't feel that I've seen or done anything really unusual my whole life."[2] Safety and sameness were antithetical to the values of 1960s youth culture, and baby boomers who grew up in those communities are still not quite sure if they should be proud or embarrassed about their hometowns and their childhood institutions, although many of them chose to raise their own children in similar places. Even as scholars are reconsidering the suburbs in a more generous light, many people maintain a critical stance toward suburban churches. Those who were and are members of those suburban congregations often hesitate to speak too positively about their own experiences, understanding that the suburban church is still a target of suspicion and even derision.

Most of the congregations in this study have seen a significant, ongoing drop in membership since a peak in the mid-1960s.[3] This is the result of demographic changes, but also reflects waning membership in mainline denominations and a reconfiguring of American church membership and attendance.[4] Members of diminishing congregations often reveal both uncertainties about the meaning of their past and concern over their future. It is not uncommon to find suburban churches built to seat three hundred with just fifty people in the pews on Sunday. In places that were once all new, the neighbors mostly young, children "all over the place," it has been disheartening to watch both buildings and people age all at once. Nimi Nord, who wrote a history of Holy Family Episcopal, Park Forest, wistfully remarked that, back then "you didn't see any gray heads . . . now it's all gray heads."[5]

Although most of the forces of decline have been beyond the control of the churches, some people wonder if the original success of the postwar church was not itself some sort of demographic accident, one that did not prepare them for what was to come. Stan Boie, of Park Forest, confessed, "I've often said that our mission was standing there on Sunday morning holding the door open . . . we thought everything should come that easy. We thought we had something to do with it and I'm pretty sure it didn't matter who was in charge"; we "would have grown by the nature of things."[6] Furthermore, the suburban church's emphasis on "fitting in" built an "unusually strong bridge between religion and culture" that was a source of strength for a time, but perhaps also religion's undoing when the culture wrenched itself away from early postwar norms.[7]

Fifty or sixty years after these churches were built, their congregations are facing a variety of circumstances and concerns. For declining congregations, questions of survival loom large. Other congregations have continued to survive and even flourish, generally because the middle-class communities around them are flourishing as well, and they have found ways to adapt to a changing religious culture. Still others, in response to demographic changes, sold to or share their buildings with new congregations. In 2014 in Park Forest, for example, Temple Beth Sholom is the Hallelujah Temple. Hope Lutheran became Celebration Ministries, and Good Shepherd United Protestant's building supports House of Prayer Ministry. These changes reflect the fact that Park Forest is now a city with a black majority population, and black churches are growing. Elsewhere, different demographic changes are apparent. At least three Stade churches in the northern Chicago suburbs (Northbrook United Methodist, Hillside Free Methodist, and St. John's Lutheran, Lincolnwood) share space with Korean congregations. Signs outside the buildings indicate the diversity of cultures and practices within (Figure 8.1).

In *Confronting Suburban Decline: Strategic Planning for Metropolitan Renewal*, William H. Lucy and David L. Phillips explain the challenges many of these once thriving suburban communities are facing today. In this "postsuburban" era, demographic patterns favor areas of newer development with greater resources and

FIGURE 8.1. Charles Stade, St. John's Lutheran, Lincolnwood, Illinois, 1962. The sign in front of the church reveals that three congregations worshipped here in 2014: the Korean Bethany Church, St. John's Lutheran Church, and the Good Shepherd Congregation (Philippine Independent Church). Photograph by the author.

resident income. Postwar suburbs, especially those with modest houses built quickly and cheaply, do not attract the investment required to continue to thrive. A decline in the value of housing stock invites new lower-income residents and immigrant groups, bringing diversity but often also reducing the community's financial resources. Shifting opportunities for employment in and near these suburbs further shape and reflect demographic changes. As these suburban communities feel more like cities—with more congestion, less visible green space, and challenges such as declining schools—their attractions fade in favor of newer suburbs farther from the urban center, or renewed core urban spaces with the benefits of a true city environment.[8] Sociologists believe that, for the most part, in the postwar suburbs settled in the fifties and sixties, "declining social infrastructure and aging or demographically changing populations" have made it difficult to establish and maintain ties, and today "complaints about lack of community are endemic among suburban residents" who are fatigued by the demands of work and consumerism.[9]

Lucy and Phillips argue that "the resiliency of a suburb, like any neighborhood, depends on lasting qualities of 'place.'"[10] Many postwar suburbs, once with a strong sense of themselves as places, have lost that coherence. What might the role of religious organizations be in establishing a contemporary sense of place and community? How is this different from the role these institutions played in the 1950s and 1960s? And how can meaningful stories of the past shape the present and future? Although Lucy and Phillips do not specifically discuss suburban religious organizations, they claim that "the suburban decline process may accelerate if an insufficient number of public and private nonprofit institutions are nearby."[11] Certainly, religious organizations will be important institutions that can contribute to the survival of these suburbs, particularly if they model renewal and faith in the sustainability of a place.

Sociologist Robert Wuthnow notes that people achieve a sense of "spatial attachment" to place by doing things locally—building, naming, and transforming their material surroundings.[12] This describes the experience of the generation that built these suburban churches according to their needs. The ongoing, weekly demands those earlier suburbanites placed on their churches, however, are not the same as today's sporadic patterns of civic engagement by residents less able or willing to make long-term commitments. Patterns of sociability and religious commitment change. Buildings adapt or disappear. Whether suburban churches contracted or expanded, their church buildings from time to time fell short of meeting their needs, and congregations did what they could to adjust either themselves or their buildings. Typical Midwestern suburban congregations that inhabit these postwar buildings today forge ahead with limited resources and try to stabilize aging structures and carve the most useful space out of their material inheritance.

When postwar congregations built churches, they did so with a sense of timeliness and urgency. Timeliness led them to build for their own day, thinking much less about the past or the future than about their contemporary concerns. Compromises in construction, inherent defects in new materials, and acceptance of imperfect solutions for the sake of economy and expediency often led to problems down the road. Most ordinary postwar builders did *not* speak about designing for the ages, and many consciously built for the short term.[13] This was deliberate in the case of first-unit churches, yet even the more "permanent" of church buildings spoke the language of contemporary need in a quickly changing, fast-paced world. Nonetheless, today many of those postwar suburban churches, their inadequacies notwithstanding, have an interest and character—a homeyness, perhaps—lacking in the plain and functional creations of the 1970s and 1980s. Many are aging better than we might have expected. Congregations are addressing questions of preservation and adaptability as they shape their ministries in tandem with building projects.

## MAKING ROOM FOR MORE: THE SUBURBAN CHURCH EXPANDS

The majority of the congregations in this study, as they anticipated, undertook subsequent expansion, ranging from the ambitious development of all facilities to simply the addition of a few classrooms or accessible restrooms. For most of these congregations, significant expansion took place soon after the construction of the original unit, when congregational membership numbers were still generally on the rise, although in a few cases building programs continue even into the twenty-first century. If the original church was a flexible first unit, expansion could be fairly straightforward, the initial sanctuary most commonly expanded into a larger sanctuary, refitted as a fellowship hall, or retained as a smaller worship space. Growing suburban congregations generally did not demolish older spaces but continued to spread out on their large sites. For instance, after a more recent membership boom, Crystal Lake United Methodist in Crystal Lake, Illinois, built a new auditorium sanctuary in 1992–94 and retained Charles Stade's 1955 A-frame as a chapel, now used for a less formal type of worship (Figures 8.2 and 8.3).

St. Luke's Methodist in Indianapolis is still growing today, and buried within the expansive church plant is the original 1956 Harold Wagoner three-hundred-seat colonial revival first unit (never considered a permanent sanctuary and always called a "fellowship hall"), a 1958 education wing, and Dart's 1967 church. In 1999, a new 1,500-seat sanctuary, education wing expansion, and large choir room grew the plant further, joined by a new youth building in 2003. In the 1950s, St. Luke's had chosen a multiple-acre site in the midst of new developments. As that suburban growth continued, St. Luke's prospered. In 2010, it was the largest Methodist church in Indianapolis, with a congregation of about five thousand. Dart's 1967 sanctuary remains a part of the church plant, beloved by members for its beauty and historical resonances and now used for smaller gatherings, more contemplative services, and non-worship activities such as drama productions. Here and elsewhere, the postwar practical wisdom of building by units is evident.

FIGURE 8.2. Charles Stade, Crystal Lake Methodist Church, Crystal Lake, Illinois, ca. 1960, sanctuary. Courtesy of First United Methodist Church of Crystal Lake, Illinois.

FIGURE 8.3. First United Methodist Church (formerly Crystal Lake Methodist Church), Crystal Lake, Illinois, sanctuary in 2014. Photograph by the author.

## CHANGING WITH THE TIMES: THE SUBURBAN CHURCH ADAPTS

Most small suburban congregations today share concerns about creating a close feeling of community in spaces that are far too large for the present assembly of the faithful. Sunday schools built for hundreds or even thousands of children now have only dozens, and many a capacious sanctuary dwarfs a small Sunday morning congregation. Congregations that built for three hundred rather than eight hundred or more often have sanctuaries and ancillary facilities better suited for today's numbers. Many of the modest churches designed by Dart, Sövik, and Stade still serve their congregations quite well. Some congregations reserve their sanctuaries for special occasions and hold regular services in their chapels or social spaces, especially if heating or cooling the larger sanctuary is a drain on resources. The size of the congregation relative to the space is important not just for the comfort of the worshippers, but as an element that will tend to attract or discourage potential new members. A small remnant of a once-booming congregation in a huge sanctuary is not generally inspiring to a visitor.

Congregations continued to change their worship preferences and practices. As we have seen, what seemed adventurous and modern in the 1950s came to appear staid and traditional as early as the 1960s. Urging "authenticity," church leaders advanced their crusade to strip away the accretions of culture and approach the essence of Christianity. Today, this ongoing desire for authenticity often manifests in the trend toward making churches even more informal, "friendly," and relaxed. The rise of the megachurch taught the older suburban churches a few valuable lessons. Megachurches succeeded in part by giving baby boomers a comfortable worship environment that was deliberately unlike the churches of their childhoods. In response, many neighborhood churches have added contemporary worship services and try to relax the fixed aspects of the traditional chancel and nave.

At the opposite end of the spectrum, critics within certain denominations, particularly Roman Catholics, have actively reversed the trend toward aesthetic and liturgical informality in design by working to recapture their rich traditions. This impulse is at bottom also a search for "authenticity," but one reclaiming tradition rather than opposing it. Part of what underlies this kind of effort is a renewed appreciation for what is distinctive in a particular religious tradition, in opposition to the rise of nondenominational megachurches.

Most churches in this study fall somewhere between the loose informality of the megachurch and the conservative backlash. They retain tradition yet look forward, just as their founders did. Because a great variety of worship practices often coexist in these spaces, adaptability for multiple functions and practices is essential. Sövik, in particular, designed sanctuaries with this kind of flexibility in mind, and although it took some time for most congregations to catch up to the potential of that idea, it is currently of concern to many. Westwood Lutheran in St. Louis

Park, Minnesota, for instance, has recently renovated its sanctuary to a flexible configuration that Sövik would have endorsed. A trend toward individual, movable seating usually means the choice of chairs over pews. Yet congregations are rarely able to replace pews with chairs without a fuss. Many people prefer pews, not just for tradition but for comfort, and sanctuaries such as the newest St. Luke's Methodist in Indianapolis use both. On the whole, people tend to be fairly conservative about matters of worship and liturgy and change is slow—a fact that makes the tremendous changes that took place in the postwar years all the more remarkable.

Two trends in worship have particularly challenged these postwar spaces: electronic music ("praise" bands) and visual technology (video screens), as seen in Figure 8.3. In 1991, Trinity Lutheran in Moorhead, Minnesota, built a "Christian Life Center," a hybrid worship and social space, furnished with tables and chairs. The congregation advertises "a celebratory service using music from our exceptional worship band in a relaxed atmosphere" and a "come as you are" openness, "dressed however you wish, carrying whatever joys and burdens you may have—only with a heart and mind open for worship!"[14] A second, informal worship space such as this is rare, however, and most congregations expect their sanctuaries to support a range of worship practices. Drums, electric guitars, and video can find a place to the side of the front of the church, yet their incorporation into worship (which is still often contested by segments of the congregation) can be an awkward fit in a more traditional space. Experimenting with new forms of worship is even more difficult when the liturgical fittings such as altar and pulpit are fixed in place, such as the permanently rooted, brick constructions common in many of Stade's A-frames.

Aesthetic preferences have also shifted over the decades, and the modernism of the postwar sanctuary has been both a challenge and an opportunity. Even when churchgoers did not tire of modernism per se, they often did find some of its typical aspects to be lacking. What looked crisply perfect in the black-and-white photographs of new churches could feel cold and barren in person, and congregations frequently added color, texture, and art. Trinity Lutheran in Park Forest attempted to make its 1959 sanctuary more inviting by adding textiles, banners, or softer floor coverings. Despite the insistence on its original "overall warmth," even in the early days some found Trinity to be a "very cold looking building," with its "bare cement floors, blond pews," cement steps to the altar, and cheap, "ugly" windows.[15] In the 1980s, the congregation added carpeting and generally tried to "warm up" its sanctuary to make it more "worship friendly" and flexible. Modern sanctuaries generally lend themselves well to the addition of art, and in this way new generations leave their mark on worship space. After several temporary art installations, in 2001 Sövik's Olivet Lutheran in Fargo, North Dakota, commissioned artist David Hetland to create an eighteen-foot olivewood *Tree of Life* for the chancel wall. This sculpture, made of wood from the Holy Land, integrates easily into the sanctuary and strengthens the congregation's identity (see Figure 5.8).

For symbolic, decorative, and historical reasons, congregations have been particularly interested in adding stained glass, which can change the interior effect dramatically. Many postwar churches incorporated colored glass into their original buildings, geometric patterned glass windows of the sort Stade so often specified, or more expensive figural stained-glass windows. Dart was less inclined to incorporate colored glass, or art in general, in his churches, perhaps because so often his buildings were self-consciously restrained works of art themselves. At the time of dedication of Dart's Holy Ghost Catholic Church in South Holland, Illinois (1971), church leaders instructed the parish to see the new church through modern eyes, and to appreciate the simplicity, spaciousness, unity, and lack of barriers and "distractions."[16] Over time, the parish became dissatisfied with the blank walls and an apparent absence of tradition. A committee of church members desiring to "beautify" the church scoured the Chicago area in 1990 looking for stained glass.[17] Today, historic stained glass from Chicago's Saints Cyril and Methodius Catholic Church is in the narthex. On the south wall of the sanctuary, the parish blasted a hole in Dart's pristine brick wall and installed another relic from Saints Cyril and Methodius, a square window with a depiction of the Holy Spirit (the church's namesake) descending like a dove (see Figure 5.26). A member of the church's liturgy committee noted that "as you walk in the church, [the stained-glass window] sets the mood . . . It's a different mood for a spiritual environment. You don't see the brick walls. They're there, but you don't see them."[18] Evidence such as this signifies a modest revolution against the simple forms and opaque symbols of the original buildings.

Some congregations have found ways to keep parishioners educated about the symbolic meaning of their midcentury spaces and symbols. Daniel Lewis, chairman of the building committee for Dart's Presbyterian Church in La Porte, Indiana, wrote a small brochure about the architecture that has circulated since 1992. This serves as a users' guide to the building, calling attention to the use of hidden light sources, the rough finish to the materials, the orientation of the sanctuary, and the spiritual significance of each feature. Lewis told the story of when one member of the church asked Dart why he did not use stained glass, because "we need something pretty to look at during worship." Dart replied that "he understood that the Presbyterian Church considers baptism, communion and preaching the Word to be the focus of worship."[19] That was enough. Several churches and one synagogue in this study have similar brochures available that decode the buildings and their symbols for members and visitors. Helen Reinkensmeyer, at Zion Lutheran, Kalamazoo, Michigan, took an early interest in the large and brilliantly colored chancel window designed by A. R. Kretzmann. She prepared a printed guide to the window and for several decades has contributed a short piece to the weekly bulletin, connecting some aspect of the window's iconography to the week's scripture readings.

Sometimes it is hard to know what to make of congregational accounts of meaning, and church members can be enthusiastic and skeptical at the same time. The racially integrated congregation at Dart's St. Augustine of Canterbury in Benton Harbor, Michigan, interprets the skylight cover on top of the church (two vertical bars connected by a horizontal element, surmounted by a cross) as a symbol of the "two races, negro and white, kneeling before the altar of God at the foot of the cross" (see Figure 3.8)[20] As the current priest suspects, however, "I think we have been the ones who've put the meaning into it."[21]

## FINDING A NEW PURPOSE: THE SUBURBAN CHURCH IN TRANSITION

Without exception, the Midwestern congregations in this study have been interested in using their facilities to serve their wider communities. At Olivet, Fargo, Carol Ferguson said at first the congregation voted against doing things like a Special Olympics breakfast, thinking "we'd be busy enough just doing things for ourselves."[22] Soon, however, they realized that "reaching into the community meant using these facilities." The form that service has taken has changed over time. Many people I spoke with identified a change in church culture that came as more and more women, the workforce of social ministries of the suburban church, were employed full-time outside the home. Hal and Clara Neugebauer, longtime Olivet members, remembered that at one time there were seventeen (!) ladies' circles, but they all disbanded. Lutheran Brotherhood also "just sort of fell apart" in the 1970s "just because people started getting so busy."[23] Within the church building, a different social world began to replace the postwar experience, one characterized by fewer clubs and weekly meetings and an opening of the facilities to the wider community.

Early-twenty-first century suburbanites experience a very different sort of rhythm to their religious lives. Even for churchgoing families, Sunday mornings might involve just a quick stop at church before running to a soccer game. The commercial-scale kitchens built by postwar congregations are often quiet, and large social gatherings are infrequent, at least relative to the postwar pattern. But the need for casual fellowship persists if worshippers are to have the kind of informal interaction that binds them together through knowledge of one another's lives and concerns. Spurred by a successful strategy of the megachurch movement and the renewed popularity of the upscale coffeehouse, congregations have upped the ante on the Sunday coffee hour, adding gourmet options and café tables. Yet it is increasingly unlikely that members of the congregation will take extra steps out of their path between car and sanctuary. Remote social facilities are ineffective; coffee and sociability need to be placed squarely in the natural flow of foot traffic. New churches build large "gathering areas" directly outside the sanctuary as a way of capturing, if only for a few minutes, a social experience. Congregations in midcentury churches often adapt by crowding such activities into a narrow narthex. In

2007, Olivet Lutheran's narthex was crammed with coffee tables. In 2014, a major building project was under way, its first objective to create an expanded, two-story narthex/reception area.

Where new building is impossible or impractical, congregations have put the functional spaces of their buildings to new and different uses. Stewart Brand, in his provocative book *How Buildings Learn*, describes the endless advantages of what he calls "low-road" buildings.[24] These structures are marked by their bland yet adaptable spaces and high degree of functionality. Whereas sanctuaries are specialized spaces difficult to repurpose, education wings, with their long hallways, multiple classrooms, and all-purpose rooms, open themselves to many purposes. Because their historical and aesthetic value is slight, few people hesitate to put them to creative new purposes. Congregations have taken these rarely occupied spaces and used them to house new programs or rented them out to other organizations. The spacious education facilities of many churches are especially likely candidates for reuse. An increasing need for full-time or part-time preschools has found a ready match with these facilities. Churches often run such preschools themselves, as a growing suburban ministry.

Other social ministries have also found a home in these postwar churches. In a response to homelessness in their communities, a growing practice is to house a shelter, often on a rotating schedule between collaborating churches. Congregations prepare meals in their kitchens and spread mattresses on the floor of the fellowship or recreation areas to give residents a bed for the night. In 2014, St. Augustine of Canterbury in Benton Harbor was hosting a shelter and running a food pantry out of its basement (Figure 8.4). The congregations at Stade's Hillside Methodist in Evanston and Villa Park Congregational also were operating substantial food pantries, serving hundreds of families a week. Volunteers come from other places in the community as well, but the churches provide key leadership, significant financial support, and physical space for the program. First United Church, Bloomington (formerly First Baptist), in 2012 made its classrooms available six hours per week for Partners, an arts-based program for Alzheimer's and early-stage dementia clients.[25] The church also provides space for Alcoholics Anonymous and drug rehabilitation programs, and serves as an emergency winter shelter. On Sunday nights, a local Mennonite church uses its small chapel for worship. Grace United Protestant in Park Forest has rented its well-lit classrooms to local artists for use as studios. These are just a few of many examples.

In 1963, Martin Marty asked the attendees of the National Conference on Church Architecture in Seattle: In the churches we build, "will there be rooms and spaces which impose on the congregation its mission to serve? Will there be space for packing of clothes and entertaining the neglected, for organizing resources? Or will all space be dictated by the logic of self-service?"[26] These "low-road" buildings—unused space with potential—have played a role in shaping, even

FIGURE 8.4. St. Augustine of Canterbury, Benton Harbor, Michigan, undercroft with food pantry, 2014. Photograph by the author.

encouraging, new ministries that serve the congregation as well as the broader community.

As the political scientist Robert Putnam has demonstrated, involvement in religious organizations prepares citizens for other kinds of civic engagement.[27] People who inhabited these suburban churches took what they learned about community service into other parts of their lives, and they still do. Religious organizations remain one of the easiest places to get involved, to meet people when new to a neighborhood, to learn to give time and resources to a community. Unlike many of the new megachurches situated along major roadways, postwar churches are around the corner and scaled for neighborhood life. On the whole, they read as inviting, manageable, and accessible places.

Not all suburban churches will remain churches. Several of Dart's churches (in Country Club Hills and West Chicago) are vacant, their futures uncertain. In Valparaiso, Indiana, the 1950s A-frame of Calvary Baptist Church was for many years the showroom of Sun Appliance and later a beauty salon, although it has recently become a church again.[28] More commonly, church complexes are reused by comparable institutions. In many cases, educational functions continue. Stade's Good Shepherd Methodist in Park Ridge was occupied for more than ten years by Embers School, an independent Catholic grade school of 120 students. Good

Shepherd relocated closer to members in 2000 and sold the building to the school. When nearby O'Hare airport gained a new runway, FAA noise-abatement funds enabled the school to add a new HVAC system (allowing the school to operate with windows closed) and renovate and reconfigure the building. The original round sanctuary was used as a multipurpose room, for preschool in the mornings, choir and band practice in the afternoons, mass once a week, parent education, and even as a gym during bad weather (Figure 8.5). In 2013, Principal Gladys Davis said the building was "working out very well" as a school.[29] The former sanctuary was especially well suited to educational purposes with its round shape and "wonderful natural light."

## MAKING THINGS NEW: RENOVATING THE SUBURBAN CHURCH

Once a month, Dan Ronning, the building superintendent of Westwood Lutheran in St. Louis Park, Minnesota, meets with more than a dozen of his peers from other congregations to talk about their buildings. Since 2003, the members of the Minnesota Association of Church Facility Managers have helped each other think

FIGURE 8.5. A fireman talks to children while sitting at former raised chancel area of Charles Stade's Good Shepherd Methodist Church, Park Ridge, Illinois, then Embers School, ca. 2013. Courtesy of Embers Elementary School.

about "facility related challenges, experiences, and solutions."[30] They share thoughts about such things as water leaks, parking lots, the care of concrete, and fuel efficiency. When Westwood replaced its old boiler with several new, smaller ones, previous building manager Wally Novak was able to inform his counterparts of the energy efficiency of this new system.[31]

All buildings require constant attention as foundations level, weather takes its toll, and materials and systems wear out. Postwar congregations often did very little to their "new" buildings for several decades; deferred maintenance or less than adequate "fixes" often led to bigger problems in the future. The single most common problem has been water leaks from the flat roofs of education and administration wings. At Stade's Lutheran Church of the Ascension in Atlanta, the congregation replaced leaking flat roofs with slightly sloped shed roofs. At Sövik's First Baptist, Bloomington (now First United), the education and administration wing's flat roof deteriorated until "water would pour through into the office of the minister."[32] As at Ascension, First United replaced its flat roof with one on a slight incline. First Baptist's 1950s pastor, Doug Rae, the visionary who hired Sövik in the 1950s, talked about "using up" the church, and the congregation nearly did so. "He thought the building might last one hundred years. The ravages of time and neglect nearly brought it down in fifty." But the congregation undertook a major $1.6 million renovation that "may last another fifty years."[33] Just as in the 1950s, members provided much of the labor.

Religious organizations are not required to meet the 1992 Americans with Disabilities Act (ADA) specifications, but many churches have improved handicapped accessibility. As suburban congregations have aged, this has been a universal concern. Ramps, accessible restrooms, and elevators are frequent additions. Further accommodations include replacing uneven flooring or removing the altar rail and allowing parishioners to remain standing for communion.

Messiah Lutheran in Burlington, Iowa, poured its energy and resources into a high-quality, $1.6 million renovation of its 1961–62 Stade church. This congregation's experience provides both a model for building renovation and proof of how such work can reenergize a community. In the postwar period, Messiah (organized in 1859) voted to move to a sixteen-acre site in a newly developing suburban quarter of the city and built a modern $550,000 church that was "the talk of the town" (Figure 8.6, also Figure 5.14).[34] For the first three decades, little maintenance was performed on the "new" building. In the 1990s, an engineering study revealed that extensive stabilization work was necessary. Even so, the cost of a major renovation was only one-third the projected cost of building a new church.[35]

The congregation had changed over the years. It was no longer necessary to partition extra Sunday school rooms out of the social hall. Despite its smaller size, the congregation valued both its building and its role in the community. A preschool, started in 1964, continues to this day. More recently, in 1998 the congregation gave

FIGURE 8.6. Charles Stade, Messiah Lutheran Church, Burlington, Iowa, sanctuary after renovation, 2012. Photograph by the author.

the adjacent land for a new senior housing community. Since 2006, a chapter of "Kids Against Hunger" packs two thousand meals a week in the social hall. The building serves as an important community center.

Following one and a half years of planning, the church embarked on a three-phase restoration. A member of the congregation, Mike Schmidt, served as contractor and a retired longtime member, Don Duke, put in forty volunteer hours a week as owner representative. A major aspect of the work was cutting three seams in each of the sanctuary side walls and installing expansion joints. Virtually all the windows were removed and replaced for energy efficiency. The glulams required considerable attention; workers cut off the rotten ends and replaced them with new steel tips engineered to keep moisture from reaching the remaining wood.

When I visited on a wintry Friday in February 2013, the education wing of the church was filled with the sounds of the preschool, original radiant heat still working to warm the floors under the active children (Figure 8.7). In the social hall of the other wing, a group of women representing the local Philanthropic Educational Organization (PEO), sat at tables to listen to a presentation, followed by a dessert they served from the remodeled kitchen (Figure 8.8). Messiah's congregation recognized that building from scratch, even with a substantial budget, would likely not have resulted in a building of the quality of Stade's original.

FIGURE 8.7. Messiah Lutheran Church, Burlington, Iowa, education/preschool classroom, in 2013. Photograph by the author.

FIGURE 8.8. Messiah Lutheran Church, Burlington, Iowa, social hall, in 2013. Photograph by the author.

Schmidt, Duke, Pastor Susanne Smith (who arrived as the project was getting started), and Jerry Smith (a member since 1957) were full of enthusiasm for this work. As they told engaging tales of the restoration, the building, and, by extension, the congregation's history as a suburban pioneer, they were justifiably proud of their past and present, and humble about the gifts they have been given. Abandoning this building would have meant losing an important part of their history. Owning that past by preserving the architecture animates the congregation for its work in the present and future.

## SAVING A LEGACY: PRESERVING THE SUBURBAN CHURCH

At the opposite of Brand's "low-road" designation is his "high-road" category—buildings distinguished for "high intent, duration of purpose, duration of care, *time*, and a steady supply of confident dictators." By spanning generations, "high-road" buildings "transcend style and turn it into history."[36] What they have going for them, even if they are not beautiful, is "layers upon layers of soul."[37] These are the buildings that last because of their own inherent qualities and because of the generations of caretakers who love them. Will any of these churches achieve "high-road" status? Some postwar sanctuaries (and even perhaps some education facilities) no doubt will, but it will likely be an unpredictable selection process shaped by a congregation's interests and fortunes as well as a community's appreciation for midcentury modern architecture and its architects.

Many of the churches by Dart, Sövik, and Stade are passing the test of time. There are good reasons to encourage the continued use of even the more ordinary of these postwar churches. Stewardship (also "creation care")—in this case, the preservation and nurturing of the built environment—has important theological meaning, as Mark Torgerson explains in his recent book *Greening Spaces for Worship and Ministry: Congregations, Their Buildings, and Creation Care.*[38] Stewardship and historic preservation are not the same thing, but both require a careful, conserving attitude toward the material world, both natural and man-made.

Within the historic preservation community, the momentum for recording, understanding, and preserving midcentury buildings is growing. Regional interest groups such as Chicago's Bauhaus and Beyond are drawing attention to postwar architecture and identifying major architects and buildings. Appreciation for the era's ordinary architecture is also on the rise; historic preservation students at the School of the Art Institute of the University of Chicago partnered with Landmarks Illinois to survey nonresidential, 1935–75 architecture in Chicago's suburbs.[39] While validation of these buildings is critical, it is likely that meeting strict historic preservation standards would overburden financially struggling congregations. Fortunately, protocol for the preservation of midcentury buildings is veering from the Secretary of the Interior's strict conservation standards toward an interest in maintaining "design intent," a more reasonable target.[40]

The work of canonized architects (such as Saarinen's Christ Lutheran Church in Minneapolis or Wright's First Unitarian Society Meeting House in Madison) has confirmed value that has led to its preservation. Of the three architects in this study, Edward Dart's place in architectural history seems most secure; the winter 2013 edition of *Preservation* magazine, the journal of the National Trust for Historic Preservation, showcased a Dart house in its cover story. The most significant of Ed Sövik's buildings are getting their due, and his voluminous writings will also assure continued interest in his work. Even Charles Stade has been rescued from oblivion; his parish churches are beginning to appear on modernism blogs and architectural history tours.

This has not stopped demolition. Sövik's award-winning Lutheran Church of the Good Shepherd in Moorhead, Minnesota, was torn down to make way for an expansion of Eventide Lutheran Retirement and Nursing Home, which bought the church building about 2006. Matthew Seymour, a preservationist who wrote a thesis on Dart, claims that nineteen of Dart's 119 custom buildings have already been demolished, including Immanuel Lutheran in the Pilsen neighborhood of Chicago. The Church of the Atonement in Barrington, Illinois, demolished Dart's first-unit building to make room for a major expansion. Stade's Pilgrim Lutheran, on the outskirts of Indianapolis, fell victim to a highway project, but not before the state department of transportation, recognizing the significance of the architect, supported extensive documentation of the building.[41]

Postwar churches may have the best chance of survival when their caretakers believe that not just the buildings but the history they embody is worth preserving. One of Edward Dart's earliest churches, St. Augustine's Episcopal in Gary, Indiana (1959), offers a hopeful story of a small congregation struggling to save its historic church, an illuminating example of how the strands of the past, present, and future come together in these midcentury modern spaces (see Figures 4.12–4.14). St. Augustine's began in 1927 as a Colored Episcopal Mission, an offshoot of Christ Episcopal in downtown Gary. Although a black congregation in a place and time still marked by racism and segregation, much about the formation of this community and its architectural setting shares the concerns of the typical suburban church. After the war, the congregation began to seriously consider moving from its tiny quarters in a repurposed city church to a new site in the Tolleston area west of downtown. Tolleston grew like many new suburbs of the period—single-family homes on wide streets, new public schools, aspiring young families looking for a middle-class, neighborhood experience—and, significantly, it was the only place in Gary where African Americans could purchase property to build new houses. St. Augustine's became the congregation of an educated, professional class of African American Episcopalians whose lives revolved around work, family, and church (Figure 8.9).

In 1951, the charismatic Wallace L. Wells, a former high-school music teacher, organist, and recent seminary graduate, took over leadership of the congregation. In 1955, the congregation initiated a fund-raising campaign—especially important for this African American congregation because mortgage discrimination prevented the acquisition of a bank loan.[42] Quentin Smith, cochairman of the building committee (a Tuskegee airman and later the first principal of Gary's West Side High School), recalls that the young members of the building committee "wanted a person who would build something that would indicate something about what the church was about by looking at the building—not just a cross or steeple."[43] In late 1955 or early 1956, the building committee interviewed several architects and traveled to view new modern churches.

Dart's first design for St. Augustine's was a long, rectangular structure of exposed steel I-beams with a rough stone wall entirely surrounding the church and its small front courtyard (see Figure 2.3). The congregation loved this design, but it turned out to be too expensive with its ten large stained-glass windows, extensive masonry work, and garden.[44] Dart came back with another design: a graceful variation on the popular A-frame. He was a good listener, Smith remembers, and when the congregation asked the building to say something about prayer, "Mr. Dart came up with this inverted ship idea." The shape of the church conveyed multiple associations; Reverend Wells quoted Dart as referencing "the tabernacle,

FIGURE 8.9. Congregation of St. Augustine's Episcopal Mission Gary, Indiana, at a baptism in the old church, ca. 1952. Father Wallace L. Wells is seated in the front row, holding the baby. Courtesy of Phillip Craig Johnson.

house of Jehovah, or tent of the meeting" or praying hands, "grasping the cross at fingertip." Other parishioners saw it as "the head of a spear, symbolizing the church militant."[45]

St. Augustine's is a beautiful little church, largely because of the graceful curve of the natural wood and the meditative interior. Unfinished red cedar roof decking, rough redwood end walls, polished oak dorsal wall and chancel furnishings, and an Indiana limestone altar all testify that quality materials could be affordable. The architectural profession immediately acknowledged the success of Dart's design with awards from the Church Architecture Guild and the American Institute of Architects. The religious press placed the church on the cover of several national magazines.[46] *Your Church* magazine called St. Augustine's "one of the most significant of America's new church buildings" in 1960, lauding the architecture that was "forged in an atmosphere of theological integrity, architectural honesty, and utilitarian sincerity."[47]

The new church drew members, totaling about three hundred by 1960, mostly professionals attracted by the strength and sophistication of the congregation and its leadership. St. Augustine's earned parish status in 1961 and reached its greatest number of members in the late 1960s, with 364 communicants in 1969.[48] Father Wells stayed until 1963. Following a series of supply priests, a young interim, Reverend Robert Hood, served the parish for four years, initiating the first folk mass in Gary, an art exhibition, and a nationally publicized Summer Urban Program for college students. At this time, improvements to the church included partitions for the basement (which for a time housed a public kindergarten), a pipe organ, stained glass above the side walls in the sanctuary, and updated office equipment. The activities of the parish, such as meetings of the Episcopal Church Women (ECW) and the Jack and Jill Club (a social and cultural organization for mothers and children of the African American, professional class), brought the members together during the week.

The church building has been a source of pride for the congregation. Parishioners, proud and protective, have "treated that building like it was a member of the family."[49] Meanwhile, the Tolleston neighborhood surrounding St. Augustine's has endured rough times. South of the church, middle-class stability holds on; properties north of the church tell a story of flight and decline. Mixed in with houses that are still well maintained are empty properties and signs of poverty. With a drop in student population, the once state-of-the-art Ernie Pyle elementary school (1960) fell vacant and plywood covers its windows.

A solid future for St. Augustine's will largely be the result of the efforts of Paula DeBois. At her father's 2008 funeral DeBois looked around the church and felt the power and peace of the architecture and the community within it.[50] Understanding the importance and vulnerability of both, she has since worked tirelessly to learn all she can about the architect, the building, and the congregation's history. As she found out more about Edward Dart and discovered the original response to the building, she knew that the congregation owned a gem and set out to gain back the recognition it deserves. In June 2013, the congregation teamed with Partners for Sacred Places to hold a workshop about honoring and preserving the congregation's architecture and history (Figure 8.10). In the fall of 2013, St. Augustine's won a listing on the National Register of Historic Places. Lisa Di Chiera, of Landmarks, Illinois, said, "It's refreshing to see a long-time congregation working to preserve its heritage by recognizing that the modernist building it commissioned is one of its most valuable assets."[51]

DeBois launched a Facebook page, now loaded with new and historical photographs, memories, and communication between past and present members. A 2013 post by Byron Ottman reads, "This church makes me proud to be from Gary, Indiana. The rich history is part of the history of Gary."[52] One of the often unrecognized things about the value of historic architecture—and these suburban churches are little by little assuming that status—is what it means to people who apparently have no connection beyond being neighbors. DeBois remembers that one day,

FIGURE 8.10. Gianfranco Grande of Partners for Sacred Places addresses members of St. Augustine's congregation in a workshop held in the undercroft of St. Augustine's Episcopal Church, Gary, Indiana, June 2013. Photograph by the author.

while she was taking pictures of the church, a neighbor walking a dog stopped to say, "Oh please, tell me it's not for sale!"[53] Dart's church is truly a landmark.

If even the best postwar modern religious buildings, such as Messiah and St. Augustine's, are to survive, some education as to their significance is proving important. Congregations are learning why restoration and preservation can be practical, theologically astute, and sensible paths for the future. They also are coming to understand the significance of the episode in American church architecture and religion that their buildings represent.

Measured against the long centuries of traditional church design, the flourishing of modern religious architecture in postwar America is striking. This transformation in building forms was inextricably connected to a highly distinctive time and type of place: the new, dramatically expanding post–World War II American suburb. The characteristics of the era, especially emerging affluence, rapid family formation, the baby boom, and a sense of the world being markedly different from what it had been a decade earlier, dovetailed perfectly with the fresh architectural visions emerging from architects and church leaders and the need for extensive church building to serve the exploding postwar revival of religion. The result was an extraordinary burst of creative church design and of communal religious life, in all its enthusiasm, piety, complexity, and variety. Contemporary architects as well as their church clients knew that they were part of a time and a movement that were changing the face of American religion.

That time is rapidly passing from living memory. As this book neared completion, the last of these three notable architects, Edward Sövik, passed away. Soon there will be few church members who personally remember what it was like, as suburban pioneers, to imagine, build, and move into new, modern sanctuaries, classrooms, and fellowship halls. Yet that common but important story, what suburban Christians of the 1950s and 1960s were thinking and doing, lives on in their buildings.

# APPENDIXES

A. National Council of Churches of Christ List of Eighteen "Outstanding" New Churches, 1956

B. Statement on Architecture and the Church, Composed at International Conference on Architecture and the Church, Ecumenical Institute of the World Council of Churches, Château de Bossey, Bogis-Bossey, Switzerland, 1959

C. Working List of Churches and Religious Buildings by Charles Edward Stade

D. List of Churches by Edward Dart

E. List of Churches by Edward Anders Sövik, 1949–69

# APPENDIX A

## *National Council of Churches of Christ List of Eighteen "Outstanding" New Churches, 1956*

In chronological order; from National Council of Churches of Christ records, RG 6, box 55, folder 18, Presbyterian Historical Society.

San Lorenzo Community Church, San Lorenzo, California (Bruce Goff, 1941 chapel at Camp Parks, moved and renovated in 1953)
Tabernacle Church of Christ, Columbus, Indiana (Eliel Saarinen, 1942)
Church of St. Clement (Episcopal), Alexandria, Virginia (Joseph H. Saunders Jr., 1948)
Christ Evangelical Lutheran Church, Minneapolis (Eliel Saarinen, 1949)
Zion Lutheran Church, Portland, Oregon (Pietro Belluschi, 1950)
Central Lutheran Church, Portland, Oregon (Pietro Belluschi, 1951)
First Methodist Church, Plainfield, Iowa (Paul Schweikher and Winston Elting, 1951)
First Presbyterian Church, Cottage Grove, Oregon (Pietro Belluschi, 1951)
Meeting House of the First Unitarian Society, Madison, Wisconsin (Frank Lloyd Wright, 1951)
Carr Memorial Chapel, Illinois Institute of Technology, Chicago (Mies van der Rohe, 1952)
First Methodist Church, Midland, Michigan (Alden B. Dow, 1952)
Wayfarer's Chapel (Church of the New Jerusalem), Palos Verdes, California (Lloyd Wright, 1952)
St. Matthew's Episcopal Church, Pacific Palisades, California (A. Quincy Jones and Frederick Emmons, 1953 remodel)
St. Stephen's Episcopal Church, Columbus, Ohio (Brooks & Coddington, 1953)
Danforth Chapel, Colorado A&M, Fort Collins, Colorado (James M. Hunter, 1954)
St. George's Episcopal Church, Durham, New Hampshire (John A. Carter, 1954)
Central Lutheran Church, Eugene, Oregon (Pietro Belluschi, 1955)
Chapel, Massachusetts Institute of Technology, Cambridge, Massachusetts (Eero Saarinen, 1955)

# APPENDIX B

## *Statement on Architecture and the Church*

## *Composed at International Conference on Architecture and the Church, Ecumenical Institute of the World Council of Churches, Château de Bossey, Bogis-Bossey, Switzerland, 1959*

1. Our twentieth-century material and scientific progress and discovery, our new ways of thought and living, do not invalidate the ageless message of Christianity. The conditions of life today are calling the Church into the common life of man, away from the enclosed sanctuary, to witness in daily work. This may create new forms of Christian community life which will also lead to expression in buildings which represent, like other buildings of our time, the thinking of modern man. New buildings are often needed to consolidate this evangelistic work and to draw men together in Christian fellowship.
2. In earlier times the church building was one of the finest expressions of the age. This does not solve our problem. We have to face our task in our time to find a new expression of Christian life today through the buildings we make.
3. The serving and not the dominating role of the Church should be kept in mind. This can be expressed, not only in the building, but in the way in which it is related to the town plan. The church building should not be a venture in personal expression, an architectural *tour de force*, or merely a sensuously satisfying achievement.
4. The Church must take account of the needs of modern society, through the use of community centres, the house church and the chapel in industrial centres.
5. The selection of architects for the church need not be on the basis of formal membership in the Christian community nor prior experience with the Church's problems. Good architecture is the essential; and the best architects are men of imagination, energy and artistic integrity who may be willing to serve the Church as ably as they do other clients. Properly run architectural competitions help the churches in making the right choice. Since the Church must speak to the world as well as to itself, men who know the world as well as the Church are to be preferred to those who know only the Church.
6. A good church building is normally the finished work of a single designer. The congregation has the obligation to brief the architect fully. Throughout the briefing process the Church must leave the designer free to speak his mind and

do his work. Good churches are never built by committees. Let the architect be the architect.

7. The architect should understand his client's need in all its aspects and endeavor to fulfill that need through the medium of the architecture he produces.
8. A dialogue must continue between Church and architect, and in this dialogue the Church should not insist on the right to make artistic decisions. The architect for his part must endeavor to serve the purpose of the Church.
9. The substance of this conversation is the work and life of the Church as a community with a mission and a living message for the modern world.
10. The place of worship should help the congregation to act corporately in the praise and service of God. Design must avoid distraction so as to focus the attention of all the worshippers on the worship and its expression through acts and symbols in the building. The fixing of the mind upon God is corporate and active. Scientific, theological, and architectural studies of this problem should be conducted by the churches through bringing specialists together within the growing agreement on the nature of worship in the ecumenical movement.
11. Fine art in the Church should not be understood as something additional or merely decorative, but as an organic part of the architecture arising from the work and worship of the church. The church must not be a museum of fine art or of archaeological relics. The highest standard of industrial design achieved in everyday life should be applied to the furnishings of the church including all the minor arts such as printing, posters, and fabrics.
12. Church authorities, theological students, building committees and congregations need to be educated in the meaning of contemporary architecture by literature, exhibitions, filmstrips and other means. Similarly, the churches must educate their architects.
13. The churches pray for the unity of the Church; let us work for it. If we prune away the habits and patterns which represent unessential differences between the churches, if we provide buildings which meet the purposes of the Christian community in today's world, we may find that in tomorrow's world we will indeed be a truer Christian community, broad enough to encompass the differences which should and will remain.

# APPENDIX C

## *Working List of Churches and Religious Buildings by Charles Edward Stade*

### STADE'S ARCHITECTURE FIRMS

1951–55 Charles Edward Stade & Associates, Chicago (Stade & Cooley, 1953–55)
1955–59 Charles Edward Stade & Associates, Park Ridge, Illinois
1960–63 Stade, Dolan, Anderson, Bonesz & Associates, Park Ridge, Illinois
1964–66 Stade, Dolan & Anderson, Park Ridge, Illinois
1966–69 Stade, Dolan, Emrich & Associates, Park Ridge, Illinois
1970–78 Charles E. Stade, Architect, Park Ridge, Illinois

### BUILDINGS

In chronological order. Date is dedication date, if known. Name is original name of congregation, with significant later name changes in parentheses.

Trinity Lutheran Church, Center Line (Warren), Michigan, 1952–53
Christ Evangelical and Reformed Church (Christ Church United Church of Christ), Des Plaines, Illinois, 1953 parish hall, 1964 sanctuary
Our Redeemer Lutheran Church, Freeport, Illinois, ca. 1953–54
Bethel (United) Methodist Church, addition, 4258 North Ridgeway Avenue, Chicago, ca. 1954
Hope Lutheran Church (Celebration Ministries), Park Forest, Illinois, first unit 1954, school 1960, new sanctuary building 1967
Pilgrim Lutheran Church, Marysville, Michigan, 1954
Portage Park Methodist Church (Irving Park United Methodist Church), Portage Park, Illinois, remodel, ca. 1954
St. Andrews Lutheran Church, Park Ridge, Illinois, 1954
St. Paul Lutheran Church, Oak Lawn, Illinois, 1954
Zion Evangelical Lutheran Church, Deerfield, Illinois, 1954
First (United) Methodist Church, Crystal Lake, Illinois, 1955
Niles Community Church (Presbyterian), Niles, Illinois, ca. 1955
Ascension of Christ Lutheran Church, Beverly Hills, Michigan, 1956
Community Presbyterian Church, Mount Prospect, Illinois, 1956, education building ca. 1959

Holy Cross Lutheran Church, Cleveland, Oho, 1956
Holy Trinity Lutheran Church, Macon, Georgia, 1956 (demolished)
The Lutheran Church of the Good Shepherd, Palos Park, Illinois, 1956
Lutheran Church of the Resurrection, Roseville, Minnesota, first unit 1956, new sanctuary 1965
Lutheran Church of the Resurrection, Yardley, Pennsylvania, 1956
St. Nicolai Evangelical and Reformed Church (St. Nicolai United Church of Christ) 3000 North Kedzie Avenue, Chicago, Illinois, 1956–57
Zion Evangelical Lutheran Church, Kalamazoo, Michigan, 1956
Church of the Reformation-Lutheran, Affton, Missouri, 1957
Edison Park Lutheran Church, 6626 North Oliphant Avenue, Chicago, Illinois, expansion and addition, 1957
Evangelical Lutheran Church of St. Matthew, Scarborough, Ontario, Canada, 1957
First Congregational Church, Lombard, Illinois, 1957
Immanuel Lutheran Church, Des Plaines, Illinois, 1957
Our Savior Lutheran Church, Norwood Park, Illinois, education building, 1957
Pilgrim Lutheran Church, Hamilton County, Indiana (Indianapolis), 1957 (demolished)
Bethel Evangelical and Reformed Church (Bethel United Church of Christ), Elmhurst, Illinois, 1958
Community Presbyterian Church (Manav Seva Mandir, Sanatan Hindu Temple), Bensenville, Illinois, 1958
First Baptist Church (First United Church), Bloomington, Indiana, 1958
First English Evangelical and Reformed Church (Old Holy Resurrection Serbian Orthodox Church), 3062 Palmer Street, Chicago, Illinois, addition, 1958
Lutheran Church of the Ascension, Atlanta, Georgia, 1958
Our Saviour's Lutheran Church, Arlington Heights, Illinois, 1958
St. Paul Lutheran Church, Albion, Michigan, 1958
St. Peter's Lutheran Church, 8550 South Kedvale Avenue, Chicago, Illinois, 1958
St. Timothy Evangelical Lutheran Church, 2100 North Killdare Avenue, Chicago, Illinois, 1958
South Baptist Church (South Church), Mount Prospect, Illinois, education building, 1958
Zion Lutheran Church, Kewanee, Illinois, 1958
Acacia Park Lutheran Church, Norridge, Illinois, 1959–60
Chapel of the Resurrection, Valparaiso University, Valparaiso, Indiana, 1959
Elston Avenue (United) Methodist Church, 5850 North Elston Avenue, Chicago, Illinois, 1959
Glenview Presbyterian Church (North Branch Bible Church), Glenview, Illinois, 1959

Immanuel United Church of Christ, Bensenville, Illinois, education building, 1959
Northlake Lutheran Church (Northlake City Centre), Northlake, Illinois, sanctuary remodel and education building, 1959
Our Redeemer Lutheran Church, Prospect Heights, Illinois, 1959
Our Savior Lutheran Church, Midland, Michigan, ca. 1959
St. Matthew Lutheran Church, Barrington, Illinois, 1959
Trinity Lutheran Church, Lombard, Illinois, 1959
Trinity Presbyterian Church, Oak Lawn, Illinois, 1959–60
Villa Park Christian Church, Villa Park, Illinois, 1959–60
Ashburn Baptist Church, 3647 West Eighty-third Street, Chicago, Illinois, 1960
Bethany Lutheran Church, Naperville, Illinois, 1960
Christ Evangelical Lutheran Church, Palatine, Illinois, ca. 1960
First Lutheran Church, Chattanooga, Tennessee, 1960
Lutheran Church of the Holy Spirit, Elk Grove Village, Illinois, 1960, education building 1963
Martin Luther Evangelical Lutheran Church, 6850 Addison Street, Chicago, Illinois, new sanctuary expansion, 1960
Northbrook (United) Methodist Church, Northbrook, Illinois, 1960
Our Saviour's (United) Methodist Church, Hoffman Estates, Illinois, 1960 (demolished)
St. James Lutheran Church, Western Springs, Illinois, ca. 1960
First Presbyterian Church, Arlington Heights, Illinois, education building, ca. 1961
Fountain of Life Lutheran Church, Tucson, Arizona, 1961
Hillside Free Methodist Church (Hillside Church), Evanston, 1961
Lake View Lutheran Church, West Addison Street, Chicago, Illinois, 1961
Messiah Lutheran Church, Burlington, Iowa, 1961
Our Savior Lutheran Church, Joliet, Illinois, 1961
Our Saviour Lutheran Church, Lansing, Illinois, 1961
St. Luke's United Church of Christ (St. Luke's Christian Community Church), Morton Grove, Illinois, first unit without sanctuary, 1961
St. Paul Lutheran Church, Mount Prospect, Illinois, 1961
St. Peter Lutheran Church, Arlington Heights, Illinois, 1961
Winnetka Presbyterian Church, Winnetka, Illinois, 1961
First Lutheran Church, Harvey, Illinois, 1962
First Presbyterian Church, La Grange, Illinois, remodel and expansion, 1962
Resurrection Lutheran Church, Franklin Park, Illinois, 1962
Salem United Church of Christ, Oak Lawn, Illinois, 1962
St. John's Lutheran Church, Lincolnwood, Illinois, 1962
Bethany Theological Seminary, Oak Brook, Illinois, 1963 (demolished)

First Evangelical Lutheran Church, Lake Geneva, Wisconsin, ca. 1963
Good Shepherd (United) Methodist Church (Embers School), Park Ridge, Illinois, 1963 (awaiting demolition)
Immanuel Lutheran Church, Seymour, Indiana, 1963
Peace Lutheran Church, Fort Wayne, Indiana, 1963
St. Paul's Evangelical Lutheran Church, Glen Burnie, Maryland, 1963
Trinity Evangelical Divinity School, Bannockburn, Illinois, ca. 1963
Martin Luther Chapel, Michigan State University, Lansing, Michigan, 1964
St. John Lutheran School, Forest Park, Illinois, 1964
St. John's Lutheran Church, Westfield, Massachusetts, 1964
Temple B'nai Torah, Highland Park, 1964–66 (probably by Irving Moses, Stade is architect of record)
Chapel of the Sermon on the Mount, Associated Mennonite Biblical Seminary, Elkhart, Indiana, 1965
St. John Lutheran Church, Janesville, Wisconsin, 1965
St. Paul Lutheran Church, Peoria, Illinois, 1966
First Evangelical Lutheran Church, Decatur, Illinois, ca. 1968
Joliet Jewish Congregation, Joliet, Illinois, 1968
St. John's Lutheran Church, La Grange, Illinois, 1968
St. Joseph Catholic Church, Summit, Illinois, 1970
St. Mary Catholic Church, Des Plaines, Illinois, 1971
St. Lawrence Seminary, Mount Calvary, Wisconsin, ca. 1972
Holy Family Catholic Church, Rockford, Illinois, 1973–75

# APPENDIX D

## *List of Churches by Edward Dart*

In chronological order. Date is dedication date, if known. Name is original name of congregation, with significant later name changes in parentheses.

St. Michael's Episcopal Church, Barrington, Illinois, 1954
Church of the Holy Family (Episcopal), Park Forest, Illinois, 1959
St. Ambrose Episcopal Church (The Emmaus Community), Chicago Heights, Illinois, 1959
St. Augustine's Episcopal Church, Gary, Indiana, 1959
Grace Lutheran Church, Bensenville, Illinois, 1961
Lutheran Church of the Atonement, Barrington, Illinois, 1961 (demolished)
St. Mark's Lutheran Church, Aurora, Illinois, 1961
All Saints Lutheran Church, Orland Park, Illinois, 1962
Calvary Lutheran Church, 11249 South Spaulding Avenue, Chicago, Illinois, 1962
St. Augustine of Canterbury Episcopal Church, Benton Harbor, Michigan, 1962
Thornridge United Church of Christ (Covenant United Church of Christ), South Holland, Illinois, 1962
Emmanuel Presbyterian Church, 1850 South Racine Avenue, Chicago, Illinois, 1963 (demolished)
Episcopal Church of the Resurrection, West Chicago, Illinois, 1963 (vacant)
House of Prayer Lutheran Church, Country Club Hills, Illinois, 1963
Lansing Presbyterian Church, Lansing, Illinois, 1963
St. Nicholas Episcopal Church, Elk Grove Village, Illinois, 1963
St. Matthew United Church of Christ, Wheaton, Illinois, 1964
Holy Apostles Greek Orthodox Church, Westchester, Illinois, 1965
St. Luke's (United) Methodist Church, Indianapolis, Indiana, 1967
Augustana Lutheran Church, 5500 South Woodlawn Avenue, Chicago, Illinois, 1968
The Presbyterian Church of La Porte, La Porte, Indiana, 1968
First St. Paul's Lutheran Church, 1301 North La Salle Drive, Chicago, Illinois, 1970
St. Procopius Abbey, Lisle, Illinois, 1970
Holy Ghost Catholic Church, South Holland, Illinois, 1971
St. John of the Cross Catholic Church, Western Springs, Illinois, 1977 (completed posthumously)

# APPENDIX E

## *List of Churches by Edward Anders Sövik, 1949–69*

Original source: Mark Torgerson, "Edward Anders Sövik and His Return to the 'Non-Church,'" Ph.D. dissertation, University of Notre Dame, 1996. This list is not exhaustive, but represents what Sövik considered to be his best work.

In chronological order. Date is dedication date, if known. Name is original name of congregation.

Riverside Bible Camp Chapel, Story City, Iowa, 1950
Northfield Moravian Church, Northfield, Minnesota, ca. 1951–52
Calvary Lutheran Church, Scottsbluff, Nebraska, 1952
Trinity Lutheran Church, Ellsworth, Iowa, 1952, education building 1959
Trinity Lutheran Church, Moorhead, Minnesota, 1952
Trinity Lutheran Church, West Concord, Minnesota, 1952
Zion Lutheran Church, Galesville, Wisconsin, education building 1952, church 1956
Bethel Lutheran Church, Newtown, North Dakota, 1953
Chatfield Lutheran Church, Chatfield, Minnesota, 1953
Hope Lutheran Church, Powell, Wyoming, 1953
First Lutheran Church, Onalaska, Wisconsin, 1954
Lutheran Church of the Good Shepherd, Moorhead, Minnesota, first unit 1954, sanctuary 1967 (demolished)
Our Savior's Lutheran Church, Austin, Minnesota, first unit 1954, sanctuary 1962
Paynesville Lutheran Church, Paynesville, Minnesota, 1954 (demolished)
First Lutheran Church, Williston, North Dakota, 1955
St. Paul's Lutheran Church, Lacrosse, Wisconsin, phase one 1956, sanctuary 1961
Zion Lutheran Church, Warroad, Minnesota, 1956
First Baptist Church, Bloomington, Indiana, 1957
Lutheran Church of the Good Shepherd, Rockford, Illinois, 1958
Zion Evangelical Lutheran Church, Dysart, Iowa, 1958–60
Augustana Lutheran Church, Denver, Colorado, 1959
Calvary Lutheran Church, Park Rapids, Minnesota, 1960
Trinity Lutheran Church, Minnehaha Falls, Minneapolis, Minnesota, 1961
Calvary Lutheran Church, Grand Forks, North Dakota, 1962
Evangelical Lutheran Church, Mount Horeb, Wisconsin, 1962

Trinity Lutheran Church, Lisbon, North Dakota, 1962
Westwood Lutheran Church, St. Louis Park, Minnesota, 1963
Olivet Lutheran Church, Fargo, North Dakota, 1965
First Presbyterian Church, Lawrence, Kansas, 1966–68
Northfield Methodist Church, Northfield, Minnesota, 1966
Zion Mennonite Church, Souderton, Pennsylvania, 1966–68
St. Leo Catholic Church, Pipestone, Minnesota, 1969

# NOTES

## INTRODUCTION

1. See *Briefs for Church Builders*, no. 10, "Multiple Church and Church School Sessions," National Council of Churches of Christ in the U.S.A., 1956. This leaflet intended for church building committees noted that the trend was toward having Sunday school for young children at the same time as church, with two full services with a full Sunday school during each service. A "relatively new solution" was to have two church services with a Sunday school hour in between.

2. Official, self-reported statistics about church attendance indicate that in the postwar period approximately half of polled Americans said they attended church regularly. Scholars are rightly skeptical of such statistics, given that people tend to report at a higher rate than actual attendance. See www.gallup.com; for overall trends in American church affiliation, see Roger Finke and Rodney Stark, *The Churching of America, 1775–1990: Winners and Losers in Our Religious Economy* (New Brunswick, N.J.: Rutgers University Press, 1992); for a deep analysis of the contemporary experience and a careful use of statistics balanced with extensive congregational studies, see Mark Chaves, *Congregations in America* (Cambridge, Mass.: Harvard University Press, 2004), and the National Congregations Study, www.soc.duke.edu/natcong. The present study is concerned primarily with the experience of postwar suburbanites who *did* bring themselves and their families to these buildings to worship, learn, and socialize.

3. Although *modern* might refer to systems and facilities as well as style, contemporaries used the term to indicate contemporary architecture in contrast to other buildings, such as those "Colonial" buildings that copied the architecture of a previous era. Throughout this book, I will employ terms such as "modern" and "contemporary" as used by ordinary postwar Americans in the congregations I studied. Ordinary Americans in the 1950s did think of modern architecture as a "style" (and spoke of the "modern style"). Experts recognized modernism more as an "approach," but common people saw modernism as the style of their day, as reflected in period documents. See William S. Clark, "Church Architecture in America: 1955–65," *Your Church* (January–February 1965): 19. For an excellent development of these themes as they relate to postwar Colonial churches, see Dale Dowling, "For God, for Family, for Country: Colonial Revival Church Buildings in the Cold War Era," Ph.D. dissertation, George Washington University, 2004.

4. Edward D. Mills, *The Modern Church* (New York: Praeger, 1956), 15.

5. Ibid.

6. Typescript of address by Professor Robert S. Baker to General Board Meeting of National Council of Churches of Christ, October 17, 1963. National Council of Churches of Christ in the U.S.A., Record Group 6, box 53, folder 1 (hereafter noted as NCC RG 6–53–1).

7. The Midwest is difficult to define, as James Shortridge explains in *The Middle West: Its Meaning in American Culture* (Lawrence: University Press of Kansas, 1989). Geographically (with a few outliers in Arizona, Maryland, and Georgia), the churches in this study range from Fargo, North Dakota, to Bloomington, Indiana, and from Sioux Falls, South Dakota, to Kalamazoo, Michigan. The majority of field research took place in suburban Chicago, which Shortridge calls the "regional capital" (17). The architecture of these churches was rooted in local building traditions, locally available materials, and religious and ethnic heritage. The *character* of this region is more slippery but important, as it also affected the religious culture of the suburbs. Shortridge identifies "Midwestern" character traits, such as pragmatism, industry, morality, and humility, and quotes an Iowa editor who in 1949 lamented the fact that "the interior of the country is strictly a bench-warmer in the national line-up" but took comfort in believing that this was the "most stable, normal and happy part of the United States" (66). These are, of course, stereotypes, but stereotypes nonetheless rooted in experience. Churches in the Midwest seemed especially concerned about helping the region to retain its strong moral character and not to capitulate to negative influences from the East and West Coasts. See also Richard Sisson, Christian Zacher, and Andrew Cayton, eds., *The American Midwest: An Interpretive Encyclopedia* (Bloomington: Indiana University Press, 2007), especially 703–91 and 1145–48.

8. Edward A. Sövik, editorial in the *Newsletter of the Guild for Religious Architecture* (hereafter, "Guild *Newsletter*") 46 (October 1966), American Institute of Architects (AIA) records, Interfaith Forum on Religion Art and Architecture (IFRAA); hereafter, AIA/IFRAA, box 5306.

9. See Pietro Belluschi, "The Meaning of Regionalism in Architecture," *Architectural Record* 118, no. 6 (December 1955): 131–39.

10. Structurally, suburban Jews followed a very similar model of activities in similar spaces. For instance, an article describing the new Beth El synagogue in Cleveland noted that the "building programs of most new synagogues exemplify this trend of stressing day-by-day religion by including not only the primary requirements for religious worship, but also ample provisions for religious instruction, social gathering, lectures and forums, club rooms for the teen agers and ample facilities for dining functions." The article further claimed that the synagogue was becoming the center of Jewish community once again. See "Synagogue That Emphasizes Day by Day Religion," *Church Management* (January 1953): 20–21.

11. Balanced and informed period accounts of the state and prospects of Jews and Catholics in the suburbs can be found in the writing of Rabbi Albert G. Isaac and Andrew Greeley. See, for instance, Isaac's *Jews in Suburbia* (Boston: Beacon Press, 1959), which includes a focus on St. Louis Park, Minnesota, and the Chicago suburb of Skokie (and also Niles and Lincolnwood) as communities with a strong postwar Jewish presence. His overall sanguine outlook is reflected in observations such as, "I believe that the suburb has strengthened Jewish family life" (84). Isaac describes the synagogue as the house of prayer, study, and assembly, a mirror image of the Christian emphasis on worship, Sunday school, and fellowship.

Of course, there were critical differences among the faiths, but structurally, the experience—and the architecture—was similar. Isaac in fact compares the suburban Protestant church and synagogue, "each . . . is increasingly emphasizing the neighborhood, the community, the ethical, moral, and social values associated with religion" (88). One difference he notes is that the suburban synagogue typically began as a social center and soon drew a rabbi and began a school, with an emphasis on the needs of children (95–96). Overall, he was heartened to find that in the suburbs a younger generation of American Jews was finding the will to deliberately claim a Jewish identity, creating a world they might have ignored or taken for granted in the cities (247). Greeley, a priest and analyst of suburban Catholicism, in *The Church and the Suburbs* (Sheed & Ward, 1959), reflected on both the challenges and the opportunities suburban living brought to a new generation of Catholics.

12. Justin Wilford, *Sacred Subdivisions: The Postsuburban Transformation of American Evangelicalism* (New York: New York University Press, 2012).

13. "The Lush New Suburban Market," *Fortune* 47, no. 11 (November 1953): 129.

14. Martin E. Marty, *The New Shape of American Religion* (New York: Harper Brothers, 1959), 98.

15. Joan Beck, "Bursting Point in Paradise: Chicago's 275 Suburbs Spilling over Their Limits as Populations Double, Triple, Quadruple," *Chicago Sun Times*, May 25, 1958 (article in records of Park Forest Public Library).

16. McGraw-Hill Department of Economics, "The Boom in Church Building," typescript dated April 29, 1958 (NCC RG 6–53–17).

17. Glenn D. Everett, "Churches Set an All-Time Building Record," *Church Management* 30, no. 6 (March 1954): 9.

18. Report of the National Conference on Church Architecture, Los Angeles, 1959 (AIA/IFRAA, box 5309). The boom hit a plateau in 1962. See Clark, "Church Architecture in America," 18. See also "Building Boom, or Christians Creating," *Christian Century* 74, no. 13 (March 27, 1957): 381–82.

19. "Roseville's Churches: How They Started, How They Grew," fragment of local news clipping in Lutheran Church of the Resurrection, Roseville, Minnesota, records (1973).

20. See, for instance, Diane Harris, ed., *Second Suburb: Levittown, Pennsylvania* (Pittsburgh: University of Pittsburgh, 2010); Kevin M. Kruse and Thomas J. Sugrue, eds., *The New Suburban History* (Chicago: University of Chicago Press, 2006); Becky Nicolaides and Andrew Wiese, eds., *The Suburb Reader* (London: Routledge, 2006).

21. Marty, *The New Shape of American Religion*, 31.

22. Ibid., 64.

23. Ibid., 100. See also Martin E. Marty, "Protestantism in Panurbia," *Christian Century* 75, no. 44 (October 29, 1958): 1232–35.

24. This may be because the scholarly focus has been on the decline of the mainline denominations since the 1970s. This decline is certainly one of the critical issues in American religion, yet a focus primarily on decline misses many dimensions of the history of the Protestant church in America in the postwar decades. The subject has been thoroughly studied by scholars from a variety of academic fields, including theology, history, and sociology. See, for example, Wade Clark Roof and William McKinney, *American Mainline Religion: Its Changing Shape and Future* (New Brunswick, N.J.: Rutgers University Press, 1987), and Robert Wuthnow, *The Restructuring of American Religion: Society and Faith since World War II* (Princeton, N.J.: Princeton University Press, 1988). The architectural history of the suburbs

has focused primarily on houses, with some work on shopping centers as well. Suburban churches (and schools) have received very little attention.

25. Cited in Marty, *The New Shape of American Religion*, 100.

26. See Harris, *Second Suburb*, 67–68.

27. A comprehensive study of the character and activities of these congregations is beyond the scope of this architectural history. But, after looking at a vast quantity of congregational documents in search of information about buildings, it became clear that the large majority of church activities had a deliberate religious component. Much of this activity, however, centered on family practice and personal piety, things notoriously difficult to measure and not the sort of activities social commentators were seeking to find.

28. Edward Sövik, "Some Notes on the Work of SMSQ," February 2, 1993, Sövik Archive, Luther Seminary (hereafter, SA), box 2, folder 4, item 7.

29. Sarah Williams Goldhagen, *Anxious Modernisms: Experimentation in Postwar Architecture and Culture* (Boston: MIT Press, 2000), 314–15.

30. Edward A. Sövik Interview, June 19, 2007.

31. Albert Christ-Janer and Mary Mix Foley, *Modern Church Architecture: A Guide to the Form and Spirit of 20th Century Religious Buildings* (New York: McGraw-Hill, 1962), 127. In the June 1953 issue of *Church Management*, editor William Leach summarized emerging denominational proclivities: "There is no parallel between theology and architectural styles. Lutheran churches are traditionally conservative in theology but among Protestants they seem to lead in contemporary and modernistic building designs. The Methodists have more than their share of theological and social liberals but their newer buildings are more apt to follow the traditional." In the Midwest, Methodists soon heartily embraced modern church designs and Episcopalians followed suit (William H. Leach, "The New American Church Building," *Church Management* [June 1953]: 26).

32. For a thorough treatment of this subject, see Dowling, "For God, For Family, For Country," 2004.

33. Edward A. Sövik, "On the Design," in Trinity Lutheran Church Dedication Week Bulletin, September 28–October 5, 1952, Trinity Lutheran Church, Moorhead, Minnesota, records.

34. Joseph Sittler, "Design for the Church in the Community," typescript of lecture, ca. 1955 (NCC RG 6–52–11).

35. This is exactly what members of the congregation of St. Augustine of Canterbury Episcopal Church in Benton Harbor, Michigan, remember telling their architect, Edward Dart (Roy Shoemaker and Priscilla Banghart interview, Benton Harbor, May 17, 2007).

36. I have been intrigued by the complexity of these organizations that is often lost in accounts that want to tell a certain story. For instance, a 1968 *McCall's* article, "The Suburb That Turned Its Back," is a critique of the insularity and increasing apathy of Park Forest, Illinois, particularly through the eyes of the booming crop of teenage residents. Yet, after stating that "a strong anti-urban attitude pervades the village and has seeped deeply into its young," the author mentions that Faith United Protestant Church study groups meet to consider the best process of integration, a group of Unitarians belong to the Chicago civil rights movement, and there are a small number of teenagers who "venture into the inner-city ghettos for volunteer work with church youth groups." Granted, this is 1968, not the 1950s, but church records and memories nonetheless indicate that even in the 1950s churches were sites of growth and change as well as conformity. See Lois Wille, "The Suburb That Turned

Its Back," *McCall's* 95, no. 10 (July 1968): 14, 124–25. None other than former first lady and secretary of state Hillary Clinton, who was thirteen in 1960, attributes the early formation of her sense of social justice and Christian responsibility to the influence of her youth pastor at First Methodist Church in suburban Park Ridge, Illinois. See http://www.cnn.com/2014/04/25/politics/clinton-methodist-minister/.

37. I am indebted to Martin Marty for his suggestion that I treat this period, centered on the 1950s, as an "episode" in the American religious experience.

## 1. THE MODERN CHURCH MOVEMENT

1. For just one example, *Your Church* magazine indicated that paperback copies of editor William S. Clark's *Building the New Church* (1957) were available for free "to help you plan for your church building or rebuilding program" (*Your Church* [January–March 1962]: 69).

2. Edward Sövik recalled that during this period there were at least eleven circulating periodicals on church art, architecture, and building (Edward Sövik interview, Northfield, Minnesota, June 19, 2007). Jay Price's *Temples for a Modern God: Religious Architecture in Postwar America* (New York: Oxford University Press, 2013) offers a sweeping account of the architecture of American religious denominations from the 1930s through 1970. Price's work is grounded in exceptionally thorough research in denominational archives and popular religious periodicals, and is an essential resource for anyone interested in the religious architecture of this period. Here I am focused on the conversations and organizations that influenced more particularly (and were influenced by) the architects in this study, and their clients.

3. For a period assessment of these sources, see Martin E. Marty, "The Test of the Tastemakers," *Christian Century* 75, no. 8 (February 19, 1958): 224–26.

4. For decades denominational bureaus had played an important role in helping congregations design, build, and pay for new churches. In 1933, the founding of an Interdenominational Bureau of Architecture began the official coordination of these efforts among Protestants. During the postwar building expansion, such efforts grew. For an excellent account of the work of these denominational bodies during the twentieth century, see Price, *Temples for a Modern God* (2103).

5. Brother Cajetan J. B. Baumann, "Behind the Renewal in Church Building," in William S. Clark, ed., *For Church Builders: A Recall to Basics* (Valley Forge, Pa.: Agora Books, 1969), 10. Article originally published in *Your Church* (May/June 1965), and the sentiment predates that publication.

6. Edward S. Frey, "Building for the Christian Community," report of National Conference on Church Architecture, Los Angeles, 1959, 1 (AIA/IFRAA, box 5309).

7. Members at the outset included twenty-five Protestant denominations and four Orthodox communions; neither Roman Catholics nor member churches of the National Association of Evangelicals (est. 1942) joined. The NCC succeeded the Federal Council of Churches, a Protestant organization established in 1908.

8. See James F. White, *Protestant Worship and Church Architecture: Theological and Historical Considerations* (New York: Oxford University Press, 1964).

9. See E. Crosby Willet, "GRA? ASCA? NCRA? Who's Who and What's What," *Journal of the American Society for Church Architecture* 12 (1971): 5–8.

10. American Institute of Architects, *A Place to Worship*, ca. 1958, American Institute of Architects and American Architectural Foundation Collection at the Library of Congress, unprocessed; see also preliminary typescript, 1958 (NCC RG 6–53–17).

11. Letter from Bill Canaday, Park Avenue Congregational Church, Arlington, Massachusetts, November 12, 1958. The congregation went on to hire Pietro Belluschi to design a contemporary church (NCC RG 6–53–17).

12. Guild *Headquarters Bulletin*, June 1962 (AIA/IFRAA, box 5306).

13. Mark Torgerson, "Edward Anders Sövik," in Richard Sisson, Christian Zacher, and Andrew Cayton, eds., *The American Midwest: An Interpretive Encyclopedia* (Bloomington: Indiana University Press, 2007), 786.

14. G. E. Kidder Smith, "Six New European Churches," *Architectural Forum* 99, no. 6 (December 1953): 104. This kind of review article is common in both architectural and church periodicals, with special attention paid to the churches of northern Europe, Germany in particular.

15. Sövik was impressed by Schwarz's work. In Sövik's 1964 address to the National Conference on Church Architecture in Dallas, "The Faith Our Forms Express," he asked his audience to think of Schwarz's church, "Remember the great, white east wall in his church at Aachen in its brilliant light, and the congregation facing it, and the altar between the wall and the people—the meeting place of the faithful people and the absolute and pure God" (typescript, SA, box 1, folder 4).

16. Elbert M. Conover, *The Church Builder* (New York: International Bureau of Architecture, 1948), 28, 32, 41.

17. "Christ Church Lutheran" is how the church refers to itself today, but in midcentury church records the church is known as "Christ Lutheran Church," so I will use that name in the text.

18. See Joseph M. Siry, *Beth Shalom Synagogue: Frank Lloyd Wright and Modern Religious Architecture* (Chicago: University of Chicago Press, 2012), 247–307.

19. Glennys Knutson, *The Cross and the Crown: An Interpretive History of Our Savior's Lutheran Church*, Our Savior's Lutheran Church, Austin, Minnesota (1990): 21; Our Savior's Lutheran Church, Austin, Minnesota, records.

20. Donald Bolles, "News Postlude: Church Architecture Breaks with the Past," in report of the National Conference on Church Architecture, Los Angeles, 1959, 4 (AIA/IFRAA, box 5309).

21. Guild *Newsletter* 12 (November 10, 1958) (AIA/IFRAA, box 5306).

22. Edward Sövik interview, Northfield, Minnesota, June, 19, 2007. Wagoner did design a number of notable modern churches, including the Community Church in Vero Beach, Florida (1955), Second Presbyterian Church in Ft. Lauderdale (1961), and Trinity Lutheran in East Grand Rapids, Michigan (1961).

23. Frederick Webber papers, Concordia Historical Institute, St. Louis; letter dated July 11, 1955, to Herbert Read, box 4, folder 8.

24. Marvin Halverson to Walter Taylor, March 21, 1958 ( NCC RG 6–53–17).

25. "GRA Now AIA Affiliate," undated memo, ca. 1966 (AIA/IFRAA, box 5306).

26. Edward A. Sövik, "New Visions for Church Builders," report of the National Conference on Church Architecture, Pittsburgh,1961, 13 (AIA/IFRAA, box 5309); subsequently published as Edward Sovik, "New Visions for Church Builders," *Church Management* 38, no. 1 (October 1961): 10, 12, 14, 26–27, 39.

27. Ibid., 13.

28. Ibid., 1.

29. Guild *Newsletter* 25 (August 1961) (AIA/IFRAA, box 5306).

30. In 1967, the Interfaith Forum on Religion, Art and Architecture (IFRAA) formed as the religious art and architecture wing of the AIA. That same year, IFRAA, in cooperation with the Guild, began publishing *Faith and Form,* primarily intended for architects, with an estimated initial circulation of twenty-four thousand. By 1979, most of the previously independent religious architecture organizations had joined forces. The descendant is still known collectively as IFRAA, part of the AIA. Other important partners in IFRAA were the Committee on Synagogue Administration of the Union of American Hebrew Congregations, the Central Conference of American Rabbis, and the Roman Catholic Liturgical Conference.

31. This division was called variously the Bureau of Church Building and Architecture or the Department of Church Building and Architecture. I will refer to it throughout as the Bureau to distinguish it from other departments.

32. Paraphrasing Paul Tillich, "Statement for Consideration and Study," "The Department of Worship and the Arts: Its Task in Christian Life and Work," typescript, n.d. (NCC RG 6–53–1).

33. Memo from the Commission on Architecture dated September 27, 1954 (NCC RG 6–53–10).

34. Notes on meeting of the Commission on Architecture, New York, May 27, 1954 (NCC RG 6–53–12). It is not uncommon in the records to find architects and theologians blaming building committees for the poor state of church architecture in the United States.

35. Ibid.

36. The record of this April 1960 meeting is found in NCC RG 6–55–11. Walter Taylor's independent report regarding the meeting is found in NCC RG 6–53–2.

37. Hudnut designed a small number of churches in historical styles in the 1920s, later claiming that this work was what pushed him toward modernism. When his church clients demanded new spaces for new functions, with no precedent he knew of, and they wanted it done on a budget, it "threw my composition completely out of balance"; quoted in Jill Pearlman, *Inventing American Modernism: Joseph Hudnut, Walter Gropius, and the Bauhaus legacy at Harvard* (Charlottesville: University of Virginia Press, 2007), 35.

38. Record of April 1960 Meeting (NCC RG 6–55–11).

39. Marvin Halverson to Roy Ross, March 21, 1962 (NCC RG 6–53–1).The purpose of this letter was to reiterate his resignation, effective July 15.

40. Undated memo, ca. 1955, probably by Halverson, "The Department of Worship and the Arts: Its Task in Christian Life and Work: Statement for Consideration and Study" (NCC RG 6–63–1).

41. Roger E. Manners, Countryside Community Church, Omaha, Nebraska, to DWA, August 31, 1956 (NCC RG 6–53–16).

42. These conferences were also called the Annual Conference on Church Architecture or the Annual Joint Conference on Church Architecture. Annual Guild meetings began in the 1940s as fairly small, one-day gatherings, often in New York. In the 1950s, the Guild initiated the practice of meeting in a different American city every year, meeting for the first time in Chicago in 1952.

43. Edward Sövik, "Reflections on the Cleveland Conference," in the Guild Newsletter 26 (April 1962), (SA, box 3, folder 5).

44. Guild *Newsletter* 8 (January 24, 1958) (AIA/IFRAA, box 5306). At the Cleveland conference in 1962, for instance, 70 percent of attendees were members of building committees.

45. Marlo N. Berger, "News Postlude" (typescript of article that originally appeared in *Telescope-Messenger*) in report of the National Conference on Church Architecture, Los Angeles, 1959, (AIA/IFRAA, box 5309).

46. Guild *Newsletter* 19 (June 1960). See also report of the National Conference on Church Architecture, Minneapolis, 1960 (AIA/IFRAA 5309). (In the conference report, this remark is attributed to Wagoner.)

47. Report of National Conference on Church Architecture, Minneapolis, 1960, 9.

48. Ibid., 13–14.

49. Ibid., 15.

50. Ibid., 1–2.

51. See Victoria M. Young, *Saint John's Abbey Church: Marcel Breuer and the Creation of a Modern Sacred Space* (Minneapolis: University of Minnesota Press, 2014).

52. Report of the National Conference on Church Architecture, Minneapolis, 1960, 37.

53. Report of National Conference on Church Architecture, Chicago, 1965, 73 (AIA/IFRRA, box 5309).

54. Edward Sövik's report on the Chicago Conference, in Guild *Newsletter* 33 (May–June 1965) (AIA/IFRAA, box 5306). Dart, a member of both the Guild and the ASCA at the time, also shows up in the conference program as one of the participants in a clinic, "Church Planning and Counsel for Building Committees."

55. Guild *Newsletter* 33 (May–June 1965).

56. Henry Willet, Manuscript "History of the Guild," ca. 1971 (AIA/IFRAA, box 5306).

57. Guild *Newsletter* 12 (November 10, 1958) (AIA/IFRAA, 5306).

58. Guild *Newsletter* 30 (February 1965) (AIA/IFRAA, 5306).

59. Guild "Headquarters Bulletin," vol. 1 (March 1962) (AIA/IFRAA 5306).

60. List found in NCC RG 6–52–12. See also "National Council Selects Outstanding Modern Churches," *Architectural Record* 120, no. 1 (July 1956): 10–12.

61. Notes regarding each building's selection are found in a typescript memo in NCC RG 6–55–18.

62. Report of the National Conference on Church Architecture, Minneapolis, 1960, 39–40.

63. Report of the National Conference on Church Architecture, Pittsburgh, 1961, 64 (AIA/IFRAA, box 5309).

64. "Plainfield Methodists Will Have Unique Church," *Waterloo Sunday Courier*, November 6, 1949; clipping in Plainfield Methodist Church, Plainfield, Iowa, records.

65. Mrs. James Roach to the Bureau, April 21, 1949, Plainfield Methodist Church records; "To the Members of the Methodist Church and the Church Board," probably by James Roach, Plainfield Methodist Church records.

66. Mrs. James L. Roach to Peter Blake, May 24, 1949, Plainfield Methodist Church records. Correspondence also reveals tension between the congregation and Conover (at the Bureau) regarding the advisability of the design, which limited the ability of the congregation to secure loans from the denomination. The congregation funded the building locally and paid off the debt by 1957.

67. Letter from Elbert Conover to Paul Schweikher, November 14, 1950; Elbert Conover to Reverend Robert Moss, December 30, 1950; "Insights into Today's Faith and Practice Incorporated into Design," *Motive* 11, no. 2. (November 1950): 1–4, Plainfield Methodist Church records.

68. Report of Building Committee of First Methodist Church, 1951, Plainfield Methodist Church records.

69. Edward and Marie Schroeder interview, St. Louis, Missouri, December 6, 2013.

70. Although English architects and critics such as Peter Hammond and J. G. Davies were leading voices of the modern church movement, England notably lagged behind, with the exception of a few important buildings such as the central-plan St. Paul's Church, Bow Common, London (Robert Maguire and Keith Murray, 1960). See William Clark, "Church Architecture in England: The Current Scene," *Journal of the American Society for Church Architecture* 3 (January 1963): 30–37. Of the Western European countries, only Spain and Portugal were considered further behind in the modern church movement.

71. Marvin Halverson, report on his recent European tour, October 11, 1960 (NCC RG 6–53–8).

72. Report on April 1960 Symposium (NCC RG 6–55–11).

73. Edward Sövik, "Art as a Kerygmatic Enterprise," Guild *Newsletter* 42 (April 1966) (AIA/IFRAA, box 5306).

74. Letter from Halverson to John Garrett of World Council of Churches, February 6 1959 (NCC RG 6–55–4).

75. Edward Sövik, "Architecture as a Mirror of Religious Conviction," typescript of March 9, 1990, talk, Storm Lake, Iowa (SA, box 1, folder 11).

76. "Statement on Architecture and the Church," with note from Halverson commending it to the American church (NCC RG 6–53–8).

77. Edward Sövik interview, Moorhead, Minnesota, 2008. Sövik's thinking on this question changed considerably during the 1950s. In 1954, the newsletter of his client, St. Paul's Lutheran Church in La Crosse, Wisconsin, quoted Sövik as arguing that the architect of a Christian church should be a believer. "If he does not believe in the Christian church," Sövik warned, "he is either going to fail in building a Christian church or he will make it a monument to another God, or he will temporarily accept the Christian view and give up his own convictions for the sake of the job. In either case the building is, I think, likely to be a profoundly dishonest thing!" (quoted in *The Bond* 4, no. 3 [May 1954], St. Paul's Lutheran Church, La Crosse, Wisconsin, records).

78. Edward Sövik interview, 2008.

79. Charles E. Stade, "New Materials for Design and Building," *Your Church* 7, no. 4 (October–December 1961): 49.

80. Marty, "Building for the Christian Parish in a Secular Culture," report of the National Conference on Church Architecture, Seattle, 1963, 10 (AIA/IFRAA, box 5309).

81. Guild *Newsletter* 11 (July 29, 1958) (AIA/IFRAA, box 5306).

82. Report of National Conference on Church Architecture, Cleveland 1962, 114 (AIA/IFRAA, box 5309).

83. Sövik, "New Visions for Church Builders," 13.

84. "The End of the Glass Box," *Time* 79, no. 21 (May 25, 1962): 87 (Academic Search Premier).

85. Ibid.

86. Report of the National Conference on Church Architecture, Los Angeles, 1959, G-6.

87. Report of the National Conference on Church Architecture, Seattle, 1963, 11.

88. Sövik, "New Visions for Church Builders," 15.

89. Dorothy Resenbrink, "Church Architecture and Social Crisis," *Tempo* (June 1, 1969); loose clipping (AIA/IFRAA, box 5306).

90. Sövik, cited in ibid.

91. Letter to Herbert Read, March 17, 1953, Webber Papers, Concordia Historical Institute, box 4, folder 8.

## 2. THE "FORM-GIVERS" OF SUBURBAN RELIGION

1. William Cooley, quoted in "Church Design: Imaginative Field," *Chicago Tribune*, January 16, 1966, D1 (ProQuest Historical Newspapers).

2. See, for instance, Michael S. Rose, *Ugly as Sin: Why They Changed Our Churches from Sacred Places to Meeting Spaces and How We Can Change Them Back Again* (Manchester, N.H.: Sophia Institute Press, 2001).

3. For an engaging account of Sövik's wartime adventures, see *Marine Wings: Stories of War and Peace as Written by the Pilots* (Rogers, Minn.: Deforest Press, 2007).

4. Edward Sövik interview, Northfield, Minnesota, June 19, 2007.

5. I have not been able to establish who this was. Sövik thought his name was "Cook" and he worked for a New York City firm (ibid.).

6. Ibid.

7. Ibid.

8. Ibid.

9. Edward Sövik interviews, 2007 and Northfield, Minnesota, August 7, 2008.

10. Sövik's Yale thesis won the prize for the best thesis of the year, which included an award of $1,200 to be spent traveling in Europe, but he graduated in January 1949 and the offer came in the summer, by which time he "was settled in Northfield heavily loaded with work and family." Sövik notes that through the 1930s a good number of graduates of the "serious architecture schools" spent a year traveling around Europe (Edward Sövik interview, 2007).

11. In "Some Notes on the Work of SMSQ," dated February 2, 1993, Sövik remembered that "from the beginning we refused, when asked, to design gothic or Georgian buildings" (SA, box 2, folder 4, item 7).

12. Edward Sövik interview, 2007.

13. Edward Sövik interview, 2008. He claimed that "most architects are not readers."

14. Ibid.

15. Ibid.

16. Edward Sövik to Carl Drake, First Baptist Church, Chattanooga, Tennessee, June 13, 1962 (NCC RG 6–53–10). I have been unable to identify the Norwegian church.

17. Mark Torgerson, *An Architecture of Immanence* (Grand Rapids, Mich.: William B. Eerdmans, 2007).

18. E. A. Sövik, *Architecture for Worship* (Minneapolis: Augsburg Publishing House, 1973).

19. Minutes of Meeting of Commission on Architecture, NCC Department of Worship and the Arts, May 27, 1954, typed transcript (approximate) of meeting (NCC RG6–53–12).

20. Edward Sövik interview, 2007.

21. These twelve articles were reprinted in *Your Church* magazine in September/October 1967, and later published as a chapter in William S. Clark, ed., *For Church Builders: A Recall to Basics* (Valley Forge, Pa.: Agora Books, 1969), 61–80.

22. Clark, *For Church Builders*, 79.

23. Edward Sövik, "Secular and Religious Architecture," Guild *Newsletter* 32 (April 1965) (AIA/IFRAA, box 5306).

24. Edward Sövik, remarks on "Building for Worship," report of the National Conference on Religious Architecture, Minneapolis, 1960, 30 (AIA/IFRAA, box 5309).

25. Edward Sövik, "Art as a Kerygmatic Enterprise," Guild *Newsletter* 42 (April 1966) (AIA/IFRAA, box 5306).

26. All biographical information is from Susan Dart, *Edward Dart, Architect* (Evanston, Ill.: Evanston Publishing, 1993). Also very helpful was Matthew Seymour's School of the Art Institute of Chicago M.A. thesis, "Edward Dart: Preserving the Works of a Mid-century Architect," 2011.

27. Edward Sövik interview, 2007.

28. Information conveyed to author by James Dart, Chicago, April 24, 2010.

29. Dart, *Edward Dart, Architect*, 135.

30. "Home Designer Makes Kitchen the Focal Point," *Chicago Tribune*, April 29, 1951, SW C5 (ProQuest Historical Newspapers).

31. "Dedication Set for New Church in Barrington," *Chicago Tribune*, November 21, 1954, NW4 (ProQuest Historical Newspapers).

32. In 1960, St. Augustine's won a merit award from the Church Architecture Guild as well as a citation from the American Institute of Architects. See also "Design for Worship," *Your Church* 6, no. 4 (October–December 1960): 19–21.

33. An undated newspaper article in St. Augustine's church records, "The Battle of the Builders—Tradition vs. Modern," ca. 1956, calls Dart "a Barrington architect who turned to church design recently after winning national awards for contemporary homes."

34. Edward Sövik to Father Michael Komechak, May 25, 1978, Edward Dart Collection, 1841–1993, Ryerson and Burnham Libraries Archives 1996, series 2, box 4.4, Art Institute of Chicago.

35. Father Michael Komechak, "An Architect's Choices: The Life of Edward Dart," *Inland Architect* 19, no. 9 (September 1975): 12.

36. Ibid., 8.

37. Quoted in ibid., 9.

38. Cited in Seymour, "Edward Dart," 9. Seymour's thesis is a very useful catalog of Dart's works: eighty-eight buildings from four offices in fourteen years of independent practice; thirty-one buildings, including St. Procopius, from 1965 to 1975, with Loebl, Schlossman, and Bennett. Seymour notes that even in Dart's earlier work his belief in the importance of site, materials, light, and form is strongly evident.

39. Virtually nothing has been published about Stade's life and work, so I include somewhat more of his biography relative to the other two architects in this study.

40. An early expression of Stade's position on church architecture is found in "Modern Church Construction Defended by Young Architect from Park Ridge," *Chicago Daily Tribune*, July 12, 1956, A4 (ProQuest Historical Newspapers).

41. It is not clear to what extent Stade desired to make his living as a church architect; his daughter believed he would have preferred to be a sculptor (Ramsey Stade Barlow interview, State College, Pennsylvania, June 3, 2006). Regarding Stade's interest in sculpture, see Charles Stade, "Chicago's Art Treasures: All Around the Town," *Chicago Tribune*, July 9, 1967, H16 (ProQuest Historical Newspapers). Stade also offered lessons in architectural

photography through the Jackson Park Photography Club: "Jackson Park to Open Free Photo Course," *Chicago Daily Tribune*, (July 18, 1952), 14 (ProQuest Historical Newspapers).

42. "Winner of Tribune Small Home Prize Is Honored Again," *Chicago Daily Tribune*, July 6, 1947, NW1 (ProQuest Historical Newspapers).

43. See Donald Drew Egbert, "Religious Expression in American Architecture," in James Ward Smith and A. Leland Jamison, eds., *Religious Perspectives in American Culture* (Princeton, N.J.: Princeton University Press, 1961), 361–411. I am grateful to the University of Minnesota Press's anonymous reader for pointing out this connection.

44. Ramsey Barlow interview, 2006. Stade's ongoing interest in historic church architecture was demonstrated consistently, for instance, in his article "Church Building, U.S.A., Part III: Historic Churches," *Your Church* (January–March 1960):17–26.

45. The records of the building committee of St. Paul Lutheran Church, Mount Prospect, Illinois, ca. 1958, indicate that he had also worked in the architectural offices of professor Kenneth Stone Kassler in Princeton and W. J. McCaughey in Park Ridge, but I have found no further documentation (St. Paul Lutheran records).

46. In 1951, Charles Edward Stade & Associates had an office at 1976 W. Balmoral in Chicago. By 1955, at age thirty-two, Stade had moved his firm to Park Ridge. In 1955–56, this firm was located at 15½ Fairview in Park Ridge; by 1958, it had moved to its permanent address at 819 Busse Highway, and remained there until the firm closed in 1981. From 1960 to 1963, the firm was Stade, Dolan, Anderson (Harry) & Associates, and from 1964 to 1965–66, Stade, Dolan & Anderson. From 1967 to 1969, the firm is listed as Stade, Dolan, Emrich & Associates. No doubt the family's Park Ridge–based construction company influenced his return to the suburbs; that business was located at 538 Busse Highway, from the early 1950s through 1973. See Park Ridge Telephone Books, 1948–80. Stade Construction Co. built St. Andrews, Park Ridge, in 1953–54.

47. Cooley, one of Stade's classmates at the University of Illinois, formed his own successful church architecture firm in partnership with Edward M. Borre and designed many suburban churches in the Chicago area out of his own Park Ridge office—for example, the Christian Church, Mt. Morris (1959); Bethel Lutheran, in Evergreen Park (1961); and St. Stephen's Lutheran, Meadowdale (1959). Many of these churches are very similar to those designed by Stade, modest L-shaped buildings with an A-frame sanctuary. Cooley was also heavily involved in national church architecture groups, serving as president of the Church Architecture Guild at the time of his accidental death in 1961. Dolan, also a University of Illinois graduate, was an engineer (Ramsey Barlow interview, 2006).

48. The exact number is hard to pin down. Sources generally claim something in the three hundred to four hundred range (including additions and modifications), but this is not verified. These reports vary widely. A 1978 interview with Stade claims he designed "more than 500 churches and temples in the United States and several foreign countries." See "Plans for St. John's Church Gain Award," *The Life: Lincolnwood Edition*, Thursday October 5, 1978; clipping in St. John's Lutheran Church, Lincolnwood, Illinois, records. Another article from 1966 claims that Stade designed "hundreds of temples, churches, and cathedrals thruout the United States, Canada, Africa, and India. Now his specialty is schools and he hopes to design hospitals." See "Architect Designs Buildings around Their Occupants," *Chicago Tribune*, August 14, 1966, D1 (ProQuest Historical Newspapers). This article claims that "some seven hundred buildings, valued at 300 million dollars have come from his drawing board." Stade's daughter believed he had designed at least one church in Africa; his

brother Robert was a Lutheran missionary in Nigeria beginning in 1946 (Ramsey Barlow interview, 2006).

49. Stade homes continue to come to light. One interesting design is a custom house for the historian Jaroslav Pelikan in Hamden, Connecticut, that incorporated a secluded study (ca. 1962).

50. Charles Stade obituary, *Chicago Sun-Times*, January 31, 1993, 68; available from Lexis-Nexis Academic, www.lexisnexis.com (April 27, 2005).

51. The fullest account of his work available online is found on Robert Powers's blog "A Chicago Sojourn," which includes many excellent photographs. See www.achicagosojourn.blogspot.com.

52. "Building Boom Revamps U.S. Church Design," *Chicago Daily Tribune*, March 9, 1959, 10 (ProQuest Historical Newspapers).

53. Records of the Building Committee of St. Peter Lutheran Church, Arlington Heights, June 19, 1958, meeting with Stade (St. Peter Church records).

54. Records of St. Paul Lutheran Church, Mt. Prospect, Illinois.

55. Advertisement, *Chicago Tribune*, September 8, 1963, C29 (ProQuest Historical Newspapers).

56. E-mail from Walter McRee to author, December 20, 2005.

57. These books include *Neue Evangelische Kirchen im Rheinland* (Dusseldorf: Werner-Verlag, 1963); Ferdinand Pfammatter, *Betonkirchen* (Zurich and Cologne: Benziger Verlag Einsiedeln, 1948); Willy Weyres et al., *Kirchen: Hanbuch für den Kirchenbau* (Munich: Verlag Georg D. W. Callwey, 1959). I have been unable to correlate particular marked pages with Stade's work, although there are numerous similarities in details of buildings. I am very grateful to Jesse Barlow for sharing these books from his father-in-law's collection.

58. Ramsey Barlow telephone interview, 2005.

59. Charles E. Stade, "An Architect's Notes: An Architect's Responsibility to His Client," *Your Church* 12, no. 2 (March–April 1966): 60.

60. Charles E. Stade, "Design for Worship:First Methodist Church, Midland, Michigan," *Your Church* 4, no. 1 (July–September, 1958): 13.

61. Ramsey Barlow remembers that her father liked everything perfectly neat at home and became distressed by visual disarray. He had expensive tastes, owned an airplane and a Rolls Royce that he kept in a specially designed, wood-floored garage, and on occasion would wear a beret around the house, yet he was also a homebody who loved cats and television (Ramsey Barlow interview, 2006).

62. Ramsey Barlow, telephone interview, 2005.

63. "Winner of Tribune Small Home Prize Is Honored Again" *Chicago Tribune* (July 6, 1947, NW1 (ProQuest Historical Newspapers). This article mentions that Stade won a contest sponsored by the Beaux-Arts Institute of Design, New York City, for a "University of Fashion" and also that he served as a "bombardier" in the air force, although other sources indicate that he was a meteorologist in the air force working in Wisconsin.

64. It is probable that Stade or Cooley (his associate at the time) also designed the parsonage on the property, a three-bedroom ranch house built between April and July 1954.

65. Stade, "Architectural Notes," Dedication Program, St. Paul Lutheran Church, Oak Lawn, records.

66. Martin Marty interview, Riverside, Illinois, June 23, 2006.

67. E-mail from Ruth McRee, December 30, 2005.

68. "Makefield Minister Likes Today's Modern Churches," *Bucks County Times*, January 5, 1967; Lutheran Church of the Resurrection, Yardley, Pennsylvania, records.

69. Charles Stade to Robert Stade, March 13, 1956; Lutheran Church of the Resurrection records. When Reverend Stade returned to Nigeria in 1958, McRee himself left the mission board to become pastor of the church, staying until 1976.

70. Charles Stade to Robert Stade, March 23, 1956; Lutheran Church of the Resurrection records.

71. Charles Stade to Robert Stade, March 13, 1956.

72. Charles Stade to Robert Stade, February 22, 1956; Lutheran Church of the Resurrection records.

73. See Gretchen Buggeln, "The Shape of a New Era: Valparaiso's Chapel of the Resurrection in Historical Context," *The Cresset* 73, no. 3 (Lent 2010): 6–14.

74. Ramsey Barlow, telephone interview, 2005.

75. Personal correspondence with Charles Johnson, March 22, 2009.

76. Labatut apparently contributed a minimal amount to the chapel, but later, at Stade's insistence, was retained as a campus planner.

77. Adalbert R. Kretzmann was the brother of O. P. Kretzmann, president of Valparaiso University at the time. As pastor of St. Luke's Lutheran Church in Chicago and in his work as a liturgical consultant, Kretzmann played an active role in contemporary discussions of church architecture, art, and liturgy.

78. See, for example, Basil Spence, "A Contemporary Expression of Cathedral Traditions," *Architectural Record* 115, no. 3 (March 1954): 144–51.

79. Martin Marty interview, 2006.

80. Three suburban Illinois churches—St. Peter's, Arlington Heights, St. John's, Lincolnwood, and Good Shepherd Methodist, Park Ridge—all won awards for architectural merit (Charles E. Stade, entry in *Who Was Who in America* 11 (New Providence, N.J.: Marquis Who's Who, 1996), 262.

81. Stade, "Church Building, U.S.A.," 17, 25.

82. Martin Marty interview, 2006.

83. Martin Marty interview, Chicago, Illinois, April, 3, 2013.

84. "Chicago Architect Stade Chides His Colleagues," *Bennington Banner*, August 13, 1966, 7 (NewspaperArchive.com).

85. Charles Stade, "An Architect's Notes: An Architect's Responsibility to His Client," *Your Church* 12, no. 2 (March–April 1966): 10.

## 3. FROM DREAM TO DEDICATION

1. William S. Clark, *Building the New Church* (Jenkintown, Pa.: Religious Publishing Co., 1957), 12; foreword by Charles Stade.

2. James Hudnut-Beumler, *In Pursuit of the Almighty's Dollar: A History of Money and American Protestantism* (Chapel Hill: University of North Carolina Press, 2007), 148–49.

3. John Scotford, *When You Build Your Church* (Great Neck, N.Y.: Doniger and Raughley, 1955), 1. Reverend Scotford was a Congregational pastor who wrote for a general audience about church architecture and decoration. He edited several journals, including the national journal of the Congregational Church, *Advance*, and served as the interim director of the Bureau of Church Building for the National Council of Churches ca. 1956–57. I quote extensively from this book in this chapter because it is practical and unsentimental and represents

a summary view of someone with firsthand knowledge of many of the new churches across the Protestant denominations.

4. Good Shepherd, Moorhead, Minnesota, Book of Early Records, January 1957; Lutheran Church of the Good Shepherd, Moorhead, Minnesota, records.

5. Letter from Pastor Sanford D. Sorgen to congregation, Easter 1953; Lutheran Church of the Good Shepherd records.

6. Dean Ferguson interview, Fargo, North Dakota, June 11, 2007. Ferguson became convinced, as time went on, that "people didn't *want* you to do that . . . didn't want to straighten up the place just for you to come over and smile a lot." When he was head of the evangelism board in the 1980s, he said door-to-door canvassing was a much less successful strategy.

7. Lansing Presbyterian Church, *Twenty-fifth Anniversary Book*, ca. 1980; Lansing Presbyterian Church, Lansing, Illinois, records.

8. See Grace B. Stoffregen, "Celebrating the Spirit: Fifty Years of the Lutheran Church of the Holy Spirit, 1958–2008; Lutheran Church of the Holy Spirit, Elk Grove Village, Illinois, records.

9. Gerry Russell interview, Elk Grove Village, Illinois, May 23, 2013.

10. St. Louis Park was the largest inner-ring suburb of Minneapolis, an independent city since 1886. Its population tripled during the 1940s, with farm population moving in for the war-related industry jobs, and doubled again in the 1950s when the vets returned home. By 1960, the population reached forty-three thousand. More than twenty thousand people moved to St. Louis Park during the period when Westwood Lutheran was established. See Robert Wuthnow, *Remaking the Heartland* (Princeton, N.J.: Princeton University Press, 2011), 234–37.

11. Nielsen left Westwood to become vice president for development at Augsburg College in 1958 and in 1962 started his own company, Norm Nielsen Homes, which built many custom homes and townhomes in west suburban Minneapolis.

12. "A Parson's Dream Come True: Hard Work, Neighborliness Key to Westwood's Success," *St. Louis Park Dispatch*, May 6, 1954; clipping, Westwood Lutheran Church, St. Louis Park, Minnesota, records.

13. See *Briefs for Church Builders*, no. 3, "The First Unit," National Council of Churches of Christ, 1957.

14. This pattern was particularly common for suburban Catholic parishes that often built a day school first.

15. See O. T. McRee, "The Role of the Pastor in a Church Building Program," *Your Church* 9, no. 1 (January–March 1963): 22–23, 38.

16. Betty Ackerman interview, La Grange, Illinois, August 18, 2010.

17. Minutes of Bishop's Committee meeting, April 20, 1961; St. Augustine of Canterbury Episcopal Church, Benton Harbor, Michigan, records.

18. "Architecture as a Mirror of Religious Conviction," March 9, 1990, typescript of talk presented at Storm Lake, Iowa (SA, box 1, folder 11).

19. Charles Stade, "An Architect's Notes: Good and Bad Church Architecture," *Your Church* 6, no. 4 (October–December 1960): 14–16.

20. Charles E. Stade, "For Pastors: A Recipe for a Good Building Committee," *Your Church* (September–October 1965): 8. Although much of Stade's published writing about building committees is optimistic, and he had a reputation for working well and respectfully with his clients, in 1966 he let his frustrations out to an audience of church architects,

admitting that "the title 'Building Committee' affects me, when I hear it, a little like chalk scraping on a blackboard, or a fingernail on glass; I tend to quiver a bit, inside" (Charles E. Stade, "The Development of Form," *American Society for Church Architecture Journal* 7 [1966]: 42).

21. Ibid., 63–64. He referenced Martin Marty, Joseph Sittler (ordained Lutheran and professor of systematic theology at University of Chicago Divininty School), Paul Tillich, Edward Frey, Peter Hammond (Anglican priest, England's leading theorist of religious architecture, and member of the New Churches Research Group), and James White (young scholar of American church history and liturgy).

22. Reverend Richard Hamilton interview, Indianapolis, Indiana, March 12, 2010.

23. Clark, *Building the New Church*, 28.

24. "Groundbreaking Attended by over 500," *Olivet Emblem*, April 1964; Olivet Lutheran Church, Fargo, North Dakota, records.

25. For monetary conversions, I used the online resource of the Federal Reserve Bank of Minneapolis, www.Minneapolisfed.org.

26. Glennys Knutson interview, Austin, Minnesota. July 22, 2007.

27. Scotford, *When You Build Your Church*, 217.

28. 1961 fund-raising brochure, Our Saviour Lutheran, Lansing, Illinois, records.

29. "Twenty Questions about the United Protestant Churches," n.d., Church files, Park Forest Public Library.

30. Fund-raising brochure, ca. 1956, First Baptist Church, Bloomington, Indiana, records.

31. Building program brochure. First Baptist Church records.

32. *Church Builder* 1, no 2. First Baptist Church records.

33. Building program brochure, First Baptist Church records.

34. Jacqueline Protsman interview, Lansing, Illinois, May 16, 2007.

35. *Church Builder* 1, no. 6, First Baptist Church records.

36. *Church Builder* 1, nos. 7 and 12, First Baptist Church records.

37. Guild *Newsletter* 46 (October 1966) (AIA/ IFRAA, box 5306).

38. Betty Ackerman interview, 2010.

39. Ramsey Barlow interview, State College, Pennsylvania, June 3, 2006. Stade also spent several months talking with the Mennonites at their seminary in Elkhart, Indiana, attending meetings, classes, and worship prior to designing their chapel (1965). He was known for his practice of studying his clients and their needs closely before designing for them. See "Architect Designs Buildings around Their Occupants," *Chicago Tribune*, August 14, 1966, D1 (ProQuest Historical Newspapers).

40. "Plans for St. John's Church Gain Award," *The Life: Lincolnwood Edition*, 1978; clipping in St. John's Lutheran Church, Lincolnwood, Illinois, records.

41. "Sticks and Stones: An Introduction to the Architecture and Building of the First Baptist Church," ca. 1957, First Baptist Church records.

42. June 1954 report in scrapbook, First Baptist Church records.

43. *Church Builder* 1, no. 8, First Baptist Church records.

44. When I asked Sövik why First Baptist chose him, a relatively young architect from Minnesota, he said he thought it might be because of a personal connection—Doug Rae was related by marriage to Albert Christ-Janer, an artist, critic, and friend (and fellow St. Olaf College graduate) of Sövik (Edward Sövik interview, 2007).

45. Report by Structure Committee, n.d., First Baptist Church records.

46. Ibid.

47. "Memoirs of Our Zion Family," Zion Lutheran Church, Galesville, Wisconsin, 1886–1986, Zion Lutheran Church, Galesville, Wisconsin, records.

48. Ibid.

49. Records of Building Committee, December 1957 to October 1958, St. Peter Lutheran Church, Arlington Heights, Illinois, records.

50. Ibid. Customary fees ranged from 6 percent to as high as 10 percent, but anything less than 6 percent Stade warned would wind up costing the congregation more in the long run.

51. Quoted in "Area Buildings Win Architectural Awards," loose newspaper clipping, 1963, St. Peter Lutheran Church, Arlington Heights, Illinois, records.

52. "Thy Kingdom Come: Centennial 1860–1960," n.p., St. Peter Lutheran Church records.

53. Sövik worked on several Catholic buildings beyond the years of this study, including renovations to Sacred Heart Church, East Grand Forks, Minnesota, 1975; St. James Catholic, Aitkin, Minnesota, 1982; Sts. Peter and Paul Cathedral, Indianapolis, 1983–86, St. Raphael, Springfield, Ohio, 1986; St. Albert the Great, Minneapolis, 1991. New Catholic churches by Sövik include the Church of the Nativity, Fargo, 1978–79; St. Bridget's, River Falls, Wisconsin, 1983; Holy Family, Clemens, North Carolina, 1983–84; St. Anthony, Cincinnati, Ohio, 1992.

54. Brian J. Willette telephone interview, November 30, 2011.

55. Ibid.

56. Sövik, "An Incarnational Church," typescript of talk delivered at St. Leo's , n.d. (SA, box 1, folder 1).

57. Ibid.

58. Edward Sovik interview, Northfield, Minnesota, June 19, 2007.

59. See Charles E. Stade, "An Architect's Notes: An Architect's Responsibility to His Client," *Your Church* 12, no. 2 (March–April 1966): 62.

60. "Report of Executive Committee for a New Church," ca. 1956, First Baptist Church records.

61. *Church Builder* 1, no. 6, First Baptist Church records.

62. "Last Service in the Old Church, the First Service in the New Church," September 8, 1957, First Baptist Church records.

63. "Sticks and Stones," First Baptist Church records.

64. Bob Stout and Helen Stout interview, Bloomington, Indiana, March 11, 2010.

65. "Groundbreaking attended by over 500," *Olivet Emblem*, April 1964, Olivet Lutheran Church, Fargo, North Dakota, records.

66. Carol Ferguson and Dean Ferguson interview, Fargo, North Dakota, June 11, 2007.

67. June Brown, Charlotte Strowhorn, and Felicia Childress interview, Gary, Indiana, June 24, 2012.

68. Edward Dart to Reverend Bruce R. Wheeler, April 21, 1961, St. Augustine of Canterbury records.

69. Paul Tritenbach, "The Suburban Church—Site Selection and Development," *Your Church* 12, no. 1 (January–February 1966): 16. See also *Briefs for Church Builders*, no. 1, "Church Parking," National Council of Churches of Christ, 1956.

70. O. T. McRee, "Preparation for Architectural Service," *Your Church* 10, no. 1 (February–March 1964): 36.

71. Ibid., 37.

72. Reverend Delwin B. Schneider, "From the Pastor," in "The New Saint Paul Lutheran Church," fund-raising brochure, 1953, St. Paul Lutheran Church, Oak Lawn, Illinois, records.

73. Faith Albano interview, Evanston, Illinois, February 27, 2013.

74. Carol Ferguson and Dean Ferguson interview, 2007.

75. Edward Sövik interview, 2007.

76. Edward Dart, "The Nature of the First Unit," *Your Church* 9, no. 1 (January–March 1963): 28ff; quotation, 28.

77. Memo from Dart's office, dated April 25, 1961, reflecting previous day's conversation between building committee and architect, St. Augustine of Canterbury records.

78. The total cost of building was $68,461; with furnishings, parking, architect's fees, and miscellaneous project costs, $105,115.

79. Roy Shoemaker, "Reflections of St. Stephens and St. Augustine's, 1958–1990," ca. 1990, St. Augustine of Canterbury records.

80. Roy Shoemaker interview, Benton Harbor, Michigan, May 17, 2007.

81. Inclusion of a basement was controversial (Roy Shoemaker interview, 2007). Over time, this has been a problem for the congregation because the basement is raised, making expansion difficult.

82. Memo in scrapbook, n.d., All Saints Lutheran Church, Orland Park, Illinois, records.

83. St. Luke's Methodist Church, "20th Anniversary Book" (1973), committee notes from 1964, St. Luke's Methodist Church, Indianapolis, Indiana, records.

84. Dr. Richard Hamilton interview, Indianapolis, Indiana. March 12, 2010. Dr. Hamilton arrived at the church in 1959.

85. Ibid.

86. Carleton Knight III, "St. Luke's Methodist Church: Building within a Building," *Indianapolis Star*, May 1967, in church scrapbook, St. Luke's Methodist Church records.

87. Pietro Belluschi, "The Importance of Simplicity in Church Design," Annual National Conference on Church Architecture, Seattle, March 5–7, 1963, 4 (typescript report, AIA/IFRAA, box 5309).

88. Robert Wuthnow, *Loose Connections: Joining Together in America's Fragmented Communities* (Cambridge, Mass.: Harvard University Press, 1998), 88.

89. Helen Danielson interview, Moorhead, Minnesota, June 9, 2007.

90. "The Park Forest Church—A Brief Sketch," typescript dated February 4, 1981, in records of First Church of Christ, Scientist, Park Forest, Illinois.

## 4. THE A-FRAME CHURCH

Many thanks to the Quadrant Center at the University of Minnesota for the opportunity to present the material in this chapter and for valuable feedback from the audience.

1. See, for example, the 1954 A-frame of suburban Temple Beth-El in Newark, Delaware (later a hair salon), and Temple Beth Elohim in Old Bethpage, New York (1959).

2. Edward Larabee Barnes, "Architecture as Witness," *Your Church* 12, no. 5 (September–October 1966): 34.

3. Ibid., 65.

4. Advertisement, *Your Church* 7, no. 1(January–March 1961): 49.

5. Chad Randl, *A-Frame* (New York: Princeton Architectural Press, 2004), 138.

6. "The Tent Form: A Village Gothic for Today," *Architectural Forum* 101, no. 6 (December 1954): 128–31.

7. See Albert G. H. Dietz, "Glued Timbers Tailored to Fit," *Architectural Record* 106, no. 6 (December 1949): 139–41.

8. Advertisement, *Church Management* 29, no. 6 (March 1953): 8.

9. Albert Christ-Janer and Mary Mix Foley, *Modern Church Architecture: A Guide to the Form and Spirit of 20th Century Religious Buildings* (New York: McGraw-Hill, 1962), 138.

10. Charles Edward Stade, "Dollars, Sense, and Square Footage," *Your Church* 11, no. 5 (July–August 1965): 9.

11. "Christ the King Lutheran Church," *Church Management* 30, no. 7 (April 1954): 26–27.

12. Henry Kamphoefer, quoted in Paul Thiry, Richard M. Bennett, and Henry L. Kamphoefner, *Churches and Temples* (New York: Reinhold, 1953), 21P.

13. "For a New College an Old Village Silhouette," *Architectural Forum* 101, no. 6 (December 1954): 133.

14. The full quote reads: "Despite Saarinen's attempt to communicate specific cultural associations through form, the A-frame church was subsequently copied by architects all around the world, divorced from the intended reference" (Eeva-Liisa Pelkonen, "The Search for [Communicative] Form," in Eeva-Liisa Pelkonen and Donald Albrecht, eds., *Eero Saarinen: Shaping the Future* [New Haven, Conn.: Yale University Press, 2006], 95–96).

15. Ibid., 95. Furthermore, Alan J. Plattus, in "Campus Plans: Context and Community," in Pelkonen and Albrecht, *Eero Saarinen,* calls it a "summer camp or state park for suburbanites" (315).

16. Abraham Eastwood Jr., "An Architect's Notes," *Your Church* 8, no. 1 (January–March 1962): 11–12.

17. Jennifer Komar Olivarez, "Churches and Chapels: A New Kind of Worship Space," in Pelkonen and Albrecht, *Eero Saarinen,* 271.

18. *Fifty Modern Churches* (London: Incorporated Church Building Society, 1947). Notably, some of the designs were explicitly intended "to make provision for vast new housing estates to come into being" (3).

19. Ibid., 144–45.

20. "Current Church Architecture," *Your Church* 2, no. 1 (January–March 1956): 11.

21. A. E. Bohlman and Herbert A. Brand, "Grace Lutheran, Western Springs, Illinois," *Church Management* 29, no. 9 (June 1953): 20.

22. http://stgeorgesdurham.org/index.php/about/church-history, October 11, 2012. See also "Design for Worship: St. George's Episcopal Church, Durham, New Hampshire," *Your Church* 1, no. 3 (October–December 1955): 12.

23. Libby Owens Ford advertisement, n.d. (author's collection).

24. An important East Coast example of the rustic, woodsy variety of A-frame is St. Gregory's Episcopal in Woodstock, New York, designed by the diocesan architect William Van Benschoten (1957). The upward-thrusting ridge line of the sanctuary jogs straight up near the front of the church to allow an intermediate clerestory window to bring light into the chancel from behind, a common variation on the A-frame seen in the United States and abroad. See also Harold Spitznagel, First Congregational Church, Spencer, Iowa (1954), a version of this type in brick.

25. "Church with a New Slant," *Indianapolis Standard,* February 23, 1957, cited in Mary Kennedy, National Register of Historic Places Evaluation for the Pilgrim Lutheran Church, Hamilton County, Indiana (Indiana Department of Transportation, February 16, 2012), 34.

26. "The Tent Form: A Village Gothic for Today," *Architectural Forum* 101, no. 6 (December 1954), 130.

27. "Thatched Hut Inspires Architecture," *Church Management* (December 1951): 26. This was a small first-unit chapel for sixty. See also "Double-Duty Roof: Cedar Hills Community Church, Oregon" *Architectural Forum* 97, no. 6 (December 1952): 94.

28. Thiry, Bennett, and Kamphoefner, *Churches and Temples*, 42P.

29. "The Tent Form," 128.

30. See Randl, *A-Frame*.

31. *Contra Costa Times*, April 9, 1953, Trinity Lutheran Church, Walnut Creek, California, records. Walter Netsch of the San Francisco office of SOM was also involved at Trinity, and the church was definitely a collaborative effort, although the congregation identified Belluschi as the architect.

32. This idea might have come from Eero Saarinen, who created a similar effect for his chapel at MIT (1955), where Belluschi was dean of the architecture school at the time.

33. Christ-Janer and Foley, *Modern Church Architecture*, 160.

34. Adalbert R. Kretzmann, "The Symbolism of Forms and Materials," *Your Church* 7, no. 1 (January–March 1961): 21, 30.

35. "Celebration of the 50th Anniversary of Grace United Protestant Church," typescript, Grace United Protestant Church, Park Forest, Illinois, records.

36. Kretzmann, "The Symbolism of Forms and Materials," 30.

37. *Briefs for Church Builders*, no. 7, "High Visibility for Your Church," National Council of Churches of Christ, 1957.

38. "Design for Worship: First Methodist Church, Warren, Michigan," *Your Church* 6, no. 2 (April–June 1960): 22–23.

39. Ibid.

40. Edward Sövik interview, Northfield, Minnesota, June 19, 2007.

41. A similar Sövik church is Zion Lutheran, in Warroad, Minnesota, 1956.

42. In another case, in 1953, Sövik designed both an A-frame and a Saarinenesque church for a congregation in Newtown, North Dakota, and built the rectangular church (SA, box 2, folder 15 [drawings]); "Partial List of Sövik Churches" (SA, box 3, folder 12).

43. See Willy Weyres and Otto Bartning, *Kirchen: Handbuch für den Kirchenbau* (Munich: Verlag Georg D. W. Callwey, 1959), 170. Sövik's design also relates visually to the Air Force Academy Chapel discussed later in this chapter.

44. "Architect Says: 'Good Church Is Witness to the Vitality of Christian Message,'" undated newspaper clipping. Calvary Lutheran Church, Park Rapids, Minnesota, records.

45. Sketch of proposed churches, St. Michael's Episcopal Church, Barrington, Illinois, records.

46. O. T. McRee to W. A. Meyer, treasurer, Church Mutual Insurance Co., November 17, 1955. McRee requested a call back to parish ministry and served Resurrection as pastor from 1958 to 1976; Lutheran Church of the Resurrection, Yardley, Pennsylvania, records.

47. Ramsey Barlow interview, State College, Pennsylvania, June 3, 2006.

48. "Lutheran Church of the Resurrection, Yardley, Pennsylvania," *Your Church* 5, no. 4 (October–December 1959): 22–23.

49. Architectural notes in dedication bulletin, May 20, 1956, Lutheran Church of the Resurrection records.

50. 125th Anniversary Book, *Celebrating 125 Blest Years*, 1996, Immanuel Lutheran Church, Des Plaines, Illinois, records.

51. Charles Stade to O. T. McRee, May 17, 1955, Lutheran Church of the Resurrection records.

52. Fred Wiedenmann, phone interview, April 2010.

53. See "Design for Worship: Good Shepherd Lutheran, Palos Park," *Your Church* 4, no. 1 (January–March 1958): 13–14.

54. "Design for Worship: Lutheran Church of the Ascension, Atlanta, Georgia," *Your Church* 7, no. 1 (January–March 1961): 13.

55. See "The Building of Zion Lutheran Church" (1981), Zion Lutheran Church, Kalamazoo, Michigan, records.

56. Mary E. Kennedy, February 16, 2012, National Register of Historic Places Evaluation for the Pilgrim Lutheran Church, Hamilton County, Indiana, in association with the U.S. 31 Road Improvement Project, INDOT Des. No. 0710215.

57. A similar church was planned for the new congregation of Trinity Presbyterian, Oak Lawn, Illinois, ca. 1958, although no church exists on the site today. See "Break Ground for Oak Lawn Church Today," *Chicago Daily Tribune*, June 1, 1958, SW3 (ProQuest Historical Newspapers).

58. Mary Rhodes, "The Founding Years: The Early History of Winnetka Presbyterian Church," n.d. (post-1994), 23, Winnetka Presbyterian Church, Winnetka, Illinois, records.

59. Ibid., 24.

60. "Design for Worship: Kahaluu Methodist Church," *Your Church* 2, no. 4 (October–December 1956): 9–10.

61. Christ-Janer and Foley, *Modern Church Architecture*, 144–45. See also Lundy's Bee Ridge Presbyterian (1958), also in Sarasota. A more dramatic Lundy A-frame is his Unitarian Church in Westport, Connecticut (1959–61).

62. E-mail correspondence with Neville Mirtschin, December 15, 2006.

63. P. Roelf Botha, "Modern Churches of South Africa," *Your Church* 7, no. 4 (October–December 1961): 20–21.

64. Minutes of Committee on Architecture Meeting, April 1, 1960 (NCC RG 6–55–11). When making a comment in print, however, Hudnut was more complimentary, calling the building "resourceful, imaginative, opportune in its technologies and, in its scenic effects, superb ("Perspectives: Air Force Academy Chapel," *Architectural Record* 122, no. 7 [December 1957]: 9.

65. William S. Clark, "The Architectural Captivity of the Church," *Your Church* 11, no. 5 (September–October 1965): 57–58 (a talk given at the American Society for Church Architecture meeting in Syracuse in May). Despite criticism, the American Institute of Architects awarded the chapel a national Twenty-five Year Award in 1996 and the chapel was included in National Historic Landmark designation in 2004. Moreover, the chapel has proved to be enduringly popular with the public, an icon of postwar American design.

66. Martin Marty interview, Riverside, Illinois, June 23, 2006.

67. Jury reports for Church Architecture Guild of America awards 1960. Report of the Annual Conference on Church Architecture, Minneapolis, 1960, 39 (AIA/IFRAA 5309). I have found a handful of instances where A-frame churches are disparagingly called "teepee" or "wigwam." These terms were used widely in the vigorous critique of Netsch's designs for the Air Force Academy Chapel. Senator Robinson, for instance, called it "an assembly of wigwams." (See Robert Allen Nauman, *On the Wings of Modernism: The United States Air*

*Force Academy* [Urbana: University of Illinois Press, 2004], 111.) Another source spoke of the A-frame as "just sort of like an overgrown pup-tent. There's nothing majestic about it" (Reverend Theodore Gerken, quoting a parishioner in "Analysis of the Worship Function," *Journal of the American Society for Church Architecture* 1, no. 1 [July 1961]: 14).

68. Brother Cajetan J. B. Baumann, cited in Guild *Newsletter* 38 (December 1965): n.p.

69. Barnes, "Architecture as Witness," 66.

70. "Neighborhood Church Uses Today's Technologies and Design Language to Convey Ancient Qualities," *Architectural Forum* 96, no. 3 (March 1952): 133.

71. Robert Woods Kennedy, "After the International Style—Then What?" *Architectural Forum* 99, no. 3 (September 1953): 132.

## 5. THE SUBURBAN SANCTUARY

1. Contemporaries used the term "sanctuary" to refer to a combination of nave and chancel.

2. John R. Scotford, *When You Build Your Church* (Great Neck, N.Y.: Doniger and Raughley, 1955), 12.

3. See James White, *Protestant Worship and Church Architecture: Theological and Historical Considerations* (New York: Oxford University Press, 1964), 118ff.

4. This configuration of worship space was also commonly called "basilican," or "longitudinal," although axial is the more common term in period records. It is associated with the "processional" or "pilgrimage" idea of worship.

5. David Ralph Bains, "The Liturgical Impulse in Mid-Twentieth Century American Mainline Protestantism," Ph.D. dissertation, Harvard University, 1999. "Divided chancel" is a term used frequently but flexibly to indicate a formal arrangement of space. Sometimes it refers to the pulpit on one side, lectern on the other; at other times it refers to the placement of the choir at the sides of the raised chancel. I found that the term as most commonly used in this period, however, refers not to a particular arrangement within the chancel but to the idea of the chancel being definitively separated from the nave.

6. Scott T. Ritenour, *Briefs for Church Builders*, no. 20, "Creating the Atmosphere of Worship," 1961, 1.

7. Reverend Richard Hamilton interview, Indianapolis, Indiana, March 12, 2010.

8. Edward Sövik, "Our Architect Discusses Church Design," in Our Savior's Lutheran *Chimes* 2, no. 3 (September 1959): n.p.; Our Savior's Lutheran Church, Austin, Minnesota, records. This text was subsequently published as Edward Sövik, "Liturgical Art and the New Churches," *Response: In Worship-Music-The Arts* 1, no. 2 (Advent 1959): 8–17.

9. See Jay Price, *Temples for a Modern God: Religious Architecture in Postwar America* (New York: Oxford University Press, 2013), 119–71.

10. Albert Christ-Janer and Mary Mix Foley, *Modern Church Architecture: A Guide to the Form and Spirit of 20th Century Religious Buildings* (New York: McGraw-Hill, 1962), 60.

11. Edward Frey, "Why What We Believe Should Determine What We Build," report of the National Conference on Church Architecture, Minneapolis (1960), 15 (AIA/IFRAA, box 5309).

12. Edward Sövik interview, June 19, 2007.

13. Notes on a meeting of the Commission on Architecture, New York, May 27, 1954 (NCC RG 6–53–12).

14. See Mark Torgerson, *An Architecture of Immanence: Architecture for Worship and Ministry Today* (Grand Rapids, Mich.: William B. Eerdmans, 2007).

15. Edward Sövik interview, 2007.

16. See E. A. Sövik, *Architecture for Worship* (Minneapolis: Augsburg Publishing House, 1973), 60–62.

17. Report of the National Conference on Church Architecture, Minneapolis, 1960, 30.

18. Ibid., 32.

19. See Price, *Temples for a Modern God*, for a summary of Catholic involvement in the arts. See also Susan J. White, *Art, Architecture, and Liturgical Reform: The Liturgical Arts Society (1928–1972)* (New York: Pueblo Publishing Co., 1990).

20. Letter from Edwin Espy, general secretary of the NCC, to Roger Ortmayer, September 2, 1966 (NCC RG 6–53–2).

21. "Building the Atmosphere of Worship," typescript, n.d. (NCC RG 6–53–17). This is an earlier version of "Creating the Atmosphere of Worship," (see note 6) and is not the same text. This earlier version was more informal and gave more particular advice, whereas the printed version was more about principle and less about specific practices. The author for the earlier, typescript version, who is not identified on the document, writes directly of the "quest for a sense of the presence of God."

22. See Richard Kieckhefer, *Theology in Stone: Church Architecture from Byzantium to Berkeley* (New York: Oxford University Press, 2004).

23. William S. Clark, "The Shape of Europe's Churches," *Your Church* (January–March 1962): 24.

24. Charles E. Stade, "The Business of Seating," *Your Church* 2, no. 4 (October–December 1956): 20, 18.

25. Second book of Building Committee records (July 1960 to January 1962), entry dated November 3, 1960, St. Peter Lutheran Church, Arlington Heights, Illinois, records.

26. Structure Committee report, ca. 1956, First Baptist Church, Bloomington, Indiana, records.

27. Reverend Glennys Knutson interview, Austin, Minnesota, July 22, 2007.

28. Gerry Russell interview, Elk Grove Village, Illinois, May 23, 2013.

29. Bob Stout and Helen Stout interview, Bloomington, Indiana, March 11, 2010.

30. Lorraine Hubley interview, South Holland, Illinois, April 30, 2010.

31. Edward Sövik interview, 2007. Thorsen remained the local construction architect on the project.

32. Jane Loeffler interview, Moorhead, Minnesota, June 9, 2007.

33. Kathy Richardson interview, Moorhead, Minnesota, June 8, 2007.

34. Dedication bulletin for Trinity Lutheran, Ellsworth, Iowa, September 20, 1953, Trinity Lutheran Church, Ellsworth, Iowa, records.

35. "Memoirs of Our Zion Family," Zion Lutheran Church, Galesburg, Wisconsin, records.

36. Jane Loeffler interview, 2007. A copy of her tour script is in the Trinity Lutheran Church records.

37. Sövik used a similar oxbow roof at Calvary, Grand Forks, North Dakota, some years later, in 1962, blending this feature with other features of his later churches.

38. Harry Shaw, "Members Helped Plan Their Church," *Louisville Courier-Journal*, n.d., article in church scrapbook, First Baptist Church records.

39. Edward Sövik interview, 2007.

40. Edward Sövik, "On the Design," in Dedication Program for Trinity Lutheran Church, Moorhead, Minnesota, October 5, 1952, Trinity Lutheran Church, Moorhead, Minnesota, records.

41. Ibid. Rudolf Schwarz uses similar language in *The Church Incarnate.*

42. Sövik, "On the Design."

43. "Reflections from Ed. A. Sövik (incomplete and provisional) on Trinity Lutheran Church Moorhead, Minnesota," ca. 2002, Trinity Lutheran Church records.

44. See Glennys Knutson, *The Cross and the Crown: An Interpretive History of Our Savior's Lutheran Church* (Our Savior's Lutheran Church: Austin, Minn.: 1990).

45. Dedication brochure, Palm Sunday, 1962, Our Savior's Lutheran Church, Austin, Minnesota, records.

46. Ibid.

47. Ronald Nelson interview, St. Louis Park, Minnesota, June 13, 2007. Recent changes to the sanctuary replaced the pews with chairs, moving closer to the flexible ideal Sövik initially had in mind.

48. Ibid.

49. Hal Neugebauer and Clara Neugebauer interview, Fargo, North Dakota, June 11, 2007.

50. Ibid.

51. Lyle Collins interview (former Olivet director of music), Fargo, North Dakota, June 11, 2007.

52. Hal Neugebauer and Clara Neugebauer interview, 2007.

53. Dedication brochure, October 22, 1967, Lutheran Church of the Good Shepherd, Moorhead, Minnesota, records.

54. Edward Sövik, "Our Architect Discusses Church Design," n.p., 1959.

55. Charles E. Stade, "Church Building, U.S.A.: Part III: Historic Churches," *Your Church* 6, no. 1 (January–March 1960): 26.

56. "Two Park Ridge Buildings Are Cited as Good," *Chicago Daily Tribune,* August 19, 1956, NW6 (ProQuest Historical Newspapers).

57. Building Committee Records, Architecture Subcommittee report, June 3, 1958, St. Paul Lutheran Church, Mount Prospect, Illinois, records.

58. "Design for Worship: St. Paul Lutheran Church, Mount Prospect, Illinois," *Your Church* 9, no. 4 (October–December 1963): 15.

59. Ibid.

60. Lorraine Hubley interview, Oak Lawn, Illinois, April 30, 2010.

61. Another artist Stade worked with in these early years was Reinhold Marxhausen, who created the carved stone decorative panels set into the outside walls of many of his A-frames—for instance, Immanuel, Des Plaines, and the first-unit Hope Lutheran, Park Forest.

62. "Joliet Jewish Congregation" informational brochure, n.d., Joliet Jewish Congregation, Peoria, Illinois, records.

63. The Jewish Joliet Congregation occupies one of two Stade synagogues; he also collaborated on B'nai Torah in Highland Park, Illinois (1966). Ramsey Stade Barlow thought her father designed three synagogues, although I have not yet located a third. It is unclear how Stade earned these commissions. The Joliet Congregation's records indicate that they also contacted well-known Chicago-area synagogue architect Walter Sobel. In the records

are documents recording the connections between church and synagogue design of the period, such as reprints, by the Union of American Hebrew Congregations, of such publications as "The Interior Designer" (from *Church Management*) and "Planning the Church Kitchen" (from *Your Church*). Although Stade is the architect of record for B'nai Torah in Highland Park, it is almost certain that the chief designer was not Stade but congregational member Irving Moses, a Chicago modernist. Stade first designed a synagogue, about 1964–65, for the congregation on its site on Lake Michigan. The proposed design, however, on piers at the edge of the bluff, was deemed inadequate by a several architects in the congregation, in part because they thought it would "fall off the cliff." Unable to get a satisfactory design from Stade, Moses himself designed the synagogue, although Stade's firm produced the construction drawings and managed the project (Toby Moses and Irving Moses telephone interview, May 13, 2013). The Joliet Congregation's records, including correspondence between Stade and Rabbi Morris Hershman, indicate that the congregation was very satisfied with Stade's work.

64. See Kenan Heise, "Charles Stade, Award-Winning Designer," *Chicago Tribune* obituary, February 1, 1993; http://articles.chicagotribune.com/1993–02–01/news/9303174491_1_nursing-homes-award-winning-designer-churches.

65. Willy Weyres et al., *Kirchen: Handbuch für den Kirchenbau* (Munich: Verlag Georg D. W. Callwey, 1959), 140–41.

66. Edward Dart, "The Architect Speaks," *Building Stone News* 4, no. 8 (February 1964): n.p.

67. Building Committee's "Charge to Architect," cited in Dedication Bulletin, February 24, 1963, Lansing Presbyterian Church, Lansing, Illinois, records. See also "Design for Worship: Lansing Presbyterian Church," *Your Church* 10, no. 1 (January–March 1964): 14–15.

68. "Design for Worship: Lansing Presbyterian Church."

69. Joyce Dykhuis interview, Lansing, Illinois, May 16, 2007.

70. Dr. Richard Hamilton interview, 2010.

71. Daniel Lewis Jr. interview, La Porte, Indiana, May 17, 2007.

72. Pastor Charles Ross, cited in "Worship Spirit Used to Guide Church's Style," *Chicago Tribune*, November 17, 1968; clipping, La Porte Presbyterian Church, La Porte, Indiana, records.

73. Notes from conference in St. Louis, 1969. Typescript provided by editor of *Tempo* magazine (SA, box 3, folder 4).

74. Church of the Holy Ghost, South Holland, dedication booklet, May 16, 1971, Holy Ghost Catholic Church, South Holland, Illinois, Parish records.

75. Brian Willette said the designers conceived it as a "journey" after European models that draw the penitent on a garden path. In the early days, the congregation would follow a processional cross through the stations, represented only by inlaid wooden crosses on the brick floor, as they moved toward the tabernacle symbolizing resurrection (Brian Willette, telephone interview, November 30, 2011).

76. A letter from Sövik to Keith Rood, June 9, 1987, mentions that he first put a font at the entrance to a nave back in 1953, in a church in Williston, North Dakota, with running water just inside the door, a radical move for the time (SA, box 1, folder 11).

77. Willette, who had volunteered on Navajo reservations, struck up a friendship with a local Lakota carver named Standing Eagle. Pipestone, in one version of the Lakota legend, represents the congealed blood of those who died in service (warriors) and signifies the

sacrament of opening and uniting with the Great Spirit. Willette spoke with Standing Eagle about Jesus's sacrifice of love and asked him if using the stone in the new church might be a respectful blending of the two traditions. Standing Eagle and his son carved the stones, and a family of Sioux construction workers placed them in the pillars.

78. "New Church Designs Reflect Changes in Liturgy," *New York Times* clipping (July 6, 1968) (SA, box 1, folder 5). Sövik's drawings of tearooms are found in SA, box 3, folder 4.

79. Patt Johnson interview, Pipestone, Minnesota, June 7, 2007.

80. Edward Sövik interview, 2007.

## 6. LIVING AND LEARNING AS A SUBURBAN CHURCH FAMILY

1. Charles E. Stade, "New Materials for Design and Building," *Your Church* 7, no. 4 (October–December 1961): 26.

2. Lois Blankenship, "Building for Christian Education," report of National Conference on Church Architecture, Los Angeles, 1959, D1–6 (AIA/IFRAA, box 5309); C. Harry Atkinson, *Building and Equipping for Christian Education* (New York: Bureau of Church Building of the National Council of Churches of Christ, 1956).

3. William Cooley, "The Historical Background of Church Building," *Your Church* 8, no. 4 (October–December 1962): 42.

4. Ibid., 42–43.

5. Atkinson, *Building and Equipping for Christian Education*, 65.

6. *Briefs for Church Builders*, no. 2, "Building on One Level—or More," National Council of Churches of Christ, 1956.

7. "The New St. Augustine's of Canterbury Episcopal Mission," 1961, St. Augustine Episcopal Church, Benton Harbor, Michigan, records.

8. Memo from Pastor Norman Hjelm to Edward Dart, August 3, 1961, All Saints Lutheran Church, Orland Park, Illinois, records.

9. Edward Sövik, "Our Architect Discusses Church Design," in Our Savior's Lutheran *Chimes* 2, no. 3 (September 1959): n.p., Our Savior's Lutheran Church, Austin, Minnesota, records. This text was subsequently published as Edward Sövik, "Liturgical Art and the New Churches," *Response: In Worship-Music-The Arts* 1, no. 2 (Advent 1959): 8–17.

10. Stephanie Coontz, *The Way We Never Were: American Families and the Nostalgia Trap* (New York: Basic Books, 1992), 106.

11. Paula S. Fass, "The Child-Centered Family? New Rules in Postwar America," in Paula S. Fass and Michael Grossberg, eds., *Reinventing Childhood after World War II* (Philadelphia: University of Pennsylvania Press, 2012), 5. For the American family in the postwar period, see also Elaine Tyler May, *Homeward Bound: American Families in the Cold War Era* (New York: Basic Books, 1988), and Coontz, *The Way We Never Were.*

12. Stephen Lassonde, "Ten Is the New Fourteen: Age Compression and 'Real' Childhood," in Fass and Grossberg, *Reinventing Childhood after World War II*, 57.

13. John Modell notes that 1950s "family building" was an especially potent cultural value, for the middle class, women in particular, largely believed that happiness and fulfillment would be achieved by marriage and child rearing. See John Modell, *Into One's Own: From Youth to Adulthood in the United States, 1920–75* (Berkeley: University of California Press, 1989), 253–62.

14. Helen Reinkensmeyer and Gil Reinkensmeyer interview, Kalamazoo, Michigan, May 15, 2013.

15. Edward Sövik interview, Northfield, Minnesota, June 19, 2007.

16. Remembrances of Vilgard Sorgen, wife of first pastor, 1953–70, in *25th Anniversary Book*, ca. 1978, Lutheran Church of the Good Shepherd, Moorhead, Minnesota, records.

17. Atkinson, *Building and Equipping for Christian Education*, 49.

18. Eleanor Vickers interview, Lansing, Illinois, May 16, 2007.

19. Martin Marty, "Building for the Christian Parish in a Secular Culture," report of Annual Conference on Church Architecture, Seattle, 1963, 11–12 (AIA/IFRAA, box 5309).

20. Atkinson, *Building and Equipping for Christian Education*, 6.

21. William Leach, "The New American Church Building," *Church Management* 29, no. 9 (June 1953): 22. See also *Briefs for Church Builders*, no. 6, "Making the Church Homelike," National Council of Churches of Christ, 1957.

22. See Sandy Isenstadt, *The Modern American House: Spaciousness and Middle-Class Identity* (New York: Cambridge University Press, 2006). For a broad view of Cold War–era domestic attitudes, see May, *Homeward Bound*.

23. See Dale Woolston Dowling, "For God, for Family, for Country: Colonial Revival Church Buildings in the Cold War Era," Ph.D. dissertation, George Washington University, 2004, 213–14. Dowling notes that these plan configurations were designed explicitly to create ease of movement between spaces.

24. Atkinson, *Building and Equipping for Christian Education*, 7.

25. Public-school release time for religious education was a real possibility and certainly on the minds of church builders as they envisioned the tasks that education buildings would have to perform. A Supreme Court ruling in 1948 declared unconstitutional the practice of released-time classes held in the public schools. Another Supreme Court decision in 1952 made it legal to hold such programs off school property (logically, in church buildings). Although the practice was not unusual, especially in remote corners of the United States, it never became common and church education buildings were rarely used for this purpose. See Robert W. Lynn and Elliott Wright, *The Big Little School: Two Hundred Years of the Sunday School* (Birmingham, Ala.: Religious Education Press, 1980), 4; J. Gordon Chamberlain, "Christian Education: Action and Meaning," report of National Conference on Church Architecture, Pittsburgh, 1961, 51 (AIA/IFRAA, box 5309). See also Dowling, "For God, for Family, for Country," 168–75.

26. Atkinson, *Building and Equipping for Christian Education*, 7.

27. See chapter 4, "Building Creativity in the Postwar School," in Amy E. Ogata, *Designing the Creative Child: Playthings and Places in Midcentury America* (Minneapolis: University of Minnesota Press, 2013). Ogata notes the emphasis on informality and domesticity in the postwar school, just as I have found in church environments in the period.

28. Blankenship, "Building for Christian Education," D2–3.

29. Atkinson, *Building and Equipping for Christian Education*, 8. See also Lynn and Wright, *The Big Little School*.

30. Blankenship, "Building for Christian Education, 60.

31. Charles E. Stade, "An Architect's Notes: Good and Bad Church Architecture," *Your Church* 6, no. 4 (October–December 1960): 14–15.

32. Atkinson, *Building and Equipping for Christian Education*, 31–32.

33. Blankenship, "Building for Christian Education," 61.

34. John Scotford, *When You Build Your Church* (Great Neck, N.Y.: Doniger and Raughley, 1955), 123.

35. John Knox Shear, ed., *Religious Buildings for Today* (New York: F. W. Dodge Corp., 1957), 137.

36. John E. Morse, *To Build a Church* (New York: Holt, Rinehart and Winston, 1969), 115.

37. Jon Pahl, *Youth Ministry in Modern America: 1930 to the Present* (Peabody, Mass.: Hendrickson Publishers, 2000), 7.

38. Structure Committee report, n.d., First Baptist Church, Bloomington, Indiana, records.

39. At the National Conference on Church Architecture held in Los Angeles in 1959, delegates debated the question of the gym, concluding that "(a) It's usually impossible to also use the same space for fellowship and dinners, etc.; (b) poorest use of church's money; (c) ping pong and shuffleboard *are* useable in regular fellowship hall; (d) Question of gymnasium really boils down to basketball. When ten play, what do the others do?; (e) It is hard to create right atmosphere for real fellowship in a gym." See "Summary of work groups on Christian education," report of National Conference on Religious Architecture, Los Angeles, 1959 (AIA/IFRAA, box 5309).

40. See Modell, *Into One's Own*, 253–62.

41. Atkinson, *Building and Equipping for Christian Education*, 138.

42. Shear, *Religious Buildings for Today*, 138.

43. Morse, *To Build a Church*, 127.

44. Edward Sövik interview, Northfield, Minnesota, August 7, 2008.

45. Persis Smith, "Adequate Social Planning for the Church," *Your Church* 4, no. 2 (April–June 1958): 20.

46. Ibid., 49.

47. Scotford, *When You Build Your Church*, 43.

48. Ibid., 44.

49. "Making the Church Homelike," 1. See also Daniel Sack, *Whitebread Protestants: Food and Religion in American Culture* (New York: St. Martin's Press, 2000).

50. "Making the Church Homelike," 3.

51. Structure Committee report, ca. 1956, First Baptist Church records.

52. Scotford, *When You Build Your Church*, 131. This point is debatable, but it seems to have been a common perception. It may be related to the disappearance of a formal dining room, rather than houses of the postwar years on the whole being smaller than they had been in the past.

53. "Making the Church Homelike," 4.

54. Persis Smith, "The Church Refreshment Hour," *Your Church* 2, no. 4 (November–December 1956): 32ff. Smith liked the fact that the atmosphere was "relaxed and religious as well" and notes that the practice extended even to Jews, citing an instance where a congregation invited members of other faiths to join them for coffee after Friday evening services (46).

55. Pamphlet for new church, ca. 1953, Our Savior's Lutheran Church, records.

56. Edward Frey, "Building for the Christian Community," report of National Conference on Church Architecture, Los Angeles, 1959, 7. See also Sack, *Whitebread Protestants*.

57. *Briefs for Church Builders*, no. 19, "Church Kitchens," National Council of Churches of Christ, 1961, 1. See also Thomas M. Bell, "The Church Kitchen," *Your Church* 1, no. 2 (July–September 1955): 16–17.

58. A number of interviewees told me that the dissolution of the men's groups, or at least their regular meeting, began when the women of the church no longer had the time or the inclination to cook dinner for them.

59. Carol Ferguson and Dean Ferguson interview, Fargo, North Dakota, June 11, 2007.

60. Betty Ackerman interview, La Grange, Illinois, August 18, 2010.

61. See "Church Kitchens."

62. Thomas Reilley, "Good Office Design," *Your Church* 14, no. 6 (November–December. 1968): 19.

63. William S. Clark, "Curtain Call," *Your Church* 1, no. 3 (October–December 1955): 6.

64. Morse, *To Build a Church*, 115–16.

65. Marty, "Building for the Christian Parish in a Secular Culture," 13.

66. Abraham Eastwood Jr., "An Architect's Notes," *Your Church* 8, no. 4 (October–December 1962): 9.

67. Blankenship, "Building for Christian Education," 60.

68. "Woman of the Week," 1966 clipping from *Park Forest Star*, Church of the Holy Family (Episcopal), Park Forest, Illinois, records.

69. David Morgan, "Introduction: The Matter of Belief," in David Morgan, ed., *Religion and Material Culture: The Matter of Belief* (London: Routledge, 2010), 6.

## 7. RELIGION, ARCHITECTURE, AND COMMUNITY IN THE CELEBRATED SUBURB OF PARK FOREST, ILLINOIS

Many thanks to William Gleason and members of the American Studies Workshop at Princeton University for helpful comments on an earlier version of this chapter.

1. James Sparkman, "Park Forest, Ill., Built to Order as Model for Future Community Growth," *Christian Science Monitor*, July 24, 1953, clipping in ACB file, Park Forest Public Library.

2. William Whyte, *The Organization Man* (New York: Simon and Schuster, 1956).

3. William Whyte, "The Future, c/o Park Forest," *Fortune*, June 1953, 127.

4. Sparkman, "Park Forest, Ill., Built to Order as Model for Future Community Growth."

5. T. Norman Mansell, "The Challenge of the Small Church," *Church Management* 29, no. 9 (June 1953): 10.

6. See Philip M. Klutznik interview with Glenda Bailey-Mershon, recorded February 5, 1981; oral history transcript, "Park Forest: An Illinois Planned Community," collection, Illinois Digital Archives: www.idaillinois.org. Klutznik raised his family of five children in Park Forest, and continued to live there after 1960 when he sold his interest in the community. He was later International President of B'nai B'rith, and president of the World Jewish Congress.

7. "Park Forest, Illinois: Proving Ground for Community Planning Techniques," *Architectural Record* 109, no. 5 (May 1951): 99–110. This is about seven hundred to nine hundred dollars per month in 2013 dollars.

8. The figure given in the 1951 *Architectural Record* article is nine Federal Housing Administration (FHA) mortgages totaling $27.6 million. A few years later, the *Chicago Sun Times* (October 24, 1954) reported that ACB had $58 million in FHA-insured loans. Other sources push the figure up to $70 million.

9. News clipping, Church of the Holy Family (Episcopal), Park Forest, Illinois, records. Whyte claims the figure was 30 percent in the rental units and 20 percent in houses (Whyte, *The Organization Man*, 301).

10. Ibid., 282–83.

11. Karen Hohbach, interview, Park Forest, Illinois, July 10, 2007.

12. Whyte, *The Organization Man*, 284.

13. See Joseph Houlihan, "Integrating the Suburbs: A Park Forest Case Study," *Cities in the 21st Century* 2, no. 1 (article 4), www.digitalcommons.macalester.edu/cities/vol2/iss1/4.

14. Loebl, Schlossman, and Bennett created other celebrated shopping centers in the Chicago area, including Old Orchard (1956) and Oakbrook Center (1962).

15. *Park Forest Reporter*, October 26, 1950.

16. Whyte, *The Organization Man*, 192. The exception was the Blackhawk School (1955), designed by Chicago architects Perkins and Will, specialists in modern school design from the late 1930s.

17. Whyte, *The Organization Man*, 194.

18. *Park Forest Reporter*, May 20, 1952.

19. Whyte, *The Organization Man*, 196.

20. *Religious Life*, promotional brochure, n.d., (ACB files, Park Forest Public Library).

21. Gregory C. Randall, *America's Original G.I. Town: Park Forest, Illinois* (Baltimore: Johns Hopkins University Press, 2003), Appendix B. I have found no evidence of any conflict between church designers and an architectural review board. Assuming there was such a board, it was likely the case that the developers and the architects of the churches were already on the same page regarding design. There is occasional evidence that the town criticized the churches because they did not plan for adequate off-street parking. See Church of the Holy Family records. The practice of large-scale developers giving land for the establishment of churches appears to have been increasingly common throughout the 1950s. See "Plan Church Sites for New Areas," *Park Forest Reporter*, February 23, 1955, a report on the plan commission's "subcommittee on church sites" efforts to spread churches around the town by inviting church groups to build in new areas, for instance, "two minimum 2-acre sites to be provided in Area 15 adjacent to each of the proposed school sites."

22. Will Herberg, *Protestant—Catholic—Jew: An Essay in American Religious Sociology* (New York: Doubleday, 1955).

23. "Minister's List of Park Forest Religious Organizations, August 5, 1963," typescript, Park Forest Churches File, Park Forest Public Library.

24. St. Irenaeus Church, *Thirtieth Anniversary Book* (1978), St. Irenaeus Catholic Church, Park Forest, Illinois, records; see also Harry C. Koenig, ed., *A History of the Parishes of the Archdiocese of Chicago*, vol. 2 (Chicago: Catholic Bishop of Chicago, 1980), 1464–68.

25. Irene Hickey interview, June 21, 2008.

26. Ibid.

27. *A History of the Parishes of the Archdiocese of Chicago*, 2:1467.

28. Ibid., 2:1468.

29. Winnie Maune and Bill Maune interview, Park Forest, Illinois, June 21, 2008.

30. *A History of the Parishes of the Archdiocese of Chicago*, 2:1467.

31. The office of chaplain existed until 1964. Leinberger left Park Forest in 1952 to become associate pastor of Flossmoor Community Church. In 1957, he was named director of planning and development for the newly merged United Congregational Church (UCC) ("Our

40th: Forward from 40 Renewing the Vision, 1951–1991," Faith United Protestant Church, Park Forest, Illinois, records).

32. "Paralysis in Park Forest," *Christian Century*, November 9, 1949, 1320.

33. Father Coogan of St. Irenaeus remembered Leinberger as a valued colleague: "We would go around together, seeking parishioners for our infant churches" (*A History of the Parishes of the Archdiocese of Chicago*, 2:1466).

34. Park Forest *Star*, November 9, 1969. In contrast, Pennsylvania's Levittown by 1953 was 41 percent Protestant, 39 percent Roman Catholic, 15 percent Jewish, 5 percent no affiliation. See Dianne Harris, ed., *Second Suburb: Levittown, Pennsylvania* (Pittsburgh: University of Pittsburgh Press, 2010), 5.

35. Laymen's Group, "Protestant Church Plans as They Have Developed," typescript, Park Forest Churches file, Park Forest Public Library.

36. Ibid.

37. Amy Hensold and Lucy Klein interview, Olympia Fields, Illinois, May 13, 2010.

38. Laymen's Group, "Protestant Church Plans as They Have Developed."

39. "Paralysis in Park Forest," 1319.

40. Ibid. In December, a reply from a young student lay leader at Trinity (Richard M. Bennett—not the architect) argued that the original article contained "a minimum of information and a maximum of exaggeration" and noted that Lutherans had a building fund of fifty thousand dollars approved by the Mission Board of the Evangelical Lutheran Church (ELC) for the "immediate construction of a Lutheran-sponsored community church in Park Forest." See "Luther in Park Forest," *Christian Century*, December 14, 1949, 1491.

41. "Paralysis in Park Forest," 1319.

42. "Sunday School Ready to Open in Park Forest," *Chicago Tribune*, February 17, 1952, SW1. The article notes the religious diversity of the congregation's first members, which included, in addition to the five organizing denominations, former members of Lutheran, Episcopal, Disciples, Dutch Reformed, LCMS, Unitarian, Mission Covenant, Evangelical-United Brethren, Quaker, Reorganized Latter-day Saints, Reformed Episcopal, Church of Brethren, Greek Orthodox, and Universalist churches.

43. Stan Boie interview, Park Forest, Illinois, May 22, 2007.

44. Ibid. Etan Diamond notes in his study of Indianapolis that is was not uncommon for there to be tensions between mainline Protestant organizations and those of more conservative groups with more independence and less bureaucracy. This explains the resistance of the Baptists and Missouri Synod Lutherans in Park Forest, but not that of the Episcopalians (Etan Diamond, *Souls of the City: Religion and the Search for Community in Postwar America* [Bloomington: Indiana University Press, 2003], 36–37). Diamond furthermore refutes William Whyte's contention that Christians would become more mainstream in suburbia (37).

45. "How And Why It All Began," Good Shepherd United Protestant Church, Park Forest, Illinois, records.

46. Richard M. Bennett, "Luther in Park Forest," *Christian Century*, December 14, 1949, 1491.

47. I found only one reference to communities following the United Church model. The *Park Forest Reporter* of February 7, 1952, reported that the Washington State Council planned to use the model for new communities along the Columbia River Basin. By 1954, Leinberger had left Park Forest and the new chaplain, Joseph Hughes, a Baptist, soon completed another set of surveys. He estimated that when the population of the town topped at 33, 217, there

would be sixteen church sites. He assumed that 50 percent of Protestants, 89 percent of Catholics, and 28 percent of Jews would be members of religious organizations, or about half the population. Of the remaining half, the vast majority would profess a religion but have no membership (*Park Forest Reporter*, February 23, 1955).

48. Herbert Gans, "Park Forest: Birth of a Suburban Jewish Community," *Commentary* 2 (April 1951): 330–39, and Herbert Gans, "Progress of a Suburban Jewish Community," *Commentary* 8 (1957): 113–22. See also Albert Gordon Isaac, *Jews in Suburbia* (Boston: Beacon Press, 1959).

49. See Victor Perlmutter, Letter to the Editor, *Commentary* (August 1951), and Samuel Z. Jaffe (rabbi) and Morris Feller (president of Beth Sholom), Letter to the Editor, *Commentary* (May 1957), Park Forest Local History Collection and Archives.

50. "Sunday school" was the term used by the congregation.

51. The Jewish Education School in 1955 promised to teach "Prayer, Bible study, religious practices, preparation for Bar and Bat Mitzvah and Confirmation, Jewish history, customs, holiday traditions, Hebrew language and literature, and related music and art craft." This does reflect a wide and somewhat generic Jewish curriculum, but also a strong component of religious education (*Park Forest Reporter*, May 4, 1955, 19).

52. Gans, "Park Forest," 332.

53. On the suburbanization of American Jews, see Karen Brodkin, *How Jews Became White Folks and What That Says about Race in America* (New Brunswick, N.J.: Rutgers University Press, 1998). See also Diane Harris, *Little White Houses: How the Postwar Home Constructed Race in America* (Minneapolis: University of Minnesota Press, 2013).

54. See Congregation Beth Sholom, *40th Anniversary Service*, May 31, 1991; Synagogue file, Park Forest Public Library.

55. *Park Forest Reporter*, November 9, 1951.

56. Gans, "Progress of a Suburban Jewish Community," 114.

57. Ibid., 115.

58. Jaffe and Feller, Letter to the Editor.

59. *Chicago Lutheran Messenger* 40, no. 10 (January 1950), in Trinity Lutheran Church, Park Forest, Illinois, records.

60. Paul Thiry, Richard M.Bennett, and Henry L. Kamphoefner, *Churches and Temples* (New York: Reinhold, 1953).

61. "First Church in Park Forest to Be Dedicated," *Chicago Daily Tribune*, May 20, 1951, SW6.

62. Henry Lehmann to Loebl, Schlossman, and Bennett, June 16, 1951, Trinity Lutheran Church records.

63. Marge Roeder interview, Park Forest, Illinois, July 10, 2007.

64. *Park Forest Reporter*, May 18, 1960.

65. Dedication Bulletin, ca. 1960. Trinity Church File, Park Forest Public Library.

66. Ibid.

67. Trinity Church Council Minutes, December 20, 1954, Trinity Lutheran Church records.

68. Lucy Klein and Amy Hensold believe that in practice people did not retain their previous denominational affiliation, so the church became simply a more ecumenical version of the sponsoring denomination (Amy Hensold and Lucy Klein interview, 2010).

69. Sparkman, "Park Forest, Ill., Built to Order as Model for Future Community Growth."

70. "Park Forest United," *Newsweek*, April 21, 1952.

71. Amy Hensold and Lucy Klein interview, 2010.

72. *Meet the United Protestant Church of Park Forest*, ca. 1953 brochure in United Protestant File, Park Forest Public Library.

73. Education building dedication bulletin, United Church file, Park Forest Public Library.

74. *Newsweek*, April 21, 1952, 116.

75. "The Future," *Fortune*, 1953, 190.

76. Amy Hensold and Lucy Klein interview, 2010.

77. Elting is often referred to as the architect of this church; he spoke at dedication events and Faith Church may possibly be more his work than Schweikher's.

78. Amy Hensold and Lucy Klein interview, 2010.

79. "Plastics Go to Church," *Monsanto Magazine*, May 1960, 9, Faith UPC file, Park Forest Public Library.

80. Amy Hensold and Lucy Klein interview, 2010.

81. Dedication of Carillon Tower, 1963, Faith UPC records.

82. It may be that this stark, modern religious architecture represented a stripped-down common denominator, a compromise for church members having a complex mix of theological backgrounds. Yet the three later UPC churches in Park Forest, equally varied in membership, erected common A-frames with typical design features. More likely, the extreme pioneering spirit of Faith, as the first UPC experiment, explains the congregation's early acceptance of this unusually and boldly modern building complex.

83. Stan Boie interview, 2007.

84. Ibid.

85. Ibid.

86. *Park Forest Reporter*, November 5, 1953.

87. First fund-raising brochure, ca. 1953, Hope Lutheran Church, Park Forest, Illinois, records.

88. Ibid.

89. Stan Boie interview, 2007.

90. First fund-raising brochure, ca. 1953.

91. Stan Boie interview, 2007.

92. Ibid.

93. "Golden and Beyond: Celebrating the Fiftieth Anniversary of Hope Lutheran Church, 1952–2002." Hope Lutheran Church records.

94. Letter from Bishop Wallace E. Conkling to congregation, April 29, 1953, Church of the Holy Family records.

95. I have not elsewhere found these requirements, but this citation alone indicates the oversight of the ACB regarding church design (Minutes of Bishop's Committee, August 15, 1950, Church of the Holy Family records).

96. Architect for the project was William Ganster of Waukegan. See scrapbooks, June 1950–December 1956, Church of the Holy Family records.

97. Ibid.

98. Holy Family is notably similar to Pietro Belluschi's design for an Episcopal church in Baltimore (Episcopal Church of the Redeemer, completed in 1958) of the same period, with its low stone wall, cruciform roof plan, transept, and steep roofline.

99. *Park Forest Star*, November 22, 1957, clipping, Church of the Holy Family records.

100. Letters from Robert Ruffie to Edward Dart, May 12, 1959, and June 4, 1959, Church of the Holy Family records.

101. In a letter from Dart to Unit Structures, Inc., he claimed that the problem was with the glulams, and was withholding payment of six thousand dollars (letter dated July 18, 1958, Church of the Holy Family records).

102. Nimi Nord interview, Park Forest, Illinois, May 22, 2007.

103. *Park Forest Star,* September 28, 1969, Church of the Holy Family records.

104. Charles Sang interview, Hazelcrest, Illinois, June 22, 2008.

105. First Baptist Dedication Bulletin, September 19, 1965, Property of Charles Sang.

106. *Park Forest Star,* January 31, 1958, First Baptist Church, Park Forest, Illinois, records.

107. Carl Palfenier and Carol Palfenier interview, Park Forest, Illinois, June 22, 2008.

108. Ibid.

109. Ibid.

110. First Baptist Dedication Bulletin, 1965.

111. Shirley Bumba and Hazel Conroyd interview, Park Forest, Illinois, May 24, 2010.

112. *A History of the Parishes of the Archdiocese of Chicago,* 2:1466.

113. See Thiry, Bennett, and Kamphoefner, *Churches and Temples.* This design was similar to Bruce Goff's chapel at Camp Parks, later the Community Church in San Lorenzo, California, on the NCC's 1956 list of notable modern churches.

114. Richard M. Bennett, "Community Synagogue: Park Forest, Illinois," in ibid., 65J.

115. Ibid., 68J.

116. Richard M. Bennett, "The Aesthetic Demands of Contemporary Architecture upon Masonry," in *Modern Masonry: Natural Stone and Clay Products* (Washington, D.C.: National Academy of Sciences Building Research Institute, publication no. 466, 1956), 7–13.

117. Undated newspaper clipping in synagogue file, Park Forest Public Library.

118. Alice T. Friedman, *American Glamour and the Evolution of Modern Architecture* (New Haven, Conn.: Yale University Press, 2010).

119. Amy Hensold and Lucy Klein interview, 2010.

120. "Catholics Asked to Give $70K for New Church," *Park Forest Reporter,* January 4, 1951.

121. *Park Forest Reporter,* October 26, 1950.

122. "An Habitation for the Mighty God," Church Dedication Bulletin, March 15, 1959, Church of the Holy Family records.

123. Karen Hohbach interview, 2007.

124. Amy Hensold and Lucy Klein interview, 2010.

125. Whyte, *The Organization Man,* 190.

126. Ibid., 188.

127. Martin Marty, *The New Shape of American Religion* (New York: Harper & Brothers, 1959), 151–52.

128. Judy Mathais interview with Dr. Gerson Englemann, August 7, 1980; "Park Forest: An Illinois Planned Community" collection, Illinois Digital Archive, p. 17 of transcript, www.idaillinois.org.

## 8. THE AFTERLIFE OF THE POSTWAR SUBURBAN CHURCH

I presented an earlier version of this chapter to the Quadrant Workshop at the University of Minnesota (March 2013) and am thankful to Anne Carter and the participants in the seminar for the many helpful suggestions.

1. I am grateful to Molly Wlodarczyk for this reference.

2. Lois Wille, "The Suburb That Turned Its Back," *McCall's* (July 1968): 14.

3. The decline in numbers of the mainline denominations (liberal and moderate Protestants and Jews, in particular) is a much-studied phenomenon. See, for example, Roger Finke and Rodney Starke, *The Churching of America, 1776–1990: Winners and Losers in Our Religious Marketplace* (New Brunswick, N.J.: Rutgers University Press, 1992), Wade Clark Roof and William McKinney, *American Mainline Religion: Its Changing Shape and Future* (New Brunswick, N.J.: Rutgers University Press, 1987), and Wade Clark Roof, *Spiritual Marketplace: Baby Boomers and the Remaking of American Religion* (Princeton, N.J.: Princeton University Press, 1999).

4. A useful account of the current demographics of American religion is provided by Mark Chaves, National Congregations Study, www.soc.duke.edu/natcong. See also Mark Chaves, *Congregations in America* (Cambridge, Mass.: Harvard University Press, 2004). This study discovered that, while megachurches are the most visible phenomenon on the American religious landscape today, the average congregation size (of all religious denominations) is in fact merely seventy-five, and 90 percent of Americans worship in congregations no larger than 350. Chaves argues that the amount of social service provided by churches in their communities is less significant that some political interests would suggest. Nonetheless, nearly all of the congregations in this study were engaged in significant outreach in their communities, and that is, of course, in addition to serving the many and varied needs of the congregation itself.

5. Nimi Nord interview, Park Forest, Illinois, May 22, 2007.

6. Stan Boie interview, Park Forest, Illinois, May 22, 2007.

7. See Roof and McKinney, *American Mainline Religion*, 27.

8. A 1998 article in the *Chicago Tribune* noted that fourteen Chicago suburbs had higher crime rates than the central city; cited in William H. Lucy and David L. Phillips, *Confronting Suburban Decline: Strategic Planning for Metropolitan Renewal* (Washington, D.C.: Island Press, 2000), 210–11; John McCarron, "Tip of the Iceberg: Only a Matter of Time before Some Suburbs Come Tumbling Down," *Chicago Tribune*, April 27, 1998.

9. Robert Wuthnow, *Loose Connections: Joining Together in America's Fragmented Communities* (Cambridge, Mass.: Harvard University Press, 1986), 85.

10. Lucy and Phillips, *Confronting Suburban Decline*, 7. Lucy and Phillips suggest that the hardest-hit suburbs are those with the majority of housing stock built in the 1945–70 period, 800 to 1,300 square feet, what they call "middle-aged" housing, while areas with pre-1940s housing often attract more investment. See chapter 8, "Housing and Neighborhood Decline: Struggles of Middle Age," 197–230.

11. Ibid, 7.

12. Wuthnow, *Loose Connections*, 88.

13. See "Church Architecture Today," *Your Church* 1, no. 2 (October–December 1955): 11. See also L. Morgan Yost, "The Case for the Contemporary," *Church Management* 29, no. 1 (October 1952): 39. As early as 1952, Yost claimed, "Today times are changing most rapidly, and the life expectancy of a church building or any other building is correspondingly less."

14. www.trinitymhd.org (February 7, 2013).

15. Karen Hohbach interview, Park Forest, Illinois, July 10, 2007.

16. Dedication Bulletin, May 16, 1971, Holy Ghost Catholic Church, South Holland, Illinois, records.

17. Erne R. and Florence Frueh, "The History of Our Memorial to Father Jim," 1983; Holy Ghost Catholic Church records.

18. Donna Kiesling, "Church's Stained Glass Casts Light on the Past," undated news clipping, Holy Ghost Catholic Church records.

19. Daniel E. Lewis Jr., *Architectural Insights: The Architecture of the Presbyterian Church of La Porte, Indiana,* Presbyterian Church of La Porte, Indiana, records.

20. William I. Carter, Vicar, "The Symbolism of St. Augustine's," ca. 1962–68, St. Augustine's of Canterbury Church, Benton Harbor, Michigan, records.

21. Father Dan Scheid interview, Benton Harbor, Michigan, May 15, 2007.

22. Carol Ferguson and Dean Ferguson interview, Fargo, North Dakota, June 11, 2007.

23. Hal Neugebauer and Clara Neugebauer interview, Fargo, North Dakota, June 11, 2007.

24. See chapter 3 of Stewart Brand, *How Buildings Learn: What Happens after They're Built* (New York: Penguin, 1994).

25. In 1967, a small United Church of Christ congregation, an outgrowth of Indiana University student ministries, lost its campus housing. First Baptist invited this church to share its space, and the two congregations integrated officially in 1973.

26. Martin E. Marty, "Building for the Christian Parish in a Secular Culture," March 6, 1963, report of National Conference on Church Architecture, Seattle, 1963, 14.14 (AIA/IFRAA, box 5309).

27. Robert D. Putnam, *Bowling Alone: The Collapse and Revival of American Community* (New York: Simon and Schuster, 2000). See chapter 4, "Religious Participation."

28. Calvary Baptist Church outgrew the original building (ca. 1949) on a smaller lot in a formerly suburban area that became more retail oriented, and in 1995 moved to a larger site elsewhere in the city.

29. Principal Gladys Davis telephone interview, January 22, 2013. The school outgrew the building. As of October 2014, it belonged to another owner and was slated for demolition.

30. E-mail correspondence with Dan Ronning, February 19, 2013. See also www.macfm.org.

31. Wally Novak interview, St. Louis Park, Minnesota, June 13, 2007.

32. Bob Stout and Helen Stout interview, Bloomington, Indiana, March 11, 2010.

33. "A Building's Past: The First Fifty Years," September 8, 2007, 5, First Baptist Church, Bloomington, Indiana, records.

34. Don Duke interview, Burlington, Iowa, February 1, 2013.

35. This is not a common problem for Stade's buildings—this is the only major structural issue I have encountered, perhaps, as the congregation supposes, having something to do with the stability of the ground at the site.

36. Brand, *How Buildings Learn,* 34–35.

37. Ibid., 49.

38. Mark Torgerson, *Greening Spaces for Worship and Ministry: Congregations, Their Buildings, and Creation Care* (Herndon, Va.: Alban Institute, 2012).

39. "Recent Past Survey: Suburban Cook County," www.landmarksil.org (February 19, 2014).

40. See Theodore H. M. Prudon, *The Preservation of Modern Architecture* (Hoboken, N.J.: John Wiley and Sons, 2008).

41. Mary E. Kennedy, February 16, 2012, National Register of Historic Places Evaluation for the Pilgrim Lutheran Church, Hamilton County, Indiana, in association with the US 31

Road Improvement Project, INDOT Des. No. 0710215. This report also contains an excellent account of postwar church building in Indianapolis.

42. Quentin Smith telephone interview, June 27, 2012.

43. Ibid.

44. Felicia Childress, June Brown, Charlotte Strowhorn, Chester Williams, and Dolores White group interview, Gary, Indiana, June 24, 2012.

45. Reverend Wallace L. Wells, "Prayerful and Militant," in *The Living Church Magazine,* January 17, 1960, St. Augustine's Episcopal Church, Gary, Indiana, records.

46. AIA Distinguished Building Award, Church Architecture Guild Honor Award in 1960.

47. "Design for Worship: St. Augustine's Episcopal Church, Gary, Indiana," *Your Church* 6, no. 4 (October–December 1960): 19–21.

48. E-mail from John Beatty, January 4, 2013, forwarded by Paula DeBois. Because of the special position of this congregation in the Gary community, the church always drew members from outside the Tolleston neighborhood.

49. Paula DeBois, telephone interview, January 24, 2013.

50. Ibid.

51. "Gary Congregation Seeks National Register Status for Midcentury Modern Church," www.wbez.org (January 9, 2013).

52. "St. Augustine's Episcopal Church," Facebook page, Byron Ottman post, January 14, 2013.

53. Paula DeBois interview, Gary, Indiana, June 24, 2012.

# SOURCES FOR RESEARCH

## ARCHIVES

American Institute of Architects Archives, Washington, D.C., Records of Interfaith Forum on Religion, Art and Architecture (IFRAA), including records of Church Architecture Guild (CAG) and Guild for Religious Architecture (GRA)

Charles E. Stade Collection, Chicago History Museum, Chicago, Illinois

Edward A. Sövik Papers, Luther Seminary Archives, St. Paul, Minnesota

Edward D. Dart Collection, Chicago History Museum, Chicago, Illinois

Edward Dart Collection, Ryerson and Burnham Libraries Archive, Art Institute of Chicago, Chicago, Illinois

National Council of Churches of Christ in the U.S.A. (NCC) Records, Presbyterian Historical Society, Philadelphia, Pennsylvania

Park Forest Public Library Historical Collections (collection recently moved to the Park Forest Historical Society collections at St. Mary's Church), Park Forest, Illinois

Frederick R. Webber Papers, Concordia Historical Institute, St. Louis, Missouri

## CHURCH RESOURCES

The following churches (listed by original name, with 2015 name in parentheses, if different) were sites of architectural and historical fieldwork. A-frame churches are designated with an A. Dates are the dedication dates (whenever possible to confirm). Church Architecture Guild (CAG) / Guild for Religious Architecture (GRA), American Society for Church Architecture (ASCA), and American Institute of Architects (AIA) awards for churches by Sövik, Stade, or Dart are noted.

### *California*

First Presbyterian Church, Concord (Donald Powers Smith, 1953) A

San Lorenzo Community Church, San Lorenzo (Bruce Goff, chapel from Camp Parks, ca. 1942, moved 1949)

Trinity Lutheran Church, Walnut Creek (Belluschi/Nestch, 1956)

### *Illinois*

All Saints Lutheran Church, Orland Park (Dart, 1962)
Augustana Lutheran Church, Chicago (Dart, 1968)
Christ Church Evangelical and Reformed Church (Christ Church Congregational), Des Plaines (Stade, parish hall 1953, church 1964)
Church of the Resurrection, Episcopal, West Chicago (Dart, 1963)
First Presbyterian Church, La Grange (Stade expansion, 1962)
First (United) Methodist Church, Crystal Lake (Stade, 1955), A
Good Shepherd Methodist Church, Park Ridge (Stade, 1963) CAG
Grace Lutheran Church, Bensenville (Dart, 1961) A
Hillside Free Methodist Church, Evanston (Stade, 1961) A
Holy Family Catholic Church, Rockford (Stade, 1973–75)
Holy Ghost Catholic Church, South Holland (Dart, 1971)
House of Prayer Lutheran Church, Country Club Hills (Dart, 1963)
Immanuel Lutheran Church, Des Plaines (Stade, 1957) A
Joliet Jewish Congregation, Joliet (Stade, 1968)
Lake View Lutheran Church, Chicago (Stade, 1961)
Lansing Presbyterian Church, Lansing (Dart, 1963) ASCA
Lutheran Church of the Atonement, Barrington (Dart, 1961) A (demolished)
Lutheran Church of the Good Shepherd, Palos Park (Stade, 1956) A
Lutheran Church of the Holy Spirit, Elk Grove Village (Stade, church 1960, education wing 1963)
Northbrook (United) Methodist Church, Northbrook (Stade, 1960) parabolic A
Our Saviour Lutheran Church, Lansing (Stade, 1961) A
Our Saviour's Lutheran Church, Arlington Heights (Stade, 1958) A
St. Ambrose Episcopal Church (The Emmaus Community), Chicago Heights (Dart, 1959)
St. Andrews Lutheran Church, Park Ridge (Stade, 1954) A, CAG
St. John's Lutheran Church, La Grange (Stade, 1968)
St. John's Lutheran Church, Lincolnwood (Stade, 1962) ASCA
St. Joseph Catholic Church, Summit (Stade, 1970)
St. Mark's Lutheran Church, Aurora (Dart, 1961) A
St. Mary Catholic Church, Des Plaines (Stade, 1971)
St. Matthew Lutheran Church, Barrington (Stade, 1959) A
St. Matthew United Church of Christ, Wheaton (Dart, 1964)
St. Michael's Episcopal Church, Barrington (Dart, 1954)
St. Nicholas Episcopal Church, Elk Grove Village (Dart, 1963)
St. Paul Lutheran Church, Mount Prospect (Stade, 1961) A
St. Paul Lutheran Church, Oak Lawn (Stade, 1954) A
St. Paul Lutheran Church, Peoria (Stade, 1966)
St. Peter Lutheran Church, Arlington Heights (Stade, church and school 1961)
Salem United Church of Christ, Oak Lawn (Stade, 1962)
Thornridge United Church of Christ (Covenant United Church of Christ), South Holland (Dart, 1962) A
Villa Park Christian Church, Villa Park (Stade, 1960) A
Winnetka Presbyterian Church (Stade, 1961) A

### PARK FOREST, ILLINOIS

Calvary United Protestant Church (first unit 1958–59, church 1963) A
Church of the Holy Family (Episcopal) (Dart, 1958) A
Congregation Beth Sholom (Hallelujah Temple)(William Bennett, 1955)
Faith United Protestant Church (Schweikher & Elting, education wing 1952, church 1958)
First Baptist Church (Robert Taylor and Derald West, education unit, 1958); William Cooley, sanctuary, 1965) A
First Church of Christ, Scientist (Rehoboth Ministries Church of God in Christ) (Albert Ramp, 1962)
Good Shepherd United Protestant Church (House of Prayer, Ministries by Faith) (Charles Draper Faulkner, 1959, education building 1962) A
Grace United Protestant Church (William Cooley, 1959; education wing 1964) A
Hope Lutheran Church (Celebration Ministries) (Stade & Cooley, A-frame 1954; Stade school 1960, new sanctuary 1967)
St. Irenaeus Catholic Church (education building 1952, church 1964) A
Trinity Lutheran Church (William Bennett, 1951, 1958) A

### *Indiana*

Chapel of the Resurrection, Valparaiso University (Stade, 1959) CAG
Chapel of the Sermon on the Mount, Associated Mennonite Biblical Seminary, Elkhart (Stade, 1965) ASCA
First Baptist Church (First United Church), Bloomington (Sövik, 1958) AIA Honorable Mention
Immanuel Lutheran Church, Seymour (Stade, 1963) A
The Presbyterian Church of La Porte, La Porte (Dart, 1968)
St. Augustine's Episcopal Church, Gary (Dart, 1959) A, CAG
St. Luke's (United) Methodist Church, Indianapolis (Dart, 1967)

### *Iowa*

First Congregational Church, Spencer (Harold Spitznagel, 1953) A, CAG
Messiah Lutheran Church, Burlington (Stade, 1961)
Plainfield Methodist Church, Plainfield (Paul Schweikher, 1951)
Riverside Bible Camp Chapel, Story City (Sövik, 1950) A, AIA
Trinity Lutheran Church, Ellsworth (Sövik, 1953)

### *Maryland*

The Church of the Redeemer (Episcopal), Baltimore (Pietro Belluschi, 1958)
St. Paul's Evangelical Lutheran Church, Glen Burnie (Stade, 1963)

### *Michigan*

St. Augustine of Canterbury Episcopal Church, Benton Harbor (Dart, 1962)
Zion Evangelical Lutheran Church, Kalamazoo (Stade, 1956) A

### *Minnesota*

Calvary Lutheran Church, Park Rapids (Sövik, 1960) A
Chatfield Lutheran Church (Sövik, 1953) A

Christ Lutheran Church (Christ Church Lutheran), Minneapolis (Eliel Saarinen, church 1949; Eero Saarinen, education wing 1962)
Lutheran Church of the Good Shepherd, Moorhead (Sövik, first unit 1954, education unit 1958, sanctuary 1967) GRA, AIA (demolished)
Lutheran Church of the Resurrection, Roseville (Stade, 1956, 1965) A
Moravian Church, Northfield (Sövik, 1949–52) A
Northfield Methodist Church, Northfield (Sövik, 1966)
Our Savior's Lutheran Church, Austin (Sövik, first unit 1954, sanctuary 1962) CAG
St. John's Lutheran Church, Austin (Sövik, 1972)
St. Leo Catholic Church, Pipestone (Sövik, 1969) AIA
Trinity Lutheran Church, Minnehaha Falls, Minneapolis (Sövik, 1961)
Trinity Lutheran Church, Moorhead (Sövik, 1952)
Trinity Lutheran Church, West Concord (Sövik, 1952)
Westwood Lutheran Church, St. Louis Park (Sövik, 1963) CAG and AIA

### *North Dakota*

Olivet Lutheran Church, Fargo (Sövik, 1965)

### *Pennsylvania*

Lutheran Church of the Resurrection, Yardley (Stade, 1956) A

### *South Dakota*

Church of St. Mary (Catholic), Sioux Falls (Spitznagel, 1956)
First Presbyterian Church, Sioux Falls (Spitznagel, 1959) A
Our Savior's Lutheran Church, Sioux Falls (Spitznagel, 1957)
Zion Lutheran Church, Sioux Falls (Spitznagel, ca. 1954)

### *Wisconsin*

Evangelical Lutheran Church, Mount Horeb (Sövik, 1962)
First Lutheran Church, Onalaska (Sövik, 1954) A
First Unitarian Society Meeting House, Madison (Frank Lloyd Wright, 1951)
St. Paul's Lutheran Church, La Crosse (Sövik, first phase completed 1956, sanctuary 1961)
Zion Lutheran Church, Galesville (Sövik, education building 1952, sanctuary 1956)

## INTERVIEWS

Ackerman, Betty. La Grange, Illinois. August 18, 2010.
Albano, Faith. Evanston, Illinois. February 27, 2013.
Banghart, Priscilla. Benton Harbor, Michigan. May 17, 2007.
Barlow, Ramsey Stade, and Jesse Barlow. State College, Pennsylvania. June 3, 2006; telephone interview, May 1, 2005.
Boie, Stan. Park Forest, Illinois. May 22, 2007.
Brown, June. Gary, Indiana. June 24, 2012.
Brown, Suzanne. Park Forest, Illinois. July 9, 2008.
Bumba, Shirley. Park Forest, Illinois. May 24, 2010.
Childress, Felicia. Gary, Indiana. June 24, 2012.

Collins, Lloyd. Fargo, North Dakota. June 11, 2007.
Conroyd, Hazel. Park Forest, Illinois. May 24, 2010.
Cribbs, Maureen. Park Forest, Illinois. August 18, 2008.
Crist, Stan. St. Louis Park, Minnesota. June 13, 2007.
Curry, Michiana. La Porte, Indiana. May 17, 2007.
Danielson, Helen. Moorhead, Minnesota. June 9, 2007.
Davis, Gladys. Telephone interview, January 22, 2013.
De Haven, Robert. Elk Grove Village, Illinois. May 23, 2013.
DeBois, Paula. Gary, Indiana, June 24, 2012. Telephone interview, January 24, 2013.
Duke, Don. Burlington, Iowa. February 1, 2013.
Dykhuis, Joyce, and Paul Dykhuis. Lansing, Michigan. May 16, 2007.
Ferguson, Carol, and Dean Ferguson. Fargo, North Dakota. June 11, 2007.
Grother, Reverend Louis. Kalamazoo, Michigan. May 15, 2013.
Hamilton, Dr. Richard. Indianapolis, Indiana. March 12, 2010.
Hanna, Bette. Seymour, Indiana. May 9, 2013.
Hausman, Reverend Robert. Roseville, Minnesota. June 14, 2007.
Hensold, Amy, with Lucy Klein. Olympia Fields, Illinois. May 13, 2010.
Hermann, Marilyn, and Don Hermann. Arlington Heights, Illinois. April 27, 2006, and May 19, 2014.
Hickey, Irene. Park Forest, Illinois. June 21, 2008.
Hohbach, Karen. Park Forest, Illinois. July 10, 2007.
Hubley, Lorraine. Oak Lawn, Illinois. April 30, 2010.
Johnson, Phillip. Telephone interview. January 15, 2013.
Klein, Lucy, with Amy Hensold. Olympia Fields, Illinois. May 13, 2010.
Knutson, Reverend Glennys. Austin, Minnesota. July 22, 2007.
Land, Donald. Park Forest, Illinois. June 21, 2008.
Lawrence, Helen. Park Forest, Illinois. June 5, 2007.
Lewis, Daniel Jr. La Porte, Indiana. May 17, 2007.
Loeffler, Jane. Moorhead, Minnesota. June 9, 2007.
Malone, John R. Park Forest, Illinois. May 30, 2007.
Marty, Martin. Riverside, Illinois, June 23, 2006; Chicago, Illinois. August 1, 2008, and April 3, 2013.
Maune, Winnie, and Bill Maune. Park Forest, Illinois. June 21, 2008.
McCarren, Evelyn. Park Forest, Illinois. June 21, 2008.
Menza, Connie. Park Forest, Illinois. June 21, 2008.
Miller, Patricia. Park Forest, Illinois. July 10, 2007.
Mirtschin, Neville. E-mail correspondence. December 15, 2006.
Moses, Toby, and Irving Moses. Telephone interview. May 13, 2013.
Nelson, Lloyd. Moorhead, Minnesota. June 11, 2007.
Nelson, Ronald. St. Louis Park, Minnesota. June 13, 2007.
Neugebauer, Hal, and Clara Neugebauer. Fargo, North Dakota. June 11, 2007.
Nord, Nimi. Park Forest, Illinois. May 22, 2007.
Novak, Wally. St. Louis Park, Minnesota. June 13, 2007.
Palfenier, Carl, and Carol Palfenier. Park Forest, Illinois. June 22, 2008.
Protsman, Jaquelyn. Lansing, Illinois. May 16, 2007.
Reinkensmeyer, Helen, and Gil Reinkensmeyer. Kalamazoo, Michigan. May 15, 2013.

Richardson, Kathy. Moorhead. Minnesota. June 8, 2007.
Roeder, Marge. Park Forest, Illinois. July 10, 2007.
Ronning, Dan. E-mail correspondence. February 19, 2013.
Russell, Gerry. Elk Grove Village, Illinois. May 23, 2013.
Sang, Charles. Hazelcrest, Illinois. June 22, 2008.
Scheid, Reverend Dan. Benton Harbor, Michigan. May 15, 2007.
Schmidt, Mike. Burlington, Iowa. February 1, 2013.
Schroeder, Edward, and Marie Schroeder. St. Louis, Missouri. December 6, 2013.
Shoemaker, Roy. Benton Harbor, Michigan. May 17, 2007.
Smith, Jerry. Burlington, Iowa. February 1, 2013.
Smith, Pastor Susanne. Burlington, Iowa. February 1, 2013.
Smith, Quentin. Telephone interview. June 27, 2012.
Sövik, Edward A. Northfield, Minnesota. June 19, 2007, and August 7, 2008; St. Cloud, Minnesota, June 2, 2010.
Stout, Bob, and Helen Stout. Bloomington, Indiana. March 11, 2010.
Strowhorn, Charlotte. Gary, Indiana. June 24, 2012.
Thompson, Patt. Pipestone, Minnesota. August 7, 2007.
Uthe, Joyce. Park Forest, Illinois. July 10, 2007.
Vickers, Eleanor. Lansing, Illinois. May 16, 2007.
Weber, John. Winnetka, Illinois. March 1, 2013.
White, Dolores. Gary, Indiana. June 24, 2012.
Wiedenmann, Fred. Telephone interview. April 2010.
Willette, Brian. Telephone interview. November 30, 2011.
Williams, Chester. Gary, Indiana. June 24, 2012.
Wolfe, Ed. Roseville, Minnesota. June 14, 2007.

## PUBLISHED MATERIAL

In 1965, Brother Cajetan J. B. Bauman claimed, "Today everything (and anything) is published everywhere!" ("Behind the Renewal in Church Building," 14). Ideas were presented in conferences and workshops, and then published and republished in journals and books. There is considerable redundancy in the documentation for this episode in church architecture. Material I found in the NCC or AIA records in unpublished form was likely later published in journals, but because I began with the archival materials I often use those references in the notes. For systematic periodical searches, I focused on *Church Management*, particularly useful for the late 1940s and 1950s, and *Your Church*, which began in 1955, because Stade served as both a consulting and an associate editor and because this publication was directed to pastors and congregations. I reviewed *Architectural Record* and *Architectural Forum* through the 1950s; one issue per year generally contained a feature on church architecture. I read through the *Journal of the American Society of Church Architecture* and the complete Guild newsletters in the AIA archive. Other journals I consulted broadly include *Progressive Architecture, Liturgical Arts, Response: In Worship-Music-The Arts, Protestant Church Building and Equipment,* and *Indiana Architect.* The NCC published a useful series of leaflets, *Briefs for Church Builders,* that I often found in church archives. The twenty individual titles (as numbered by the NCC) indicate concisely the chief concerns of church builders (anonymous, unless noted):

1. Church Parking, 1956
2. Building on One Level—or More, 1956
3. The First Unit, 1957
4. Arrangements for Music, 1956
5. Light and Color, 1957
6. Making the Church Homelike, 1956
7. High Visibility for Your Church, 1957
8. Sound Control, 1957
9. Motivation for Building Better Churches, 1957
10. Multiple Church and School Sessions, 1956
11. A Place for Everything, 1958
12. A Home for the Minister, 1958
13. Rooms for Preschool Children, 1958
14. Rooms for Primary and Junior Children, 1958
15. Rooms for Youth and Adults, 1958
16. Program, Committee, and Architect, 1961 (by Edward Frey)
17. Financing the Building Program, 1961
18. Church Offices, 1961
19. Church Kitchens, 1961
20. Creating the Atmosphere of Worship, 1961 (by Scott T. Ritenour)

Allitt, Patrick. *Religion in America since 1945: A History*. New York: Columbia University Press, 2003.

"Anarchy in Our Churches." *Architectural Forum* 97, no. 6 (December 1952): 93.

Archer, John. *Architecture and Suburbia: From English Villa to American Dream House, 1690–2000*. Minneapolis: University of Minnesota Press, 2005.

"Architect Designs Buildings around their Occupants," *Chicago Tribune*, August 14, 1966, D1. ProQuest Historical Newspapers.

Armstrong, Harris. "A Church's Challenge to an Architect." *Your Church* 5, no. 1 (January–March 1959): 28–29, 52–55.

Atkinson, C. Harry. *Building and Equipping for Christian Education*. New York: Bureau of Church Building of the National Council of Churches of Christ, 1956.

Bains, David Ralph. "The Liturgical Impulse in Mid-Twentieth-Century American Mainline Protestantism." Ph.D. dissertation, Harvard University, 1999.

Barnes, Edward Larabee. "Architecture as Witness." *Your Church* 12, no. 5 (September–October 1966): 34–35, 64–71.

Baumann, Brother Cajetan J. B., O.F.M. "Behind the Renewal in Church Building." *Your Church* 11, no. 3 (May–June 1965): 14–15, 27–32.

Beauregard, Robert A. *When America Became Suburban*. Minneapolis: University of Minnesota Press, 2006.

Beck, Joan, "Bursting Point in Paradise: Chicago's 275 Suburbs Spilling over Their Limits as Populations Double, Triple, Quadruple." *Chicago Sun Times*, May 25, 1958.

Bell, Thomas M. "The Church Kitchen." *Your Church* 1, no. 2 (July–September 1955): 16ff.

Belluschi, Pietro. "The Meaning of Regionalism in Architecture." *Architectural Record* 118, no. 6 (December 1955): 131–39.

Bendroth, Margaret. *Growing Up Protestant: Parents, Children, and Mainline Churches*. New Brunswick, N.J.: Rutgers University Press, 2002.

Bennett, Richard M. "Luther in Park Forest." Letter to the editor. *Christian Century* 66, no. 50 (December 14, 1949): 1491.

Bennett, Richard Marsh "The Aesthetic Demands of Contemporary Architecture upon Masonry." In *Modern Masonry: Natural Stone and Clay Products,* 7–13 (Washington, D.C.: National Academy of Sciences Building Research Institute, publication no. 466, 1956).

Bieler, Andre. *Architecture in Worship: The Christian Place of Worship.* Trans. Odette and Donald Elliott. Philadelphia: Westminster Press, 1965.

Bohlman, A. E., and Herbert A. Brand. "Grace Lutheran, Western Springs, Illinois." *Church Management* 29, no. 9 (June 1953): 20.

"Bold Forms Control Light in Protestant Church: Faith United Protestant Church." *Architectural Record* 125, no. 4 (April 1959): 183–86.

Botha, P. Roelf. "Modern Churches of South Africa." *Your Church* 7, no. 4 (October–December 1961): 17–34, 39, 41.

Brand, Stewart. *How Buildings Learn: What Happens after They're Built.* New York: Penguin, 1994.

"Break Ground for Oak Lawn Church Today." *Chicago Daily Tribune,* June 1, 1958, SW3. ProQuest Historical Newspapers.

Brodkin, Karen. *How Jews Became White Folks and What That Says about Race in America.* New Brunswick, N.J.: Rutgers University Press, 1998.

Buggeln, Gretchen T. "Form, Function, and Failure in Postwar Christian Education Buildings." In David Morgan, ed., *The Matter of Belief,* 193–213. London: Routledge, 2009.

———. "The Shape of a New Era: Valparaiso's Chapel of the Resurrection in Historical Context." *The Cresset* 73, no. 3 (Lent 2010): 6–14.

———. "Teen Spaces." In *Making Suburbia: New Histories of Everyday America,* ed. John Archer, Paul J. P. Sandul, and Kate Solomonson, 227–39. Minneapolis: University of Minnesota Press, 2015.

"Building Boom, or Christians Creating." *Christian Century* 74, no. 13 (March 27, 1957): 381–82.

"Building Boom Revamps U.S. Church Design." *Chicago Daily Tribune,* March 9, 1959, 10. ProQuest Historical Newspapers.

Caudill, William. *Toward Better School Design.* New York: F. W. Dodge Corp., 1954.

Chaves, Mark. *Congregations in America.* Cambridge, Mass.: Harvard University Press, 2004.

———. National Congregations Study, www.soc.duke.edu/natcong.

Chiat, Marilyn J. *America's Religious Architecture: Sacred Places for Every Community.* New York: John Wiley and Sons, 1997.

"Chicago Architect Stade Chides His Colleagues." *Bennington Banner,* August 13, 1966, 7. NewspaperArchive.com.

"Christ Church, Minneapolis." *Architectural Forum* 93, no. 1 (July 1950): 79–85.

Christ-Janer, Albert, and Mary Mix Foley. *Modern Church Architecture: A Guide to the Form and Spirit of Twentieth Century Religious Buildings.* New York: McGraw-Hill, 1962.

"Christ the King Lutheran Church, Reseda, California." *Church Management* 30, no. 7 (April 1954): 26–27, 29.

"A Church Designed and Built in the Attitude of Prayer." *Architectural Forum* 97 (December 1952): 85–92.

"Church Architecture Today." *Your Church* 1, no.3 (October–December 1955): 11–15.

Clark, William S. "The Architectural Captivity of the Church." *Your Church* 11, no. 5 (September–October 1965): 36–37, 56–62.
———. *Building the New Church*. Jenkintown, Pa.: Religious Publishing Co., 1957.
———. "The Cathedral at Coventry." *Your Church* 8, no. 3 (July–September 1962): 16–19, 34–37.
———. "Church Architecture in America, 1955–65." *Your Church* 11, no. 1 (January–February 1965): 18–19, 38–39, 41–44.
———. "Church Architecture in England: The Current Scene." *Journal of the American Society for Church Architecture* 3 (January 1963): 30–37.
———. "Church Building, U.S.A., Part I: Modern Churches." *Your Church* 5, no. 1 (January–March 1959): 13ff.
———. "Curtain Call." *Your Church* 1, no. 3 (October–December 1955): 6.
———. "The Shape of Europe's Churches." *Your Church* 8, no. 1 (January–March 1962): 22–25, 44–47.
———, ed. *For Church Builders: A Recall to Basics*. Valley Forge, Pa.: Agora Books, 1969.
Clausen, Meredith L. *Spiritual Space: The Religious Architecture of Pietro Belluschi*. Seattle: University of Washington Press, 1992.
Coffman, Elesha. *The Christian Century and the Rise of the Protestant Mainline*. New York: Oxford University Press, 2013.
Cohen, Lizbeth. *A Consumer's Republic: The Politics of Mass Consumption in Postwar America*. New York: Vintage, 2003.
Conklin, William. Society for Arts, Religion, and Contemporary Culture Web site: www.sarcc.org (April 2, 2010).
Conover, Elbert M. *The Church Builder*. New York: Interdenominational Bureau of Architecture, 1948.
Cooley, William. "The Historical Background of Church Building," *Your Church* 8, no. 4 (October–December 1962): 24–27, 42–43.
"Current Church Architecture: The Lutheran Church of the Atonement, Florissant, Missouri." *Your Church* 2, no. 1 (January–March 1956): 11.
"Dart, Edward. The Nature of the First Unit." *Your Church* 9, no. 1 (January–March 1963): 28–29.
Dart, Susan. *Edward Dart, Architect*. Evanston, Ill.: Evanston Publishing, 1993.
"Dedication Set for New Church in Barrington." *Chicago Tribune*, November 21, 1954, NW4. ProQuest Historical Newspapers.
"Design for Worship: First Methodist Church, Warren, Michigan." *Your Church* 6, no. 2 (April–June 1960): 22–23.
"Design for Worship: Good Shepherd Lutheran, Palos Park." *Your Church* 4, no. 1 (January–March 1958): 13–14.
"Design for Worship: Kahaluu Methodist Church." *Your Church* 2, no 4 (October–December 1956): 9–10.
"Design for Worship: Lansing Presbyterian Church, Lansing, Illinois." *Your Church* 10, no. 1 (January–March 1964): 14–15.
"Design for Worship: Lutheran Church of the Ascension, Atlanta, Georgia." *Your Church* 7, no. 1 (January–March 1961): 13–15.
"Design for Worship: The Lutheran Church of the Resurrection, Yardley, Pennsylvania." *Your Church* 5, no. 4 (October–December 1959): 22–23.

"Design for Worship: St. Augustine's Episcopal Church, Gary, Indiana." *Your Church* 6, no. 4 (October–December 1960): 19–21.

"Design for Worship: St. George's Episcopal Church, Durham, New Hampshire." *Your Church* 1, no. 3 (October–December 1955): 12.

"Design for Worship: St. Paul Lutheran Church, Mount Prospect, Illinois." *Your Church* 9, no. 4 (October–December 1963): 15.

Diamond, Etan. *Souls of the City: Religion and the Search for Community in Postwar America.* Bloomington: Indiana University Press, 2003.

Dietz, Albert G. H. "Glued Timbers Tailored to Fit." *Architectural Record* 106, no. 6 (December 1949): 139–41.

Dodson, Dan W. "Religion in Suburbia." *Journal of Educational Sociology* 32 (April 1959): 365–73; http://www.jstor.org/stable/2264196.

"Double-Duty Roof: Cedar Hills Community Church, Oregon." *Architectural Forum* 97, no. 6 (December 1952): 94.

Dowling, Dale Woolston. "For God, for Family, for Country: Colonial Revival Church Buildings in the Cold War Era." Ph.D. dissertation, George Washington University, 2004.

Eastwood, Abraham, Jr. "An Architect's Notes." *Your Church* 8, no. 1 (January–March 1962): 11ff.

———. "An Architect's Notes." *Your Church* 8, no. 4 (October–December 1962): 9, 71.

Egbert, Donald Drew. "Religious Expression in American Architecture." In *Religious Perspectives in American Culture,* ed. James Ward Smith and A. Leland Jamison, 361–411. Princeton, N.J.: Princeton University Press, 1961.

Ellwood, Robert S. *The Fifties Spiritual Marketplace: American Religion in a Decade of Conflict.* New Brunswick, N.J.: Rutgers University Press, 1997.

Elman, Kimberly J., and Angela Giral, eds. *Percival Goodman: Architect—Planner Teacher—Painter.* New York: Columbia University, Miriam and Ira D. Wallach Art Gallery, 2001.

"The End of the Glass Box." *Time* 79, no. 21 (May 25, 1962): 87. Academic Search Premier, 54208265.

Engelhardt, N. L., N. L. Engelhardt Jr., and Stanton Leggett. *Planning Elementary School Buildings.* New York: F. W. Dodge Corp., 1953.

Englemann, Gerson. Interview with Judy Mathais, August 7, 1980. "Park Forest: An Illinois Planned Community" collection, Illinois Digital Archive, www.idaillinois.org.

Everett, Glenn D. "Churches Set All-Time Building Record." *Church Management* 30, no. 6 (March 1954): 9–10.

*Fifty Modern Churches.* London: Incorporated Church Building Society, 1947.

Finke, Roger, and Rodney Starke. *The Churching of America, 1776–1990: Winners and Losers in Our Religious Marketplace.* New Brunswick, N.J.: Rutgers University Press, 1992.

"First Congregational Church, Spencer, Iowa." *Architectural Record* 118, no. 6 (December 1955): 184–85.

"First Methodist Church, Plainfield, Iowa." *Architectural Record* 106, no. 6 (December 1949): 124–27.

"For a New College an Old Village Silhouette." *Architectural Forum* 101, no. 6 (December 1954): 132–37.

Frey, Edward S. *This before Architecture.* Jenkintown, Pa.: Foundation Books, 1963.

Friedman, Alice T. *American Glamour and the Evolution of Modern Architecture.* New Haven, Conn.: Yale University Press, 2010.

Gans, Herbert. "Park Forest: Birth of a Suburban Jewish Community." *Commentary* 2 (April 1951): 330–39.
Gerken, Reverend Theodore, quoting a parishioner in "Analysis of the Worship Function." *Journal of the American Society for Church Architecture* 1, no. 1 (July 1961): 14.
Geva, Anat. *Frank Lloyd Wright's Sacred Architecture: Faith, Form, and Building Technology*. London: Routledge, 2011.
Goldhagen, Sarah Williams. *Anxious Modernisms: Experimentation in Postwar Architecture and Culture*. Boston: MIT Press, 2000.
Gordon, Albert Isaac. *Jews in Suburbia*. Boston: Beacon Press, 1959.
Greeley, Andrew M. *The Church and the Suburbs*. New York: Sheed & Ward, 1959.
Halverson, Marvin. "The Artist and the Church." *Arts in Society* (spring–summer 1962): 102–6.
Hammond, Peter. *Liturgy and Architecture*. New York: Columbia University Press, 1961.
———. *Towards a Church Architecture*. London: Architectural Press, 1962.
Harris, Dianne. *Little White Houses: How the Postwar Home Constructed Race in America*. Minneapolis: University of Minnesota Press, 2013.
———, ed. *Second Suburb: Levittown, Pennsylvania*. Pittsburgh: University of Pittsburgh Press, 2010.
Herberg, Will. *Protestant—Catholic—Jew: An Essay in American Religious Sociology*. New York: Doubleday, 1955.
"Home Designer Makes Kitchen the Focal Point." *Chicago Tribune*, April 29, 1951, SW C5. ProQuest Historical Newspapers.
Hudnut-Beumler, James. *In Pursuit of the Almighty's Dollar: A History of Money and American Protestantism*. Chapel Hill: University of North Carolina Press, 2007.
"Insights into Today's Faith and Practice Incorporated into Design." *Motive* 11, no 2. (November 1950): 14.
Isenstadt, Sandy. *The Modern American House: Spaciousness and Middle Class Identity*. New York: Cambridge University Press, 2006.
Jackson, Kenneth. *Crabgrass Frontier: The Suburbanization of the United States*. New York: Oxford University Press, 1985.
Jaffe, Samuel Z. (rabbi), and Morris Feller (president of Congregation Beth Sholom, Park Forest, Illinois), letter to the editor. *Commentary* (May 1957).
Jester, Thomas C., ed. *Twentieth-Century Building Materials: History and Conservation*. New York: McGraw-Hill, 1995.
Kennedy, Mary. "National Register of Historic Places Evaluation for the Pilgrim Lutheran Church, Hamilton County, Indiana. Indiana Department of Transportation." February 16, 2012.
Kennedy, Robert Woods. "After the International Style—Then What?" *Architectural Forum* 99, no. 3 (September 1953): 130ff.
Kidder Smith, G. E. *The New Churches of Europe*. New York: Holt, Rinehart and Winston, 1963.
———. "Six New European Churches." *Architectural Forum* 99, no. 6 (December 1953): 104ff.
Kieckhefer, Richard. *Theology in Stone: Church Architecture from Byzantium to Berkeley*. New York: Oxford University Press, 2004.
Kilde, Jeanne Halgren. *Sacred Power: Sacred Space: An Introduction to Christian Architecture and Worship*. New York: Oxford University Press, 2008.

———. *When Church Became Theatre: The Transformation of Evangelical Architecture and Worship in Nineteenth-Century America.* New York: Oxford University Press, 2002.

Klutznick, Phillip M. Interview with Glenda Bailey-Mershom, February 5, 1981. "Park Forest: An Illinois Planned Community" collection, Illinois Digital Archive, www.idaillinois.org.

Koenig, Harry C., ed. *A History of the Parishes of the Archdiocese of Chicago.* Vols. 1–2. Chicago: Catholic Bishop of Chicago, 1980.

Komechak, The Rev. Michael E. "An Architect's Choices: The Life of Edward Dart." *Inland Architect* 19, no. 9 (September 1975): 8-13.

Kretzmann, Adalbert R. "The Liturgical Consultant." *Your Church* 4, no. 1 (January–March 1958): 22–23, 41.

———. "The Symbolism of Forms and Materials." *Your Church* 7, no. 1 (January–March 1961): 20–21, 30–31, 33.

Kruse, Kevin M., and Thomas J. Sugrue, eds. *The New Suburban History.* Chicago: University of Chicago Press, 2006.

Lane, George A., SJ. *Chicago Churches and Synagogues: An Architectural Pilgrimage.* Chicago: Loyola University Press, 1981.

Leach, William. "The American Church Building." *Church Management* 29, no. 4 (January 1953): 16–18, 41.

———. "The New American Church Building." *Church Management* 29, no. 9 (June 1953): 22–32.

———. "Steps Towards a New Building." *Church Management* 30, no. 1 (October 1953): 14ff.

Longstreth, Richard W. *Looking beyond the Icons: Midcentury Architecture, Landscape, and Urbanism.* Charlottesville: University of Virginia Press, 2015.

Lucy, William H., and David L. Phillips. *Confronting Suburban Decline: Strategic Planning for Metropolitan Renewal.* Washington, D.C.: Island Press, 2000.

"The Lush New Suburban Market." *Fortune* 47, no. 11 (November 1953): 129.

Lynn, Robert W., and Elliott Wright. *The Big Little School: Two Hundred Years of the Sunday School.* Birmingham, Ala.: Religious Education Press, 1980.

Maddex, Diane. *Alden B. Dow: Midwestern Modern.* Midland, Mich.: Alden B. Dow Home and Studio, 2007.

Mansell, T. Norman. "The Challenge of the Small Church." *Church Management* 29, no. 9 (June 1953): 10–11.

———. "The Shape of the Church." *Your Church* 10, no. 6 (November–December 1964): 14–15, 24–26, 31–33.

Marty, Martin E. "Church Building, U.S.A.: Part II, College Chapels." *Your Church* 5, no. 2 (April–June 1959): 17, 27–29, 47–50.

———. *The New Shape of American Religion.* New York: Harper & Brothers, 1959.

———. *Pilgrims in Their Own Land: 500 Years of Religion in America.* Boston: Little, Brown, 1984.

———. "Protestantism in Panurbia." *Christian Century* 74, no. 44 (October 29, 1958): 1232–35.

———. *Righteous Empire: The Protestant Experience in America.* New York: Harper & Row, 1977.

———. "The Task of Church Architecture." *Your Church* 7, no. 2 (April–June 1961): 20–21, 30–35.

Marty, Martin, and William Cooley, interview with Studs Terkel, April 27, 1965. http://conversations.studsterkel.org.

May, Elaine Tyler. *Homeward Bound: American Families in the Cold War Era.* New York: Basic Books, 1988.

McClinton, Katharine Morrison. *The Changing Church: Its Architecture, Art, and Decoration.* New York: Morehouse-Gorham, 1957.

McRee, O. T. "Preparation for Architectural Service: Part 1, Basic Considerations." *Your Church* 10, no. 1 (January–March 1964): 18–19, 34–39.

———. "The Role of the Pastor in a Church Building Program." *Your Church* 9, no. 1 (January–March 1963): 22–23, 38.

Mills, Edward D. *The Modern Church.* New York: Praeger, 1956.

Morgan, David, ed. *Religion and Material Culture: The Matter of Belief.* London: Routledge, 2010.

Morse, John E. *To Build a Church.* New York: Holt, Rinehart and Winston, 1969.

"Multiple Use Space Created with Flexible Partitions in an Open, Single-Level Plan, First Methodist Church, Plainfield, Iowa." *Architectural Forum* 97, no. 6 (December 1952): 99–101.

"National Council Selects Outstanding Modern Churches." *Architectural Record* 120, no. 1 (July 1956): 10–12.

Nauman, Robert Allen. *On the Wings of Modernism: The United States Air Force Academy.* Urbana: University of Illinois Press, 2004.

"Neighborhood Church Uses Today's Technologies and Design Language to Convey Ancient Qualities." *Architectural Forum* 96, no. 3 (March 1952): 133–35.

*Neue Evangelische Kirchen im Rheinland.* Dusseldorf: Werner-Verlag, 1963.

"The New Lutheran." *Time* 71, no. 14 (April 7, 1958): 60ff. Academic Search Complete.

Nicolaides, Becky, and Andrew Wiese, eds. *The Suburb Reader.* London: Routledge, 2006.

Oakley, J. Ronald. *God's Country: America in the Fifties.* New York: Dembner Books, 1986.

Ogata, Amy. *Designing the Creative Child: Playthings and Places in Midcentury America.* Minneapolis: University of Minnesota Press, 2013.

Pahl, Jon. *Youth Ministry in Modern America, 1930 to the Present.* Peabody, Mass.: Hendrickson Publishers, 2000.

"Paralysis in Park Forest." *Christian Century* 66, no. 45 (November 9, 1949): 1319–21.

"Park Forest United." *Newsweek,* April 21, 1952.

"Park Forest, Illinois: Proving Ground for Community Planning Techniques. *Architectural Record* (May 1951): 99–110.

Patterson, James T. *Grand Expectations: The United States: 1945–1974.* New York: Oxford University Press, 1996.

Pearlman, Jill. *Inventing American Modernism: Joseph Hudnut, Walter Gropius, and the Bauhaus Legacy at Harvard.* Charlottesville: University of Virginia Press, 2007.

Pelkonen, Eeva-Liisa, and Donald Albrecht, eds. *Eero Saarinen: Shaping the Future.* New Haven, Conn.: Yale University Press, 2006.

Perlmutter, Victor. Letter to the editor. *Commentary* (August 1951).

"Perspectives: Air Force Academy Chapel." *Architectural Record* 122, no. 6 (December 1957): 9ff.

Pfammatter, Ferdinand. *Betonkirchen.* Zurich and Cologne: Benziger Verlag Einsiedeln, 1948.

Powers, Robert. "A Chicago Sojourn." www.achicagosojourn.blogspot.com (April 26, 2013).

Price, Jay. *Temples for a Modern God: Religious Architecture in Postwar America.* New York: Oxford University Press, 2013.

"Progress of a Suburban Jewish Community." *Commentary* 8 (1957): 113–22.

Promey, Sally M. "Taste Cultures: The Visual Practice of Liberal Protestantism, 1940–1965." In *Practicing Protestants: Histories of the Christian Life in America*, ed. Laurie Maffly-Kipp, Leigh Schmidt, and Mark Valeri, 250–93. Baltimore: Johns Hopkins University Press, 2006.

Prudon, Theodore H. M. *The Preservation of Modern Architecture*. Hoboken, N.J.: John Wiley and Sons, 2008.

Putnam, Robert D. *Bowling Alone: The Collapse and Revival of American Community*. New York: Simon and Schuster, 2000.

Randall, Gregory. *America's Original G.I. Town: Park Forest, Illinois*. Baltimore: Johns Hopkins University Press, 2003.

Randl, Chad. *A-Frame*. New York: Princeton Architectural Press, 2014.

"Recent Past Survey: Suburban Cook County." www.landmarksil.org.

Reilley, Thomas. "Good Office Design." *Your Church* 14, no. 6 (November–December 1968): 18–19, 21.

Roof, Wade Clark. *Spiritual Marketplace: Baby Boomers and the Remaking of American Religion*. Princeton, N.J.: Princeton University Press, 1999.

Roof, Wade Clark, and William McKinney. *American Mainline Religion: Its Changing Shape and Future*. New Brunswick, N.J.: Rutgers University Press, 1987.

Rose, Michael S. *Ugly as Sin: Why They Changed Our Churches from Sacred Places to Meeting Spaces and How We Can Change Them Back Again*. Manchester, N.H.: Sophia Institute Press, 2001.

Saarinen, Eero. "Eero Saarinen on the Broad Currents of Modern Architecture." *Architectural Forum* 99, no. 1 (July 1953): 110–15.

Sack, Daniel. *Whitebread Protestants: Food and Religion in American Culture*. New York: St. Martin's Press, 2000.

Schmertz, Mildred F. "Recent European Churches." *Your Church* 6, no. 3 (July–September 60): 11–16.

Schwarz, Rudolf. *The Church Incarnate*. English translation, Chicago: H. Regnery, 1958 (1938, in German as *Vom Bau der Kirche*).

Scotford, John R. "Multiple Services Influence Architecture." *Church Management* 28, no. 1 (October 1951): 24ff.

———. *When You Build Your Church*. Great Neck, N.Y.: Doniger and Raughley, 1955.

Seymour, Matthew. "Edward Dart: Preserving the Works of a Mid-century Architect." M.A. thesis, School of the Art Institute of Chicago, 2011.

Shear, John Knox, ed. *Religious Buildings for Today*. New York: F. W. Dodge Corp., 1957.

Shippey, Frederick A. *Protestantism in Suburban Life*. New York: Abingdon Press, 1964.

Shortridge, James. *The Middle West: Its Meaning in American Culture*. Lawrence: University Press of Kansas, 1989.

Sisson, Richard, Christian Zacher, and Andrew Cayton, eds. *The American Midwest: An Interpretive History*. Bloomington: Indiana University Press, 2007.

Siry, Joseph M. *Beth Shalom Synagogue: Frank Lloyd Wright and Modern Religious Architecture*. Chicago: University of Chicago Press, 2011.

———. *Unity Temple: Frank Lloyd Wright and Architecture for Liberal Religion*. Cambridge: Cambridge University Press, 1998.

Smith, Persis. "Adequate Social Planning for the Church." *Your Church* 4, no. 2 (April–June 1958): 20ff.
———. "The Church Refreshment Hour." *Your Church* 2, no. 4 (October–December 1956): 32ff.
Sövik, E. A. *Architecture for Worship*. Minneapolis: Augsburg Publishing House, 1973.
———. "The Faith Our Forms Express." *Protestant Church Buildings and Equipment* 12, no. 1 (May 1964): 11, 30–31, 33, 48–50.
———. "Fundamentals for Church Builders." *Your Church* 7, no. 3 (July–September 1961): 18–19, 29–37.
———. "Liturgical Art and the New Churches." *Response: In Worship-Music-The Arts* 1, no. 2 (Advent 1959): 8–17.
———. "New Visions for Church Builders." *Church Management* 38, no. 1 (October 1961): 10, 12, 14, 26–27, 39.
———. "A Portfolio of Reflections on the Design of Northfield Methodist Church." *Your Church* 13, no.5 (September–October 1967): 16–17, 46–59.
———. "The Shape of Our Places of Worship." *Protestant Church Buildings and Equipment* 8, no. 1 (May 1960): 12ff.
Spence, Basil. "A Contemporary Expression of Cathedral Architecture." *Architectural Record* 115, no. 3 (March 1954): 144–51.
———. *Phoenix at Coventry: The Building of a Cathedral*. London: Geoffrey Bles, 1962.
"Stade, Charles." In *Who Was Who in America*, vol. 11, 262. New Providence, N.J.: Marquis Who's Who, 1996.
Stade, Charles E., "An Architect's Notes," Your Church 11, no. 1 (January–February 1965): 7, 45–47.
———. "An Architect's Notes: The Adventures of Misty, the Church Mouse, part I." *Your Church* 12, no. 1 (January–February 1966): 11ff.
———. "An Architect's Notes: The Adventures of Misty, the Church Mouse, part II." *Your Church* 12, no. 3 (May–June 1966): 8ff.
———. "An Architect's Notes: An Architect's Responsibility to His Client." *Your Church* 12, no. 2 (March–April 1966): 10, 12, 60–63.
———. "An Architect's Notes: Dollars, Sense, and Square Footage." *Your Church* 11, no. 4 (July–August 1965): 8–9, 40.
———. "An Architect's Notes: For Pastors: A Recipe for a Good Building Committee." *Your Church* 11, no. 5 (September–October 1965): 8, 10, 63–64.
———. "An Architect's Notes: Good and Bad Church Architecture." *Your Church* 6, no. 4 (October–December 1960): 14–16.
———. "The Architect and the Congregation." *Your Church* 3, no 2 (April–June 1957): 16, 46–52.
———. "Chicago's Art Treasures: All around the Town." *Chicago Tribune*, July 9, 1967, H16. ProQuest Historical Newspapers.
———. "Church Building, U.S.A., Part III: Historic Churches." *Your Church* 6, no. 1 (January–March 1960): 17–26, 51–53.
———. "Design for Worship: First Methodist Church, Midland, Michigan." *Your Church* 4, no. 3 (July–September 1958): 11–13.
———. "'Modern' Church Construction Defended by Young Architect from Park Ridge." *Chicago Tribune*, July 12, 1956, A4. ProQuest Historical Newspapers.

———. "New Materials for Design and Building." *Your Church* 7, no. 4 (October–December 1961): 26–27, 44–47, 49.
———. Review of Albert Christ-Janer and Mary Mix Foley, *Modern Church Architecture Your Church* 9, no. 1 (January–March 1963): 61–62.
———. Review of G. E. Kidder Smith, *The New Churches of Europe. Your Church* 11, no. 3 (May–June 1965): 8–9, 39–40.
———. "This Business of Seating." *Your Church* 2, no. 4 (October–December 1956): 18–19, 21–23, 41–43.
Stade, Charles E., and John Psiris Jr. "The Church Building as a Fallout Shelter." *Your Church* 9, no. 1 (January–March 1962): 30–31, 50–53.
"St. Andrew's Lutheran Church, Park Ridge, Illinois." *Architectural Record* 119, no. 6 (June 1956): 198–201.
"St. Stephen's Episcopal Church, Columbus, Ohio." *Architectural Forum* 99, no. 6 (December 1953): 85–87.
"A Synagogue That Emphasizes Day-by-Day Religion: Beth El Synagogue, Akron, Ohio." *Church Management* 29, no. 4 (January 1953): 20–21, 28.
"The Tent Form: A Village Gothic for Today." *Architectural Forum* 101, no. 6 (December 1954): 128–31.
Thiry, Paul, Richard M. Bennett, and Henry L. Kamphoefner. *Churches and Temples.* New York: Reinhold, 1953.
Torgerson, Mark A. *An Architecture of Immanence: Architecture for Worship and Ministry Today.* Grand Rapids, Mich.: William B. Eerdmans, 2007.
———. "Edward Anders Sövik and His Return to the 'Non-Church.'" Ph.D. dissertation, University of Notre Dame, 1995.
———. *Greening Spaces for Worship and Ministry: Congregations, Their Buildings, and Creation Care.* Herndon, Va.: Alban Institute, 2012.
Travis, Paul. "Thatched Hut Inspires Architecture." *Church Management* 28, no. 3 (December 1951): 26.
"Trinity Lutheran Church, Walnut Creek, California." *Architectural Record* 116, no. 6 (December 1954): 147–48.
Tritenbach, Paul. "The Suburban Church—Site Selection and Development." *Your Church* 12, no. 1 (January–February 1966): 16–19, 44–46.
Wagoner, Harold. "Church Architecture: What Next?" Reprint of article published in *Protestant Church Buildings and Equipment* (February 1961), National Council of Churches of Christ records (RG 6, box 52, folder 12), n.p.
Weyres, Willy, et al. *Kirchen: Handbuch für den Kirchenbau.* Munich: Verlag Georg D. W. Callwey, 1959.
White, James F. *Protestant Worship and Church Architecture.* New York: Oxford University Press, 1964.
———. *Roman Catholic Worship: Trent to Today.* New York: Paulist Press, 1995.
Whyte, William. "The Future, c/o Park Forest." *Fortune* (June 1953): 127.
———. *The Organization Man.* New York: Simon and Schuster, 1956.
Wilford, Justin. *Sacred Subdivisions: The Postsuburban Transformation of American Evangelicalism.* New York: New York University Press, 2012.
Wille, Lois. "The Suburb That Turned Its Back." *McCall's* 95, no. 10 (July 1968): 14, 124–25.

Willet, E. Crosby, "GRA? ASCA? NCRA? Who's Who and What's What." *Journal of the American Society for Church Architecture* 12 (1971): 5–8.
Willet, Henry Lee. "An Ancient Craft in the Modern Manner." *Your Church* 2, no. 2 (April–June 1956): 16–17, 32–35.
Williams, J. Paul. *What Americans Believe and How They Worship*. Rev. ed. New York: Harper and Row, 1962.
Williams, Peter W. *Houses of God: Region, Religion and Architecture in the United States*. Urbana: University of Illinois Press, 2000.
Wilson, Sloan. *The Man in the Gray Flannel Suit*. 1955. 4th ed. Boston: Da Capo Press, 2002.
"Winner of Tribune Small Home Prize Is Honored Again." *Chicago Tribune*, July 6, 1947, NW1. ProQuest Historical Newspapers.
Winter, Gibson. *The Suburban Captivity of the Churches*. New York: Macmillan, 1962.
Wise, Michael Z. "America's Most Prolific Synagogue Architect." *Forward*, March 9, 2001. www.michaelzwise.com (March 18, 2010).
Wright, Frank Lloyd. "First Unitarian, Madison, Wisconsin." *Architectural Forum* 88, no. 1 (January 1948): 118–19.
Wuthnow, Robert. *Loose Connections: Joining Together in America's Fragmented Communities*. Cambridge, Mass.: Harvard University Press, 1998.
———. *Remaking the Heartland*. Princeton, N.J.: Princeton University Press, 2011.
———. *The Restructuring of American Religion: Society and Faith since World War II*. Princeton, N.J.: Princeton University Press, 1988.
Yost, L. Morgan. "The Case for the Contemporary." *Church Management* 29, no. 1 (October 1952): 39–40.
Young, Victoria M. *Saint John's Abbey Church: Marcel Breuer and the Creation of a Modern Sacred Space*. Minneapolis: University of Minnesota Press, 2014.
Zelinsky, Wilbur, and Stephen A. Matthews. *The Place of Religion in Chicago*. Chicago: University of Chicago Press for Columbia College Chicago Press, 2011.

# INDEX

GRETCHEN BUGGELN holds the Phyllis and Richard Duesenberg Chair in Christianity and the Arts in Christ College at Valparaiso University. Her book *Temples of Grace: The Material Transformation of Connecticut's Churches, 1790–1840* received the Abbott Lowell Cummings Prize from the Vernacular Architecture Forum.